A HANDBOOK
of
NEW
TESTAMENT
EXEGESIS

A HANDBOOK

of

NEW TESTAMENT EXEGESIS

Craig L. Blomberg
with Jennifer Foutz Markley

Baker Academic
a division of Baker Publishing Group
Grand Rapids, Michigan

Published by Baker Academic
a division of Baker Publishing Group
P.O. Box 6287, Grand Rapids, MI 49516-6287
www.bakeracademic.com

Printed in the United States of America

Library of Congress Cataloging-in-Publication Data

Blomberg, Craig.
    A handbook of New Testament exegesis / Craig L. Blomberg with Jennifer Foutz Markley.
        p.   cm.
    Includes bibliographical references and index.
    ISBN 978-0-8010-3177-9 (pbk.)
    1. Bible. N.T.—Hermeneutics. I. Markley, Jennifer Foutz. II. Title.
BS2331.B56 2010
225.601—dc22   2010021512

15   16   7   6   5   4

for Jonathan and Jonathan

Contents

Acknowledgments

I am grateful to Jim Kinney, editorial director at Baker Academic, for convincing me of the need for this volume and for supporting us throughout the project. When he first approached me, I had just completed most of the work for a book that I coauthored with a recent graduate of Denver Seminary who had been my research assistant for two years. I had such a good experience that I was hoping for a chance to work on another book with one of our "best and brightest." At that time, I suggested the idea to Jennifer Foutz, a brand new MDiv graduate, and she was eager to be involved. She worked as a research assistant for me for half a year and then for a year as a New Testament department graduate assistant. She was then accepted into a well-known PhD program in New Testament but deferred that acceptance as her life circumstances changed. For the past three years she has been an admissions officer for the seminary. Having written exemplary exegetical papers for several classes, Jenn was well poised to be the primary author for five of the ten chapters, and I tackled the first drafts of the other five. We read and commented on each others' chapters, but I took over the project at the stage of creating the final drafts, to complete a few small sections of chapters Jenn did not have time to finish, to add some clarifying comments to her work, to create uniform style throughout the whole manuscript, and to substantially beef up the footnotes. I added the front matter, introduction, and summary, and tidied up a few other loose ends as well. I was also the one involved in the minor revisions that editor Brian Bolger requested after we first submitted the manuscript, including adding the bibliographies. The appendix and sidebars were created by Baker Academic.

I am further grateful to Denver Seminary for its distinguished professor's fund that allows me to employ research assistants and, for one year when we were particularly shorthanded, to create the temporary position of New

Testament graduate assistant that Jenn was able to fill. Dr. Keith Wells and the rest of his staff at our Carey S. Thomas Library have continued to provide excellent services for all of my writing projects. So too did Kimberly Claire and her staff at our bookstore until it was outsourced two years ago and her position eliminated. I am likewise grateful to our board of trustees for a sabbatical term during the fall of 2008 (just before they indefinitely suspended all further sabbaticals due to the recession), which enabled me to finish several smaller projects so that I could return to this one and put the finishing touches on it during the first half of 2009. It would be remiss of me not to mention further my current full-time colleague, Dr. Bill Klein; the senior professor in our department, Dr. Kermit Ecklebarger; and my late predecessor, Dr. Donald Burdick, whose convictions about exegetical method at Denver Seminary over the years have shaped my thinking and our current departmental assignments in more ways than I can enumerate. Erin Heim also read the entire manuscript, made excellent suggestions for improvement, and caught numerous typos and infelicities of expression.

During the four years of the gestation of this project, Jenn met, dated, and married her husband, Jonathan Markley, thus explaining her name change. During the identical period, my daughter Elizabeth met, dated, and married her husband, Jonathan Little. Besides sharing the same first name, both are excellent men for whom we are grateful to God that they have joined our respective families. We are therefore dedicating this volume to Jonathan and Jonathan, with hopes and prayers for decades of wonderful marriages. But to God be all the glory!

Introduction

"This is how we know who the children of God are and who the children of the devil are: Those who do not do what is right are not God's children; nor are those who do not love their brothers and sisters" (1 John 3:10). This sounds pretty cut and dried, but don't most people fall somewhere in between doing what is right and not doing so? "Son though he [Jesus] was, he learned obedience from what he suffered and, once made perfect, he became the source of eternal salvation for all who obey him" (Heb. 5:8–9). Christ had to learn to obey God? He was *made* perfect? Wasn't he God from all eternity past and therefore always perfect? And doesn't this passage, like the last one, clearly teach salvation through obedience to God's commandments? Isn't salvation entirely by grace through faith? "But women will be saved through childbearing—if they continue in faith, love and holiness with propriety" (1 Tim. 2:15). Good grief! Now half the human race is saved not only by good works but by one particular deed—having kids? What about all those women who can't or don't have children? "Peter replied, 'Repent and be baptized, every one of you, in the name of Jesus Christ for the forgiveness of your sins. And you will receive the gift of the Holy Spirit'" (Acts 2:38). Here it sounds like all people, including women and men alike, must be baptized to be saved. At least that's easier than having children. Moreover, then we'll receive a gift from the Spirit. Hmm, I wonder which gift it is. The Scriptures certainly seem confusing.

The Protestant Reformers, on the one hand, regularly stressed what they called the perspicuity or clarity of Scripture. What they meant was that anyone who was reasonably literate and had a well-translated copy of the Bible in their native language could discover in its pages everything they needed to be right with God and live a life pleasing to him. Anyone who read from Genesis to Revelation, or even just the New Testament from Matthew to Revelation, would capture the main contours of the story of God, his creation, their fall into sin, and his plan of redemption for them. They would see Jesus as the heaven-sent deliverer, recognize their need to trust in him and follow him in discipleship, and claim the promises of eternal life—a new quality of human existence in this world and unending happiness with God and all the company of the redeemed for an eternity.

On the other hand, the Reformers never claimed that all passages in the Bible were equally clear. They never claimed that readers would not run across texts that appeared to conflict with the overall gist of the Bible's story line and theology. They never claimed that we could cite individual verses, out of context and apart from a knowledge of the entire revelatory word we call Scripture, and not risk grave misinterpretation. Indeed, beginning in the sixteenth century it was the Protestant Reformation that emphasized—against the previous millennium of Roman Catholic and Eastern Orthodox tradition and to an extent not seen since the first five centuries of Christianity—the discipline of biblical exegesis.[1]

Exegesis comes from two Greek words, ἐξ ("from, of, out of") and ἄγω ("to lead"), referring to the process of leading out from a text its original meaning. Exegesis is closely related to the art and science of hermeneutics (from Gk. ἑρμενεύω, "interpret, translate"). As it turns out, perusing the tables of contents of recent works on these two topics often discloses considerable overlap. Traditionally, hermeneutics developed more as a subset of philosophy, dealing with larger, theoretical questions about whether one can determine the meaning of someone else's utterances or communicative acts and, if so, to what extent and how, whereas exegesis is the actual practice of doing the interpretation.[2] In some contexts, "exegesis" is the term reserved for working with the biblical texts in their original language as one seeks to grasp their intent.[3] But we want our textbook to be widely useful to specialists and nonspecialists alike, so we have written it for New Testament readers who have studied Greek as well as for those who haven't.

The etymology of "handbook" suggests a small volume, though not all that goes by that label today is necessarily short or succinct. This little book was inspired by Gordon Fee's highly successful and useful introductory textbook, *New Testament Exegesis*, which has gone through three editions and helped

1. See further esp. James P. Callahan, *The Clarity of Scripture: History, Theology and Contemporary Literary Studies* (Downers Grove, IL: InterVarsity, 2001). Cf. also Mark D. Thompson, *A Clear and Present Word: The Clarity of Scripture* (Leicester: Apollos; Downers Grove, IL: InterVarsity, 2006).

2. Cf., e.g., the issues treated in Gerhard Maier, *Biblical Hermeneutics* (Wheaton: Crossway, 1994).

3. Over thirty years ago the Denver Seminary Biblical Studies faculty decided to label all Bible book electives based on the English text of Scripture "Analysis of . . ." but all classes requiring the translation and interpretation of the Hebrew, Aramaic, or Greek text "Exegesis of . . ." The nomenclature remains unchanged to this day.

a generation or more of theological students and practitioners.[4] Fee wrote what in many ways can be thought of as a "how-to manual," with numerous short, prescriptive instructions in each chapter but without an abundance of illustrations from Scripture elaborated in detail. In our experience, exegesis is caught as much as it is taught, or, better put, it is learned inductively at least as much as deductively. In other words, there are really only a fairly small number of unvarying rules or principles with which one needs to acquaint oneself; the rest of the skill comes from repeated practice and from the evaluation of the work of other practitioners. So we have written a work of more expansive prose than Fee's, emphasizing examples of the various exegetical tasks from significant New Testament passages, with motivational comments en route. We did so because we recognize the barriers, logistically and emotionally, that Bible students face in faithfully elaborating a full-orbed exegesis of a given passage of Scripture.

There are plenty of other books related to the New Testament with "exegesis" or one of its cognates in their titles, but some focus on the whole range of biblical criticisms rather than function as an exegetical textbook per se.[5] Many produce excellent, detailed explorations of a select number of the key tasks involved in exegesis but don't work the student step by step through the full exegetical process.[6] Occasionally, a work excels in presenting extended examples from New Testament texts, but doesn't treat methodology in much detail.[7] In several instances among these various volumes, genre criticism (highlighting the distinctive interpretive principles for different literary forms), more appropriately dealt with in introductory hermeneutics texts, occupies a large percentage of the work.

We have tried to avoid each of these potential pitfalls and to create a ten-chapter work, not too long overall, that proceeds in a sequential fashion according to the logic of the exegetical task itself and devotes approximately the same amount of attention to each step. We have discussed methodology to what extent is necessary to get the introductory theological student under way in the process. But we have used abundant illustrations from the New Testa-

---

4. Gordon D. Fee, *New Testament Exegesis: A Handbook for Students and Pastors*, 3rd ed. (Louisville: Westminster John Knox, 2002).

5. E.g., Stanley E. Porter, ed., *Handbook to the Exegesis of the New Testament* (Boston and Leiden: Brill, 2002).

6. As with Richard Erickson, *A Beginner's Guide to New Testament Exegesis: Taking the Fear out of Critical Method* (Downers Grove, IL: InterVarsity, 2005); George H. Guthrie and J. Scott Duvall, *Biblical Greek Exegesis* (Grand Rapids: Zondervan, 1998); Michael J. Gorman, *Elements of Biblical Exegesis: A Basic Guide for Students and Ministers*, rev. ed. (Peabody, MA: Hendrickson, 2009); Walter C. Kaiser Jr., *Toward an Exegetical Theology: Biblical Exegesis for Preaching and Teaching* (Grand Rapids: Baker, 1981); and John H. Hayes and Carl R. Holladay Jr., *Biblical Exegesis: A Beginner's Handbook*, 3rd ed. (Louisville: Westminster John Knox, 2007).

7. E.g., Werner Stenger, *Introduction to New Testament Exegesis* (Grand Rapids: Eerdmans, 1993).

ment itself, focusing on those where getting exegesis right makes a significant difference because of what is at stake in the text. Of course, many students will recognize that we have not shied away from at times using biblical illustrations that themselves have been interpreted in competing ways. Interpreters who wish to disagree with the conclusions in our specific illustrations are obviously free to do so, but hopefully they will recognize the kinds of principles and methods they will need to employ in defending alternative interpretations. They will also learn why one pair of writers has chosen the particular interpretations they have, and they will understand the kinds of arguments they would have to counter in order to argue for alternative approaches.

Overview

First, the foundation for the exegesis of any ancient document is *textual criticism*. Rarely do the "autographs," or original manuscripts, still exist. Unless we have reason to believe we have a largely accurate reconstruction of what those originals contained (and a reasonably accurate identification of those places where we do not have this confidence), there is little point in continuing with the remaining nine steps. Second, once we have such a reconstruction, we must then create a reliable *translation* in the modern language or languages in which we wish it to be read. Different translations have different objectives in view, objectives that we need to understand and evaluate so that we can choose the right kind of translation for each different modern context in which the Bible is used. Third, still before turning to an explanation of the meaning of the text, we must investigate its *historical-cultural background*. This includes whatever information can be known about the circumstances of the composition of the book overall—such as author, audience, date, provenance, purposes, and setting—as well as specific historical and cultural information pertinent to the most important topics or details of the passage. With the burgeoning of social-scientific analysis of texts, sociology and cultural anthropology must not be neglected in our acquisition of relevant historical and cultural information.

The fourth step is to analyze the *literary context* of the passage at hand. This includes its most immediate contexts within the document itself, as well as more remote ones within the same book or, as with an anthology like the Bible, the most relevant surrounding literature. Identification of any figures of speech, distinctive literary forms or genres, or overall species of rhetoric is also important, lest we miss or misinterpret important nuances of the text that are less straightforward and clear than others. Fifth, we must determine those words in the passage for which the translations are disputed, for which the theology proves crucial, or for which the contexts suggest an unusual meaning. *Word studies* of such terms, which examine their meaning over time in the Greek language leading up to the period of the biblical writer and their function in the literary context in which they appear, can shed important light on how the terms are to be rendered and understood. Sixth, constructions with ambiguous *grammar* (or crucial theological implications that depend on the correct identification of the grammatical form employed) must be investigated in a manner akin to word studies.

The final four steps are more synthetic in nature. The analysis of *interpretive problems* addresses the exegetical questions often asked of a text that cannot be simply answered by one of the previous methods but may require a combination of several of them. The ways the historical and literary contexts interact with each other and with the meanings of words and important grammatical constructions often make these problems more complex. Discerning an *outline* of the individual passage being studied, preferably according to the structure of the original Greek, can afford an opportunity to synthesize the results of preceding sections. Discussing a passage's *theology* requires at least an introductory awareness of the major topics of systematic theology, and an assessment of how any given biblical text can be viewed legitimately as contributing to the sum total of the Bible's teaching. Finally, no exegesis is complete without reflection on contemporary *application* of the text at hand. To what specific issues or situations in the twenty-first century is a given passage relevant and in what ways? The more specific the answers to those questions can be, the more likely the exegesis will be not just accurate but also useful and pertinent.

Students in theological colleges and seminaries will typically write one or more in-depth exegetical papers, and this book can serve as a handbook for a step-by-step process for them. As noted earlier, it is particularly useful for those who have had some Greek, but it can pay rich dividends even in English Bible courses. The authors are schooled particularly in the methods that Denver Seminary has promoted for at least the last thirty years. Throughout that time exegetical papers have been assigned in second-year, second-semester Greek exegesis courses, in which students have employed all ten of these processes to a selected passage from the letters of James or Romans and written up the results of their research in a prescribed format, with material on each of the various procedures. English Bible students have for at least as long undertaken and written up the results of "inductive Bible studies," with the same steps, minus textual criticism and translation. Some exegetical manuals give in-depth instruction for how such papers can be composed.[8] Individual professors, however, inevitably want to put their own unique stamps on their assignments, so we are not sure this is one of the more helpful parts of exegetical handbooks. Invariably, different passages from different sections and genres of the New Testament literature will require more stress on certain steps in the exegetical process and less on others.

---

8. E.g., Fee, *New Testament Exegesis*, 5–38.

We would prefer, therefore, to think of this slim volume not so much as a precise how-to manual, in which strict, unvarying conformity to a long set of rules and policies will produce award-winning exegetical papers and Bible studies, but rather as a tool box. Just as the construction worker or repair-person selects a hammer and nails for some jobs, screws and screwdrivers for others, and nuts, bolts, and a monkey wrench for still others, so Bible students, teachers, and pastors will seldom need to apply all ten steps (or apply them to the same degree) to all New Testament passages. Lack of time and inadequate access to the best reference works are the most common hindrances to a thor-ough process, but the fact that so many other people have repeatedly gone through similar processes for all major parts of the Bible means that many issues have been reasonably settled. When time or interest does not justify utilizing all ten "tools," choose those that are the most necessary for a given passage, based on what is least agreed on about that passage by scholars and commentators in the recent past. Here is where one will need to expend the most energy, in forming convictions on the most controversial and debated issues. Interpreters who have familiarity and practice with *all* of the tools, however, will not have to shy away from trying to answer important questions about a given passage just because they are less skilled in using the tools most needed to answer those questions.

Preliminary Applications of the Method

We return to the four questions, then, with which we began this introduction. There are a number of proposed solutions to the problem of the apparent claims of sinlessness in 1 John 3; one of the most common involves under-standing the *grammar* of the Greek present tense, especially with nonindica-tive mood verbs, as implying ongoing, characteristic behavior. True believers do not continue constantly in a state of sin (cf. [T]NIV).[9] For Hebrews 5:8 an understanding of the overall *theology* of the New Testament doctrine of the incarnation is important. Jesus did not retain the independent exercise of his divine attributes apart from those occasional circumstances when it was his father's will that he do so.[10] So there were many things he had to learn as a human being, without being able to draw on divine omniscience. For 1 Timothy, a *word study* of "saved," especially in the Pastoral Epistles, shows that this verb is by no means limited to spiritual redemption. Paul may be referring in 1 Timothy 2:15 to the restoration of the female gender to its divinely appointed role, overall, after the fall. When we recognize from the

9. Marianne Meye Thompson, *1–3 John* (Leicester and Downers Grove, IL: InterVarsity, 1992), 95.
10. Gordon R. Lewis and Bruce A. Demarest, *Integrative Theology*, vol. 2 (Grand Rapids: Zondervan, 1990), 284–86.

historical context that false teachers in Ephesus were promoting celibacy as a Christian ideal (1 Tim. 4:3), this explanation makes good sense of 1 Timothy 2:15, without us having to take the first part of the verse as a mandate to every woman or as the means of salvation from sin.[11] The *literary context* of Acts 2 discloses that Peter's next evangelistic sermon climaxes in the call to repentance without a word about baptism, suggesting that baptism itself is neither salvific nor normative, though it appears to have been normal, following belief, throughout the New Testament.[12]

Much more could be said about each of these four texts, which would bring additional elements of the exegetical process into play, but these brief hors d'oeuvres should at least whet readers' appetites for the main course to come. Some of these issues will be explored in more detail in the course of our handbook. So let us proceed to the entrées. Each chapter is largely a self-contained unit for those who wish to dip into the book at different places or read chapters selectively or out of order. But, as sketched above, there is a logic to the sequence of topics. Readers not yet familiar with the entire exegetical process should benefit most by perusing the topics in the order we have presented them. Enjoy the feast!

11. Somewhat similarly, cf. Andreas J. Köstenberger, "Ascertaining Women's God-Ordained Roles: An Interpretation of 1 Timothy 2:15," *Bulletin of Biblical Research* 7 (1997): 107–44.
12. Cf. also Luther McIntyre, "Baptism and Forgiveness in Acts 2:38," *Bibliotheca Sacra* 153 (1996): 53–62.

Abbreviations

b.	Babylonian Talmud
BDAG	*A Greek-English Lexicon of the New Testament and Other Early Christian Literature*, ed. Walter Bauer, Frederick W. Danker, William F. Arndt, and F. Wilbur Gingrich, 3rd ed. (Chicago: University of Chicago Press, 2000)
CEV	Contemporary English Version
ESV	English Standard Version
GNT	Good News Translation
HCSB	Holman Christian Standard Bible
JB	Jerusalem Bible
KJV	King James Version
LXX	Septuagint
The Message	*The Message*, trans. Eugene H. Peterson (Colorado Springs: NavPress, 2002)
NA, NA²⁷	*Novum Testamentum Graece*, ed. Eberhard Nestle, Erwin Nestle, Kurt Aland, and Barbara Aland, 27th ed. (Stuttgart: Deutsche Bibelgesellschaft/German Bible Society, 1993)
NAB	New American Bible
NASB	New American Standard Bible
NEB	New English Bible
NET	New English Translation
NIDNTT	*New International Dictionary of New Testament Theology*, ed. Colin Brown, 4 vols. (Grand Rapids: Zondervan, 1978–85)
NIrV	New International Readers' Version
NIV	New International Version
NIVAC	New International Version Application Commentary
NJB	New Jerusalem Bible

NKJV	New King James Version
NLT	New Living Translation, 2nd ed.
NRSV	New Revised Standard Version
NWT	New World Translation of the Holy Scriptures
par(s).	and parallel(s)
REB	Revised English Bible
RSV	Revised Standard Version
TDNT	*Theological Dictionary of the New Testament*, ed. Gerhard Kittel and Gerhard Friedrich, 10 vols. (Grand Rapids: Eerdmans, 1964–76)
TLB	*The Living Bible* (Wheaton: Tyndale House, 1971)
TNIV	Today's New International Version
UBS, UBS⁴	*The Greek New Testament*, ed. Barbara Aland, Kurt Aland, Johannes Karavidopoulos, Carlo M. Martini, and Bruce M. Metzger, 4th rev. ed. (Stuttgart: Deutsche Bibelgesellschaft/ United Bible Societies, 1993)
YLT	Young's Literal Translation

1

Textual Criticism

The term "textual criticism" may sound more like students complaining about their reading assignments than a shorthand reference to the artful science of establishing a probable original text. The practice of textual criticism often takes a back seat to some of the more "glamorous," or at least better known, exegetical endeavors. It is certainly not a discernible element in most sermons. Relatively few laypeople are aware of how the manuscripts of the Bible have been copied and passed down to us throughout the generations. However, because we do not possess Scripture as it was originally written, the exegete who is interested in handling the Bible with as much accuracy as possible needs to know that the ancient copies of the New Testament sometimes disagree with one another as to the precise wording of a given text. After acknowledging this, he or she needs to assess the various options and determine which of the different readings is most likely the original one.[1]

It is not our intention to give a comprehensive explanation of the entire field of textual criticism; many other works treat such issues with the detail

---

1. Not all New Testament textual criticism experts agree that the primary goal of textual criticism should be to determine the original as the author of each New Testament book first wrote it, but this is certainly the dominant perspective. For a discussion of the opinions of various contemporary scholars on the topic, see Eldon Jay Epp, "The Multivalence of the Term 'Original Text,'" in *Perspectives on New Testament Textual Criticism: Collected Essays, 1962–2004* (Leiden and Boston: Brill, 2005), 551–93. For a definition of the term "original text" as we will use it throughout our discussion, see below, pp. 5–6.

that this brief chapter will not permit.[2] Instead we aim to introduce the topic in a way that will allow students and pastors to engage in the practice, thereby improving their understanding and exposition of Scripture. We will therefore define textual criticism and the relevant terms used in its practice, look at the history of how the various texts available for study have been transmitted, and then examine a few pertinent characteristics of these texts. With these items in place, we can move to a discussion of how one practices textual criticism as part of the exegetical process.

What Is Textual Criticism?

Our contemporary ease of communication makes it difficult to appreciate the painstaking process of textual transmission in antiquity. In a world of photocopiers, e-mail, and word processing that offers automatic correction of misspelled words and cut-and-paste options, it is easy to overlook the mistakes that come with copying documents by hand. Since the autographs (the original documents) of each of the writings in the Bible were lost or discarded long ago, we must rely on manuscripts that represent the originals copied many times over. If these copies agreed at all points, our discussion could end here. The exact text would be established for us. However, the copies do not agree, hence the need for textual criticism.

Simply defined, textual criticism is the practice of comparing the various copies of a work in order to determine, as best as possible, the exact wording of an original text that is either undiscovered or no longer exists. Textual criticism is both a science and an art. It is a scientific practice because it requires the critic to collect data and compare the various options and then to apply certain rules for determining the original reading. However, not all the rules apply equally to each instance of textual variation, so the critic must artfully balance the evidence and incorporate common sense in order to assimilate the relevant information and arrive at sound conclusions.

The ancient documents that are used to reconstruct the New Testament text as we have it today have been grouped into three main headings for ease of reference: *Greek manuscripts, ancient translations*, and *patristic citations*.[3]

2. Particularly useful, in ascending order of detail, are David A. Black, *New Testament Textual Criticism: A Concise Guide* (Grand Rapids: Baker, 1994); J. Harold Greenlee, *Introduction to New Testament Textual Criticism*, rev. ed. (Peabody, MA: Hendrickson, 1995); Kurt Aland and Barbara Aland, *The Text of the New Testament*, rev. ed. (Grand Rapids: Eerdmans, 1989); Bruce M. Metzger and Bart D. Ehrman, *The Text of the New Testament: Its Transmission, Corruption, and Restoration*, 4th ed. (New York and Oxford: Oxford University Press, 2004); and D. C. Parker, *An Introduction to the New Testament Manuscripts and Their Texts* (Cambridge: Cambridge University Press, 2008).

3. Other, less central resources include ancient Greek lectionaries, of which there are over 2,400 (books with Scripture readings for each Sunday in church) and the Diatessaron (a late

The Greek manuscripts are further subdivided into *papyri* (about 120), *majuscules* (about 320), and *minuscules* (nearly 2,900). Papyri (papyrus is an ancient form of paperlike material) comprise some of the oldest manuscripts available for scrutiny. A papyrus is usually designated in the scholarly literature by a Gothic *p* (𝔓), followed by a numerical superscript (𝔓[45], for example). Greek manuscripts written on material besides papyrus (usually parchment and, much later, paper) were subdivided by writing style into majuscules (also called *uncials*) and minuscules. Uncials are the earliest codices (pages bound into books) and were written in capital letters, for the most part without spacing, word division, or punctuation. The most famous, oldest, and/or most reliable are represented by capital letters from the Hebrew, Latin, and Greek alphabets as well as by numbers with a "0" prefix, while the others are designated solely by numbers with a "0" prefix. Of the approximately 310 uncials, the most important are codices Sinaiticus (ℵ/01), Alexandrinus (A/02), Vaticanus (B/03), Ephraemi Rescriptus (C/04), Bezae (D/05), and Washingtonianus (W/032), all dating to the fourth or fifth century, and Koridthi (Θ/038), dating to the ninth century.[4] Minuscules are manuscripts written in the later lowercase, cursive style that was developed in the eighth or ninth century to speed the copying process. Minuscules begin to introduce some occasional spacing between sections of text and a little punctuation. They are labeled with simple Arabic numerals with groups of extremely similar manuscripts collected together in families. Families 1 and 13 (designated f^1 and f^{13}, respectively) are often viewed as the most reliable or important for the text-critical process.[5]

A second category of source material for textual criticism involves translations of parts or all of the Greek New Testament into other ancient languages in the early centuries of church history. These include Latin, Syriac, Coptic, Armenian, Georgian, Ethiopic, and Slavonic. Because the Latin "Vulgate" (meaning "common" [language]), produced by Jerome in the fourth and fifth

> ### Sidebar 1.1
> **Types of Ancient Documents**
>
> Greek manuscripts
> - papyri
> - majuscules (or uncials)
> - minuscules
>
> Ancient translations
> - Latin (esp. the Vulgate)
> - Syriac
> - Coptic
> - Armenian
> - others
>
> Patristic citations
> - Irenaeus
> - Clement of Alexandria
> - Origen
> - Athanasius
> - others

---

second-century harmonization of all four Gospels). For a complete overview of the documents cited in the United Bible Societies or Nestle-Aland Greek New Testaments and their age and place of origin, see the introductions to each of those works.

4. Cf. Metzger and Ehrman, *Text of the New Testament*, 48; Michael W. Holmes, "Textual Criticism," in *Interpreting the New Testament: Essays on Methods and Issues*, ed. David A. Black and David S. Dockery (Nashville: Broadman & Holman, 2001), 48–49, who omit C.

5. Aland and Aland, *Text of the New Testament*, 106–7.

centuries, became the standard Roman Catholic Bible worldwide for over a millennium, its readings have been very influential. More significant for textual criticism, however, are the "old italic" or "old Latin" translations that predate the Vulgate. Syriac readings are significant for the Gospels because at times Syriac vocabulary and syntax closely resemble Aramaic, the language Jesus would have spoken before his words were translated into Greek by the Gospel writers. Occasionally, a divergent Syriac rendering may therefore enable us to pick up on a nuance of Jesus's words that is not as clear from the Greek.[6] The other translations are less significant, except that some of the earliest ones do come from the third through fifth centuries so that, to the extent they were translated very literally, they represent testimony to the state of the Greek manuscripts in the period for which we have noticeably fewer Greek texts themselves than in the centuries that followed.

Finally, patristic citations of the New Testament are found in the writings of the earliest post–New Testament Christian leaders (often called church fathers), such as Justin Martyr, Irenaeus, Clement of Alexandria, Origen, Eusebius, Athanasius, and Cyril of Alexandria. Because these writers were so dependent on what would later become the New Testament canon, if the New Testament as we have it today were somehow lost or destroyed it could be reconstructed virtually in its entirety from its quotation by the church fathers.[7] These citations, however, are somewhat limited in their usefulness for reconstructing the exact autographs of Scripture because we do not always know how literally they were "quoting" the Bible, and they were not always based on what we would consider the most reliable manuscripts of their day. Before we can determine the helpfulness of patristic citations, they too must undergo the process of textual criticism. Their greatest contribution to the field is that textual critics can approximate how the text appeared at different times and places by seeing how it was used in the writings of these church fathers.[8] Because patristic writings begin emerging as early as the second century, their information proves invaluable in assessing the history of the text in the earliest days of its transmission.[9]

Three other basic terms related to textual criticism remain to be defined before we can proceed in our discussion. First, as different copies of New

6. The scholar best known for proposing a large number of such insights is George M. Lamsa. See esp. his *Gospel Light*, rev. ed. (Covington, GA: Aramaic Bible Society, 2002). Many of his proposals go beyond what can be demonstrated with any confidence, but he often captures a key component of the original meaning; e.g., "baptism of fire" probably does not mean "free from sin" in its New Testament contexts (as p. 1 argues), but "pure in heart" does mean "pure in mind" (p. 4).

7. Paul D. Wegner, *A Student's Guide to Textual Criticism of the Bible: Its History, Methods and Results* (Downers Grove, IL: InterVarsity, 2006), 236.

8. For detailed criteria of how to use and assess these materials, see esp. Carroll D. Osburn, "Methodology in Identifying Patristic Citations in New Testament Textual Criticism," *Novum Testamentum* 47 (2005): 313–43.

9. Aland and Aland, *Text of the New Testament*, 176–78.

Testament manuscripts generate different readings of the same passages, these differences are labeled *textual variants* or *variant readings*. Variant readings may involve changes in a letter, a word, a phrase, or even additions and omissions of whole sentences or paragraphs, although changes of this magnitude are extremely rare. Indeed, there are only two places in the New Testament where textual variants affect whole paragraphs or chapter portions: the longer ending of the Gospel of Mark (Mark 16:9–20) and the account of the woman caught in adultery (John 7:53–8:11).[10] Among the textual variants that affect an entire verse or two, only a handful have been moved to the footnotes of modern editions of the Greek New Testament so that we should probably doubt their authenticity.[11] Second, after weighing the options, the textual critic will establish which of the variant readings is the *preferred reading*. Finally, certain distinguishing characteristics occur in the copies of the New Testament, allowing experts to group the numerous copies into a particular *text type*. Copies within a text type are probably based on a parent copy that originated in a particular geographical area. The major text types and their representative characteristics will be discussed below.

One final definition is required. What exactly is the original text? While the chief goal of textual criticism is to determine the text as the author originally wrote it, the spurious readings that are ruled out by careful criticism are not useless and in fact can represent a different sort of "original." Scholars recognize various levels of "originals" or, better stated, different "dimensions of originality."[12] First, there is the *precanonical original* of certain New Testament texts, which represents the earliest stages in the composition of what later would become the canonical text. For example, the Gospel of John may well contain not only material by John himself but possibly some by a community that added

10. Both are unlikely to have been in the autographs. Mark either intended to end at verse 8 or his original ending has been lost. For state-of-the-art discussion of all major options here, see David A. Black, ed., *Perspectives on the Ending of Mark: 4 Views* (Nashville: Broadman & Holman, 2008). Most Christians will be relieved to discover that vv. 9–20 need not be treated as part of the inspired, authoritative originals, since they promise snake handlers and venom drinkers no harm. Snake handling cults throughout church history have regularly appealed to this passage and have always had fatalities. Modern translations like the NRSV and TNIV helpfully relegate these passages to footnotes or smaller print, and almost all modern translations insert comments alerting the reader to their absence from older and more reliable manuscripts. The account of the woman caught in adultery may well represent an authentic incident from the life of Jesus; it is just highly unlikely that it forms part of what John originally wrote, not least because it seems to be an episode in search of a home, appearing in some ancient manuscripts after John 7:36 or 21:25, or even after Luke 21:38 or 24:53. For an excellent overview of the issue, see Chris Keith, "Recent and Previous Research on the *Pericope Adulterae* (John 7.53–8.11)," *Currents in Biblical Research* 6 (2008): 373–404.

11. See Aland and Aland, *Text of the New Testament*, 298–305. The examples they discuss are Matt. 17:21; 18:11; 23:14; Mark 7:16; 9:44, 46; 11:26; 15:28; Luke 17:36; 23:17; John 5:3b–4; Acts 8:37; 15:34; 24:6b–8a; 28:29; and Rom. 16:24.

12. Epp, "Multivalence of the Term 'Original Text,'" 567.

to and/or edited his work, probably after his death.[13] The precanonical original would be the words of John and the separate words of the community before they were joined and subsequently circulated for the purpose of instruction. Second, there is the *author's original*, that is, the text as it was when it left the hand of, say, Paul or Luke and was delivered to the recipients. Third, there is the *canonical original*, or the text when a given writing was recognized as authoritative or its canonicity was established, such as the time when the letters of Paul or the four Gospels were gathered together into larger collections. Finally, there exist *interpretive originals* or Scripture as it came to be known and used in the life, instruction, and worship of the church throughout its history. Each of these categories really qualifies as original.[14] It is the second one, the author's original, that we are most interested to find,[15] but it is sometimes admittedly difficult to extract this original from the others. Likewise, it is unfair to act as if the other originals are not useful in our study of Scripture, especially as these four levels of originals closely overlap the majority of the time.

From now on, when we mention originals it will be helpful to remember that the authorial original is in primary view, but that we encounter and interact with the others in every variant of the New Testament. To fail to recognize this is to discount the rich history and the journey of the text from its initial writing to today. By involving oneself in the practice of textual criticism, the interpreter becomes a historian, interested not only in the author's original but also in the traditions leading up to the penning of a particular writing and its history within the life of the church. Analyzing why textual variants may have appeared in individual texts can serve as a way to further engage the historical-cultural situation of the church as it passed on its sacred writing from generation to generation. What was happening in the church at various stages of manuscript production that would cause intentional changes—changes deemed important enough by scribes that they would introduce them into the text and by doing so elevate those alterations to the status of Scripture? Answering this question when encountering text-critical problems has the potential to enrich our understanding of church history throughout the ages and alerts us not only to how the text was written but also to how it was read at various points throughout its history.[16]

13. See, e.g., Craig L. Blomberg, *Jesus and the Gospels: An Introduction and Survey*, 2nd ed. (Nashville: B&H; Nottingham: Apollos, 2009), 200.

14. Eldon J. Epp, "Textual Criticism in the Exegesis of the New Testament, with an Excursus on Canon," in *A Handbook to the Exegesis of the New Testament*, ed. Stanley E. Porter (Boston and Leiden: Brill, 2002), 87–89. In "Multivalence of the Term 'Original Text,'" 586–88, Epp gives new labels to these various dimensions of reality, which are more technical and "careful," but his former titles for each category still communicate their essence.

15. For a good defense of why this should remain so, see Paul Ellingworth, "Text, Translation, and Theology: The New Testament in the Original Greek?" *Filología Neotestamentaria* 13 (2000): 61–73.

16. Bart D. Ehrman, "The Text as Window: New Testament Manuscripts and the Social History of the Early Christianity," in *The Text of the New Testament in Contemporary Research:*

The Bible is not the only ancient literature that requires the work of textual criticism in order to establish the wording of the text, but biblical text criticism is distinguished from other textual criticism for at least three reasons. First, the wealth of copies available for scrutiny is far greater for biblical writings than for any other ancient document. This is especially true for the New Testament writings, whose existing hand-copied Greek manuscripts alone number over 5,700.[17] In the interest of preserving what they considered sacred writing, scribes across many geographical areas and throughout many centuries committed themselves to copying New Testament texts. Such abundant resources are not available for most other literature of antiquity. Many critics of ancient documents would consider even a dozen different manuscripts for any one work thrilling.[18] While the vast New Testament manuscript resources are undoubtedly a blessing and a testimony to the early church's belief in the truth and relevance of Scripture, they also create a web of complexity that requires the devoted attention of many text-critical specialists.[19]

Second, New Testament textual criticism in particular is distinct because even when there are multiple manuscripts of other ancient documents, there is often a considerable time gap between the initial composition of the text and the earliest manuscript available. For example, there are only nine or ten good manuscripts from Caesar's *Gallic Wars*, and the most ancient of these derives from about nine hundred years after Caesar's day.[20] The New Testament, on the other hand, enjoys the existence of multiple early papyri. One papyrus fragment ($\mathfrak{P}^{52}$), which contains a portion of a few verses of John 18, has been dated to the first third of the second century, making it likely no more than forty years later than the original Gospel of John, which probably dates to the 90s. More than thirty other papyri are dated to the late second through early third centuries, and some of these contain the Gospels and Acts (esp. $\mathfrak{P}^{45}$) or

---

Essays on the Status Quaestionis, ed. Bart D. Ehrman and Michael W. Holmes (Grand Rapids: Eerdmans, 1995), 361.

17. Metzger and Ehrman, *Text of the New Testament*, 52.

18. Compare the 5,700 New Testament manuscripts with the quantity of extant manuscripts of other ancient Greek and Roman writers and their ages: 27 surviving manuscripts for Livy, the oldest from the fourth century (400 years after he wrote); 3 from Tacitus, the oldest from the ninth century (700 years after he wrote); just over 200 for Suetonius, beginning in the ninth century (600 years after he wrote); 20 for Thucydides, starting in the first century (400 years after he wrote); and 75 for Herodotus, starting in the first century (again 400 years after he wrote). See J. Ed Komoszewski, M. James Sawyer, and Daniel B. Wallace, *Reinventing Jesus: What the* Da Vinci Code *and Other Novel Speculations Don't Tell You* (Grand Rapids: Kregel, 2006), 71.

19. The fullest text-critical data has been assembled and continues to be analyzed in detailed, technical volumes produced by the Institut für neutestamentliche Textforschung in Münster, Westfalia, Germany, known as Novum Testamentum Graecum: Editio Critica Maior. Four volumes have appeared to date covering James–Jude and are published in the United States by Peabody: Hendrickson, 1997–2006.

20. F. F. Bruce, *The New Testament Documents: Are They Reliable?* 6th ed. (Grand Rapids: Eerdmans, 2003), 11. See also the data in n. 18 above.

the Pauline Epistles (esp. $\mathfrak{P}^{46}$) in almost their entirety. Reliable copies of most or all of the entire New Testament date from the fourth (א and B) and fifth centuries (esp. A and C).[21]

Third, textual criticism within the field of biblical studies stands apart because of the conviction of Christians throughout the centuries that the Bible is the uniquely inspired word of God. If we are dealing with the very words of God, we had better do our best to determine what those words are! At the same time, such convictions also led to a care in the preservation of the text usually not found to the same degree elsewhere in antiquity.[22]

Perhaps all this talk about text-critical specialization and the abundance of manuscripts seems a bit overwhelming. There is no need for the pastor or student to worry or be intimidated. Don't shut the doors of your church or neglect the people in your life and ministry in order to collect and compare manuscript data! It has been the calling of the experts to do the work of manuscript collection and comparison so that you don't have to. Their findings are easily accessible to the student of Greek who will spend some time learning to use the basic text-critical tools, of which the text-critical apparatuses of the United Bible Society's *Greek New Testament*, 4th revised edition (hereafter UBS[4] or simply UBS) and Nestle-Aland's *Novum Testamentum Graece*, 27th edition (hereafter NA[27] or simply NA) are the most important. Also eminently helpful for explaining why the UBS translation committee chose the preferred readings that occur in the text and thus for guiding one's own approach to text-critical decisions is Bruce Metzger's *A Textual Commentary on the Greek New Testament*.[23] We will give a brief introduction to these tools below.

Textual criticism, then, is not just for experts but also for interpreters of Scripture who have a basic knowledge of Greek and want to deal with the text as it was written by the original, inspired authors. Making the task of textual criticism even less daunting is the fact that in the instances where texts present variant readings, very few of these (probably less than 1 percent) require the exegete's attention.[24] Textual variants can be divided into three categories. First, there are variants that do little to change the meaning of the text. These often include unintentional scribal errors such as the omission or addition of letters or other misspellings. The most common of all involve the "movable nu"—the

21. Cf. Aland and Aland, *Text of the New Testament*, 67–71.

22. See, e.g., Darrell L. Bock and Daniel B. Wallace, *Dethroning Jesus: Exposing Popular Culture's Quest to Unseat the Biblical Christ* (Nashville: Nelson, 2007), 43–52. Parker (*New Testament Manuscripts and Their Texts*, 158) observes that five changes per one thousand words are typical for early New Testament scribal activity.

23. Bruce Metzger, *A Textual Commentary on the Greek New Testament*, 2nd ed. (Stuttgart: Deutsche Bibelgesellschaft/German Bible Society, 1994). See also Roger L. Omanson, *A Textual Guide to the Greek New Testament* (Stuttgart: Deutsche Bibelgesellschaft/German Bible Society, 2006). Omanson's work has a similar format but is designed to be somewhat more user-friendly for Bible translators.

24. Bock and Wallace, *Dethroning Jesus*, 58.

Greek letter "n" that may or may not occur on the end of certain noun and verb forms.[25] Second are variants that affect the meaning of the text yet are unattested or very poorly attested by the most reliable text types or in the older manuscripts. This kind of variant occurs especially in contexts in which the scribes felt more liberty to "correct" by adding or omitting words or phrases to make the texts harmonize more easily with one another, particularly among Gospel parallels.[26] Third are variants that significantly affect the meaning of the text and are well attested by the most reliable text types. Of the three kinds of variants, this last is the one with which exegetes should concern themselves. Modern-language translations of the Bible typically present only a small selection of this third category of variants in their footnotes or marginal references. The Greek New Testaments present a fuller selection, including some from the second category, with which teachers should familiarize themselves. Neither the UBS nor the Nestle-Aland committee, however, claims to represent the original text with absolute certainty, and often their decisions reflect split votes, leaving room for exegetes to make their own decisions about which reading is most probably original.[27]

Sidebar 1.2

Types of Textual Variants

1. Insignificant variants that do little to change the meaning of the text (e.g., scribal errors of omission or addition of letters, misspellings, "movable nu")
2. Variants that affect the meaning of the text but are unattested or poorly attested in the best manuscripts (e.g., scribal decisions to add or omit words in order to make certain texts harmonize more easily, especially among Gospel parallels)
3. Variants that significantly affect the meaning of the text and are well attested

---

Text Types

When it comes to reliability and closest approximation to the original text, not all text types are created equal. Three major text types emerged in the early centuries of the church: (1) the Western, (2) the Alexandrian, and (3) the

---

25. Ibid., 55. In this category, too, are the mere substitutions of synonyms for each other.

26. Or take as an example James 2:20, in which some manuscripts change the otherwise unparalleled ἀργή (useless) to the common νεκρά (dead). In other words, instead of reading "faith without works is useless," involving a clever pun that might better be captured in English as "faith without works doesn't work," the scribes wanted to harmonize James's texts with his other declarations that "faith without works is dead" (see vv. 17 and 26).

27. Expressing concern that modern editions of the Greek New Testament not become a new *Textus Receptus* (see below, p. 13) is Rodney R. Reeves, "What Do We Do Now? Approaching the Crossroads of New Testament Textual Criticism," *Perspectives in Religious Studies* 23 (1996): 61–73.

Byzantine (see table 1.1).[28] Before we examine these text types in detail, a brief history of textual transmission from its earliest days may prove helpful for understanding how variants were introduced into the New Testament text.

Table 1.1: Major Text Types, Characteristic Features, and Examples

Text Type	Characteristic Features	Examples
Alexandrian	• Copied with meticulous care and accuracy • Earliest exemplars are dated to the second century • Generally preferred over Western and Byzantine text types, due to characteristic accuracy	• $\mathfrak{P}^{75}$ and $\mathfrak{P}^{66}$ • Codex Vaticanus (B) • Codex Sinaiticus (ℵ) • Various Coptic translations
Western	• Early dating (some as early as the second century) • Use of loose paraphrase, harmonization with other New Testament texts • Enrichment of narrative through inclusion of extra and/or explanatory material	• Codex Bezae (D) • Old Latin or italic manuscripts • $\mathfrak{P}^{48}$ and $\mathfrak{P}^{38}$
Byzantine	• Continual development from third century through early Middle Ages • Clarity and completeness • Conflated preexistent divergent readings by expanding the text and smoothing out word difficulties • Became the dominant Greek text type from seventh century onward • Represents 80 percent of existing manuscripts today	• Majority Text • *Textus Receptus*

Imagine the excitement of any one of the fledgling Christian communities upon receiving a letter from Paul, the missionary who had first preached the gospel to them. In an act to preserve the writing, a literate, but not necessarily professional, copyist was put to the task of copying the entire document so that the church might have additional records of this letter.[29] As news trickled out

28. It should be noted that some scholars recognize a Caesarean text type as a fourth textual family. It is a mixture of the Alexandrian text and the Western text. The compiler of the Caesarean text followed the Alexandrian text and incorporated the Western text where it did not seem too improbable. Its editor was interested in harmonization and flow of thought, as was the Western text, but was also committed to modified reproduction of the Alexandrian text. Larry W. Hurtado (*Text-Critical Methodology and the Pre-Caesarean Text: Codex W in the Gospel of Mark* [Grand Rapids: Eerdmans, 1981], 88) argues that this text type is "a form of Western text as it was shaped in the East." We will limit our discussion to the three major types listed above for two reasons: (1) compared to the other textual families, relatively few traces remain of this original text type; and (2) the Caesarean type can be understood after a thorough discussion of the Alexandrian and Western families.

29. The fullest study of copying texts during the first few Christian centuries is now James R. Royse, *Scribal Habits in Early Greek New Testament Papyri* (Leiden and Boston: Brill, 2008).

across Asia Minor of the church's apostolic document, other communities who recognized Paul's authority and perhaps even inspiration also wished to obtain these truths in written form for themselves. So the copying tradition continued, and it proceeded all the more fervently after the death of Paul. The same principle of rapid copying and dispersal throughout the far reaches of the Roman empire would be true for the writings of the other New Testament authors as well.[30]

Interestingly, the variant readings in the earliest manuscripts are somewhat greater in number than those in the later copies. This indicates that at some point the process of copying was professionalized and subjected to standards by which the earliest copyists did not abide.[31] Yet even the greater number of variants at this earlier period seldom discloses a reading not known from the later period, reassuring us that important readings have not been lost. Regarding the progress modern textual critics have made in evaluating the variants to determine the best form of the text, Bart Ehrman summarizes:

> Textual scholars have enjoyed reasonable success at establishing, to the best of their abilities, the original text of the NT. Indeed, barring extraordinary new discoveries (e.g., the autographs!) or phenomenal alteration of method, it is virtually inconceivable that the physiognomy of our printed Greek New Testaments is ever going to change significantly.[32]

The writings of the early church fathers are helpful for determining that, from as early as the second century, different major text types emerged and were being used in different locales of the empire. For example, the Western text-type is represented in the writings of Justin Martyr, Irenaeus, and Tertullian; the Alexandrian text can be found in the writings of Origen and Athanasius; and a nascent form of the Byzantine text appears in the writing of Basil the Great and Chrysostom.[33] While at some point the text types began to interact with one another as copies were compared and used to correct one another, most manuscripts retained a number of the characteristics of the textual parent(s) from which they originated.

The Alexandrian Text Type

Alexandria, Egypt, was known as one of the major centers for learning and classical scholarship. Not surprisingly, the copying tradition of the

---

30. For details, see Michael B. Thompson, "The Holy Internet: Communication between Churches in the First Christian Generation," in *The Gospels for All Christians: Rethinking the Gospel Audiences*, ed. Richard Bauckham (Grand Rapids and Cambridge: Eerdmans, 1998), 49–70; and Loveday Alexander, "Ancient Book Production and the Circulation of the Gospels," in ibid., 71–111.

31. Metzger and Ehrman, *Text of the New Testament*, 275–76.

32. Ehrman, "Text as Window," 375.

33. Metzger and Ehrman, *Text of the New Testament*, 277–79.

manuscripts originating in this region shows meticulous care and accuracy.[34] Evidence for this text type's high quality of transmission is best demonstrated by comparing $\mathfrak{P}^{75}$ and Codex Vaticanus (B). $\mathfrak{P}^{75}$ is dated to around AD 200 while the more elegant codex is dated to around AD 350. That $\mathfrak{P}^{75}$ and B are nearly identical shows a straight line of transmission across generations from the papyrus to the codex. While the $\mathfrak{P}^{75}$–B line demonstrates remarkable excellence of transmission, changes in the text are evident in other copies within the Alexandrian family. Despite these changes, the manuscripts in the Alexandrian family reveal a commitment to preserving the accurate form of the text in ways that the other two major families do not. Other important manuscripts in this tradition include $\mathfrak{P}^{66}$, Codex Sinaiticus ($\aleph$), and various Coptic translations. This text type thus has the advantages of both the early dating of its oldest exemplars (second century) and the demonstrated care of transmission.[35]

The Western Text Type

The Western text type shares the advantage of early dating with the Alexandrian text tradition, with citations of its text appearing in the writings of the church fathers as early as the second century. But fondness for loose paraphrase, harmonization with other New Testament texts, and enrichment of narrative through the inclusion of extra and/or explanatory information are also distinctive characteristics of this text type. Western scribes felt free to smooth out the rough edges and add further clarification to the text, especially in the book of Acts, in ways that the Alexandrian tradition did not.[36] In general, therefore, the Alexandrian text type is to be preferred to the Western text type, though there are occasional key exceptions. Important early manuscripts from the Western textual family include Codex Bezae (D), the Old Latin or italic manuscripts, and $\mathfrak{P}^{48}$ and $\mathfrak{P}^{38}$, all of which demonstrate the Western tendency to add, omit, or change words, phrases, or whole accounts as the scribes saw fit.[37]

The Byzantine Text Type

The Byzantine text type, hardest to date because of its continual development through the early Middle Ages, is characterized by clarity and completeness. There is no clear evidence of the existence of this family before the fourth

---

34. Gordon D. Fee, "Textual Criticism of the New Testament," in *The Expositor's Bible Commentary*, ed. Frank E. Gaebelein, vol. 1 (Grand Rapids: Zondervan, 1976), 7.

35. Metzger and Ehrman, *Text of the New Testament*, 278.

36. See Eldon J. Epp, *The Theological Tendency of Codex Bezae Cantabrigiensis in Acts* (Cambridge: Cambridge University Press, 1966); and David C. Parker, *Codex Bezae: An Early Christian Manuscript and Its Text* (Cambridge: Cambridge University Press, 1992).

37. Metzger and Ehrman, *Text of the New Testament*, 279–80.

century.[38] Its popularity as the most favored text among copyists in the early Middle Ages was due to the fact that the Byzantine textual tradition had worked to conflate preexisting divergent readings by expanding the text and smoothing out difficulties. This approach is even less tempered in its discipline than the Western type and noticeably less literal in manuscript reproduction than the Alexandrian type.[39] Because the Byzantine textual family was received in Byzantium (which became Constantinople and eventually Istanbul), the capital and heart of the Eastern Orthodox world, it was copied and distributed throughout the Byzantine empire. The result was that the Byzantine text type came to be the dominant Greek text type from the seventh century onward, so that the majority of the manuscripts surviving today (some 80 percent of existing manuscripts) were generated from this textual tradition. From this tradition came the Majority Text (so named for the vast number of manuscripts in the tradition) and the so-called *Textus Receptus* (i.e., "received text"), a collection of very similar Byzantine manuscripts on which Reformation-era translations— such as the King James Version in English, the *Reina Valera* in Spanish, or the *Lutherbibel* in German—were largely based. Although this tradition is well attested by its large number of existing manuscripts, quantity does not equal quality with regard to the best material for establishing the original reading.[40]

How Does One Practice Textual Criticism?

Getting to Know the Relevant Tools

Familiarity with the available tools will arm the willing exegete with the information he or she needs to make informed judgments about the original text. The text-critical apparatus of the UBS[4] *Greek New Testament* is a good place to start.[41]

The United Bible Societies' Greek New Testament, 4th Revised Edition

The UBS[4] critical apparatus is structured to be friendly for the pastor or student who is familiar with Greek. It is the presupposition of the editorial

---

38. D. A. Carson, *The King James Version Debate: A Plea for Realism* (Grand Rapids: Baker, 1979), 44.

39. Wegner, *Student's Guide to Textual Criticism*, 244.

40. Metzger and Ehrman, *Text of the New Testament*, 280.

41. The editors of the UBS[4] explain the changes from the third edition in their preface. The text remains unchanged not because the committee is certain they have recovered the original wording, but because at the time of publication the committee found no evidence indicating that the previously established preferred readings should be altered. The major shift between the editions occurred in the textual apparatus. Besides eliminating less helpful and including more helpful text-critical problems, as discussed above (pp. 5–6), the fourth edition has drastically reduced the number of "D" ratings given to a text-critical problem by solidifying their decisions somewhat on difficult texts.

committee that the interpreter should be able to be involved in the process of text criticism without that process becoming such an overwhelming task that there remains no time for the exegete to engage in translation and interpretation. Therefore, the committee has selected 1,438 passages that they consider most important for showing textual variants and manuscript support for those variants. The variants represent only about 1 percent of the New Testament text, and of these only about four hundred have a significant bearing on the meaning of the text.[42] These are the text-critical issues that most interest the exegete.

Perhaps the best way to become acquainted with the UBS[4] critical apparatus is to look at each of its components. Here is an example of the text along with the apparatus taken from Romans 5:2, which contains a small set of minor textual variants (compared with the many that the UBS includes):

δι' οὗ καὶ τὴν προσαγωγὴν ἐσχήκαμεν [τῇ πίστει][2] εἰς τὴν χάριν ταύτην ἐν ᾗ ἑστήκαμεν καὶ καυχώμεθα ἐπ' ἐλπίδι τῆς δόξης τοῦ θεοῦ.

through whom also we have had access [by faith][2] into this grace in which we have stood and boast in the hope of the glory of God.

[2] 2 {C} τῇ πίστει ℵ[*,2] C Ψ 6 33 81 104 256 263 365 424 436 459 1175 1241 1319 1506 1573 1739 1852 1881 1912 2127 2200 2464 *Byz* [K L P] *Lect* it[ar, b, d2, mon, o] vg syr[p, h, pal] cop[bo] arm eth geo slav Origen[lat2/5] Chrysostom[1/2] Cyril // ἐν τῇ πίστει ℵ[1] A 1962 *l* 597 vg[mss] Chrysostom[1/2] Hesychius // *omit* B D F G 0220 it[d*, f, g] cop[sa] Origen[lat3/5] Basil; Ambrosiaster Julian-Eclanum Augustine

The superscripted number that appears in the Greek text points the reader to the same number in the critical apparatus at the bottom of the page. In the apparatus, the bold number occurring after the superscript reference indicates the verse of the text under consideration. The bracketed letter that follows is the UBS committee's degree of certainty about the reading they have chosen as most likely original, on a scale of A through D. An "A" indicates a high degree of certainty that the reading chosen is superior to the variants, while a "D" indicates the least amount of certainty. Therefore, a "C" or "D" rating invites the interpreter to engage in his or her own evaluation to a greater degree than an "A" or a "B."[43] However, because the UBS has included the text-critical evidence even for the variants in which the degree of certainty about the solution is relatively high, the interpreter may evaluate the committee's choices for all readings.[44] The UBS

42. UBS[4], v.

43. Elizabeth G. Edwards, "On Using the Textual Apparatus of the UBS Greek New Testament," *Bible Translator* 28.1 (1977): 122–23. Although this article was based on the third edition of the UBS, it is still an excellent introduction to using the textual apparatus overall.

44. Indeed, some textual critics think the current UBS committee has been too confident of their decisions too often. See esp. Kent D. Clarke, *Textual Optimism: A Critique of the United Bible Societies' Greek New Testament* (Sheffield: Sheffield Academic Press, 1997).

system of rating variants thus forms a handy reference tool for interpreters to know which of the text-critical problems most merit their sustained attention.

Following the letter indicating the degree of certainty for the preferred reading, the apparatus offers the variant readings along with the most important manuscripts that support each reading. The preferred reading (in this case, τῇ πίστει) with its supporting manuscripts is always listed first in the apparatus. Parallel slanted lines (///) divide the variants from each other. The introduction to the UBS *Greek New Testament* gives lists of abbreviations enabling the student to decode the symbols for the various manuscripts, including superscripts that differentiate the original form of a manuscript (indicated with an asterisk) from later corrections to it, or that distinguish between different manuscripts from a given church father or different editions or dialects of a version from another language (along with virtually everything else one might want to know about the apparatuses of this edition).[45]

Using this information, we may look at our example from Romans 5:2 and see that there are three possible readings for this text-critical problem. Option one is what the text reads (τῇ πίστει, "by faith"); option two has the addition of the preposition ἐν (ἐν τῇ πίστει, making the "by" explicit rather than just indicated by the case ending of "faith"); and option three omits the phrase altogether. Each of the variants is attested by several important manuscripts. Later, in our final section on evaluating external evidence, we will consider the manuscript weight for each option. For now, it will suffice to note that there are three possibilities, and the preferred reading is granted only a "C" for the committee's degree of confidence or consensus, which leaves plenty of room for the textual critic to evaluate the various options. In fact, in this rare case the committee was tentative enough regarding this conclusion that they chose to bracket the phrase in question in the text in order to represent the balance of the evidence.[46] Interpreting the text-critical apparatus has given us the necessary external evidence to begin making a decision on this variant reading.

A Textual Commentary on the Greek New Testament, 2nd Edition

The United Bible Societies was not content to leave the exegete with only external evidence to make a text-critical decision. Therefore they have published a companion volume to the *Greek New Testament* that gives a brief description of why the committee of the UBS[4] chose the preferred reading in each of the 1,428 texts treated in the apparatus. The *Textual Commentary* explains

---

45. UBS, 1*–52*.

46. Bracketing the phrase denotes that the committee had difficulty reaching the decision (as indicated by the "C" rating) and that the words in the brackets "may be regarded as part of the text, but that in the present state of New Testament textual scholarship this cannot be taken as completely certain" (UBS, 2*).

the significance of the external evidence and evaluates manuscript attestation. It also discusses internal evidence, showing what rules of interpretation are most relevant for the passage at hand. This is an especially useful resource for the exegete in situations where the committee decided against the witness of the most reliable early manuscripts, for in these cases the grounds for choosing a contrary reading is almost always based on internal evidence. The logic employed in these instances is not always as obvious to the beginning student. Thus, the *Textual Commentary* is an invaluable tool to help the amateur interpreter begin to think like a textual critic and is handy for helping the more seasoned student formulate arguments either for or against the decisions of the UBS[4] committee. These discussions are listed in the order in which the affected texts occur in the New Testament canon and can be accessed by looking up the New Testament book, chapter, and verse(s) involved. For Romans 5:2, the *Textual Commentary* explains the balanced external evidence for both τῇ πίστει and its omission, alerts the reader that the committee decided to keep the phrase because it was most likely dropped by a copyist who thought it was superfluous after ἐκ πίστεως (from faith) in 5:1, and mentions that ἐν τῇ πίστει was a scribal error caused by dittography—recopying the last two letters (ἐν) of the previous word (ἐσχήκαμεν).[47]

THE NESTLE-ALAND *NOVUM TESTAMENTUM GRAECE*, 27TH EDITION

In the late nineteenth and early twentieth centuries, a number of critical editions began to emerge as scholars gathered and compared manuscript evidence.[48] Eberhard Nestle's version was outstanding among these texts because of its careful work with the various text types and its critical apparatus, which mentioned far more variant readings among manuscripts than had previous editions of the Greek New Testament. Such a thorough apparatus allowed the user to form independent opinions about the text, no longer having to rely

47. Metzger, *Textual Commentary on the Greek New Testament*, 452–53.
48. Critical Greek New Testament texts such as those compiled by late nineteenth-century scholars Constantin von Tischendorf, Samuel Prideaux Tregelles, and, consummately, Cambridge professors Brooke Foss Westcott and Fenton John Anthony Hort, evaluated various early manuscripts in order to achieve a text that most likely represented the original. They laid the groundwork for Nestle's meticulous work, which did little more than compare the Westcott-Hort edition with the Tischendorf edition. Where the readings differed, Nestle consulted a third edition (either Richard Frances Weymouth's or Bernhard Weiss's), and in doing so was able to establish the text by majority. Because the editions Nestle consulted were based for the most part on early reliable manuscripts, Nestle's edition was outstandingly accurate. The work of these critics triggered the downfall of reliance on the so-called *Textus Receptus*, which, although the dominant text from the 400s to the 1800s, was based on much later, more-corrupt manuscripts. Scholars could now begin to explain how and why variations had crept in and offer conjectures about which reading could best account for all of the textual variants. For a succinct history of the various editions of the Greek New Testament, see Parker, *New Testament Manuscripts and Their Texts*, 191–223.

on the Majority Text or even on scholarly consensus. It was the production of such a work that slowly began to replace previous editions that were often overly dependent on the abundant but later Byzantine manuscripts. Now in its 27th edition and supplemented by the contributions of Kurt Aland, the Nestle-Aland text remains the foundation for other critical editions, especially the UBS text. Today the UBS[4] and NA[27] have identical texts but different apparatuses. The NA includes considerably more instances of textual variants than the UBS does but then gives much briefer representative manuscript attestation, lest the apparatus grow so large as to overwhelm the text itself.[49] Additionally, the NA does not include a "grading" system like the UBS does, and it lacks the companion volume that explains committee decisions. The extra information in the NA proves handy for the interpreter who typically works with the UBS text and finds no variant readings for a given passage (James 3:13–18, for example) and yet is still interested in seeing if and how manuscript traditions diverge from one another in that particular text, even if in more minor ways. The reverse is also true: the information in the UBS is helpful for the textual critic who most often works with the NA but desires a fuller listing of evidence for the variants or would like to see which of the variants listed in the NA apparatus the UBS committee considered the most significant (Rom. 5:1–11, for example, has eleven variants listed in the NA apparatus but only three in the UBS).

As we did with the text-critical apparatus of the UBS[4], we will do here with the NA[27]. The sample passage and explanation of its apparatus will again come from Romans 5:2.

δι' οὗ καὶ τὴν προσαγωγὴν ἐσχήκαμεν ⸂[τῇ πίστει]⸃ εἰς τὴν χάριν ταύτην ἐν ᾗ ἑστήκαμεν καὶ καυχώμεθα ἐπ' ἐλπίδι τῆς δόξης ᵀ τοῦ θεοῦ.

through whom also we have had access ⸂[by faith]⸃ into this grace in which we have stood and boast in the hope of the glory ᵀ of God.

2 ⸂– B D F G 0220 sa; Ambst ¦ εν τη π. ℵ[1] A *pc* vg[mss] ¦ *txt* ℵ[*.2] C Ψ 33. 1739. 1881 𝔐 lat | ᵀ filiorum lat

---

49. Note that although the wording in the text is the same in the UBS and NA, the punctuation differs at points, since punctuation and word division do not appear in ancient manuscripts. The UBS also divides the text into smaller passages and provides English titles that capture the main idea of each passage. It is particularly important that the exegete realize that the punctuation and the passage division and titles are not inspired. Therefore, when the interpreter practices literary context analysis, he or she may decide against the division of the passage as it is represented in the UBS text. Likewise, punctuation can change the meaning of the text and may indeed constitute an interpretive problem that must be considered by the student or pastor. Again, in this case the interpreter is not constrained to the punctuation as listed in either the UBS or the NA.

The number listed directs the reader to the verse in which the variant reading appears. Next, different symbols point the reader to the place in the verse where this variant occurs. These symbols represent the four dominant types of variants in the New Testament, namely additions, omission, substitutions, and transpositions.[50] Many verses have multiple variants, but the symbols allow the reader to match the variant reading in the text with its apparatus information.[51] Additionally, multiple variant readings within a single verse are divided from each other by a single vertical line. Any textual variant (as opposed to the preferred reading that occurs in the text) is offered first in the NA, followed by a very short list of manuscript support. Alternative textual variants for one specific part of a verse are divided from each other by a broken vertical line. The reading chosen for the text is preceded by the designation *txt* in the apparatus and is then followed by a list of manuscript support, but only when there is any reasonable uncertainty. Where passages would have merited a high level of confidence in the UBS apparatus, the NA lists only the variants and leaves the reader to infer that all other significant texts follow the reading chosen for inclusion in the text itself. One can see that although the NA offers considerably less manuscript attestation for the variants in Romans 5:2, it does include one more textual variant (in Latin) for this verse than the UBS[4].

Weighing Evidence and Making Decisions

With all our discussion about gathering witnesses, weighing evidence, determining whose testimony is most reliable, and making final judgments about which variants most likely represent the original text, perhaps we should invoke a courtroom analogy to help us better understand the practice of textual criticism. Just as a careful judge and jury listen to different witnesses and make decisions on who is telling the most accurate version of the truth, so textual critics adjudicate among existing textual variants. As in the justice system, verdicts can never be proved beyond a shadow of a doubt, that is, with 100 percent certainty. The jury will convict where there is proof of guilt beyond a *reasonable* doubt. The text critic deals with less than 100 percent certainty simply because the original autographs of Scripture are not available to be consulted. Nonetheless, great degrees of accuracy are achievable in the careful practice of textual criticism. Even if the text established by the preferred readings of the critical editions of the Greek New Testament or chosen by the translator or exegete does not always perfectly represent the originals, the odds are exceedingly high that the original reading is represented *among* the textual variants. The person trained in textual criticism is therefore at least aware

50. See the introduction in NA, 45*–47*, for a legend of which symbols represent the changes mentioned here.
51. Consult the introduction in NA, 49*–69*, for a key to understanding the remaining symbols used in the text and apparatus.

Sidebar 1.3

Guidelines for Weighing the Evidence

Evaluating External Evidence

- Prefer the reading attested by the earliest reliable manuscripts.
- Prefer the reading that occurs across a wide geographical spread in a number of different text types or kinds of sources.
- Prefer the reading that originates from the more accurately preserved textual traditions.

Evaluating Internal Evidence: Transcriptional Principles

- Prefer the more difficult reading (the *lectio difficilior*) as original.
- Prefer the shorter reading.

Evaluating Internal Evidence: Intrinsic Principles

- Prefer the reading that most easily fits with the author's style and vocabulary.
- Prefer the reading that best fits in the context and in the author's overall theological and narrative framework.
- Where parallel passages with variants exist (such as in the Gospels), prefer the less-harmonious reading.

---

of the original reading, even if he or she is not certain which one of several options it is. Textual criticism puts the original text more within the reach of the interpreter, even if absolute certainty remains elusive. The textual critic must balance external and internal evidence in the process and avoid giving too much weight to any single argument among a larger number.

EVALUATING EXTERNAL EVIDENCE

By examining the various witnesses, textual critics have come up with principles, also called "canons," for evaluating external evidence. These may sound familiar because we have implicitly alluded to them throughout our discussion. Here we state them explicitly:[52]

1. *Prefer the reading attested by the earliest reliable manuscripts.* The rationale in general is that the earlier the text, the closer it will be to the original since there has been less opportunity for corruption. However, this should be applied with discernment, since there are some early manuscripts with significantly corrupted texts and some later manuscripts that reflect reliable early readings. For example, manuscript 1739 from the tenth century preserves a text very similar to $\mathfrak{P}^{46}$ (second century).[53] Even more important than

---

52. Cf. Black, *New Testament Textual Criticism*, 32–35.
53. Wegner, *Student's Guide to Textual Criticism*, 241.

the date of the manuscript itself is the date and quality of the text type it represents. An early manuscript based on an early or more accurate text type should be given priority over others.[54] Still, blind preference for one manuscript when there is a wealth of reliable manuscripts is irresponsible, because no one manuscript can be followed mechanically in all places in establishing the original text. The most dramatic example of this first principle appears in the words added to 1 John 5:7–8 about the Father, the Word, and the Holy Spirit being three witnesses in heaven who agree, words which appear in no known Greek manuscript before the fourteenth century.[55] In extreme cases like this, it scarcely matters what the internal evidence might demonstrate; with no external evidence that the reading was known in earlier centuries, the reading cannot be considered original.

2. *Prefer the reading that occurs across a wide geographical spread in a number of different text types or kinds of sources.* A reading that is attested by papyri, uncials, and patristic citations from a broad cross section of the ancient world is more likely to be original than a reading found in only one area. So if a reading can be found in manuscripts from North Africa, Rome, and Asia Minor, it is more likely to be original than that which appears in only one of those regions. This is especially true if the readings from these different locations are from different text types.[56] These factors would indicate that the reading occurs in a manuscript that predates widespread geographical distribution. Thus, for example, some Western manuscripts omit Luke 22:19b–20, but others contain it, as do almost all Byzantine and Alexandrian manuscripts, so these additional statements about the Lord's Supper (from the so-called Words of Institution) should be accepted.[57]

3. *Prefer the reading that originates from the more accurately preserved textual traditions.* Text-critical scholars have identified which of the traditions are more prone to copying mistakes, harmonizations, and secondary additions. The textual traditions that avoid these errors in any given passage should be preferred; however, it is vital to remember that original readings can be found in all text types, which is why the critic should always make comparisons. Far more often than not, readings on which Alexandrinus and Sinaiticus agree will be preferred, though occasionally, they may be rejected if little or no other external evidence supports their readings. Romans 4:19 offers the textual critic two options, which also affect how the verse should be understood: "[Abraham's] faith did not weaken when he considered . . ."

54. See, e.g., Metzger and Ehrman, *Text of the New Testament*, 305–6.
55. Robert W. Yarbrough, *1–3 John* (Grand Rapids: Baker, 2008), 293.
56. Cf. Metzger and Ehrman, *Text of the New Testament*, 302.
57. For a fuller discussion of this variant, see Bradly S. Billings, *Do This in Remembrance of Me: The Disputed Words in the Lukan Institution Narrative (Luke 22.19b–20): An Historico-Exegetical, Theological, and Sociological Analysis* (London and New York: T&T Clark, 2006).

and "[Abraham] was so strong in faith that he did *not* consider. . . ." Here the external evidence for the former rendering includes not only ℵ and B, but also A and C, while the latter is supported primarily by the Western and Byzantine traditions. The former reading is therefore preferred.[58] But only a few verses later in 5:1, despite very strong external evidence for the subjunctive ἔχωμεν ("let us have") over against the indicative ἔχομεν ("we have"), only the latter fits the context, which is talking about the results of justification, which believers "have." The reading "let us have" is explicable as an accidental substitution of one kind of Greek "o" for another. In this case, strong external evidence for one reading cannot by itself justify choosing that reading.[59]

In other words, these canons for employing external evidence must be used together, and never in isolation from one another. And even when taken together, these principles *by themselves* will usually not be sufficient to point the textual critic to the most likely original reading. After analyzing the external evidence, the critic will need to evaluate the internal evidence as well in order to reach a sound judgment on the text in question.[60]

EVALUATING INTERNAL EVIDENCE

Internal evidence must be evaluated on two levels, in terms of both *transcriptional* and *intrinsic* probabilities. Transcriptional probabilities have to do with the process of copying and transmission. They deal with scribal tendencies toward mistakes or accuracy. A good example of this is the accidental omission or addition of a letter. Intrinsic probabilities have to do with the author's style of writing and typical vocabulary. For example, if a single reading emerged using atypical Pauline vocabulary in one of Paul's epistles, even if that reading was from an early, generally reliable manuscript, the reading would be suspect because of the unlikelihood of Paul suddenly or dramatically changing his style.[61] However, this alone would not render the reading inauthentic; it would merely raise questions in the reader's mind about what other options might be available that would fit Paul's typical patterns. Internal evidence can be best evaluated by applying the transcriptional and intrinsic principles listed below.[62]

Transcriptional Principles

1. *Prefer the more difficult reading (the* lectio difficilior) *as original.* The principle of determining the reading that best explains the existence of the others comes into play here. Because scribes were interested in smoothing out

---

58. Metzger, *Textual Commentary on the Greek New Testament*, 451.

59. Ibid., 452.

60. A table of witnesses dividing the more important manuscripts into their respective textual families appears in Black, *New Testament Textual Criticism*, 63–65.

61. Wegner, *Student's Guide to Textual Criticism*, 241; Metzger and Ehrman, *Text of the New Testament*, 302.

62. Cf. Black, *New Testament Textual Criticism*, 52–55.

the text and having it be as clear as possible, the textual critic should generally prefer the more difficult reading as the original text.[63] The most puzzling reading for us was likely the most puzzling reading for the scribe and hence prompted the scribe to change the wording (for example, Matt. 5:22, in which some variants seek to soften Jesus's difficult words by inserting "without cause" after "whoever hates his brother"). However, there are points at which a reading is too difficult (such as when one variant ending to the parable of the two sons in Matt. 21:29–31 identifies the son who promised to work in the vineyard but then didn't as the one who did his father's will). Then the exegete should reject the hardest reading.

2. *Prefer the shorter reading.* Scribes tended to add to the text, in order to clarify, rather than to delete material, especially when they believed they were dealing with God's Word. While a transcriptional error may have led to the omission of a phrase because of mistakes such as *homoeoteleuton* (Greek for "similar ending," meaning that a scribe accidentally skipped from a letter or word to the same letter or word farther down the page, leaving out material in between), the addition of explanatory material by the scribe occurs more frequently.[64] By far the most common examples are references to Jesus that attract one or more titles to themselves, such as "the Lord Jesus," "Jesus Christ," and "the Lord Jesus Christ."[65] Preference for the shorter reading should be disregarded, however, where the context and other variants indicate that a shorter reading has occurred because a textual difficulty has been smoothed over by a scribe who decided to omit rather than include or change the difficult phrase (see John 3:13 for a good example). Additionally, certain early papyri tend to abbreviate rather than expand.[66] Above all things, remember that we are seeking the reading that best explains the presence of the other variants.

Intrinsic Principles

1. *Prefer the reading that most easily fits with the author's style and vocabulary.* As mentioned earlier, a reading reflecting an abrupt change in style from

63. Metzger and Ehrman, *Text of the New Testament*, 302–3; Wegner, *Student's Guide to Textual Criticism*, 247.

64. Other frequent mistakes that will aid the textual critic in assessing transcriptional probabilities are (1) faulty word division, since there were no breaks in the early texts; (2) haplography—writing a letter or word once where it appeared twice in the text being copied; (3) dittography—writing a letter or word twice where it appeared only once in the previous copy; (4) metathesis—changing the order of words or letters; and (5) itacism—writing the wrong vowel letter that sounds like another, such as replacing an omicron with an omega. For examples of places where such errors occur in the New Testament text, see Black, *New Testament Textual Criticism*, 59–60.

65. See esp. Bart D. Ehrman, *The Orthodox Corruption of Scripture: The Effect of Early Christological Controversies on the Text of the New Testament* (Oxford and New York: Oxford University Press, 1993).

66. See the thorough demonstration of this tendency for six early papyri in Royse, *Scribal Habits in Early Greek New Testament Papyri*.

the author's typical form of expression should generally be rejected if other, good readings exist.[67] The longer ending of Mark is an excellent example of longer, more awkward sentences that do not much resemble the simple, straightforward Greek of the rest of the Gospel.

2. *Prefer the reading that best fits in the context and in the author's overall theological and narrative framework.* If the theology appears different from what is encountered in the rest of the book, it may be the handiwork of a scribe who was interested in promoting certain theological convictions.[68] The rest of the exegetical process must be considered here too. For example, literary analysis would be supremely important in a decision of this sort, in order to determine the author's flow of thought (see chap. 4). Not only does textual criticism inform exegesis, but also proper exegesis will help determine difficult text-critical decisions, so that no one part of the interpretive process can become the exegete's sole focus.

A highly controversial example involves 1 Corinthians 14:34–35. Because in a handful of manuscripts these verses on women being silent in the churches appear at the end of the chapter (after vv. 39–40), some scholars have argued that they may not have been written by Paul at all. After all, Paul clearly envisions women praying and prophesying in church in 11:5, even while insisting that they respect their husbands with culturally appropriate head coverings. However, the seemingly disruptive location of these verses, in the middle of Paul's discourse on tongues and prophecy, more than adequately explains why some scribes would move them to just after Paul had finished that discussion, and there are no known manuscripts in which the verses are actually absent. As for the apparent disruption of the narrative, that may in fact be the exegetical key to their interpretation—that a much more circumscribed form of speaking is in view.[69]

3. *Where parallel passages with variants exist (such as in the Gospels), prefer the less-harmonious reading.* The scribes were more likely to harmonize seemingly discrepant parallels than to introduce new problems into their texts.[70] The various authors of Scripture, however, should be granted the right to express themselves in their own characteristic fashion. In the later exegetical step of biblical theology (see chap. 9), the interpreter can determine how seemingly discordant passages can be reconciled, but that is not the task of a scribe or copyist. So when a large number of manuscripts add to the shorter, Lukan version of the Lord's prayer in Luke 11:2 "your will be done, on earth as it is

---

67. Metzger and Ehrman, *Text of the New Testament*, 313–14.

68. Black, *New Testament Textual Criticism*, 36.

69. The two most likely options are the evaluation of prophecy (a complementarian argument) or interruptions by uneducated women (an egalitarian argument). See further Craig L. Blomberg, "Neither Hierarchicalist nor Egalitarian: Gender Roles in Paul," in *Paul and His Theology*, ed. Stanley E. Porter (Leiden and Boston: Brill, 2006), 304–5.

70. Metzger and Ehrman, *Text of the New Testament*, 314.

in heaven," it is clearly to bring the prayer in line with the Matthean or more common liturgical form (Matt. 6:10).

The Relationship between Internal and External Evidence

There is no complete scholarly consensus on the way in which external and internal evidence should be used together to determine the original reading. The method we are following throughout this chapter is called *reasoned eclecticism*.[71] It gives equal consideration to both external and internal evidence and seeks to establish whether external, internal, or some combination of both types of evidence answers the question of which reading accounts for the rise of the others. This is by far the most common approach. Some, however, favor the internal evidence of a text as more important than the external evidence. *Rigorous* or *thoroughgoing eclecticism* prefers to determine the probable original by giving almost exclusive consideration to the contextual demands and the style of the author. Finally, a few scholars passionately promote *radical conservatism* or the *Majority Text/Byzantine Priority approach*. They consider only external evidence and give priority to the Byzantine text type, arguing that the text should be established according to the support of the majority of manuscripts.[72] Charted on a continuum, the various major approaches would look like this:

rigorous/thoroughgoing	reasoned	radical
eclecticism	eclecticism	conservatism

The methods on the ends of the continuum do not incorporate the text's history of transmission into the text-critical decision.[73] Yet these two methods are prevalent enough in New Testament scholarship that we must briefly explain why we have not chosen them and then turn to the rationale for the mediating view that we prefer.

WEAKNESSES OF THE BYZANTINE PRIORITY / MAJORITY TEXT APPROACH

While it is true that about 80 percent of extant manuscripts are Byzantine in character, the proliferation of manuscripts of this sort is explained by the text type's adoption by the religious leaders of the Byzantine empire that flourished

---

71. See esp. Michael W. Holmes, "Reasoned Eclecticism in New Testament Textual Criticism," in Ehrman and Holmes, *Text of the New Testament in Contemporary Research*, 336–60.

72. For a volume that includes articles by defenders of each of these different approaches, see David A. Black, ed., *Rethinking New Testament Textual Criticism* (Grand Rapids: Baker, 2002).

73. Holmes, "Textual Criticism," 56.

from the fifth to the twelfth centuries.[74] As long as this geographical region proved central to the developing Christian faith, we would expect it to produce and preserve the greatest number of Greek New Testament manuscripts.

In fact, most in the Majority Text movement, which so heartily decries the "subjectivity" of internal evidence, base their arguments on a theological presupposition that the inspiration of Scripture demands not only inerrant originals but also providentially preserved, inerrant copies. Though Scripture itself makes no such claims for the providence of God functioning in this way, Majority Text proponents typically think God simply must have acted like this.[75] Ironically, there is no comparable tradition of "preservation by majority rule" for Old Testament manuscripts, so this approach is demonstrably unworkable for that larger portion of Scripture.[76] As with every other area of exegesis, the interpreter must do his or her best to arrive at conclusions that are not already predetermined by presuppositions.[77]

WEAKNESSES OF RIGOROUS ECLECTICISM

A text-critical method that relies solely on internal evidence errs in the opposite direction. The biggest difficulty with a rigorous eclectic approach is that individual scholars' preference for various readings based on internal criteria can be highly subjective where it remains unbalanced by a good measure of external evidence. Further, in this practice the author's style is usually preferred irrespective of transcriptional probabilities. In effect, this robs the original author of his voice, since he very well may have used something contrary to his usual diction or style to emphasize a point.[78] A later scribe who then found difficulty with the break in authorial style could have made a change in order to smooth out the text and harmonize the concept with the rest of the author's work. Rigorous eclecticism would then wind up choosing the corrupted reading.

A RATIONALE FOR REASONED ECLECTICISM

Reasoned eclecticism, however, gives consideration to both external and internal evidence. How widely and early the external evidence supports a

74. Metzger and Ehrman, *Text of the New Testament*, 220.

75. The promise in 2 Tim. 3:16, which Majority Text proponents like to cite in support of their view, would apply to Old Testament Scripture rather than the entire Bible as we have it today. This historical-cultural fact makes the use of this verse by Majority Text proponents an unwarranted proof text. Even then, it says nothing about the inerrant preservation of the text.

76. Daniel B. Wallace, "The Majority-Text Theory: History, Methods and Critique," *Journal of the Evangelical Theological Society* 37 (1994): 203.

77. For an outstanding history and critique of the resurgent Majority Text argument, more generally, see Wallace's entire article (ibid., 185–215).

78. Eckhard J. Schnabel, "Textual Criticism: Recent Developments," in *The Face of New Testament Studies: A Survey of Recent Research*, ed. Scot McKnight and Grant R. Osborne (Grand Rapids: Baker Academic, 2004), 71.

reading determines how seriously to take it. Internal evidence is then used to adjudicate among variants that all have reasonably strong external support. Nuancing our earlier criterion, we may now affirm that reasoned eclecticism thus always asks, "Which reading best explains, *in terms of both external and internal evidence*, the origins of the other readings?"[79] Of course there is some measure of subjectivity even here, but there are far more checks and balances than in the other two approaches. Moreover, reasoned eclecticism is willing to grapple with historical evidence, rather than dismissing it in favor of a purely internal analysis of the text (as in rigorous eclecticism) or in favor of a reading in which the external evidence has been merely counted instead of weighed (as in the Majority Text approach).

Implications for Pastoral Ministry

Where does this discussion of textual criticism leave the believer who has a high view of Scripture? It seems that so many existing versions of the text and the lack of the originals, not to mention all of our language about "probabilities," "approximations," and "most likely readings," undercut the notion that the New Testament as we have it is God's very word to his church. In fact, the circumstances are not nearly as dire as we might first imagine. More than 99 percent of the original Greek New Testament can be reconstructed beyond any reasonable doubt. As noted above, only about four hundred variants (less than one per page in an average English translation) have any significant bearing on the meaning of the passage at hand, and the committees that produced modern-language translations usually note the most theologically significant of these variants in footnotes, so that even those who do not read Greek know the major options. Furthermore, no mainstream Christian doctrine is founded solely, or even primarily, on any textually disputed passage.[80] The average reader of Scripture is not at any great peril if he or she does not understand the text-critical process; however, the pastor or teacher who wants to instruct with the greatest amount of accuracy and precision but who bypasses this step in exegesis risks relying on an inferior text at some point without even knowing it. Ignorance of textual criticism will become a more serious obstacle for pastors or teachers when they are unable to answer parishioners' questions about how the text has come to us in the forms in which we have it, or about why different modern-language translations opt for different textual variants. They will be unable to respond to the charges of the "far right" that contemporary translations have corrupted the supposedly pure, inerrant King James Version, and of the "far left" that careless copying or theologically motivated distor-

79. Holmes, "Textual Criticism," 56, italics ours.
80. Bruce M. Metzger, *The New Testament: Its Background, Growth, and Content*, 2nd ed. (Nashville: Abingdon, 1983), 281.

tions prove so pervasive that we cannot be confident that anything remaining resembles the original documents.[81]

As useful as textual criticism can be in ministry, a word of caution is in order. Often, many people in a congregation have never learned much about it. Some may have no idea that anything exists other than a single Greek text from which their English translation derives. Some may even act as if they think the Bible was originally written in English, or whatever modern language they speak. A few words regarding the use of textual criticism in teaching and preaching are thus in order. If in the course of exegesis a text-critical issue presents itself as important enough to include in a message, devote some serious time to introducing the issue to your audience so that it is not confusing. Otherwise, most text-critical work should be done behind the scenes, rather than discussing the practice at length in your preaching and teaching. As a given audience becomes familiar with the discipline, it will become easier simply to say, "The oldest and most reliable texts here read . . ." or "Probably a scribe understood x as follows and therefore changed it to y." But even with a seasoned congregation, be alert to newcomers, visitors, young Christians, or others who are unfamiliar with the concept of textual variants, and make adjustments accordingly.[82]

Taking Our Text-Critical Skills for a Test Drive

There is no better way to test the understanding and potential fruitfulness of practicing textual criticism than to dive right in. We have found that a helpful way to assess the evidence is to create a chart that puts the most important witnesses of each of the different text types in parallel columns. Brief sentences in three boxes at the bottom of the sheet can then be created to summarize the external evidence, along with the internal evidence under both intrinsic and transcriptional headings. A final decision as to the preferred reading may then be made. One possible template for compiling text-critical observations and a chart categorizing many of the most important witnesses to each text-type are provided at the end of the chapter.[83]

81. Contra the former, see esp. James R. White, *The King James Only Controversy: Can You Trust the Modern Translations?* 2nd ed. (Minneapolis: Bethany, 2009). Contra the latter, see esp. Timothy P. Jones, *Misquoting Truth: A Guide to the Fallacies of Bart Ehrman's* Misquoting Jesus (Downers Grove, IL: InterVarsity, 2007).

82. Walter L. Liefeld (*New Testament Exposition: From Text to Sermon* [Grand Rapids: Zondervan, 1984], 143–44), e.g., suggests limiting the topic to small groups, where there is plenty of time for discussion once these principles are introduced. We are indebted to Liefeld for several of his astute pastoral observations on how to use this tool to benefit maximally the spiritual lives of churchgoers.

83. Note that some manuscripts vary text type from one part of the New Testament to another.

The following example from 1 Thessalonians 2:7 provides the kind of information that could be recorded in a text-critical chart.[84]

δυνάμενοι ἐν βάρει εἶναι ὡς Χριστοῦ ἀπόστολοι. ἀλλὰ ἐγενήθημεν νήπιοι[1] ἐν μέσῳ ὑμῶν, ὡς ἐὰν τροφὸς θάλπῃ τὰ ἑαυτῆς τέκνα,

. . . being able to be weighty as apostles of Christ, but we became babes[1] in your midst, as whenever a nursing mother takes care of her own children.

[1]7 {B} νήπιοι 𝔓⁶⁵ ℵ* B C* D* F G I Ψ* 0150 104* 263 459 1962 *l* 147 *l* 592 *l* 593 *l* 603ᶜ itᵃʳ, ᵇ, ᵈ, ᶠ, ᵍ, ᵐᵒⁿ, ᵒ vgᶜˡ, ʷʷ copˢᵃᵐˢ, ᵇᵒ eth Origen⁽ᵍʳ¹/³⁾, ˡᵃᵗ; Ambrosiaster Jerome Pelagius Augustine // ἤπιοι ℵᶜ A C² D² Ψᶜ 075 6 33 81 104ᶜ 256 365 424 436 1241 1319 1573 1739 1852 1881 1912 2127 2200 2464 *Byz* [K L P] *Lect* vgˢᵗ (syrᵖ, ʰ) copˢᵃᵐˢˢ, ᶠᵃʸ arm (geo) slav Clement Origen²/³ Basil Chrysostom Theodoreˡᵃᵗ

The two options for the original text are νήπιοι ("babes") and ἤπιοι ("gentle"). The external evidence is relatively evenly divided. Although "gentle" has the Byzantine tradition (*Byz*) and hence the Majority Text in support of it, the earliest manuscripts line up more with "babes"—a third-century papyrus (𝔓⁶⁵), the two key fourth-century Alexandrian witnesses, Sinaiticus and Vaticanus (ℵ* B), and several other important early uncials. One sees also a large number of old italic manuscripts, which with Codex Bezae (D) give the Western text type good representation as well. Complicating matters, however, are the number of early witnesses that were later altered from "babes" to "gentle." On the one hand, the fact that "babes" was written by the initial copyist in so many texts (asterisked in the apparatus) that were later changed to "gentle" suggests "babes" as the original reading. On the other hand, so many potentially independent correctors could indicate knowledge of one or more earlier manuscripts that did in fact read "gentle." The varied weights of the minuscules, translations, and church fathers add few further insights.

When one turns to the internal evidence, it appears that "babes" is the harder reading that would more likely have generated "gentle" than vice versa. Intrinsically, it is more likely that scribes would find Paul's mixed metaphor very jarring, as he likens himself to young children in one clause and nursing mothers caring for those children in the next, and would try to alter it. But is "babes" too hard a reading to be the original? Probably not, given Paul's ability to switch metaphors abruptly elsewhere (e.g., in the middle of 1 Cor. 3:9, in which believers shift from being a field to a building, without even a

84. On this verse, cf. esp. Jeffrey A. D. Weima, "'But We Became Infants among You,'" *New Testament Studies* 46 (2000): 547–61; Timothy B. Sailors, "Wedding Textual and Rhetorical Criticism to Understand the Text of 1 Thessalonians 2.7," *Journal for the Study of the New Testament* 80 (2000): 81–98; and Stefano Cotrozzi, "1 Thessalonians 2:7—A Review," *Filología Neotestamentaria* 12 (1999): 155–60.

conjunction separating the two predicates). Transcriptionally, the evidence is almost equal for each option. A scribe could easily have missed the nu (ν) at the beginning of νήπιοι when the words ἐγενήθημεν νήπιοι were originally run together without spacing, because ἐγενήθημεν ends with the same letter. But dittography—writing a letter (or sometimes even a word) twice by accident—was also common, so the transcriptional evidence proves indecisive.

With the external evidence and the intrinsic part of the internal evidence both largely favoring "babes," though not overwhelmingly so, the UBS committee opted for νήπιοι but only with a B level of confidence.[85] Had one of these two lines of reasoning been more indecisive, they probably would have opted for a C; had all the arguments been finely balanced, a D. What is intriguing for readers of the NIV, however, is that this English translation reads "gentle." The translators were probably thinking the mixed metaphor was too blatantly contradictory for Paul to have written, but, against its usual practice with a reading this uncertain, there is no footnote to tell the reader of the other option. The TNIV has now chosen to follow the UBS, doubtless an improvement, but equally surprisingly gives no footnote supplying the option that the NIV had adopted. There could scarcely be stronger justification for learning the basics of textual criticism—enough to make sense of these changes in English translations—than an example like this one.

Conclusion

Although textual criticism is a complex and sometimes arduous task, it is not impossible to understand. Even the committed beginner can employ the field of study in order to understand the choices made by the different editions of the Greek New Testament and different modern-language translations. Through knowledge of the terminology, theory, and tools of textual criticism, students can become reasonably assured that they are dealing with the text as it was originally written by the author. While we should not assume that this degree of accuracy is guaranteed, we should never give up the quest to find the words of God as they were written to communities by the original, inspired authors of Scripture.

---

85. Indeed, Metzger (*Textual Commentary on the Greek New Testament*, 562) notes that he and Allen Wikgren argued for the reading "gentle," finding "babes" too harsh a juxtaposition of metaphors in the context. The rest of the committee outvoted them, however, pointing out Gal. 4:19 as an equally jarring passage in which Paul likens his concern to a mother in labor.

Table 1.2: Textual Criticism Worksheet (James 1:3)

Reading	Alexandrian		Western		Caesarean		Byzantine		Misc.	
	Manuscript	Date (century)	Manuscript	Date	Manuscript	Date	Manuscript	Date	Manuscript	Date
1. δοκίμιον (testing)	א	4th	it^ar	9th			K	5th	$\mathfrak{P}^{74}$	7th
	A	5th	it^ff	9th			L	9th	436	11th/12th
	B	4th	it^s	6th			P	9th	945	11th
	C	5th	syr^p	5th			Byz*		1505	12th
	Ψ	9th/10th	syr^h	616			Lect**		1611	12th
	33	9th					vg	4th/5th	2138	1072
	81	11th					slav	9th	syr^pal	6th
	322	15th							arm	5th
	323	12th							eth	6th
	1067	14th							geo	5th
	1175	10th							Cyril	444
	1243	11th								
	1292	13th								
	1409	14th								
	1735	10th								
	1739	10th								
	1852	13th								
	2298	12th								
	2344	11th								

Reading	Alexandrian		Western		Caesarean		Byzantine		Misc.	
	Manuscript	Date (century)	Manuscript	Date	Manuscript	Date	Manuscript	Date	Manuscript	Date
	2464	9th								
	Didymus³/⁴	4th								
2. δόκιμον (genuineness)	1241	12th								
	Didymus¹/⁴	4th								

Evaluation:

External Evidence

Major Alexandrian and Byzantine uncials, old translations into other languages in the Western tradition, and the vast majority of all later manuscripts overwhelmingly make δόκιμον the probable original reading.

Internal: Transcriptional

1. *Unintentional*
Easy to drop one letter from hearing or memory
2. *Intentional*
– Possible harmonization with δόκιμος v. 12
– Similar meaning—one use

Internal: Intrinsic

δόκιμον—means of testing fits passage best

Conclusion:

δόκιμον is best—external and internal, both support it.

*Byz = The reading of the *Byzantine* witnesses, that is, the text of the great majority of all Greek manuscripts, especially of the second millennium.

**Lect = The *majority* of the selected *lectionaries* together with the lectionary text of the Greek church (i.e., the text of the edition published by Apostoliki Diakonia, Athens).

Chart prepared by Kermit A. Ecklebarger, William W. Klein, and Erin M. Heim.

Table 1.3: Important Witnesses Arranged by Text Type

	Gospels	Acts
Alexandrian	**Papyri:** $\mathfrak{P}^1$ $\mathfrak{P}^3$ $\mathfrak{P}^4$ $\mathfrak{P}^5$ $\mathfrak{P}^{22}$ $\mathfrak{P}^{39}$ ($\mathfrak{P}^{66}$) $\mathfrak{P}^{75}$ **Lettered Uncials:** ℵ B C L T (W Lk. 1–8:12, Jn.) Z Δ Ξ Ψ **Numbered Uncials:** 059 060 0162 **Minuscules:** 33 579 892 1241 (1342 Mk.) **Versions:** Bohairic Coptic, cop^bo; (Sahidic Coptic, cop^sa) **Fathers:** Athanasius, Didymus, Jerome (in part), Origen (in part) The Vulgate, vg (in part)	**Papyri:** $\mathfrak{P}^8$ $\mathfrak{P}^{45}$ ($\mathfrak{P}^{50}$) **Lettered Uncials:** ℵ A B C Ψ **Numbered Uncials:** 048 076 096 **Minuscules:** 33 81 326 1175 **Versions:** Bohairic Coptic, cop^bo; (Sahidic Coptic, cop^sa) **Fathers:** Athanasius, Clement of Alexandria, Jerome (in part), Origen (in part)
Caesarean	**Papyri:** $\mathfrak{P}^{37}$ $\mathfrak{P}^{45}$ **Lettered Uncials:** Θ (W Mk. 5ff.) **Minuscules:** Family 1, f^1 = 1 118 131 209; Family 13, f^{13} = 13 69 124 174 230 (174 & 230 not used in Mk.) 346 543 788 826 828 983 1689; 28 157 565 700 1071 1604 **Versions:** Georgian, geo; Armenian, arm **Fathers:** Eusebius, Origen (in part)	**Papyri:** $\mathfrak{P}^{45}$ **Lettered Uncials:** I? *Text Type Not Certain in Acts* **Minuscules:** I? **Fathers:** Eusebius

Gospels

	Gospels	Acts
Western	**Papyri:** $\mathfrak{P}^{25}$ $\mathfrak{P}^{69}$ **Lettered Uncials:** ℵ (John 1:1–8:38) D (W Mk. 1–5?) **Numbered Uncial:** 0171 **Versions:** Old Latin, it, especially it^k&e; Sinaitic Syriac, syr^s; Curetonian Syriac, syr^c (in part) **Fathers:** Justin, Marcion, Hippolytus (except in Rev.), Tatian's Diatessaron, Tertullian, Irenaeus, Augustine (in part), Early Latin Fathers* and Syrian Fathers to AD 450** (except as otherwise noted), witnesses from the 6th century onward (e.g., Primasius, Cassiodorus, Bede)	**Papyri:** $\mathfrak{P}^{29}$ $\mathfrak{P}^{38}$ $\mathfrak{P}^{48}$ **Lettered Uncials:** D E **Numbered Uncials:** 066 **Minuscules:** 383 614 1611 1739 2138 2298 **Versions:** Old Latin, it; marginal readings in the Harclean Syriac^hmg, syr; The Peshitta, syr^p **Fathers:** Early Latin Fathers* and Syrian Fathers to AD 450** (except as otherwise noted), witnesses from the 6th century onward (e.g., Primasius, Cassiodorus, Bede Commentary of Ephraem)
Byzantine	**Lettered Uncials:** A E F G H K P S V (W Mt, Lk. 8:12ff.) Π Ψ Ω **Minuscules:** 1006 and most other minuscules not listed elsewhere **Versions:** Ethiopian, eth; Gothic, goth; Old Church Slavonic, slav (also contains some Western and Caesarean readings); and later versions **Fathers:** Jerome (in part), Chrysostom (in part), later fathers from AD 450 onward (except as noted elsewhere) The Vulgate, vg (in part) The Majority Text, *Textus Receptus*, 𝔐	**Lettered Uncials:** H L S P **Numbered Uncial:** 049 **Minuscules:** Most minuscules not listed elsewhere **Versions:** Ethiopian, eth; Gothic, goth; Old Church Slavonic, slav (also contains some Western and Caesarean readings); and later versions **Fathers:** Jerome (in part), Chrysostom (in part), later fathers from AD 450 onward (except as noted elsewhere) The Majority Text, *Textus Receptus*, 𝔐

N.B. A text with a superscribed character, e.g., 424^c, is a corrector and must be considered as a separate ms. of a different text type than that of its exemplar.

	Pauline Epistles and Hebrews	General Epistles	Revelation
Alexandrian	**Papyri:** $\mathfrak{P}^{10}$ $\mathfrak{P}^{13}$ $\mathfrak{P}^{15}$ $\mathfrak{P}^{16}$ $\mathfrak{P}^{27}$ $\mathfrak{P}^{32}$ $\mathfrak{P}^{46}$ $\mathfrak{P}^{65}$ most papyrus fragments **Lettered Uncials:** ℵ A B C H I P Ψ **Numbered Uncials:** 048 081 088 0220 **Minuscules:** 6 33 81 104 326 424ᶜ 1175 1739 1908 **Versions:** Bohairic Coptic, cop^bo; (Sahidic Coptic, cop^sa) **Fathers:** Jerome (in part), Origen (in part) The Vulgate, vg (in part)	**Papyri:** $\mathfrak{P}^{20}$ $\mathfrak{P}^{23}$ $\mathfrak{P}^{72}$ **Lettered Uncials:** ℵ A B C P Ψ **Numbered Uncials:** 048 056 0156 **Minuscules:** 33 81 104 323 326 424ᶜ 1175 1739 2298 **Versions:** Bohairic Coptic, cop^bo; (Sahidic Coptic, cop^sa) **Fathers:** Athanasius, Clement of Alexandria, Jerome (in part), Origen (in part) The Vulgate, vg (in part)	**Papyri:** $\mathfrak{P}^{18}$ $\mathfrak{P}^{24}$ $\mathfrak{P}^{47}$ **Lettered Uncials:** ℵ A C **Numbered Uncials:** 0169 0207 **Minuscules:** 61 1006 1611 1841 1854 2053 2344 2351 **Fathers:** Jerome (in part), Origen (in part) The Vulgate, vg (in part)
Caesarean	Text type not determined for Paul and Hebrews	Text type not determined for the General Epistles	Text type not determined for Revelation
Western	**Lettered Uncials:** D E F G **Numbered Uncial:** 048 (Tim., Titus, Phm.) **Minuscules:** 88 181 915 917 1836 1912 **Versions:** Old Latin, it **Fathers:** Greek Fathers to the end of the 3rd cent., Early Latin Fathers* and Syrian Fathers to AD 450** (except as otherwise noted)	**Papyri:** $\mathfrak{P}^{38}$ **Lettered Uncials:** D E **Numbered Uncials:** 066 **Versions:** Old Latin, it; marginal readings in the Harclean Syriac, syr^hmg, The Peshitta, syr^p **Fathers:** Tertullian, Irenaeus, Cyprian, Augustine, Epiphanius, Early Latin Fathers* and Syrian Fathers to AD 450**	**Lettered Uncial:** **Versions:** Old Latin, it

Byzantine

Pauline Epistles and Hebrews	General Epistles	Revelation
Lettered Uncials: K L **Numbered Uncial:** 049 **Minuscules:** Most minuscules not listed elsewhere **Versions:** Ethiopian, eth; Gothic, goth; Old Church Slavonic, slav (also contains some Western and Caesarean readings); and later versions **Fathers:** Jerome (in part), Chrysostom (in part), Later Fathers from AD 450 onward (except as noted elsewhere) The Vulgate, vg (in part) The Majority Text, *Textus Receptus*, 𝔐	**Lettered Uncials:** H K L **Numbered Uncial:** 049 **Minuscules:** 398 and most minuscules not listed elsewhere **Versions:** Ethiopian, eth; Gothic, goth; Old Church Slavonic, slav (also contains some Western and Caesarean readings); and later versions **Fathers:** Jerome (in part), Chrysostom (in part), Later Fathers from AD 450 onward (except as noted elswehere) The Vulgate, vg (in part) The Majority Text, *Textus Receptus*, 𝔐	**Numbered Uncials:** 046 051 052 **Minuscules:** Family 1, f^1 = 1 118 131 209; 82 93 104 254 296 424 429 469 808 920 1778 1828 (1854) (2020) 2042 2048 2049 2050 2053 2057 2081 2302 and most other minuscules not listed elsewhere **Versions:** Ethiopian, eth; Gothic, goth; Old Church Slavonic, slav (also contains some Western and Caesarean readings); and later versions **Fathers:** Jerome (in part), Chrysostom (in part), Later Fathers from AD 450 onward (except as noted elsewhere) The Vulgate, vg (in part) The Majority Text, *Textus Receptus*, 𝔐

*Early Latin Fathers: Tertullian, Cyprian, Novatian, Victorinus-Pettau, Juvencus, Hilary, Lucifer, Tychonius, Priscillian, Ambrose, Macarius, Magnes, Epiphanius, Gaudentius, Chromatius, Rufinus, Pelagius, Jerome, Augustine

**Syrian Fathers to about AD 450: Eusebius, Aphraates, Ephraem, Basil the Great, Cyril of Jerusalem, Gregory of Nazianzus, Gregory of Nyssa, Chrysostom, Theodore of Mopsuestia, Euthalius

Chart prepared by Elodie B. Emig and Erin M. Heim

2

Translation and Translations

First-year students of New Testament Greek often imagine that they will quickly discover all kinds of hidden secrets of Scripture that few in their churches know. They think they will be able to solve the major doctrinal and exegetical controversies of the faith, or at least know which of the existing options is "right." More careful reflection on these issues, however, should suggest to them that, if all it took to attain such depths of insight were a year or two of Greek, then the tens of thousands of students who had traversed this path before them, with the identical resources, would all have come to agreement on most every important exegetical question.

In fact, what Greek students quickly do discover is that (1) they begin to appreciate the complexity of the language and the exegetical issues; (2) they start to understand why interpretations differ; and (3) they become aware of alternate interpretations for texts that they previously thought had undisputed meanings. These realizations should instill a certain humility into the interpreter, which is itself an important accomplishment. By the end of two years of Greek (and sooner for many), most students should be able to use a dictionary and a grammar textbook to work out for themselves a rough-and-ready translation of most parts of the New Testament and be able to understand why other translations, including published versions of the Bible and renditions in commentaries, vary. The students also should be able to make reasonable assessments as to the relative merits of these translations. This chapter will consider both of these objectives in turn.

Creating a Translation

Different instructors will have different goals for students with respect to how polished a translation they desire for the passages from the Greek New Testament. But all students should at least aim to achieve a literal translation insofar as intelligibility in English (or another modern language) permits. The term "literal," however, can mislead. There are no two languages in the world in which the semantic domains (or range of meanings) of individual words or multiword constructions entirely overlap. The closer the languages are to each other in the history of their linguistic development, the greater the overlap, but it will never be 100 percent.[1] For example, Portuguese translates into Spanish much more readily than into German. Most European languages translate more directly into one another than they do into African or Asian languages. Greek translates reasonably well into Latin and, via Latin, into the Romance languages (Spanish, Portuguese, French, Italian, and Romanian), not too poorly into Teutonic and Anglo-Saxon languages, but with greater difficulty into East Asian ones.

To take just one example, for as simple a task as finding one English word to correspond to a key Greek word, consider the important theological term δικαιοσύνη. Spanish translators have a straightforward task; the word to use is *justicia*. But in English, two different words each capture part of the concept implied by the Greek: "righteousness" and "justice." Most English readers of the New Testament do not automatically recognize that when Jesus commands us to seek God's δικαιοσύνη (Matt. 6:33), the "righteous" living we should pursue includes seeking "justice" for those who do not have it in this world.[2]

In addition to the problem of finding words or expressions that fit what is meant in a different language is the issue of syntax or word order. English tends to follow the word order of subject–verb–direct object (or predicate complement) with modifiers placed fairly closely to what they modify. Greek, with its use of case endings, is not nearly as dependent on syntax to determine function. Especially in the more exalted prose and longer sentences of classical Greek, the word order could easily be direct object–verb–subject, with modifiers sometimes several words distant from what they modify. The accusative case would nevertheless identify a word as the direct object; the nominative

1. The best primer on the application of general linguistic theory to New Testament Greek remains Peter Cotterell and Max Turner, *Linguistics and Biblical Interpretation* (Leicester and Downers Grove, IL: InterVarsity, 1989). On ten main universals of language, see pp. 19–25. On the variables of semantics, see pp. 37–53. At the more technical level, the key work is Eugene A. Nida and Johannes P. Louw, *Lexical Semantics of the Greek New Testament* (Atlanta: Scholars Press, 1992).

2. Elsa Tamez, *The Amnesty of Grace: Justification by Faith from a Latin American Perspective* (Nashville: Abingdon, 1993).

case, the subject; and agreement in case endings would show which words modified others.

Thus a word-for-word translation of James 3:3a (εἰ δὲ τῶν ἵππων τοὺς χαλινοὺς εἰς τὰ στόματα βάλλομεν εἰς τὸ πείθεσθαι αὐτοὺς ἡμῖν) might read, "If but of the horses the bridles into the mouths we put in order the to be persuaded them by us." This is as "literal" a translation as one can make, but it is virtually unintelligible. At the very least, we have to change the word order of the first part of the giant conditional clause to "But if we put the bridles of the horses into the mouths." The article before "mouths," however, is used as a substitute for the possessive pronoun, so we should probably translate "their mouths." The final prepositional phrase requires the deletion in English of the definite article, which is untranslated in an articular infinitive. But then we either have to change "in order" to "for" and recognize the accusative pronoun as the subject of the infinitive ("for them to be persuaded by us") or change "in order" to "in order that" and render the infinitive as an English subjunctive ("in order that they might be persuaded by us"). When we realize that "to persuade" in the passive voice in the Greek (as often in English) is equivalent in meaning to "obey," we could then translate the clause even more intelligibly as "for them to obey us" or "in order that they might obey us." If we wanted to preserve something of the passive construction of the original but found "obey" a better contextual fit, we could use the cognate adjective of "obey" and translate, "in order that they might be obedient to us." And all these translations are "literal" compared to those that might introduce translations for individual words that are less appropriate in context, or parts of speech or multiword expressions that are less semantically equivalent (e.g., "Now consider the situation where y'all stick a little bit into that part of an equine that opens to chew its food, so that y'all can run roughshod over it"—we drastically exaggerate for the sake of making the point clearly).[3]

Linguists, therefore, prefer to speak not of more or less literal translation but of *formal* versus *functional equivalence*.[4] Sometimes functional equivalence is also called *dynamic equivalence*. Formal equivalence preserves the form of the original language as much as the new "receptor" language into which one is translating permits, while functional equivalence translates using words or expressions that duplicate the original function even if less exactly equivalent word by word. In the above example, "for them to be persuaded by us" would be about as formally equivalent as English would permit, while "for them to obey us" would be an excellent functional equivalent. When a large amount of text is translated, it will include a spectrum of or degrees of adherence to

---

3. On this verse and its role in context, see further Craig L. Blomberg and Mariam J. Kamell, *James* (Grand Rapids: Zondervan, 2008), 147–55.

4. Gordon D. Fee and Mark L. Strauss, *How to Choose a Translation for All Its Worth* (Grand Rapids: Zondervan, 2007), 26–27.

either formally or functionally equivalent translations, with many intentionally mediating options in between the two poles.[5]

Consider the much more difficult example of Ephesians 1:3–14, arguably all one sentence in the Greek.[6] This is virtually impossible to preserve in English, which requires at least periodic sentence breaks. The King James Version (KJV, orig. 1611) comes the closest, putting periods only after verses 6 and 12, which makes the next sentence in each instance technically incomplete by beginning with "In whom . . ." rather than "In him. . . ." The Revised Standard Version (RSV, orig. 1952) breaks these twelve verses up into six sentences, putting periods after verses 4, 6, 8, 10, and 12. The New American Standard Bible (NASB, orig. 1960) creates six sentences, with breaks near the ends of verses 4, 8, and 10, and after verses 6 and 12. The New Revised Standard Version (NRSV, 1989) creates seven independent clauses with periods after verses 4, 6, 10, and 12, and in the middle of verse 8, and with a semicolon where a period could have more naturally occurred after verse 13. The English Standard Version (ESV, 2001), based on the RSV, reverts to longer sentences at one point by deleting the break after verse 8. The New Living Translation (NLT, orig. 1996; 2nd ed. 2004), which is completely functionally equivalent, creates no fewer than fifteen sentences, thus averaging more than one per verse. Notice how different are the renderings of the KJV and the NLT:

Ephesians 1:3–14 KJV Blessed *be* the God and Father of our Lord Jesus Christ, who hath blessed us with all spiritual blessings in heavenly *places* in Christ: According as he hath chosen us in him before the foundation of the world, that we should be holy and without blame before him in love: Having predestinated us unto the adoption of children by Jesus Christ to himself, according to the good pleasure of his will, To the praise of the glory of his grace, wherein he hath made us accepted in the beloved. In whom we have redemption through his blood, the forgiveness of sins, according to the riches of his grace; Wherein he hath abounded toward us in all wisdom and prudence; Having made known unto us the mystery of his will, according to his good pleasure which he hath purposed in himself: That in the dispensation of the fulness of times he might gather together in one all things in Christ, both which are in heaven, and which are on earth; *even* in him: In whom also we have obtained an inheritance, being predestinated according to the purpose of him who worketh all things after the counsel of his own will: That we should be to the praise of his glory, who first trusted in Christ. In whom ye also *trusted*, after that ye heard the word of truth, the gospel of your salvation: in whom also after that ye believed, ye were sealed with that holy Spirit of promise, Which is the earnest of our inheritance until the redemption of the purchased possession, unto the praise of his glory.

5. See the chart in ibid., 28, which places the major current translations on a spectrum from the most formally equivalent translations to the least formally equivalent ones.

6. William W. Klein, "Ephesians," in *The Expositor's Bible Commentary*, ed. Tremper Longman III and David E. Garland, rev. ed. (Grand Rapids: Zondervan, 2005), 12:47.

Ephesians 1:3–14 NLT All praise to God, the Father of our Lord Jesus Christ, who has blessed us with every spiritual blessing in the heavenly realms because we are united with Christ. Even before he made the world, God loved us and chose us in Christ to be holy and without fault in his eyes. God decided in advance to adopt us into his own family by bringing us to himself through Jesus Christ. This is what he wanted to do, and it gave him great pleasure. So we praise God for the glorious grace he has poured out on us who belong to his dear Son. He is so rich in kindness and grace that he purchased our freedom with the blood of his Son and forgave our sins. He has showered his kindness on us, along with all wisdom and understanding. God has now revealed to us his mysterious plan regarding Christ, a plan to fulfill his own good pleasure. And this is the plan: At the right time he will bring everything together under the authority of Christ—everything in heaven and on earth. Furthermore, because we are united with Christ, we have received an inheritance from God, for he chose us in advance, and he makes everything work out according to his plan. God's purpose was that we Jews who were the first to trust in Christ would bring praise and glory to God. And now you Gentiles have also heard the truth, the Good News that God saves you. And when you believed in Christ, he identified you as his own by giving you the Holy Spirit, whom he promised long ago. The Spirit is God's guarantee that he will give us the inheritance he promised and that he has purchased us to be his own people. He did this so we would praise and glorify him.

The KJV reads like a gigantic run-on sentence by today's standards. The NLT breaks the text down into "kernels," rephrases them in modern English, and indicates the connections between clauses by the introductory words and phrases used in each verse. Many grade school children can make sense of the NLT; many adults remain baffled by the KJV.

Occasionally, editions of the Bible appear that become even more "literal" than a purely formally equivalent translation like the KJV. The *Concordant Version* of Titus 3:4–6, first published in 1926, for example, reads "Yet when the kindness and fondness for humanity of our Saviour, God, made its advent, not for works which are wrought in righteousness which we do, but according to His mercy, He saves us, through the bath of renascence and renewal of holy spirit, which He pours out on us richly through Jesus Christ, our Saviour."[7] Similarly, nineteenth-century scholar Robert Young, better known for his famous concordance of the KJV, created his own Young's Literal Translation (YLT, orig. 1862) based on the notion that the more one could translate word by word and tense by tense, the closer one's version was to being inspired. His rendition of Matthew 5:17–20, for example, reads:

---

7. *Concordant Literal New Testament*, 6th ed. (Canyon Country, CA: Concordant Publishing Co., 1976), 501.

Do not suppose that I came to throw down the law or the prophets—I did not come to throw down, but to fulfill; for, verily I say to you, till that the heaven and the earth may pass away, one iota or one tittle may not pass away from the law, till that all may come to pass. Whoever therefore may loose one of these commands—the least—and may teach men so, least he shall be called in the reign of the heavens, but whoever may do and may teach *them*, he shall be called great in the reign of the heavens. For I say to you, that if your righteousness may not abound above that of the scribes and Pharisees, ye may not enter to the reign of the heavens.

No contemporary linguists would recommend creating such rugged renderings, and few readers could be expected to make sense of them!

Figure 2.1: Types of Translations

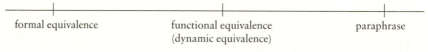

formal equivalence   functional equivalence   paraphrase
                                (dynamic equivalence)

More commonly, at the opposite end of the spectrum, one will find paraphrases of the Bible that prove freer even than a functionally equivalent translation like the NLT. Eugene H. Peterson's *The Message* is the best known example today. First Corinthians 13:4–7, for example, reads:

Love never gives up. Love cares more for others than for self. Love doesn't want what it doesn't have. Love doesn't strut, doesn't have a swelled head, doesn't force itself on others, isn't always "me first," doesn't fly off the handle, doesn't keep score of the sins of others, doesn't revel when others grovel, takes pleasure in the flowering of truth, puts up with anything, trusts God always, always looks for the best, never looks back, but keeps going to the end.

The Living Bible (TLB) was not as free as *The Message* but still free enough that a large team of scholars was solicited to revise it and create the NLT. Created solely by Ken Taylor (to produce something his teenagers would read, understand, and enjoy) from the old American Standard Version (1901, revision of the KJV), TLB caught the eye of many young adults in the 1970s and won them over to regular Bible reading when there were far fewer options on the market. By way of illustration, Luke 1:1–4, comparatively convoluted in Luke's syntax, became the very clear:

Dear friend who loves God: Several biographies of Christ have already been written using as their source material the reports circulating among us from the early disciples and other eyewitnesses. However, it occurred to me that it would be well to recheck all these accounts from first to last and after thorough investigation to pass this summary on to you, to reassure you of the truth of all you were taught.

Still other paraphrases go even further to service a "niche" audience. *The Aussie Bible* renders some of the most famous stories from Scripture in Australian slang, partly to be humorous and partly to reach an audience that might never otherwise pay attention to them. Introducing the story of the feeding of the five thousand, Mark 6:31–33 turns into:

> Jesus said to his team, "Come on out to the desert for a bit, so you can have some kip." (There was such a big mob hanging around they didn't even have time for a bite to eat.) They hopped in the skiff and rowed around the shore to a quiet spot in the scrub. But the mob saw them leave, and recognised them, and took off on foot. So people from all the townships got there ahead of them.[8]

Finally, there are "versions" that completely contemporize Bible stories, making them about other people in different times and places, like the famous *Cotton Patch Version* of the Civil Rights era, in which "Jesus is born in Gainesville, Georgia, and lynched in Atlanta by the state governor and his religious cronies."[9]

With rare exceptions, serious students of Scripture should stick to Bible versions that stay within the spectrum of formal to functional equivalence. The biggest interpretive payoff for students to create their own formally equivalent translations of Scripture is for them to discover for themselves the exact structure and diction of the Greek. They can then observe when the same Greek word appears more than once in a given context (even if certain translations appropriately use different English words); when there may be a play on words that translations mask where there is parallelism of language or structure within the text; when the original case, person, and/or number of a noun is not disclosed by the translation; and when the parsing of a verb is not immediately obvious or perhaps even obscured by a given translation. Likewise one can recognize when genitives have been interpreted (rather than the all-purpose "of" appearing before the noun in question) or when participles have been classified and so translated with finite verb forms introduced by adverbs like "because," "while," or "in order that" (rather than occurring as the one-word "-ing" form of the verb in English).[10]

First Thessalonians 1:3 in the New International Version (NIV, orig. 1978) and Today's New International Version (TNIV, orig. 2005) waxes almost

8. Kel Richards, *The Aussie Bible (Well, Bits of It Anyway!)* (North Ryde: Bible Society NSW, 2006), ad loc.

9. Fee and Strauss, *How to Choose a Translation*, 33. See, e.g., Clarence Jordan, *The Cotton Patch Version of Matthew and John* (El Monte, CA: New Win Publishing, 1970).

10. The value of formally equivalent translations is well articulated, though at times exaggerated, in Leland Ryken, *The Word of God in English: Criteria for Excellence in Bible Translation* (Wheaton: Crossway, 2002). Cf. Craig L. Blomberg, review of ibid., *Denver Journal* 6 (2003), http://www.denverseminary.edu/article/the-word-of-god-in-english-criteria-for-excellence-in-bible-translation/ (accessed March 10, 2010).

poetic with its beautiful rendering, "your work produced by faith, your labor prompted by love, and your endurance inspired by hope." Turning to the Greek, on the one hand, enables one to see that there are no separate verbs that were translated as "produced," "prompted," or "inspired." Instead, the three genitive nouns (often translated simply as "of faith," "of love," and "of hope") were correctly identified as subjective genitives, and functional equivalents were used to make this clear.[11] On the other hand, the NIV of Philemon 6a ("I pray that you may be active in sharing your faith") takes the expression "fellowship of your faith" as containing an objective genitive. But if, with most commentators, this should be understood as a subjective genitive instead (akin to those just noted in 1 Thess. 1:3), then the NIV misleads the reader into thinking Paul is talking about the need for evangelism when instead he is talking about Philemon's hospitable character. Thus the TNIV corrects the NIV to "I pray that your partnership with us in the faith may be effective . . ."[12]

Examples of intratextual connections that the student may discern by examining the Greek include the nice play on words in James 2:20. The Greek reads θέλεις δὲ γνῶναι, ὦ ἄνθρωπε κενέ, ὅτι ἡ πίστις χωρὶς τῶν ἔργων ἀργή ἐστιν. Most translations render the last clause as "that faith without works is useless." But "useless" (ἀργή) is a compound word formed from ἀ + ἔργον ("not" + "work"). The only way to bring out the play on words in English is to say something like "faith without works doesn't work," which is just a little freer than most functionally equivalent translations. But formally equivalent translations could never say "faith without works is not-work," because no one would understand it. So English versions invariably mask the original pun.[13]

Or consider a more substantial exegetical issue. First Peter 3:18–22 portrays Jesus preaching to the spirits in prison some time after his death. Of many enigmas in this passage, we may consider just one here. There is a growing consensus today that this text does not describe Jesus offering people a chance to be saved in the underworld but rather that he is announcing his victory over the evil spirits because of his atoning death. But does this happen between the crucifixion and resurrection or at some later point? His conquest of death is not complete until the resurrection. Jews at times envisioned the unseen, demonic realm as located above the earth between the atmosphere and what we would call heaven (cf. Eph. 2:2 and 2 Cor. 12:2). So perhaps Jesus announced his victory over the demons as he was returning to his Father's side during his ascension. Might the diction of 1 Peter in any way actually support this interpretation? Looking at English translations does not normally suggest anything. But the verbs used in 3:19 and 22 for Jesus's "going" are identical—the

11. Cf., e.g., F. F. Bruce, *1 and 2 Thessalonians* (Waco: Word, 1982), 12.

12. Cf., e.g., Douglas J. Moo, *The Letters to the Colossians and to Philemon* (Grand Rapids and Cambridge: Eerdmans; Nottingham: Apollos, 2008), 390–92.

13. Cf. further William R. Baker, "James," in *James-Jude: Unlocking the Scriptures for You*, by William R. Baker and Paul Carrier (Cincinnati: Standard, 1990), 62–63.

masculine nominative singular aorist deponent passive participle πορευθείς (having gone). When Jesus was made alive in (or by) the Spirit, *having gone*, he preached to the imprisoned spirits (vv. 18–19); after the resurrection, *having gone*, he is at the right hand of God (vv. 21–22). No one would translate these sentences so woodenly in a published Bible, but the matching words and forms enable the reader of Greek to suspect that the two "goings" are to be equated.[14] So, in the words of William Larkin's exegetical handbook title, "Greek is great gain."[15]

In short, every aspect of grammar typically studied in first- and second-year Greek classes[16] may, sooner or later, be hidden by English translations, or at least left ambiguous. Even students who cannot yet work out by themselves the translation of an entire passage of the New Testament can at least identify the various parts of speech and, where relevant, their parsings. Thus, the students can better understand why translations differ and why scholars disagree over interpretations. The students can recognize when a given word in English translates a corresponding Greek word (or is added in order to represent accurately its parsing) and when the term has been inserted because it corresponds to the translators' interpretation concerning, for example, what kind of genitive is present (or dative or participle or infinitive or use of a tense or clause, and so on). In the latter instances, students can suggest alternative translations utilizing grammatical classifications that are equally probable, especially where scholars already have lobbied for competing options. We will return to some of these issues in our chapter on grammar; meanwhile, we must proceed to the question that students, with or without the ability to translate the Greek of a New Testament text, regularly must answer: which modern-language translations should I utilize in which settings or under which circumstances? To answer this question we must also survey the breadth of available options and the strengths and weaknesses of each (see table 2.1 for types of translations and their typical uses).

Choosing Translations

The implication of all we have discussed so far is that it is valuable for serious students of the Bible, once they have studied enough Greek, to work out their own formally equivalent translations (even to the point of being woodenly literal, as long as they utilize grammatical and intelligible English). Bible readers who have not had the opportunity to learn Greek should consult regularly one

---

14. For a full defense of this view, see William J. Dalton, *Christ's Proclamation to the Spirits: A Study of 1 Peter 3:18–4:6*, 2nd ed. (Rome: Pontificio Istituto Biblico, 1989).

15. William J. Larkin, *Greek Is Great Gain: A Method for Exegesis and Exposition* (Eugene, OR: Wipf & Stock, 2008).

16. As reflected, e.g., in David A. Black, *It's Still Greek to Me: An Easy-to-Understand Guide to Intermediate Greek* (Grand Rapids: Baker, 1998).

or more of the available formally equivalent translations (see below), especially the NASB, NRSV, or ESV. The public reading, exposition, and teaching of Scripture, however, is another matter. Unless one has a highly educated, biblically literate audience with considerable homogeneity of theological background, the very literal or formally equivalent translations may go over their heads or at least be very difficult for some to understand. The KJV, for example, requires a twelfth-grade reading level (and acquaintance with a fair number of archaic English words and forms); the NASB, a tenth-grade level; but the NIV, only a seventh-grade level. These "levels" do not refer to what students in these grades actually learn, but to what ideal educational objectives prescribe. Thus the same scale that made these determinations assessed "the average adult reading level" to be between sixth and ninth grades.[17]

Table 2.1: Choosing the Best Type of Translation

Type of Translation	Typical Uses
Formally equivalent	• Serious Bible students who have not learned to use the original languages and who want the most "literal" translation (i.e., most closely corresponds word by word to the Greek New Testament) • When key doctrinal issues, controversial texts, or important theological words are involved • Students who want to check the accuracy of their own translation or see how it could be smoothed out while still largely retaining formal equivalence
Intermediate (between formally and functionally equivalent)	• Preachers, teachers, and other Christian leaders when engaging a broad cross section of public contexts • Pulpit Bibles
Functionally equivalent	• Youth groups and adult congregations with a fair percentage of people who have not gone to college
Functionally equivalent (or paraphrase)	• When freer but often clearer or fresher renderings are needed • Special contexts in which one wants a new take on an old, well-known passage
Multiple translations of different kinds	• When readers cannot adjudicate the strengths and weaknesses of a given translation by comparing it with the Greek

Completely functionally equivalent translations, however, give many fresh insights but often prove a little too free for demonstrating the kinds of exegetical observations that the preacher or teacher wants to make. The public use of Scripture, therefore, proceeds best when it utilizes good translations designed to occupy an intermediate position between fully formal and fully functional equivalence. The NIV, TNIV, and Holman Christian Standard Bible (HCSB,

---

17. Paul D. Wegner, *The Journey from Texts to Translations: The Origin and Development of the Bible* (Grand Rapids: Baker, 1999), 392.

1999) are particularly helpful in this respect. Note the differences, for example, between the NASB and the TNIV for Romans 3:25–26:

> whom God displayed publicly as a propitiation in His blood through faith. *This was* to demonstrate His righteousness, because in the forbearance of God He passed over the sins previously committed; for the demonstration, *I say*, of His righteousness at the present time, so that He would be just and the justifier of the one who has faith in Jesus. (NASB)

> God presented Christ as a sacrifice of atonement, through the shedding of his blood—to be received by faith. He did this to demonstrate his justice, because in his forbearance he had left the sins committed beforehand unpunished—he did it to demonstrate his justice at the present time, so as to be just and the one who justifies those who have faith in Jesus. (TNIV)

The TNIV is five words longer than the NASB, but it is also clearer in several places. The NASB itself is eleven words longer than the Greek, because of the specific kinds of terms and forms used in the original that simply cannot be reproduced in fluent English by a single word.

Completely functionally equivalent translations prove ideal for those at lower levels of English comprehension, such as children and young teens, people for whom English is a second language, or adults whose literacy skills are below average. Such translations can also help longtime Bible readers gain fresh insight into Scripture and renewed enthusiasm for well-worn texts, and they can make the Bible come alive for competent readers, including non-Christians, who for some reason become bored with or alienated from the Bible while reading more traditional translations. For good models here, consider especially the NLT, Good News Translation (GNT; formerly Good News Bible, orig. 1976), and Contemporary English Version (CEV, 1995). The GNT, for example, renders Romans 3:25–26 as follows:

> God offered him, so that by his blood he should become the means by which people's sins are forgiven through their faith in him. God did this in order to demonstrate that he is righteous. In the past he was patient and overlooked people's sins; but in the present time he deals with their sins, in order to demonstrate his righteousness. In this way God shows that he himself is righteous and that he puts right everyone who believes in Jesus.

The GNT is sixteen words longer than the TNIV but is even more straightforward in its vocabulary and syntax.

Specific Debates

Three issues merit extra attention before we make some summary comments about the full range of current English-language Bibles and give additional reasons for using one kind of translation in one context and another in a different one.

Translating Metaphors, Idioms, and Euphemisms

Even the most formally equivalent translations have to make exceptions in their methodology when it comes to expressions that become nonsensical if translated literally. If contemporary speakers try to render "you're pulling my leg" literally in a foreign language, they will almost certainly convey not the idea of "you're kidding me" but rather just that "you are tugging on the part of my body that I walk with." The equivalent idiom in Spanish is "*Me estás tomando el pelo*," which in English is literally, "You're taking my hair." Some languages do not have a corresponding idiom at all, so that the expression would have to be rendered nonidiomatically with the literal equivalent in that language of "you're kidding me." Functionally equivalent translations render such expressions more freely, to ensure understanding of the meaning rather than merely preserving the form. In some cases, however, even formally equivalent translations have to make some concessions.[18]

Consider Christ's words to Saul of Tarsus according to the KJV rendering of Acts 26:14: "It is hard for thee to kick against the pricks." In contemporary English slang, this would create a graphic metaphor indeed, but not the one Luke intended with the Greek word κέντρον, which means "sting" or "goad." The New King James Version (NKJV, orig. 1979), like most modern translations, uses "goad," but how many people today know that this is a kind of whip used to prod an ox? If they do, does that make the meaning of the idiom any clearer? One might envision the futility of a four-legged creature trying to raise a leg so as to kick a whip, but would one necessarily think of the possible harm it could inflict on itself if it missed? Thus, less than fully literal, earlier twentieth-century translations included, "You hurt yourself by kicking at the goad" (James Moffatt's translation, orig. 1924) and "By kicking against the goad you are punishing yourself" (Twentieth Century New Testament, orig. 1901), while J. B. Phillips's paraphrase (orig. 1958) tried to explain how God prods us, by writing, "It is not easy for you to kick against your own conscience," and Olaf Norlie's *Simplified New Testament* (1961) wanted to explain the kicking as well, with "It will be hard for you to rebel and resist." More recently, the GNT decided on "You are hurting yourself by hitting back, like an ox kicking against its owner's stick," whereas the NLT prefers "It is useless for you to fight against my will." *The Message*, as a full-fledged paraphrase, substitutes one entire metaphor for another one, but accurately grasps the sense: "Why do you insist on going against the grain?"[19]

18. Still very helpful on translating metaphor and simile is John Beekman and John Callow, *Translating the Word of God* (Grand Rapids: Zondervan, 1974), 137–50.

19. Translations not already cited before this paragraph are quoted from *The Bible from 26 Translations*, ed. Curtis Vaughan (Grand Rapids: Baker, 1967), an excellent resource that

Or take 2 Corinthians 6:12b. A "literal" translation would read, "But you have narrow room in your intestines [or kidneys]."[20] The KJV says the same thing in Elizabethan English: "But ye are straitened in your own bowels." Even highly touted modern translations that typically stay quite close to the original languages cannot let this pass. Thus the NASB reads, "But you are restrained in your own affections," while the ESV substitutes "restricted" for "restrained." A more functionally equivalent translation can opt for "You have withheld your love from us" (NLT). Victor Furnish's translation in his Anchor Bible commentary announces, "You are cramped, rather, in your feelings," replacing one kind of gut-wrenching experience for another.[21] The GNT substitutes the more common modern metaphor for the seat of one's emotions and translates, "It is you who have closed your hearts to us."[22]

REPRODUCING STYLE AND RHETORICAL EFFECT

One of the most common arguments in favor of using the KJV involves its elegance and beauty. For those who can understand the Elizabethan English of the early 1600s, there is a poetry, a memorizability, and a stylistic and aesthetic delight to much of Scripture phrased in archaic English that modern translations lack. The problem with this observation is that such elegance and stylistic sophistication would not have been perceived in much of the original Hebrew and Greek text because they were written in the common, ordinary language of the person on the street. To be sure, there are poetic parts to the Bible, especially in the Old Testament in the Psalms and Proverbs and in the New Testament in short paragraphs that apparently reproduce early Christian creedal or confessional material. But a sizable majority of the Old Testament and an overwhelming majority of the New Testament was not written in a high, literary style like the classical Attic poets and playwrights, but in much more straightforward Hebrew or Hellenistic/Koine (= "common") Greek.[23] Even the majestic tones of the KJV in many instances sounded much more ordinary in 1611 than they do today.

It is certainly true, however, that one can move too consistently in the direction of colloquialisms and miss some of the style of the original language.

---

presents a selection of noticeably different renderings of the Scriptures, verse by verse, from English-language translations already in print by 1966. A revised edition (1988) includes additional versions current by that date.

20. The Greek σπλάγχνα refers to the internal abdominal organs, believed in antiquity to be the seat of the emotions.

21. Victor P. Furnish, *II Corinthians* (Garden City, NY: Doubleday, 1984), 359.

22. The last two paragraphs are taken, with slight adaptation, from Craig L. Blomberg, *The Historical Reliability of the Gospels*, 2nd ed. (Nottingham and Downers Grove, IL: InterVarsity, 2007), 163–64.

23. See further Stanley E. Porter, "The Greek Language of the New Testament," in *A Handbook to the Exegesis of the New Testament*, ed. Stanley E. Porter (Boston and Leiden: Brill, 2002), esp. 105–10.

Readers who depend on functionally equivalent translations, if possible, should aim to progress in their understanding of English so that they can eventually handle intermediate and perhaps even formally equivalent translations. At the same time, it is often the functionally equivalent translations that manage to preserve the shock value of intentionally arresting language in the original, not domesticated by the desire to avoid offense as often prevails among formally equivalent translations. Thus J. B. Phillips's "paraphrase" better captures the force of Acts 8:20, and in this case the meaning also, when Peter rebukes Simon the Magician: "May you and your money go to hell!" Most translations offer something like, "May your money perish with you," which hardly shocks anyone and may not even suggest the concept of eternal damnation as the Greek does.

The opposite problem can occasionally occur as well, when a formally equivalent translation sounds ruder than the corresponding expression in the original language. Literal renditions of Jesus's address to Mary in John 2:4 begin with the word "Woman," which does not sound at all courteous in English. In Greek and Aramaic, however, it was a much more neutral term of address. Jesus is distancing himself to a certain degree from his mother at the wedding in Cana, but the expression was not an impolite one.[24] The NIV and NLT try to deal with this by using "Dear woman," but would any contemporary English speaker use this form of address at all? The TNIV may reflect the best compromise, as it preserves the literal vocative, "Woman," but then explains in a footnote that the term "does not denote any disrespect."

INCLUSIVE LANGUAGE FOR HUMANITY

No controversy has stirred up greater passions or spawned more misunderstanding in recent years than the debate over terms like "men," "man," "brothers," "he," and so on, when the original biblical languages unambiguously refer to men and women alike. Prior to the late 1960s, English speakers almost uniformly used these terms generically, that is, to refer to both genders. But today the language is very much in flux. Almost no one any longer, in oral communication, would say, "Everyone should bring *his* Bible to class tomorrow." Instead we use "his or her" or "their." It would sound downright inappropriate for a speaker to address a mixed audience with an exhortation for everyone present by saying, "Let every man here tell the truth." Indeed, almost everyone would assume that males were being singled out for some reason. In other contexts, words like "men" or "mankind" are still used generically, as in stock phrases like the "evils of mankind" or "men of virtue." The problem is compounded by the fact that different geographical regions have

---

24. D. A. Carson (*The Gospel according to John* [Grand Rapids: Eerdmans; Leicester: Apollos, 1991], 170) suggests the polite use of "Ma'am" as an almost exact American equivalent except in those places, usually in the South, where children *are* taught to address their mothers this way.

different practices. English outside the United States has introduced inclusive language for humanity more slowly than American English; speakers in the American South (roughly contiguous with the heart of the "Bible belt") also more often preserve older forms of speech, especially in church. So residents of these areas may be puzzled over the insistence that the language has changed dramatically.

What should Bible translators do? Is their main obligation to please traditionalists within Christian circles or achieve the greatest amount of intelligibility and positive response among outsiders? "Man" may preserve the masculine *form* of ἄνθρωπος but, when either gender is in view, "person" best reproduces the *meaning* in English. Increasing numbers of Bible readers, especially among younger generations, do not naturally think of both genders when they read or hear these distinctively masculine words in English. If they are reading Scripture without study helps or others around who can explain things to them, how will they know when such language is truly gender-exclusive and when it is not, unless translators make the differentiation for them?

Objections to the use of gender-inclusive language[25] include the claim that masculine forms were used in the biblical languages to teach the representative role of men as "heads" over women in the home and in the church. But there is no linguistic evidence for this claim, nor does Scripture itself ever make such an affirmation. Given that not all languages throughout history have had generic masculine forms, and given that Christians believe God wants the Bible translated into as many tongues of the world's people as possible, it seems highly unlikely that the grammar of gender by itself intends to teach anything about supposed male representative headship.[26]

Another argument against inclusive-language translations is that substituting a plural form like "they" for a singular like "he" could make people think that certain teachings were only for a group of people, not for each individual within the group. But who misunderstands a command like "let those who want to live long lives exercise daily" to mean that people must gather together in a group for workouts every day? But real people do often hear "let him who wants to live a long life . . ." and think, at least initially, just of males.[27]

---

25. See esp. Vern S. Poythress and Wayne A. Grudem, *The Gender-Neutral Bible Controversy: Muting the Masculinity of God's Words* (Nashville: Broadman & Holman, 2000); and the substantial revision and expansion of this book as idem, *The TNIV and the Gender-Neutral Bible Controversy* (Nashville: B&H, 2004).

26. See esp. D. A. Carson, *The Inclusive Language Debate* (Grand Rapids: Baker Books, 1998), 77–98. Carson puts the point much more strongly: "The argument that attaches a particular formal equivalent in gender assignment to faithfulness to the Word of God is profoundly mistaken in principle. It understands neither translation nor gender systems. Even when the criticism is telling with respect to a particular passage, it does not follow that the undergirding assumptions about language and translation are believable" (p. 98).

27. See the studies referenced in Mark L. Strauss, *Distorting Scripture? The Challenge of Bible Translation and Gender Accuracy* (Downers Grove, IL: InterVarsity, 1998), 141–46.

Other times, when the text of Scripture itself contains a second-person form and then moves to a generic third-person form, inclusive-language translations will preserve the second person ("you"), which does not suggest just men. For example, James 1:5 reads literally, "But if anyone of you lacks wisdom, let him/her ask from the God giving generously to all and not reproaching, and it will be given to him." This kind of change from second to third person in the middle of a sentence is considered poor style in English. The NRSV avoids the exclusive language of older versions by translating, "If any of you is lacking in wisdom, ask God, who gives to all generously and ungrudgingly, and it will be given you." But this creates an abrupt shift to commands without explicit subjects. The TNIV therefore renders, "If any of you lacks wisdom, you should ask God, who gives generously to all without finding fault, and it will be given to you." Interestingly, if those who object to changing person or number in translation were consistent, they should object to all English translations that have abandoned the old "thous" and "thees" that enabled readers to distinguish between second-person singular and plural forms. As it is, readers without Greek in our modern individualized West regularly misinterpret the plural "you" in the Bible, even in the most formally equivalent translations, as referring to individuals rather than groups, but no one hears any outcry against this problem.[28]

Even more telling is an examination of the New Testament quotations of the Old Testament and of one Gospel's use of another. Frequently, one person, number, or even gender is substituted for another, suggesting that the inspired authors saw no problem in doing what some modern critics find objectionable. Unwittingly, these critics are impugning God himself and his practices in inspiring his Scripture![29] The counterargument, that God can do whatever he wants, but that we as translators are not allowed similar freedom,[30] is an arbitrary one, not based on any scriptural mandate and reflecting the erroneous claim that form is the only or the most important element in reproducing meaning as one moves from one language to another.

Still others complain that inclusive-language translations make it easier to promote Christian feminism or that we will proceed down a slippery slope

---

28. A classic example is Matt. 6:33: "But seek first the kingdom of God and his righteousness, and all these things [food, drink, clothing] will be added to you" (ESV). But what about the tens of thousands of faithful Christians over the centuries who have starved to death? Recognition of the plurals behind "seek" and "you" moves us in the direction of an answer—as the church collectively seeks God's righteous or holy standards, it will by definition share with the needy in its midst so that destitute Christians will be helped. Cf. Craig S. Keener, *A Commentary on the Gospel of Matthew* (Grand Rapids and Cambridge: Eerdmans, 1999), 237.

29. See further Craig L. Blomberg, "*Today's New International Version*: The Untold Story of a Good Translation," *Bible Translator* 56 (2005): esp. 205–8.

30. Poythress and Grudem, *TNIV and the Gender-Neutral Bible Controversy*, 45–46; Ryken, *Word of God in English*, 31.

in which inclusive language for the Godhead (God as "Mother and Father" or "He or She") will soon prevail. But, in fact, no translation concerned with inclusive language simply for humanity has changed the English translation of any of the famous, controversial passages in the gender roles debates (or even more than one or two of the alternative readings supplied in footnotes) in any way that makes it easier to defend egalitarianism or harder to defend complementarianism, for those for whom that is a concern.[31] As for inclusive language for deity, while one or two fringe translations outside the mainstream Bible translation projects have attempted this,[32] the biggest discussion about using masculine and feminine language for God in Bible translations occurred twenty or more years ago, and it was decided in most circles that such a move was inappropriate.[33] For those so inclined, commentators, interpreters, or readers could choose to make such substitutions, but not even more functionally equivalent translations would be faithful to their task if they introduced such language into Scripture itself. There has been no slope in the years since this dialogue, much less a slippery one. Any subsequent efforts to change this situation will come from those whose agenda is quite different from simply ensuring gender accuracy in translating words for human beings in the Bible.

The Spectrum of Contemporary Translations

The KJV remains as consistent an exemplar of formal equivalence as any major English translation in print. Its two major weaknesses are its archaic English, which increasing numbers of people cannot readily understand, and its faulty textual base (discoveries since 1611 have enabled us to determine the original text to reflect readings from manuscripts not known or available to early seventeenth-century translators). The NKJV remedies a large part of the first weakness, but not the second, although it does include footnotes with some of the most important alternate readings that other translations accept

31. Inclusive-language translations typically use "deacon" or "deaconess" for διάκονος in Rom. 16:1, but the RSV already introduced this translation long ago. They also use the word "women" in 1 Tim. 3:11, leaving the door open for the view that the women in question are women deacons, not deacons' wives. But "women" is exactly what γυναί means, and again the noninclusive RSV already afforded precedent. The translations that use "wives" are the ones making an interpretive move away from the literal meaning of the text. Even complementarian scholars are increasingly recognizing that these two passages most likely are referring to women deacons. See, e.g., Thomas R. Schreiner, "Women in Ministry: Another Complementarian Perspective," in *Two Views on Women in Ministry*, ed. James R. Beck, rev. ed. (Grand Rapids: Zondervan, 2005), 281–82.

32. Most notably, *The Inclusive Bible* (Lanham, MD, and London: Sheed and Ward, 2007). Produced by a group called "Priests for Equality," this translation typically just repeats "God" rather than using a pronoun, when one occurs in the text, and substitutes "Parent" for "Father."

33. Strauss, *Distorting Scripture?* 171–93.

as original.[34] The three current, very worthwhile English translations with a consistently high degree of formal equivalence are the NASB, the NRSV, and the ESV. The NASB was produced first in the 1960s by a large team of evangelical scholars when there were not nearly the proliferation of translations that are available today, in part to avoid the handful of places in the RSV that were perceived to reflect a more liberal bias and a less accurate translation. The RSV was later thoroughly revised again, creating the NRSV, the first major translation to introduce inclusive language for humanity. Like its predecessor, the NRSV was ecumenical in its orientation, international in its representation, and widely heralded in academic circles (especially outside of evangelicalism) as the most readable translation that was still primarily formally equivalent, even if not quite to the same degree as the RSV.

When the RSV went out of print, a team of evangelical scholars wanted to create a translation modeled on it that preserved the older and more poetic language in numerous places, was thoroughly evangelical in those passages where liberal bias had been perceived, was very formally equivalent and aesthetically pleasing to read, and introduced inclusive language for humanity only in those places where no "representative male headship" could possibly have been intended. The result was the English Standard Version. The term "standard" was retained because it was used in the RSV; the term "English" was introduced because of the concern for elegance in the language. Unfortunately, in Bible translations, "English" rather than "American" often means "British" English, which this version is not. And, as an entirely new publishing venture going beyond a mere second revision of the old RSV, it was rather presumptuous to call it "standard." Mark Strauss, in a recent, thorough examination of the ESV, points out many inconsistencies in application of the stated translation philosophy and many infelicities of language that still remain, leading him to coin the clever title for his study, "Why the English Standard Version Should Not Become the Standard English Version."[35]

Most major translations used today occupy the middle ground between primarily formally equivalent and primarily functionally equivalent translation. These include the New American Bible (NAB, 1970), New English Bible (NEB, 1970), Revised English Bible (REB, 1989), Jerusalem Bible (JB, 1966), New Jerusalem Bible (NJB, 1986), New English Translation (NET, 2005), HCSB, NIV, and TNIV. In Roman Catholic circles for several centuries the English translation of choice had been the Douay-Rheims translation

34. Contra the handful of bona fide scholars who argue for the superiority of the KJV textual base, see D. A. Carson, *The King James Version Debate: A Plea for Realism* (Grand Rapids: Baker, 1979); and James R. White, *The King James Only Controversy: Can You Trust the Modern Translations?* 2nd ed. (Minneapolis: Bethany, 2009).

35. Mark Strauss, "Why the English Standard Version Should Not Become the Standard English Version" (paper presented at the annual meeting of the Evangelical Theological Society, Providence, RI, November 20, 2008).

(orig. 1610), a highly literal rendering of the Latin Vulgate—the standard Latin translation of the Bible going back to the days of Jerome in the fifth century—which therefore did not reflect the original Greek and Hebrew in places where they were not well translated into ancient Latin. Only in the last half-century have Catholics authorized and produced new translations that bypass the Latin and translate directly from the Greek and Hebrew. Internationally, the main such version was the JB, now updated as the NJB. In American circles, a slightly less fluent but slightly more literal counterpart has been the NAB.[36]

In British circles, the ecumenically motivated NEB moved more in the direction of functional equivalence while not fully embracing that end of the spectrum. It was also rendered in distinctive British English. It has been updated as the REB, which has removed some of the most idiomatic language of its predecessor. At the same time that the inclusive-language controversy first broke out, the Southern Baptist Convention in the United States decided to create its own version (HCSB) that, like the ESV, was only partially inclusive in its language but, unlike the ESV, more contemporary and understandable in its English, thus earning it a place in the intermediate position between predominantly formal and predominantly functional translation. The NET, organized by several scholars and others associated with Dallas Seminary, was designed specifically for online use with storyboarding study notes of different kinds and varying amounts of detail. It also appears in hard copy form. Its acronym can be read as the New English Translation or just understood as a reference to the Inter*net*. It is a little more up to date in its language than many translations but still occupies the intermediate space between formal and functional translations.[37] The God's Word Translation (formerly God's Word to the Nations) adheres to what it calls "closest natural equivalence" and also occupies this intermediate space, though at a simpler reading level than the other versions discussed in this category.

No modern English translation of the Bible, however, comes anywhere close to having become as popular or "standard" as the NIV—today nearly 30 percent of all Bibles sold or distributed are NIVs. As the second major translation (along with the NASB) to be undertaken by a uniquely evangelical team of scholars, it included British as well as Americans on its "Committee on

36. An earlier form of which was first known as the Confraternity Version.
37. Excellent sources for the origins, contents, and evaluations of most of these (and many other older or lesser known) English translations of the Bible include Wegner, *Journey from Texts to Translations*, 271–394; Jack P. Lewis, *The English Bible from KJV to NIV: A History and Evaluation*, 2nd ed. (Grand Rapids: Baker, 1991); Bruce M. Metzger, *The Bible in Translation: Ancient and English Versions* (Grand Rapids: Baker Academic, 2001), 55–190; Sakae Kubo and Walter Specht, *So Many Versions? Twentieth Century English Versions of the Bible*, rev. ed. (Grand Rapids: Zondervan, 1983); and David Dewey, *A User's Guide to Bible Translations: Making the Most of Different Versions* (Leicester and Downers Grove, IL: InterVarsity, 2004).

Bible Translation" (unlike the NASB).[38] The NIV's remarkable combination of accuracy, fluency, and intelligibility have convinced many in more-ecumenical circles to use it as well.[39] Its inclusive-language update, the TNIV, also introduced a large number of minor revisions, about two-thirds of which move the translation back in a more formally equivalent direction. This fact has been largely eclipsed by the controversy over inclusive language, as has the fact that the revisions that replaced "he" with "they" or "brothers" with "brothers and sisters," and the like, comprised a fairly small minority of the total changes. The passages in which the NIV was most legitimately faulted for being too free with the text have almost all been corrected in the TNIV.[40]

Fully functionally equivalent translations began with the GNT produced by the United Bible Societies, the main international and ecumenical organization for modern-language Bible translation. Better known in evangelical circles is the NLT, with one of the largest committees (ninety scholars) ever organized to produce a new translation. Given the immense popularity of *The Living Bible*, Tyndale House Publishers wanted to preserve Ken Taylor's freshness of language wherever possible but make all necessary revisions to ensure the new edition would be a bona fide translation. With only occasional exceptions, since its publication in 1996 the NLT has ranked third (after the NIV and KJV) in all English-language Bible sales and distributions (and, like the KJV, typically garnering roughly 20 percent of the market share).[41] The CEV more resembles the GNT in that it did not originate with any existing English translation but with the Greek and Hebrew alone. But it achieves a minimal fifth-grade reading level, lower even than the GNT's sixth-grade level.[42]

We could continue, but that would belabor the points already made. Some Bible translations have aimed at an extremely basic vocabulary level and sentence structure so that they can be read by the even younger elementary schoolchild—for example, the New International Readers' Version (NIrV, 1998).[43] New Testaments produced by Messianic Jews have sometimes preserved in English transliteration the Hebrew names for Jewish characters and for key Jewish customs or traditions.[44] George Lamsa, a well-known scholar of

38. For its origins, see further Kenneth L. Barker and Edwin H. Palmer, *The NIV: The Making of a Contemporary Translation* (Grand Rapids: Zondervan, 1986).

39. Statistics on percentages sold and ecumenical use reported by representatives of Zondervan at the meeting of the Committee on Bible Translation, Grand Rapids, MI, June 2009.

40. See Blomberg, "*Today's New International Version*," esp. 191–98.

41. Statistics announced by representatives of Tyndale House Publishers at the annual dinners for translators held in conjunction with the annual meetings of the Society of Biblical Literature at various locations throughout the 2000s.

42. Cf. Wegner, *Journey from Texts to Translations*, 374; with Dewey, *User's Guide*, 75–76. At a comparable level also is the New Century Version (NCV, 1991)

43. Dewey, *User's Guide*, 75–76.

44. See esp. David H. Stern's *Jewish New Testament* (Clarksville, MD: Jewish New Testament Publications, 1989).

Syriac, has created some idiosyncratic versions based on the translation of the Syriac New Testament into English (recall above, p. 4 and 4n6). Lamsa believes that where the Syriac differs from the Greek it may reflect its sister language, Aramaic, especially for the teachings of Jesus, and represent an earlier stage of the New Testament text than do our existing Greek manuscripts.[45] Most scholars doubt that he is correct except perhaps in a few instances. Still other translations or paraphrases are similarly the work of a given individual, almost by definition guaranteeing that it will not be as reliable as those that rely on committees of scholars, especially in our era of highly compartmentalized education.[46]

Distinctive in yet another respect is The Amplified Bible, which inserts in parentheses after most key theological terms one to four other possible English renderings of the word. For example, John 3:16 reads, "For God so greatly loved and dearly prized the world that He [even] gave up His only begotten (unique) Son, so that whoever believes in (trusts in, clings to, relies on) Him shall not perish (come to destruction, be lost) but have eternal (everlasting) life."[47] The problem is that most readers who use this version assume that all options are equally likely or, worse still, that all are implied simultaneously by the single Greek word in the context in which it appears. Finally, some translations reflect the distinctively sectarian theologies of a particular heterodox offshoot of Christianity—for example, the New World Translation (NWT, 1961) of the Jehovah's Witnesses[48] or the Joseph Smith Translation (produced between 1830 and 1844, published in 1867) of the Church of Jesus Christ of Latter-Day Saints, more popularly known as Mormonism.[49]

45. George M. Lamsa, *Holy Bible: From the Ancient Eastern Text* (New York: Harper & Row, 1985).

46. In addition to those cited earlier in this chapter, see esp. the translations by William F. Beck, *The New Testament in the Language of Today* (St. Louis: Concordia, 1963); Richard F. Weymouth, *The Modern Speech New Testament* (London: James Clarke, 1903); Charles B. Williams, *The New Testament in the Language of the People* (Boston: Bruce Humphries, 1937); Ronald Knox, *The New Testament of Our Lord and Saviour Jesus Christ* (New York: Sheed and Ward; London: Burns & Oates, 1944); and Edgar J. Goodspeed, *The New Testament: An American Translation* (Chicago: University of Chicago Press, 1923).

47. *The Amplified Bible* (La Habra, CA: The Lockman Foundation, 1987).

48. For a presentation and debunking of the idiosyncratic translational principles, esp. related to deity and to the use of the article in the NWT, see Robert H. Countess, *The Jehovah's Witnesses' New Testament: A Critical Analysis of the New World Translation of the Christian Greek Scriptures* (Phillipsburg, NJ: P&R, 1982).

49. Although the KJV is the only translation of the Bible deemed fully canonical in LDS circles, some Mormons would agree with Bruce R. McConkie (*A New Witness for the Articles of Faith* [Salt Lake City: Deseret, 1985], 393): "The Joseph Smith Translation—an inspired version—both corrects errors and reintroduces lost passages, all by the spirit of revelation, thus making this version the best source of biblical knowledge."

Conclusion

As already noted, serious Bible students who have not learned to use the original languages should consult a formally equivalent translation when they want the most "literal" translation, that is, when they want to see what most closely corresponds word for word to the Greek New Testament. Formally equivalent translations are usually the most helpful to consult, particularly when key doctrinal issues, controversial texts, or important theological words are involved. Students who have learned to work out for themselves a translation from the Greek will still find these translations useful for checking the accuracy of their translation or seeing how overly wooden renderings can be smoothed out and yet still retain formal equivalence.

For a pulpit Bible, however, or for a version that a preacher, teacher, or other Christian leader regularly uses in a broad cross section of public contexts, one of the translations in the intermediate category is best. Unless one has reason to cater to a particular population, such as a Catholic or British or Southern Baptist audience, either the NIV or the TNIV is probably most useful for capturing the best balance between accuracy and normal contemporary English. Unless the audience simply cannot cope with inclusive language for humanity, the TNIV should be preferred to the NIV because of how clearly it reads in current English.[50]

For still freer but often clearer or fresher renderings, adopt a functionally equivalent translation. Youth groups, adult congregations with a fair percentage of people who have not gone to college, or special contexts in which one wants a new take on an old, well-known passage all afford ideal settings for one of these translations. The NLT is the premier example of functional equivalence in English, while the GNT and CEV are additional, stalwart examples. Bible paraphrases, most notably *The Message*, should never be presented as if they give insights into the authorial meaning of the biblical writers, but should be used only in comparison with bona fide translations. When a paraphrase at a given point provides the semantic equivalent to an actual translation, then that paraphrase can work just like a functionally equivalent translation and give a fresh perspective or new insights. But when it is clear that the paraphrase has gone beyond what the text itself actually says, no theology, ethics, or any other didactic point should be based on the distinctive form of the paraphrase.[51]

All this presupposes that a reader has access to more than one Bible translation. We should not allow the comments of this chapter to be taken out of

50. See further D. A. Carson, "The Limits of Functional Equivalence in Bible Translation—and Other Limits, Too," in *The Challenge of Bible Translation: Communicating God's Word to the World*, ed. Glen G. Scorgie, Mark L. Strauss, and Steven M. Voth (Grand Rapids: Zondervan, 2003), 65–113.

51. Cf. Dewey, *User's Guide*, 42–43.

perspective. Any one of the translations discussed here is sufficiently close to the original Scriptures that readers can learn all that they need in order to come to Jesus, become his followers, grow in Christian living, and understand the story of his mighty acts in history. But to whom much is given, much shall be required (Luke 12:48). All it takes today is Internet access and one may search for and consult just about any translation of the Bible. Readers who cannot adjudicate the strengths and weaknesses of a given translation by comparing it with the Greek should especially be sure to compare three or four translations of different kinds before confidently proclaiming anything at all controversial out of Scripture, lest they make a point that really can't be defended from the text at hand (usually due to misunderstanding how the *English* is functioning in one particular translation).

People unfamiliar with the Bible's contents increasingly ask Christian leaders questions along the lines of "How can we trust that we know what the biblical authors first wrote when there are so many different English translations?" Such a question betrays their lack of familiarity with how similar all the major translations are to one another. Differences deal with nuances, not with the fundamental truths of Christianity. Just as was the case with textual criticism (see chap. 1), no doctrine of the faith depends on the unique rendering of some modern translation.[52]

Illustrations

To illustrate the similarities and differences among the major English translations, we conclude this chapter by comparing select versions. Readers can then continue the process for themselves.

Matthew 1:18

KJV: Now the birth of Jesus Christ was on this wise: When as his mother Mary was espoused to Joseph, before they came together, she was found with child of the Holy Ghost.

ESV: Now the birth of Jesus Christ took place in this way. When his mother Mary had been betrothed to Joseph, before they came together she was found to be with child from the Holy Spirit.

TNIV: This is how the birth of Jesus the Messiah came about: His mother Mary was pledged to be married to Joseph, but before they came together, she was found to be pregnant through the Holy Spirit.

---

52. Even the NWT demonstrates the deity of Christ because both Jehovah God and Jesus refer to themselves as "the Alpha and the Omega" or "the First and the Last" (Rev. 1:8, 18; 22:13).

NLT: This is how Jesus the Messiah was born. His mother, Mary, was engaged to be married to Joseph. But before the marriage took place, while she was still a virgin, she became pregnant through the power of the Holy Spirit.

Acts 20:28

NKJV: Therefore take heed to yourselves and to all the flock, among which the Holy Spirit has made you overseers, to shepherd the church of God which He purchased with His own blood.

NRSV: Keep watch over yourselves and over all the flock, of which the Holy Spirit has made you overseers, to shepherd the church of God that he obtained with the blood of his own Son.

HCSB: Be on guard for yourselves and for all the flock, among whom the Holy Spirit has appointed you as overseers, to shepherd the church of God, which He purchased with His own blood.

NJB: Be on your guard for yourselves and for all the flock of which the Holy Spirit has made you the guardians, to feed the Church of God which he bought with the blood of his own Son.

2 Corinthians 3:10

NASB: For indeed what had glory, in this case has no glory because of the glory that surpasses it.

NIV: For what was glorious has no glory now in comparison with the surpassing glory.

NAB: Indeed, what was endowed with glory has come to have no glory in this respect because of the glory that surpasses it.

NET: For indeed, what had been glorious now has no glory because of the tremendously greater glory of what replaced it.

1 Timothy 2:12

KJV: But I suffer not a woman to teach, nor to usurp authority over the man, but to be in silence.

ESV: I do not permit a woman to teach or to exercise authority over a man; rather, she is to remain quiet.

TNIV: I do not permit a woman to teach or to assume authority over a man; she must be quiet.

NLT: I do not let women teach men or have authority over them. Let them listen quietly.

Revelation 3:20

YLT: Lo, I have stood at the door, and I knock; if any one may hear my voice, and may open the door, I will come in unto him, and will sup with him, and he with me.

HCSB: Listen! I stand at the door and knock. If anyone hears My voice and opens the door, I will come in to him and have dinner with him, and he with Me.

NJB: Look, I am standing at the door, knocking. If one of you hears me calling and opens the door, I will come in to share a meal at that person's side.

CEV: Listen! I am standing and knocking at your door. If you hear my voice and open the door, I will come in and we will eat together.

Addendum

As this book goes to press, the Committee on Bible Translation is nearing completion of its work on the 2011 edition of the NIV. This edition of the NIV will incorporate many improvements over the 1984 NIV, many of which have appeared in the TNIV. It will also feature the results of a thorough re-analysis of the best way to handle gender language in contemporary English. There is every reason to believe that the 2011 NIV should be the English Bible translation suitable for the broadest range of contexts for years to come.

3

Historical-Cultural Context

After establishing as best as possible the original text and generating a reliable translation, we turn to a task that offers deep, immediately clarifying insights for most passages of Scripture. Understanding the historical context of a passage removes the haze of obscure cultural traditions that often shrouds the text for modern interpreters of Scripture. Reading the Bible can seem like listening to one side of a phone conversation or reading an e-mail addressed to someone else. The intended recipient shares many implicit agreements and understandings with the person who initiates the verbal or written communication. The "eavesdroppers" on the conversation may find it difficult to discern the message accurately and can easily interpret the speaker as implying something that was never intended. As readers who are not the original recipients of the New Testament writings, we who "eavesdrop" on the Bible must do a little investigation to make sure we understand the message through the cultural framework of the original hearers. The natural human tendency to interpret all things according to one's own location, culture, and worldview poses a threat to good biblical interpretation. This is especially true when such vast distances in time, geography, and values exist as those we find between the first-century Mediterranean world and the twenty-first-century Western world.[1]

The job of the responsible exegete, therefore, is to overcome the obstacle of cultural distance by understanding the relevant aspects of the social atmo-

---

1. Cf. further William W. Klein, Craig L. Blomberg, and Robert L. Hubbard Jr., *Introduction to Biblical Interpretation*, rev. ed. (Nashville: Nelson, 2004), 13–16, who also give numerous biblical examples.

sphere as the authors and the audience of Scripture would have understood them. The reader who is willing to grapple with the historical context will also be better able to separate situation-specific details from timeless principles that God sought to give to his people through the Bible. The exegete will then be equipped to discover comparable, if different, applications of those principles for godly and powerful Christian living in today's societies (see further chap. 10). It is our intention in this chapter to discuss the exegetical tool of historical-cultural analysis in a way that makes it accessible to the pastor and the student.[2]

We will begin by discussing the importance and methodology of historical criticism in general. Then we will consider how the interpreter can best understand the historical context of a specific biblical book and employ that information in analyzing given passages within it. This will include an introduction to the primary and secondary literature to be consulted and will also suggest the most helpful questions to ask of the text itself. No discussion of historical context is complete without an introduction to the subdiscipline of social-scientific criticism, so we will turn to that next. Finally, we must demonstrate how this practice enlivens the spiritual life of the exegete and those among whom he or she ministers.

The Objectives and Importance of Discerning the Historical-Cultural Context

The main goal in analyzing the historical-cultural setting of a biblical book or passage is not the acquisition of knowledge for knowledge's sake. Rather, biblical scholars speak of the exegete focusing on two horizons.[3] The first horizon is the meaning of the original text; the second is contemporary application. Commentary series are increasingly devoted to the process of determining present-day significance so that the contemporary relevance of the ancient Bible is readily accessible to students of Scripture (scholars and nonscholars alike).[4] But to apply texts properly to the contemporary horizon,

---

2. Cf. further ibid., 229–40; Richard Erickson, *A Beginner's Guide to New Testament Exegesis: Taking the Fear out of Critical Method* (Downers Grove, IL: InterVarsity, 2005), 98–113; W. Randolph Tate, *Biblical Interpretation: An Integrated Approach*, rev. ed. (Peabody, MA: Hendrickson, 1997), 29–63; Paul N. Jackson, "Background Studies and New Testament Interpretation," in *Interpreting the New Testament: Essays on Methods and Issues*, ed. David A. Black and David S. Dockery (Nashville: Broadman & Holman, 2001), 188–208.

3. For a detailed, technical defense, see Anthony C. Thiselton, *The Two Horizons: New Testament Hermeneutics and Philosophical Description* (Exeter: Paternoster; Grand Rapids: Eerdmans, 1980).

4. The New International Version Application Commentary series from Zondervan and the Two Horizons New Testament Commentary series from Eerdmans are the two best, most intentional, and methodologically thoughtful contemporary commentary series applying these insights.

we must first focus on the horizon of original context and enter, as much as possible, into the world of the biblical text, leaving behind our own cultural assumptions.

So, for example, for 1 Corinthians 8 we need to know the historical context surrounding Paul's instructions about meat sacrificed to idols, which is not an issue that most twenty-first-century Westerners face. When was the last time you sat down with a Big Mac and thought, "I wonder if this was sacrificed to a pagan deity before they fried it up"?[5] However, when we understand that the socioeconomic situation of the poorest in the Corinthian church meant that they could not often afford to buy meat, so that they typically consumed it, free of charge, only as part of public, Greco-Roman festivals, then a clearer picture begins to emerge. Furthermore, some Corinthian Christians may have believed that to eat meat that had been sacrificed to the gods was idolatrous participation in the imperial cult, which contravened the absolute lordship of Christ.[6] While the text indicates that some Christians could participate with clear consciences, able to separate the act of eating meat from pagan worship, others were not able to distinguish the two but chose to participate in the activity anyway. This compromise of conscience constituted infidelity to Christ himself. Observing a concrete situation that seems foreign to us in terms of its original historical context helps us to understand the principle. Paul is not arguing that meat is bad and we should all become vegetarians, but that Christians should refrain from activities in which they feel free to participate if others present would join them without clear consciences and, in doing so, violate their allegiance to Christ.[7]

5. This rhetorical question is primarily directed to those who interpret and apply the Bible in a thoroughly Western society. The issue of idol worship and sacrificed foods remains pressing for Christians in some African, Latin American, and Asian cultures, including some immigrant subcultures in the Western world.

6. For an overview of the major perspectives adopted in recent scholarship, see Wendell Willis, "1 Corinthians 8–10: A Retrospective after Twenty-Five Years," *Restoration Quarterly* 49 (2007): 103–12.

7. Even the historical background from Paul's world is varied enough that interpreters do not entirely agree on which parts are most relevant for understanding Paul. But the most nuanced and persuasive approach seems to include three main contexts: in a private home, eating meat that had been blessed by a pagan priest before it was sold in the marketplace (normally acceptable unless specifically told otherwise); during temple services, eating meat as part of worshiping pagan gods (always wrong); and in the temple precincts, eating meat dedicated to idols as part of other civic or community activities held there, all of which had at least some nominal or token religious dimension (the gray area that varied depending on who else was present). See esp. Bruce N. Fisk, "Eating Meat Offered to Idols: Corinthian Behavior and Pauline Response in 1 Corinthians 8–10," *Trinity Journal* 10 (1989): 49–70. Cf., with only slight variation, E. C. Still, "The Meaning and Uses of ΕΙΔΟΛΟΘΥΤΩΝ in First Century Non-Pauline Literature and 1 Corinthians 8:1–11:1: Toward Resolution of the Debate," *Trinity Journal* 23 (2002): 225–34; and Joseph A. Fitzmyer, *First Corinthians* (New Haven and London: Yale University Press, 2008), 332.

This is the overarching principle. Now we look for ways to apply it to our contemporary scene. The opportunities for application of this principle abound, especially in activities that can lead to excess and sin but do not have to do so. Drinking alcohol, certain forms of dress (or undress), and playing games that sometimes but not always involve gambling are some such activities that quickly come to mind. Where some Christians may be induced to sin—either by participating against their conscience at the behest of other Christians who flaunt their involvement in these otherwise morally neutral actions, or by participating in a morally neutral practice that develops into sin—the Christian freedom to participate in these activities in moderation must be curbed.[8]

With this quick look at 1 Corinthians 8 we have climbed and descended a helpful tool called the *ladder of abstraction* (see further below, pp. 251–57). It serves to bridge the gap between the original situation addressed in the Bible and the situations we have today. It functions like this:

abstract principle: Christians should live in liberty but must avoid Christian freedom where it might induce other Christians to sin.	
situation: Christians can eat food sacrificed to idols, but there are qualifications.	*situation*: Christians can drink alcohol in moderation, but there are qualifications.
first-century world	contemporary world

The concrete situations point to an abstract principle that is equally relevant in contemporary ethical Christian living as it was to first-century Christians. Finding this more abstract or timeless principle is one objective of engaging in historical-cultural analysis. The formulation of legitimate applications to other situations forms a major focus of chapter 10 below. But the overarching principle that governs contemporary life cannot be uncovered without knowledge of the historical context in which it first appeared. The importance of historical-context analysis is that it helps us to understand the cultural husk in which the kernels of more timeless principles are often wrapped. Plenty of other insights even at the level of original meaning similarly result, and the chance of misinterpreting the text is minimized when one has a detailed understanding of the historical-cultural background to a given part of Scripture.

The Components of Historical-Cultural Analysis

Thus far we have labeled the practice of gathering background information for biblical texts simply as historical-cultural analysis. However, as the label implies, the practice involves two subdisciplines: historical-context analysis and cultural analysis. The second of these closely overlaps with social-scientific

8. Craig Blomberg, *1 Corinthians* (Grand Rapids: Zondervan, 1994), 167–69.

criticism. In the remainder of this chapter, we will treat each of these two main sub-disciplines in turn, while recognizing that in many ways they are intertwined.

Historical-context analysis is primarily concerned with the history *behind* the text; social-scientific analysis is interested in the history *at the same time as* the text.[9] That is, historical-context analysis is involved primarily in *diachronic* (throughout time) aspects of the text such as its date, author, recipients, and the historical events that affected or necessitated the writing of New Testament documents—those things that situate the writing in the broader context of history. Social-scientific analysis deals primarily with *synchronic* (within time) aspects of the text, namely implicit cultural values, social relationships, religious and political systems, and other social events or patterns of behavior from the time of the biblical account that help to clarify the text as it stands. Sometimes it means that models from the modern practice of the social sciences are applied to the New Testament. This is true especially where the text and the raw historical data do not provide a wealth of background information to aid the interpretive process.

While the subdisciplines of historical-context analysis and social-scientific criticism overlap, there are at least two reasons for treating them separately. First, the practice of historical-context analysis predates social-scientific criticism by many centuries. It has been only in the past fifty years that the social sciences and New Testament study have joined hands to reconstruct the social contexts in which the New Testament writings were composed. While the merger has been fitful at points, when the social sciences are used responsibly the understanding of the first-century Mediterranean social environment clarifies the Bible's meaning and subsequent application considerably. Much of the secondary literature on New Testament backgrounds divides into these two distinct disciplines with the older volumes focusing solely on historical contexts and the newer volumes incorporating social-scientific perspectives with historical analysis but still under separate headings.[10]

Sidebar 3.1

Subdisciplines of Historical-Cultural Analysis

Historical-Context Analysis

- History *behind* the text (*diachronic*, throughout time)
- Examples: date, author, recipients, historical events that affected the writing

Social-Scientific Analysis

- History *at the same time* as the text (*synchronic*, within time)
- Examples: implicit cultural values, social relationships, religious and political systems

---

9. Cf. John H. Hayes and Carl R. Holladay Jr., *Biblical Exegesis: A Beginner's Handbook*, 3rd ed. (Louisville: Westminster John Knox, 2007), 45.

10. Indeed, entire extensive bibliographies treat these two broad areas separately. See esp. Watson E. Mills, *New Testament History and Background* (Lewiston, NY, and Lampeter, Wales:

A second reason for treating the subdisciplines separately is for the sake of methodological explanation. Whereas historical-context analysis remains dependent on the biblical text along with extrabiblical historical information to determine pertinent background material, social-scientific analysis reaches beyond both of these collections to incorporate social-scientific models, economic patterns, and relevant discoveries of cultural artifacts. With these newer resources comes a greater danger of misapplication, whereby the biblical material is forced into categories that may skew rather than elucidate the intended meaning of the text. Therefore, a different set of criteria is required to evaluate applications of the two subdisciplines because of the caution needed when applying data from outside the biblical text and/or ancient world.[11]

We will begin with approaches to historical-context analysis and then discuss social-scientific analysis. After each subdiscipline has been introduced, explained, and illustrated, the two will be combined to show how both fields interact in reconstructing the probable historical-cultural circumstances of Scripture.

Historical-Context Analysis

Historical analysis is noticeably more dependent on secondary literature than other steps in the exegetical process; understanding the circumstances in lands so far removed from us in both time and distance is a full-time enterprise and itself a distinct academic discipline. There is a fine assortment of Bible-background works and commentaries that collate information from the primary sources surrounding the New Testament era, making the relevant information accessible to students and pastors alike. We will explore these helps later. Before the exegete turns to secondary literature, however, it is always important first to mine a given New Testament text itself for any clues, explicit or implicit, that it might offer about the historical context in which it was written.

Using the Bible to Gain Historical-Context Information

When time permits, it is helpful to read in one sitting the entire biblical book in which the chosen passage occurs. That way, historical features from earlier or later in the book, which inform the passage at hand, will more likely be noticed. Take notes as you read through the text so that you can write down the explicit references to historical circumstances, cultural practices specific to the audience, worldviews that are correct or need changing, or

---

Edwin Mellen, 2002); and David M. May, *Social-Scientific Criticism of the New Testament: A Bibliography* (Macon, GA: Mercer, 1991).

11. See esp. Edwin Yamauchi, "Sociology, Scripture and the Supernatural," *Journal of the Evangelical Theological Society* 27 (1984): 169–92.

anything else that helps reconstruct the historical situation.[12] Sometimes the statements regarding historical circumstances are as explicit as the aside in Mark 7:3–4, a parenthetical comment about the handwashing practice of the Pharisees that might not have been well known to Mark's audience.[13] Other times passing references are made to events or circumstances that would have been familiar to both author and recipients, but that may be unknown to other readers. Take, for example, Jesus's reference to Pilate mixing the blood of certain Galileans with their sacrifices and the eighteen people who died when the tower in Siloam fell on them (Luke 13:1–5). These two events do not appear in other ancient historical sources. What we do know of Pilate, especially from Josephus, demonstrates that the first incident is consistent with his behavior on other occasions.[14] And as for the second, buildings fall down in almost every culture.

The book or context in which a passage appears is not the interpreter's only biblical resource. The study of parallel or complementary passages will also shed much light on historical matters. This type of comparison is especially useful with the Gospels. What is implicit in one Gospel might be explicit in another. For example, Luke 11:14–23 gives an account of the religious leaders' accusations against Jesus. Their claim is that his authority to cast out demons has been given by Beelzebul (Satan) rather than by God. Luke mentions that it was "some" of the religious leaders (11:15), while Mark (3:22–27) is slightly less vague, describing his accusers as scribes from Jerusalem. Matthew (12:22–30) is most specific, attributing the accusatory words to the Pharisees (some of whom were also scribes).[15] For more background on the Pharisees, the interpreter could then consult other passages in the Gospels in which the Pharisees appear. Reading the Gospels side by side will help one glean more *historical* background relevant to each, but it will also illuminate the evangelists' distinctive themes, which will be important for summarizing a passage's contribution to *theology* (see chap. 9). This passage in Matthew 12, like many others in this Gospel, highlights Matthew's theme of the blindness of the Jewish religious leaders, especially the Pharisees, to Jesus's messianic mission.[16]

12. For an excellent model, see John D. Grassmick, *Principles and Practice of Greek Exegesis*, rev. ed. (Dallas: Dallas Theological Seminary, 1976), 51–59.

13. The wording and details of the aside may raise new questions for the audience. For the problems and probable solutions, see M. Eugene Boring, *Mark: A Commentary* (Louisville and London: Westminster John Knox, 2006), 199–200.

14. Cf. the judicious conclusions of I. Howard Marshall, *The Gospel of Luke* (Exeter: Paternoster; Grand Rapids: Eerdmans, 1978), 553.

15. The Greek-English synopsis edited by Kurt Aland (*Synopsis of the Four Gospels*, 7th ed. [Stuttgart: German Bible Society, 1984]) will save the interpreter much time by presenting parallel Gospel accounts side by side in both English and Greek. An English-only edition is also available.

16. See esp. D. A. Carson, "The Jewish Leaders in Matthew's Gospel: A Reappraisal," *Journal of the Evangelical Theological Society* 25 (1982): 161–74; cf. also John Nolland, "Matthew

Another area where parallel and complementary reading proves helpful is in a comparison of Acts and the Pauline Epistles. Most of Paul's letters and each of his missionary journeys can be dated by a combination of historical material in Acts, references to events in Paul's life from his epistles, and dates gleaned from extrabiblical sources. For example, Paul's first evangelistic activity in Corinth appears in Acts 18:1–17, on his second missionary journey. Because of rising tension due to the conversion of Jewish leaders to Christianity during Paul's ministry in Corinth, he was arraigned before the proconsul Gallio, whose reign can be dated as the summer of 51 to the summer of 52, based on a stone inscription at Delphi.[17] This relatively fixed point, along with various references to the passage of time within the book of Acts, allows us to date numerous events in Paul's life with reasonable precision. Other fixed extrabiblical events such as the death of Herod Agrippa I (explained in Acts 12) in AD 44 and the height of the famine in Judea in AD 46 or 47 are recorded by the Jewish historian Josephus in his work *Jewish Antiquities*.[18]

The comparison of Acts and the epistles can then be used to date Paul's letters. Relying on the inscription at Delphi about Gallio, it is easy to date 1 Corinthians. Along with the mention of Gallio in Acts 18:12–17, Luke indicates that Paul stayed for a year and a half with the small believing community he had helped to establish in Corinth, teaching the Corinthians the word of God (v. 11). After this initial stay in Corinth during his second missionary journey, Paul moved on to Ephesus, where he spent three years (Acts 19:10 and 20:31). In 1 Corinthians 16:8, we learn that as Paul writes this letter to the Corinthians, he is at the end of his stay in Ephesus, hoping to visit Corinth again soon but wanting to wait until after the spring festival of Pentecost. Putting all the numbers together, we add the year and a half Paul spent in Corinth to the year AD 51, the first year in which Gallio was proconsul in Corinth, and then add Paul's three years in Ephesus, factoring in the information in 1 Corinthians 16:8 that Paul is writing before Pentecost. Hence, we can date the letter to late winter or early spring of AD 55.[19] We have used fixed points in extrabiblical history and testimony in Acts and in 1 Corinthians to find a relatively precise date for this letter. Other Pauline letters can be dated, even if not quite so precisely, using the same method: determining fixed extrabiblical points and matching internal references in Acts with information available in the epistles themselves.

---

and Anti-Semitism," in *Built upon the Rock: Studies in the Gospel of Matthew*, ed. Daniel M. Gurtner and John Nolland (Grand Rapids and Cambridge: Eerdmans, 2008), 154–69.

17. Rainer Riesner, *Paul's Early Period: Chronology, Mission Strategy, Theology* (Grand Rapids: Eerdmans, 1998), 208–11.

18. See throughout ibid. Cf. also F. F. Bruce, *Paul: Apostle of the Heart Set Free* (Grand Rapids: Eerdmans, 1977).

19. There is enough flexibility between the fixed points that some scholars vary these and similar dates in one direction or the other. For the full range of options, see Anthony C. Thiselton, *The First Epistle to the Corinthians* (Carlisle: Paternoster; Grand Rapids: Eerdmans, 2000), 31–32.

As mentioned earlier, we are not content with acquiring this knowledge simply for the sake of knowing when the letter was written. Instead, we want to know how such information will help us in the interpretive task. Continuing our focus on 1 Corinthians, the rewards for our sleuthing emerge in 1 Corinthians 7:26, in the context of Paul's commending celibacy for those who are unmarried. There Paul comments, "Because of the present crisis, I think that it is good for you to remain as you are" (NIV), and he explains in verse 28 that his advice is because "those who marry will face many troubles in this life," which singleness would spare them. What is the "present crisis" that causes Paul so heartily to recommend celibacy for the unmarried in his congregation? That depends on the date of the letter. Some commentators argue that Paul advises celibacy due to the residual scarcities from the severe famine in the mid-to-late 40s. In this case, Paul sees the lack of wisdom in marriage and eventual procreation when there is not even enough food for those who are already living.[20] Yet, based on our compilation of evidence, Paul writes to the Corinthians nearly a decade later, a significant enough time to doubt that Paul deems famine-induced poverty the "present crisis." Perhaps the commendation to celibacy is more than culture-bound to a period of famine. Paul further clarifies his thought on the present crisis in 7:29, saying, "What I mean, brothers and sisters, is that the time is short." In a generation that got further and further away from the resurrection and ascension of Jesus, the expectation was that the return of Jesus was imminent. It is the same mindset that Paul urges Christians to adopt throughout his letters. A single and therefore celibate lifestyle lends itself toward single-minded devotion to God rather than being invested in the interests of a spouse or children.[21]

Today, we as Christians share the expectation that the days are short and that the return of our Lord is imminent, the very statement Paul makes in 1 Corinthians 7:29. Application of this principle to ministry comes right on the heels of this realization. By recognizing the date of the letter, we better understand the situation that Paul was addressing, and we can offer the same words of encouragement to the unmarried individuals in our ministries without wondering if we are applying a culture-bound principle. Rather than singleness being a plague or an indication of a defective personality, it may be a call on the lives of some of God's followers to devote themselves to ministry in ways that a married person could only dream of.[22] And so dating of the historical

20. See esp. Bruce W. Winter, *After Paul Left Corinth: The Influence of Secular Ethics and Social Change* (Grand Rapids and Cambridge: Eerdmans, 2001), 216–25.

21. On these and related concerns, see esp. Vincent L. Wimbush, *Paul: The Worldly Ascetic* (Macon, GA: Mercer, 1987).

22. See the very helpful pastoral comments in Mark Dever, *Twelve Challenges Churches Face* (Wheaton: Crossway, 2008), 71–74; and Lyle D. Vander Broek, *Breaking Barriers: The Possibilities of Christian Community in a Lonely World* (Grand Rapids: Brazos, 2002), 70–71.

kind leads us to valuable conclusions and an encouraging word for singles about dating of the romantic kind!

Using Other Ancient Material to Gain Historical-Context Information

After mining the Bible itself for pertinent historical information, it is wise to turn to other authors from that time period to get a feel for the political and social atmosphere of the New Testament world. The primary sources emerge from authors who wrote concerning their Jewish or Greco-Roman contexts during or close to the first century.[23]

PRIMARY JEWISH SOURCES

We have already mentioned the work of the Jewish historian Josephus as a valuable resource for extrabiblical information.[24] Other Jewish primary sources include the works of Philo, a first-century Jewish philosopher who intermingled Jewish and Greek concepts and who was especially interested in the lives of philosophers throughout the Jewish Diaspora.[25] The Dead Sea Scrolls are a valuable resource for understanding the sect of Jews known as the Essenes, who produced the documents at Qumran. These texts are especially valuable for reconstructing what was happening in the temple shortly before and during the time of Jesus because of their critique of the existing priestly aristocracy. The Dead Sea Scrolls also help to confirm the Jewishness of numerous details in the New Testament.[26] For example, extended beatitudes appear, "Son of God" emerges as a title equivalent to Messiah, attitudes equally critical of the temple hierarchy to those of Jesus and Paul can be found, and

23. For succinct introductions to both Jewish and Greco-Roman material, see Warren Heard, "New Testament Background," in *Introducing New Testament Interpretation*, ed. Scot McKnight (Grand Rapids: Baker, 1989), 21–51; and Joseph D. Fantin, "Background Studies: Grounding the Text in Reality," in *Interpreting the New Testament Text: Introduction to the Art and Science of Exegesis*, ed. Darrell L. Bock and Buist M. Fanning (Wheaton: Crossway, 2006), 167–96.

24. The most convenient edition in English translation is *The Works of Josephus Complete and Unabridged*, trans. William Whiston, updated ed. (Peabody, MA: Hendrickson, 1987). An excellent work that excerpts and explains the sections most relevant for New Testament interpretation is Cleon L. Rogers Jr., *The Topical Josephus: Historical Accounts That Shed Light on the Bible* (Grand Rapids: Zondervan, 1992).

25. The companion edition to the English translation of Josephus (Whiston, *Works of Josephus*) is *The Works of Philo Complete and Unabridged*, trans. C. D. Yonge, updated ed. (Peabody, MA: Hendrickson, 1993). For a good primer for his work, see Kenneth Schenck, *A Brief Guide to Philo* (Louisville: Westminster John Knox, 2005).

26. A standard translation of the Scrolls and their fragments is Florentino García Martínez, ed., *The Dead Sea Scrolls Translated: The Qumran Texts in English* (Leiden: Brill, 1994). A Hebrew-English edition is also available. Perhaps the best general introduction is James C. VanderKam, *The Dead Sea Scrolls Today*, rev. ed. (Grand Rapids: Eerdmans, 2010); see also C. Marvin Pate, *Communities of the Last Days: The Dead Sea Scrolls, the New Testament and the Story of Israel* (Downers Grove, IL: InterVarsity, 2000).

apocalyptic literature helpful for understanding Revelation dots the Scrolls' literary landscape.[27]

Certain writings within the Old Testament Apocrypha provide useful background for understanding Judaism at the time of Jesus's life and ministry. Despite the bad press the Apocrypha has typically received in Protestant circles because of its exclusion from Scripture's canon (contra Roman Catholic tradition), it remains a valuable testimony to Judaism from the third century BC through the first century AD. This is especially helpful because this is a time period on which our Bible remains silent. The Apocrypha contains a variety of different genres for the historical analyst to enlist in interpretation. Some of the apocryphal books are historical in nature, such as 1 Esdras, which retells the return of the Jewish exiles from Babylon (overlapping with the canonical books of Ezra and Nehemiah). Likewise, 1 and 2 Maccabees give histories of the Jewish resistance to empire-wide Hellenization from roughly 175 BC onward, and the Jewish liberation movement to take back Israel from the Syrians after the desecration of the temple in 167 BC. Such revolts made the scene ripe for the later fall of the Jewish temple in AD 70, an event that was very much on the mind of Jesus and his disciples even before it happened (see esp. Mark 13 pars.). Other apocryphal books contain wisdom literature similar to that found in Proverbs, Ecclesiastes, and some of the psalms. The most notable of these books are the Wisdom of Sirach (or Ecclesiasticus) and the Wisdom of Solomon. Still other apocryphal books contain the liturgies of the Jewish people throughout this time period.[28]

Not only does the Apocrypha offer important insights into Judaism before and during the time of Jesus; the authors of Scripture also show a familiarity with these writings. For example, Matthew and James repeat themes from the Wisdom of Sirach (e.g., Matt. 6:12, 14–15; James 3:13–18) while in Matthew 11:25–30 Jesus may well be alluding to teachings scattered about Sirach 51.[29] The author of Hebrews knows the suffering of believers who would not recant their faith, as depicted in the history of the Maccabees (Heb. 11:35b), as well as the pseudepigraphon (see below, p. 74) on Isaiah's martyrdom by being sawn in two in the *Ascension of Isaiah* (v. 37b).[30] The apocryphal writ-

27. See also the helpful overview of Michael O. Wise, "Dead Sea Scrolls: General Introduction," in *Dictionary of New Testament Background*, ed. Craig A. Evans and Stanley E. Porter (Downers Grove, IL, and Leicester: InterVarsity, 2000), 252–66.

28. A standard English translation and edition is *The New Oxford Annotated Apocrypha*, ed. Bruce M. Metzger and Roland E. Murphy (New York: Oxford, 1991). For good introductions, see David A. deSilva, *Introducing the Apocrypha* (Grand Rapids: Baker, 2002); and Daniel J. Harrington, *Invitation to the Apocrypha* (Grand Rapids and Cambridge: Eerdmans, 1999).

29. On which, see esp. Celia Deutsch, *Hidden Wisdom and the Easy Yoke: Wisdom, Torah and Discipleship in Matthew 11.25–30* (Sheffield: JSOT Press, 1987).

30. Particularly detailed in tracing the influence of later Jewish tradition on the portrayals of the heroes of faith in Heb. 11 is Pamela M. Eisenbaum, *The Jewish Heroes of Christian History: Hebrews 11 in Literary Context* (Atlanta: Scholars Press, 1997).

ings were fundamental in shaping the community of early Christians, and we do ourselves a favor if we immerse ourselves in their passages to understand the biblical canon more deeply.

The Old Testament Pseudepigrapha, which is a collection of writings composed almost entirely between 200 BC and AD 200, mostly attributed to much earlier individuals who feature in the Old Testament, contributes to our historical understanding in much the same way as the Apocrypha.[31] The Pseudepigrapha reconstructs the history and growing zeal of the Jewish people in the conflict-ridden intertestamental period, and in the years surrounding the composition of the New Testament, as the Jews were repeatedly occupied by Gentile nations, especially the Greeks and Romans, and suffered intermittent attacks from the Parthians, Syrians, and Egyptians. These writings reflect the belief that although things were far from the way they were promised in the covenants between God and Israel, God would arrive on the scene at the end times in apocalyptic fashion and right all the world's wrongs. Therefore, such literature can give us a good idea of the tradition within which some of the apocalypticists of both the Old and New Testaments wrote. Furthermore, we begin to understand the events that made the nation of Israel expect a warrior messiah, which sheds light on how the person of Jesus Christ failed to meet these evolving messianic aspirations. In short, through the Pseudepigrapha we see the religious development of Judaism for a nearly four-hundred-year period in ways that are not discernible simply through the Bible.[32]

Rabbinic literature has often been used to reconstruct Judaism at the time of Jesus and the New Testament authors. The Palestinian and Babylonian Talmuds incorporate both Mishnah and Tosefta. Taken together, these works contain countless applications, some quite ingenious, of how Old Testament texts can enable devout Jews in later times and different places to employ Scripture in everyday life. The Mishnah is dominated by *halakah*, or legal pronouncements; the Tosefta contains more *haggadah*, or illustrative stories, often from the life experiences of the rabbis, although both Mishnah and Tosefta contain both kinds of material. Material in the Mishnah is potentially the most relevant to the first century because it codified already-existing oral laws and traditions at the end of the second century. The rabbinic literature also contains numerous works of *Midrash* (plural, *Midrashim*), which are among the oldest biblical commentaries and help with the interpretation of authoritative books, and of *targum* (plural, *targumim*)—Aramaic translations/paraphrases of numerous parts of the

---

31. The standard English translation is James H. Charlesworth, ed., *The Old Testament Pseudepigrapha*, 2 vols. (Garden City, NY: Doubleday, 1983).

32. See further esp. Gerbern S. Oegema and James H. Charlesworth, eds., *The Pseudepigrapha and Christian Origins: Essays from the Studiorum Novi Testamenti Societas* (London and New York: T&T Clark, 2008).

Hebrew Scriptures often containing substantial additions consisting of interpretive commentary.[33]

Contemporary scholarship has taken major strides in understanding the nature of the rabbinic literature. The great difficulty in using any of it as historical background for the New Testament is that its dates range from as early as the first century to as late as the tenth century AD. Because of the way many of the documents were edited, especially to harmonize discrepant portions in both content and form, it is often impossible to determine if a given segment represents early-enough tradition to give an accurate description of Judaism during the time in which the New Testament was written.[34] Unfortunately, many pastors and teachers have used rabbinic literature indiscriminately in teaching and sermons, sometimes following commentaries that proceed in the same fashion, thinking it is all equally relevant.[35] Even academic scholarship predating about 1970 regularly utilized rabbinic literature that substantially postdates the New Testament in order to "understand" the biblical text. Recent biblical scholarship is more aware of this potential trap and less likely to depend on the latest or least reliable of rabbinic literature, but there are still plenty of exceptions to this trend.

The only way to be optimistic that rabbinic materials either predate or are contemporary to the New Testament is to consult the dates of the lives of the rabbis to which various traditions are ascribed, when they are indeed attributed to someone. The closer they are to the first century, or the earlier the document originated in which they appear, the more likely it preserves oral traditions that go back as far as the lives of the New Testament char-

33. The standard overview of Mishnah, Talmud, and Midrashim, complete with references to various modern translations and to studies of each work, is Hermann L. Strack and Günter Stemberger, *Introduction to the Talmud and Midrash*, trans. and ed. Markus Bockmuehl (Edinburgh: T&T Clark, 1991). See also Jacob Neusner, *Introduction to Rabbinic Literature* (New York: Doubleday, 1994); and Charlotte E. Fonrobert and Martin S. Jaffee, eds., *The Cambridge Companion to the Talmud and Rabbinic Literature* (Cambridge: Cambridge University Press, 2007). An excellent introduction to the targums with sample extracts from theologically interesting expansions of the Old Testament is Pierre Grelot, *What Are the Targums? Selected Texts* (Collegeville, MN: Liturgical, 1992). An important reference work is Shmuel Safrai, Zeev Safrai, Joshua Schwarz, and Peter J. Tomson, eds., *The Literature of the Sages*, vol. 2, *Midrash and Targum, Liturgy, Poetry, Mysticism, Contracts, Inscriptions, Ancient Science, and the Languages of Rabbinic Literature* (Minneapolis: Fortress, 2006).

34. See esp. Jacob Neusner, *Rabbinic Literature and the New Testament: What We Cannot Show, We Do Not Know* (Valley Forge, PA: Trinity Press International, 1994). No one has campaigned more tirelessly to make this point than Neusner, in his literally hundreds of published books.

35. A classic, still popular exemplar of this indiscriminate method is Alfred Edersheim, *The Life and Times of Jesus the Messiah* (1883; repr., Peabody, MA: Hendrickson, 1993). Paradoxically, orthodox Jews, including Messianic Jews, are often most guilty here when they uncritically assume that all the traditions they have learned, sometimes from childhood, must go back to the time of the New Testament.

acters.[36] Much of the remaining material has the potential to be misleading. Perhaps the best advice to the busy pastor or student is to stick primarily to the valuable information on Judaism available in the Apocrypha, Pseudepigrapha, and Dead Sea Scrolls, most of which demonstrably come from the first century or earlier, when looking for reliable information on historical context. It is equally important to depend on the most recent scholarship and commentaries that make similar distinctions in their use of ancient Jewish primary sources.

Finally, the Septuagint (abbreviated LXX), the Greek translation of the Hebrew Scriptures from about 200 BC, provides key insight into the world of the authors of New Testament Scripture. The translation was produced after the Mediterranean world was Hellenized (permeated with Greek language and culture) by the Greek conqueror Alexander the Great. It is this Greek translation rather than the Hebrew Scripture that the New Testament authors most often used because they were writing in Greek. With a copy of the Septuagint, an interpreter can consult the passages that New Testament writings quote or to which they allude.[37] It becomes evident, for example, that when Paul uses verbatim Greek phrases from Isaiah 45:22–23 in the Septuagint that speak of God himself in his Christ hymn in Philippians 2:10, he is attributing God's divinity to Christ. While it is still important to know the Old Testament based on the most reliable Hebrew texts, we must remember in New Testament studies that the LXX was frequently the Scripture consulted by the Christian writers who produced the works that we now revere as sacred Scripture.[38]

PRIMARY GRECO-ROMAN SOURCES

Although the New Testament has deep historical and theological roots in Judaism, it is also set in the context of the Greco-Roman world, which profoundly shaped the ethos of its audience and writers. The Greco-Roman backdrop becomes especially important for understanding the politics of the world in which the New Testament was written. It also offers invaluable background information for understanding the Gentile author Luke and his writing, and for properly interpreting Paul's writings, as they stemmed from his predominantly Gentile mission and addressed problems and solutions in a world driven by Greco-Roman values. Even Palestinian Jewish-Christian

---

36. Brad H. Young, *Meet the Rabbis: Rabbinic Thought and the Teachings of Jesus* (Peabody, MA: Hendrickson, 2007), 109. For a table that will enable the exegete to quickly reference the dates of the lives of the rabbis, see Herbert Danby, *The Mishnah* (Oxford: Clarendon, 1933), 799–800.

37. Excellent introductions include Karen H. Jobes and Moisés Silva, *Invitation to the Septuagint* (Grand Rapids: Baker; Carlisle: Paternoster, 2000); and Martin Hengel, *The Septuagint as Christian Scripture* (Grand Rapids: Baker, 2002). Narrower in focus but equally helpful is R. Timothy McLay, *The Use of the Septuagint in New Testament Research* (Grand Rapids and Cambridge: Eerdmans, 2003).

38. Jobes and Silva, *Invitation to the Septuagint*, 26.

authors were influenced, especially in their later years, by the dominant Greco-Roman milieu.[39]

The materials of first-century historians Suetonius and Tacitus are especially pertinent as they convey the general mood and particulars of the Roman empire. Suetonius, for example, was employed as the historian and literary advisor of emperors Trajan (AD 98–117) and Hadrian (AD 117–138) and invested much of his writing time in biographies of twelve of Rome's emperors, from Augustus to Domitian. The Jews and Judea show up in ten of the twelve biographies, and in each case Suetonius is reasonably even-handed in his treatment of the Jews, unlike many of the biographers of his day. A notable excerpt recounts Emperor Claudius's expulsion of the Jews from Rome in AD 49 because of a riot provoked by one *Chrestus*. Suetonius is usually understood as referring to Christ, using a variant spelling of *Christus*, so that his perhaps slightly garbled account means that Jewish Christians and non-Christian Jews were causing unrest by their disputes over Jesus's identity. Suetonius most likely confirms the historicity and gives a precise date of the account of the expulsion mentioned in Acts 18:2.[40]

The eviction of Jews from Rome likewise provides valuable background to one of Paul's main concerns in the letter to the Romans—that Jews and Gentiles be united as one people in Christ. This concern makes good sense if Paul is writing in 57, only three years after the expulsion of Jews was rescinded at the time of Claudius's death in 54. The historical circumstances surrounding the writing of Romans could then be that Jews have returned to the Roman congregation that they had helped to build, only to find it in the hands of the Gentiles to whom they had first preached the gospel. The Roman congregation had been predominantly Gentile for a full five years before the influx of returning Jewish Christians. There was undoubtedly tension between these two ethnic groups, as some of the Jewish Christians might have expected their leadership positions back. Paul's commitment to see the gospel permeate and ameliorate this tense situation colors the entire epistle.[41]

For the moral atmosphere of the Greco-Roman world, Epictetus, Seneca, and Plutarch are helpful primary sources. Many of their ideas find parallels in the teachings of Paul and Jesus. Because the Greco-Roman and Christian authors

---

39. Good introductions include Loveday C. A. Alexander, "The Relevance of Greco-Roman Literature and Culture to New Testament Study," in *Hearing the New Testament: Strategies for Interpretation*, ed. Joel B. Green, 2nd ed. (Grand Rapids: Eerdmans; Carlisle: Paternoster, 2010), 85–101; Gregory E. Sterling, "Hellenistic Philosophy and the New Testament," in *A Handbook to the Exegesis of the New Testament*, ed. Stanley E. Porter (Boston and Leiden: Brill, 2002), 313–58; and David W. J. Gill, "The Roman Empire as a Context for the New Testament," in ibid., 389–406.

40. Cf. esp. Andrew Wallace-Hadrill, *Suetonius: The Scholar and His Caesars* (London: Duckworth; New Haven: Yale University Press, 1983).

41. As indeed do numerous issues reflecting imperial counterclaims to the gospel. See esp. throughout Robert Jewett, *Romans* (Minneapolis: Fortress, 2007).

were contemporaries and likely not literarily dependent on one another, the existence of literary parallels makes a strong case that the shared ideas were part of the moral fabric of society, adapted and applied in different ways by different philosophies and religions. For example, Paul and Epictetus, a Cynic, both employ the imagery of citizens as part of a body; share the persuasion that although they may be ineloquent speakers the content of their message speaks for itself; exhibit a positive attitude toward death and suffering and living life in order to serve God;[42] and commend prayer and thanksgiving to God in all circumstances whether in want or in plenty.[43] Likewise, although Plutarch paid little attention to the burgeoning Christian movement in his own lifetime, parallels between composition, language, and topics such as ethics and theology show numerous similarities between early Christian literature and the writings of this Stoic philosopher. Thus, his philosophical commitment that the end goal of humanity is to increase in likeness to God resembles the Pauline conviction that a Christian's ultimate goal is to become like Christ. Likewise, an understanding of the Epicureans and Stoics is helpful in seeing how Paul contextualizes the gospel in a philosophical environment like Athens; not surprisingly, both groups appear in the account of Paul and the Areopagus (or Mars Hill) in Acts 17:16–34.[44]

Many reliable surveys are available that compile and assess the primary materials of antiquity to acquaint students with the more pertinent aspects of the Jewish and Greco-Roman societies as they relate to the New Testament. Many of these secondary sources are Bible dictionaries or encyclopedias that organize articles by topic, listing New Testament passages in which such historical background information proves most relevant. Not only do these sources provide excellent information on a wide variety of topics, but they also serve to show the aspiring exegete how to move from mere knowledge of a particular social or historical reality to the use of that knowledge in interpreting the New Testament.[45]

42. C. Forbes, "Epictetus," in Evans and Porter, *Dictionary of New Testament Background*, 323.

43. C. K. Barrett, ed., *The New Testament Background: Selected Documents*, rev. ed. (San Francisco: HarperSanFrancisco, 1989), 71.

44. On the various Greco-Roman philosophies and more overtly religious options, see esp. Hans-Josef Klauck, *The Religious Context of Early Christianity: A Guide to Greco-Roman Religions* (London: T&T Clark, 2000; Minneapolis: Fortress, 2003).

45. Outstanding among such works are Geoffrey W. Bromiley, ed., *The International Standard Bible Encyclopedia*, 4 vols., rev. ed. (Grand Rapids: Eerdmans, 1979–86); and David N. Freedman, ed., *The Anchor Bible Dictionary*, 6 vols. (New York: Doubleday, 1993). Equally helpful though narrower in coverage are Evans and Porter, eds., *Dictionary of New Testament Background*; Joel B. Green, Scot McKnight, and I. Howard Marshall, eds., *Dictionary of Jesus and the Gospels* (Downers Grove, IL, and Leicester: InterVarsity, 1992); Gerald F. Hawthorne, Ralph P. Martin, and Daniel G. Reid, eds., *Dictionary of Paul and His Letters* (Downers Grove, IL, and Leicester: InterVarsity, 1993); and Ralph P. Martin and Peter H. Davids, eds., *Dictionary of the Later New Testament and Its Developments* (Downers Grove, IL, and Leicester:

Historical-Context Analysis of Specific Books

Thus far we have discussed the primary materials, biblical and extrabiblical, that are useful for immersing ourselves in the biblical times and places so different from our own. Beginning with the more general context and moving to the more specific, the interpreter will next want to determine the historical context of the entire book in which the passage appears and then, finally, consider background to specific details in that passage. While it is not always possible to reconstruct all the information the interpreter might desire, it is worth determining wherever possible who wrote the book, who was the originally intended audience, the purpose(s) and occasion for the writing, and any additional historical circumstances relevant to the interpretation of that book.[46]

For the books of the New Testament, if one accepts the traditional ascriptions of authorship, only Hebrews comes without any early consensus as to who wrote it. In the early centuries, Petrine authorship of 2 Peter was also questioned at times because of its dramatically different Greek style from that of 1 Peter. Among contemporary scholars, especially outside evangelical circles, many doubt the ascriptions of the Gospels and Acts to Matthew, Mark, Luke, and John. The Pauline authorship of 2 Thessalonians, Colossians, Ephesians, and the Pastoral Epistles is often doubted, as are the traditional claims concerning all of the General Epistles and Revelation. New Testament introductions along with the more detailed commentaries on these various books will present the most prominent and viable arguments for the different theories about authorship.[47] After the interpreter forms an opinion on authorship, it is then possible to ask more specific questions of the text: Where does the book fit into the life of the author? What are the author's circumstances

---

InterVarsity, 1998). Keyed to particular passages of Scripture is the enormously helpful work by Craig S. Keener, *IVP Bible Backgrounds Commentary: New Testament* (Downers Grove, IL: InterVarsity, 1993). For a survey and introduction of specifically Jewish backgrounds see Larry R. Helyer, *Exploring Jewish Literature of the Second Temple Period: A Guide for New Testament Students* (Downers Grove, IL: InterVarsity, 2002). For specifically Greco-Roman background information, see James S. Jeffers, *Greco-Roman World of the New Testament Era: Exploring the Background of Early Christianity* (Downers Grove, IL: InterVarsity, 1999).

46. Particularly useful here are the standard New Testament introductions and surveys; see esp. the evangelical works by D. A. Carson and Douglas J. Moo, *An Introduction to the New Testament*, 2nd ed. (Grand Rapids: Zondervan, 2005); David A. deSilva, *An Introduction to the New Testament: Context, Methods and Ministry Formation* (Downers Grove, IL, and Nottingham: InterVarsity, 2004); and Gary M. Burge, Lynn H. Cohick, and Gene L. Green, *The New Testament in Antiquity: A Survey of the New Testament within Its Cultural Contexts* (Grand Rapids: Zondervan, 2009).

47. For the standard critical consensus, see Carl R. Holladay, *A Critical Introduction to the New Testament* (Nashville: Abingdon, 2005). Excellent centrist offerings are Mark A. Powell, *Introducing the New Testament: A Historical, Literary, and Theological Survey* (Grand Rapids: Baker Academic, 2009); and Luke T. Johnson, *The Writings of the New Testament*, 3rd ed. (Minneapolis: Fortress, 2010).

while writing? How is the relationship between the author and recipients best characterized?

Using Philippians as an example, Paul is in prison (1:7, 13), probably under house arrest in Rome, between AD 61 and 62 (cf. Acts 28:30–31), having thought at one point he was near the end of his ministry (1:22–23; 2:17) only to have God encourage him that there was still more for him to do (1:24–25). Nevertheless, his relationship with the Philippians apparently brings both of them much joy (1:3–11; 4:10). The Philippians were concerned to help him, sent Epaphroditus to him in that context (2:25–30), and had recently sent a gift of money for which Paul is thanking them (4:10–20). He has also learned that they are being troubled by Jewish false teachers (3:2–6). These and related circumstances determine the tone of the letter throughout, where Paul expresses sorrow and yet is joyful and tender with the Philippians, who are a direct product of Paul's missionary labor. Toward the false teachers, however, he is much harsher because he knows their message can prove damning.[48]

Romans does not disclose the same extremes of emotion; rather, it has become known as Paul's most systematic presentation of the gospel. It too is an "occasional" document, written in part at least in response to specific circumstances. But it makes sense that Paul would write this way when there is no preexisting relationship between Paul and the Roman congregation apart from the members of the congregation Paul has met on his various journeys and greets in chapter 16. This detail accounts for the more matter-of-fact tone of Romans and for the more careful and thorough explication of Paul's understanding of the Christian message.[49]

Next, consider the recipients. For letters, in most cases the addressees are named in the opening greetings. From the book itself we can often determine any special circumstances that necessitated the writing. Good questions to ask of the text include: Who is the audience? What can be said about its ethnic makeup, age, economic situation, gender, social status, and the like? Are the recipients' circumstances immediately evident? What are the key problems they are facing? Issues in the letter to the Hebrews become much clearer when we conclude that the recipients were primarily Jewish Christians facing hostility from the Roman government because of their Christian faith. The temptation to revert back to Judaism would have been strong because Judaism at the time enjoyed the status of a legal religion, which could be maintained without fear of punishment.[50] Hence, the five strong warning passages against apostasy that occur throughout Hebrews (2:1–4; 3:7–4:13; 5:11–6:12; 10:19–39; 12:14–29) can

---

48. Of many good commentaries that treat this material in their introductions and under the relevant verses throughout, see, e.g., Markus Bockmuehl, *The Epistle to the Philippians* (London: A&C Black; Peabody, MA: Hendrickson, 1998).

49. Of many good commentaries that treat this material, see, e.g., Douglas J. Moo, *The Epistle to the Romans* (Grand Rapids and Cambridge: Eerdmans, 1996).

50. See esp. William L. Lane, *Hebrews*, 2 vols. (Dallas: Word, 1991).

be read and more clearly understood against this backdrop. Or take Galatians. This letter is written in response to a specific group of Judaizers who were adding stipulations such as circumcision (and thus, most likely, law-keeping as a whole) to the requirements for salvation. Paul's adamant language and the lack of thanksgiving in the letter zero in on the fact that the audience was facing a problem that threatened their faith, and it was imperative that they deal with the issue immediately and decisively.[51]

Finally, and a bit overlapping with the two previous categories, the exegete should seek to determine the purpose or occasion of the writing. Sometimes this is directly stated; other times it is implied. First Corinthians is written to remedy the problems of divisiveness and Christian immaturity in the Corinthian congregation (see esp. 1:10–17). Second Corinthians, at least in its final form, is a defense of Paul's authority to the Corinthians in the midst of "super apostles"—those who asserted themselves as more knowledgeable than Paul himself in matters of salvation (see esp. chaps. 10–13). The Gospels of Luke and John have directly stated purposes: Luke claims that his Gospel is an orderly investigation so that Theophilus "may know the certainty of the things you have been taught" (Luke 1:4), while John writes so that his hearers might "believe that Jesus is the Messiah, the Son of God, and that by believing you may have life in his name" (John 20:31). The purpose of these works remains the same as we read them today. Other books may lack explicitly stated occasions for writing. Sometimes these can still be inferred from the text; in other instances early church tradition makes claims that merit evaluation. Although not expressed directly, the purpose of James's epistle, as indicated by much of the material, is to encourage the beleaguered poor to persevere in the midst of trials, while working out their faith in practical ways. The extreme circumstances of these recipients necessitated the letter.[52] For the Gospel of Mark, we have to turn to external tradition, which suggests that John Mark was writing to Christian churches in and around Rome in the 60s as persecution, either official or unofficial, was increasing.[53]

Historical-Cultural Analysis of a Specific Passage

The mistake many beginning interpreters make is to dwell too long on the general historical-cultural context or the overall circumstances behind the writing of the book. It should be evident from the length of time that we have spent on these details thus far that these elements are fundamentally important to the interpretive task. But in writing an exegetical paper, or in preaching or teach-

51. Cf., e.g., Gordon D. Fee, *Galatians* (Blandford Forum, UK: Deo, 2007), 21–29.
52. Cf. esp. throughout Craig L. Blomberg and Mariam J. Kamell, *James* (Grand Rapids: Zondervan, 2008).
53. This dovetails with the internal hints as to audience more readily than is often noticed. See Robert H. Stein, *Mark* (Grand Rapids: Baker Academic, 2008), 9–15.

ing a specific passage, or even a series on a whole book, one should present to others only that information that directly impinges on interpretation, and explain how it so impinges. Otherwise, the material may come across as boring, extraneous, or irrelevant. Additional background information is important for those of *us* who study, preach, and teach, providing the necessary framework in which we can view the specific historical-cultural details of a passage. However, we make a grave mistake and truncate our understanding if we do not discern which historical details relate *specifically* to the passage we are interpreting. Therefore, in any exegesis, the interpreter must resist the urge to offer overall background information either about the culture or the book in general where that information is not immediately relevant to the passage at hand.[54]

Thus, information about the author might be pertinent to a specific passage, but it sometimes is not. If one understands Ephesians to be pseudonymous, post-Pauline, and a regression from Paul's putative egalitarianism to a context of repatriarchalizing Christianity, then one may interpret the command concerning wives' submission in Ephesians 5:22 to be a less authoritative regression that does not invalidate the more timeless interchangeability of role relationships promised by Paul himself in Galatians 3:28.[55] If Paul wrote both letters, however, one will typically look for a different explanation of the two passages.

In other instances, information about the recipients may prove indispensable for understanding a particular passage. First Peter 1:1 notes that this epistle's addressees are scattered about the western and central parts of what we would today call Turkey, which were largely unaffected by Nero's imperial persecution in the 60s, the most probable decade for 1 Peter's composition. So when we read about submitting to the political authorities in 2:13–17, we should probably not envision a context of overt state persecution. We can understand in 3:13–17 why Peter thinks it is comparatively unlikely that his audience will suffer for doing good. First Peter 4:2–4 confirms that the hostility experienced by some in the churches is local and unofficial—the rejection that often comes from friends and family when a person converts. But when one reads Peter's commands to slaves in 2:18–25, there is nothing obviously unique to the provinces in which his recipients were living that would explain his instruction any differently than had he been writing to Italy or Greece.[56]

54. One of us once attended a home Bible study on the Pastoral Epistles in which the leader spent an entire hour presenting all known information about the named individuals besides Jesus and Paul in these three letters, but never once reflected on the significance, if any, of this information either for understanding the overall message of the letters or for Christian living today!

55. This is the approach taken with all of the disputed Pauline letters, and their teaching on gender roles, by Dennis R. MacDonald, *There Is No Male and Female: The Fate of a Dominical Saying in Paul and Gnosticism* (Philadelphia: Fortress, 1987).

56. See further, e.g., throughout Karen H. Jobes, *1 Peter* (Grand Rapids: Baker Academic, 2005).

Almost always, however, there are specific issues or themes within a given passage that can be illuminated by historical background, beyond what applies to the entire biblical book. Staying with 1 Peter, consider 3:1–7. To read Peter's commands as his original audiences would have, we need to understand the roles of men and women in the ancient Greco-Roman world. Above all, it was a milieu that afforded wives comparatively few rights. Six verses addressed to wives on submission (vv. 1–6) would have caused no surprise, but even one verse, and a detailed one at that, with the command for husbands to be considerate to their wives (v. 7) would have proved countercultural in its day. Patriarchal societies simply did not have the same standard of treatment for women as we enjoy in the Western world in the twenty-first century. Women had little or no right to choose their own faith. That choice was made for them by their fathers or husbands. Therefore, the mixed marriage described in verses 1–2 indicates most likely that the wife had become a convert to the newly emerging Christian faith even though her husband had not. This was enough to seriously upset societal expectations of a wife's behavior and plague the home with strife. Her silent submission and witness through action would go a long way to quell her husband's suspicion toward Christianity. In that society, it would prove a much more appropriate way to evangelize than for her to challenge her husband's authority even further by nagging him to convert.[57]

In some cases, historical information illuminates an often misunderstood detail of a text. For example, the seven churches of Revelation would have had little trouble grasping Jesus's statement to the church in Laodicea that, because they are "lukewarm—neither hot nor cold," Jesus is about to spit them out of his mouth (Rev. 3:15–16). Some interpreters have inappropriately deduced that Jesus would rather have people stand in complete opposition to him and his message (cold) than have them vacillating about whether to follow him wholeheartedly (lukewarm). Intuitively, we should suspect that something is wrong with a declaration that God is happier about those clearly on their way to hell than those on the threshold of heaven. Historical background information confirms the misinterpretation of Christ's metaphors. Laodicea was far enough away from fresh water sources that aqueducts were constructed to transport water into the city. The cold and refreshing waters from the mountain streams near Colossae warmed up as they flowed to the city, while the hot and therapeutic waters from the nearby thermal springs at Hierapolis cooled off, leaving the water that reached the city tepid and undesirable no matter where it came from. In the metaphor, then, cold and hot are both positive attributes, while lukewarm is disgusting and useless. Little wonder that Jesus feels like spitting this water out of his mouth. He is looking for useful members of his kingdom, zestfully cold or soothingly hot. He does not mean that he would

---

57. Jeannine K. Brown, "Silent Wives, Verbal Believers: Ethical and Hermeneutical Considerations in 1 Peter 3:1–6," *Word and World* 24 (2004): 395–403.

rather have someone be completely set against him rather than expressing possible interest. When historical-cultural background is considered, such an interpretation finds no support.[58]

Sometimes even the vocabulary of the text reflects a mutual understanding between the author and the recipient that we do not share. At this point a lexical analysis, or word study, may prove necessary to determine the original meaning (see chap. 5). But historical-contextual analysis may also be necessary to strip away the meaning of a word in one's own culture that masks older meanings. For example, many modern definitions of love do not do justice to the biblical model that is demonstrated by God. Love in the Bible is defined as a committed interest in the well-being of others (e.g., John 15:9–17; 1 John 3:16–18). Too often in modern terms, love means a feeling one has about something or someone, and it is trivialized to the point of confessing love for inanimate objects that are unworthy of love as it is depicted in the Bible. This phenomenon can be observed in such statements as "I love ice cream" (or chess or New Mexico or gardening, etc.). Therefore, the interpreter must ignore how words or concepts are used in today's contexts, seeking only ancient usages germane to the biblical contexts.[59]

What features of New Testament texts potentially merit historical-background study? A short list would include worldview (values, mindset, outlook of the writer or editor, recipients or other people mentioned in the text, or in the larger society); societal structures (marriage and family patterns, gender roles, and racial issues); physical features (climate and weather, buildings and structures, implements, or ease and means of transportation); economic structures (means of earning a living, issues of wealth and poverty, slavery, or economic mobility); political climate (its structures, loyalties, and personnel); behavior patterns (dress and customs); and religious practices (their implicit power centers and explicit convictions, rituals, or affiliations).[60] Not all come into play in every passage, but such a checklist is useful to think through when we consider background questions. In many instances these items contain both historical and sociological dimensions, so it is time to turn to our second main subdivision of historical-cultural analysis: social-scientific criticism.

58. See esp. M. J. S. Rudwick and E. M. B. Green, "The Laodicean Lukewarmness," *Expository Times* 69 (1957–58): 176–78; and Stanley E. Porter, "Why the Laodiceans Received Lukewarm Water (Revelation 3:15–18)," *Tyndale Bulletin* 38 (1987): 143–49.

59. Cf. esp. D. A. Carson, *The Difficult Doctrine of the Love of God* (Wheaton: Crossway, 2000).

60. Cf. Klein, Blomberg, and Hubbard, *Introduction to Biblical Interpretation*, 239. For excellent introductions to such cultural issues, see Albert A. Bell Jr., *A Guide to the New Testament World* (Scottdale, PA, and Waterloo, ON: Herald, 1994); Ralph Gower, *The New Manners and Customs of Bible Times*, rev. ed. (Chicago: Moody, 2005); and Stanley E. Porter and Craig A. Evans, eds., *Dictionary of New Testament Background* (Downers Grove, IL, and Leicester: InterVarsity, 2000).

Social-Scientific Criticism

The plea in each of the previous sections is to realize not only the vast distance in time between the world of the New Testament and our own contemporary setting, but also the geographical, cultural, and language differences. Beyond the important historical information about the New Testament writings— such as date, authorship, intended audience, and specific historical events that shaped each passage—the realm of sociology and its cognate disciplines remains to be considered for maximum historical-cultural payoff. Social-scientific criticism of the Scriptures during the past three decades has developed into a major segment of biblical criticism. Much as sociologists look at the social trends of our day and comment on the values and institutions of culture, those in the field of New Testament social-scientific criticism offer key insights into a number of social phenomena of the ancient Mediterranean world.[61]

Social-scientific criticism is not an entirely separate practice from historical-context analysis, and the two often considerably overlap. Social-scientific criticism is the branch interested in ancient social and cultural systems implicit in the writings of the New Testament.[62] It steps beyond the question "What did the text mean then and there?" and asks how and why the text was designed to function and how it might have impacted its recipients and author in light of their social, economic, political, and cultural surroundings.[63] It can be used to overcome the interpreter's innate tendency to read the Bible from his or her own cultural perspective. Social-scientific criticism can help one to recognize the cultural scripts of the New Testament world and how the inspired text either fits those cultural scripts or breaks from them in revolutionary ways. This approach also safeguards against the tendency to turn the New Testament into a collection of abstract principles divorced from time and history.[64] Because God chose to express truth in written form through a particular time and culture, the more abstract biblical truths cannot fully be determined without first analyzing the historical-cultural settings; this is analogous to how the Godhead cannot fully be understood without first considering the incarnation of the Second Member of the Trinity as a

61. Of many good resources, cf. esp. Jerome H. Neyrey and Eric C. Stewart, eds., *The Social World of the New Testament: Insights and Models* (Peabody, MA: Hendrickson, 2008); John J. Pilch, ed., *Social-Scientific Models for Interpreting the Bible* (Leiden and Boston: Brill, 2001); David A. deSilva, *Honor, Patronage, Kinship and Purity: Unlocking New Testament Culture* (Downers Grove, IL: InterVarsity, 2000); and Richard L. Rohrbaugh, ed., *The Social Sciences and New Testament Interpretation* (Peabody, MA: Hendrickson, 1996).

62. John H. Elliott, *What Is Social-Scientific Criticism?* (Minneapolis: Fortress, 1993), 8.

63. John H. Elliott, *A Home for the Homeless: A Sociological Exegesis of 1 Peter, Its Situation and Strategy* (Philadelphia: Fortress, 1981; London: SCM, 1982), 7–8.

64. Stephen C. Barton, "Historical Criticism and Social-Scientific Perspectives in New Testament Study," in Green, *Hearing the New Testament*, 34–64.

Jewish man whose life was set within the cultural confines of first-century
Palestinian Judaism.[65]

Methods for Practicing Social-Scientific Criticism

The interpreter of Scripture should approach social-scientific criticism with
due caution. When attempting to discern the social world of the original hearers
and get closest to the original meaning, one always runs the risk of imposing
on the text inaccurate frameworks or sociological assumptions derived from
other cultural settings that are not sufficiently parallel to the biblical ones to
be transferable. But when the ancient Mediterranean cultures yield inadequate
data from which to derive our social theories, such transfers from incongruous
cultural parallels at times appear inevitable. So it is always worth asking: if
a social-scientific study talks about social stratification or marriage customs
or interpersonal dynamics or political systems, is it applying models derived
strictly from information from the ancient culture in question, or is it relying
on models of interpretation developed in the analysis of other cultures in
other times and places? The latter approach is not necessarily invalidated, but
it must be treated with greater caution. Throughout the following discussion
of the main categories of social-scientific criticism, we will offer concrete
examples of both appropriate and inappropriate ways to apply the findings
from social-scientific analysis to New Testament texts.[66]

At the least speculative end of the spectrum is the practice of *social description*. This branch of sociology is entirely a subcategory of historical-context
criticism that is interested in the pervasive sociological and cultural values of the
New Testament world. Social description can be tested because it is observable
in the pages of Scripture or other ancient sources. For example, social description uses demonstrably common values in the first-century Mediterranean
world to illuminate Jesus's radical statement in Mark 3:31–35 that his family
consists of those who do God's will rather than his blood kin. Sociological
factors such as group loyalty, identity in a community rather than individual
self-actualization, and social obligations throw light on this situation that
would not be immediately recognizable to a person from a quite different
culture. When these factors are taken into account it becomes obvious that
Jesus's actions would have been considered rude and shocking to his family
yet remarkably affirming to his disciples, while at the same time creating social obligations to him and his cause.[67] Social description is the area in which

65. M. Robert Mulholland Jr., "Sociological Criticism," in Black and Dockery, *Interpreting
the New Testament*, 170.
66. Our three categories of sociology in biblical studies and their labels come from Thomas
E. Schmidt, "Sociology and New Testament Exegesis," in McKnight, *Introducing New Testament Interpretation*, 118–21.
67. David M. May, "Mark 3:20–35 from the Perspective of Shame/Honor," *Biblical Theology
Bulletin* 17 (1987): 83–87.

Sidebar 3.2

Methods for Practicing Social-Scientific Criticism

Least speculative	Social description	e.g., sociological factors such as group loyalty; the institution of patronage
↕	Sociological clarification	e.g., study of societies throughout history that demonstrate the same socioeconomic stratification as that of the first-century world
Most speculative	Sociological analysis	e.g., application of Marxist economics to the first-century church; appeal to rabbinic models of memorizing Scripture

---

the practical exegete (i.e., pastors and students) will likely engage the most consistently and fruitfully.

Moving past the historical information we have examined in historical-context analysis, let us employ in some detail an example of the significant contributions of social description to our historical-cultural methods.[68] Consider the institution of patronage, which permeates the New Testament writings. It was rooted in the belief that when a favor was done on behalf of a client (a poorer or socially subordinate person) by a wealthier or socially superior patron, the client would then repay the favor in ways that promoted the fame or well-being of the patron.[69] The system of reciprocity was invoked, so that while the service remained unreturned the client was socially indebted to the patron for the favor. Favors accepted without appropriate responses called the client's character into question, bringing shame rather than honor not just to the individual but also to the tightly knit social group with whom he or she was associated. The quest to maintain honorable character was placed far above economic prosperity or success in business, as a contemporary Western reader would envisage it. In capitalistic twenty-first-century America, where individuals expect personal merit to earn them success, actions driven by the desire to reciprocate favors and so maintain one's honorable reputation

---

68. See the chart in John J. Pilch and Bruce J. Malina, ed., *Handbook of Biblical Social Values* (Peabody, MA: Hendrickson, 1998), xxxii–xxxix, for a comparison of major values that shape culture and how they are viewed differently in a Mediterranean first-century culture than they are in twenty-first-century American culture.

69. Everett Ferguson, *Backgrounds of Early Christianity*, 3rd ed. (Grand Rapids and Cambridge: Eerdmans, 2003), 67.

strike the contemporary reader as countercultural and, in some contexts, even unethical. Ancient Mediterranean audiences would have responded in diametrically opposite ways. *Not* to curry favor with superiors by what we would call "brownnosing" would have stood out as unusual.[70]

This often underlying cultural value affects our understanding of Paul's letter to the Philippians. More than once, Paul praises the Philippian believers for their financial generosity toward him and his mission. But although his gratitude is sincere, Paul never offers outright thanks to them for their gift, precisely due to the cultural value of reciprocity. Had Paul directly thanked them, in their mind they would have become patrons and he their client, indebted to repay them a favor of their choosing, including potentially what he did or did not preach in his ministry. Paul shows his keen awareness of this by commending their kindness and concern but framing their participation in his own ministry as giving to God rather than to him (see Phil. 4:18–19). In this way, if the Philippians were to demand service in return for their gift, they would have to make the demand of God himself, whom they recognized as their own patron. So the lack of a direct "thank you" on Paul's part was not rudeness but a skillful rhetorical maneuver to avoid ingratiating himself to any particular group in such a way that the gospel might be hindered by their restrictions on him (see also 1 Cor. 9:1–18).[71]

Reciprocity is also the underlying cultural value in the Gospel account of Jesus healing the ten men with leprosy (Luke 17:11–19). After visiting the priests as commanded by Christ (v. 14), only one of them returns to thank Jesus, and he was a Samaritan at that. (Also notice how the historical reality of the tense relationship between Jews and Samaritans in New Testament times, and their resultant disdain for each other, informs this passage and others, such as Luke 10:25–37 and Acts 8:4–25). The other nine were willing to receive the healing, but not to return and express thanks in a way that would confirm their client-patron indebtedness to Jesus in response to the healing he granted them.[72]

Slightly more speculative is the second category of *sociological clarification*, located midway on the continuum of methodologies. Any sociological practice that looks at phenomena in the New Testament and attempts to explain it in light of other known phenomena throughout history is attempting social clarification. For example, a social-scientific analyst might reference Max Weber's study of the growth of new sects from charismatic groups to institutionalized organizations. Applying this to the New Testament, the sociologist

70. On the whole system of patronage, see esp. Andrew Wallace-Hadrill, *Patronage in Ancient Society* (London and New York: Routledge, 1989).

71. Cf. esp. Gerald W. Peterman, "'Thankless Thanks': The Epistolary Social Convention in Philippians 4:10–20," *Tyndale Bulletin* 42 (1991): 261–70.

72. Bruce J. Malina and Richard L. Rohrbaugh, *Social-Science Commentary on the Synoptic Gospels*, 2nd ed. (Minneapolis: Fortress, 2003), 297.

might recognize Jesus as the early charismatic leader, the church of Acts with its loose organization as an intermediate phase, and the later Pastoral Epistles' detailed criteria for church offices as the beginning of institutionalization.[73] The nature of church organization in other New Testament documents might then be dated on the basis of where on this trajectory it appears. Jude, for example, has been called "early Catholic" and placed late in the first century in part because of its reference to "the faith" as a fixed deposit of teaching delivered once for all to God's people, a view that is supposedly not likely to have developed within the first generation of Christianity.[74]

As impressive as the parallels between Max Weber's theory and the biblical data might initially seem, complete application of his sociological theory to the Bible faces some problems. The Jewish culture out of which the ministry of Jesus grew already had both synagogue elders and teachers/rabbis among its leaders. Early Christianity adopted somewhat institutionalized language when James and others were recognized as elders and apostles in Jerusalem at least by the late 40s (Acts 15:2, 6, 22–23). Paul and Barnabas appointed leaders everywhere they ministered (Acts 14:23); deacons and overseers were offices in letters as early as Philippians (1:1), which was written no later than AD 62; and the Gospel of John may have been written in part as a protest against institutionalization of the church that occurred at the end of the first century. All this shows that some forms of hierarchy appeared already in the infancy of the church, and no straight-line trajectory of growth in institutionalization accounts for all the New Testament data.[75] If, then, there are other reasons for dating Jude earlier, its ecclesiology should not by itself stand in the way of such dating.[76]

Another attempt at sociological clarification might include the study of societies throughout history that demonstrate the same socioeconomic stratification as the first-century world. From behavioral and relational patterns, certain connections can be made between other ancient imperial cultures and the cultural milieu of the Bible that may prove helpful for the interpreter. This social clarification seems to be more promising than appealing to Weber's theory of the evolution of a sect. Bypassing the economic system that will be most familiar to the majority of this book's audience (industrial/technological capitalism) and embracing the mindset of an agrarian society would give the interpreter greater clarity. A useful exercise, therefore, is to look at the culture of agrarian societies with no sizable middle class or upward mobility and with

73. See Max Weber and Samuel N. Eisenstadt, *Max Weber on Charisma and Institution Building* (Chicago: University of Chicago Press, 1968).

74. E.g., James D. G. Dunn, *Unity and Diversity in the New Testament: An Enquiry into the Character of Earliest Christianity*, 3rd ed. (London: SCM, 2006), 341–61.

75. See esp. Ronald Y. K. Fung, "Charismatic versus Organized Ministry: An Examination of an Alleged Antithesis," *Evangelical Quarterly* 52 (1980): 195–214.

76. Similarly Richard Bauckham, *Jude, 2 Peter* (Waco: Word, 1983), 8–14.

"zero-sum" economies in which one person's increased wealth necessarily implies another's increased poverty.[77] Although generalized from the study of numerous ancient empires, this economic model is sufficiently congruent with what we know of the first-century Roman Empire that it seems appropriate to employ this model. Because such a cultural experience does not resonate with the typical American lifestyle, it is necessary to consider carefully the way the Bible might be heard in such a society. For example, we might imagine that the "rich fool" who simply built bigger storage facilities to preserve his unexpected bumper crop (Luke 12:16–21) was acting prudently, whereas the average Jew would have assumed the man had the responsibility to share from his harvest with the 70 to 80 percent of the "people of the land" who barely eked out a marginal existence.[78]

Finally, and most speculative of all, is what has been called *sociological analysis*. This approach takes a theoretical model that is not supported in any culture or society with significant parallels to the New Testament world and applies it to biblical phenomena. By its very nature, this is the approach out of the three that is most likely to yield misleading results. The ambiguity of what constitutes a significant parallel, however, makes it less than straightforward to know when a theory should be assigned to this category. A well-known example that likely belongs here is the application of Marxist economics to the first-century church, which existed in a world long before either communism or capitalism had been conceived as a full-blown system or philosophy.[79] Even more suspect is a comparison of the New Testament church to "cargo cults" in colonial Melanesia, where sects believing in the immediate end of the world as they knew it rallied and grew even after failed prophecy.[80] However, appeal to certain models of oral transmission—such as rabbinic models of memorizing Scripture, twentieth-century traditional pre-literate Middle-Eastern peasant village models of oral variation in recounting unwritten but cherished tribal stories, and studies of social memory in the modern world—holds good hope for informing the processes of oral traditions about the historical Jesus between his lifetime and the time of the first written Gospels or Gospel sources.[81]

77. See esp. Gerhard E. Lenski, *Power and Privilege: A Theory of Social Stratification* (New York: McGraw-Hill, 1966).

78. Cf. Douglas E. Oakman, "The Radical Jesus: You Cannot Serve God and Mammon," *Biblical Theology Bulletin* 34 (2004): 122–29.

79. See, e.g., José P. Miranda, *Communism in the Bible* (Maryknoll, NY: Orbis, 1982).

80. For principles or good questions to ask to determine if a sociological theory is appropriate for part of the Bible, see Klein, Blomberg, and Hubbard, *Introduction to Biblical Interpretation*, 84–86. For excellent models of sociological application to specific New Testament texts, see John J. Pilch, ed., *Social Scientific Models for Interpreting the Bible: Essays by the Context Group in Honor of Bruce J. Malina* (Boston and Leiden: Brill, 2001).

81. See esp. Richard Bauckham, *Jesus and the Eyewitnesses: The Gospels as Eyewitness Testimony* (Grand Rapids and Cambridge: Eerdmans, 2006).

Merging the Worlds of Sociology and Theology

Is sociological study compatible with a high view of Scripture? No more and no less so than with historical-cultural analysis, some commentators have suggested. It is true that certain forms of study presuppose an anti-supernatural worldview or deny spiritual causation, but sociology in general is simply a neutral tool that can be used in a variety of ways. Stripped to its most basic essence, sociology is the study of the interrelationships among humans and how those interrelationships define and shape the behavior of individual persons and cultures. The God who entrusted his Word to human beings to write it down, and who became incarnate in a world filled with social systems and customs, expects us to do our best to understand that world in order to interpret his Word and to apply it to other times and places as well, and nothing in Christianity would suggest otherwise. Furthermore, both theologians and sociologists are guilty when it comes to making exclusive claims about who has the corner on the market for explaining the behavior of people throughout history.[82] The two do not have to remain mutually exclusive. In light of this, let us state explicitly that in introducing historical-cultural criticism, involving both historical context and sociological findings, we do not prescribe relegating theology to the back burner. Simply because some event or cultural phenomenon can be explained by sociological or historical factors does not mean that God in his sovereignty is not working in and through those circumstances to accomplish his will. Indeed, texts like Genesis 50:20 and Romans 8:28 explicitly assert that he *is* doing so. However, in order to see first-century details for what they truly were, interpreters must be aware of the theological presuppositions that inevitably color the exegete's entire experience, including how he or she interprets ancient texts. Then the exegete should proceed carefully so that those presuppositions do not unduly skew the sociological data. At the same time, Christian interpreters will want to pray for and be sensitive to the guidance of God's illuminating Spirit throughout the entire process, with the constraints of clear, biblical doctrine in mind.

Conclusion

Now that we have looked at how historical-context analysis and sociological studies can enhance the exegete's understanding of particular texts, examined several examples of how these practices clarify the distant world of the New Testament, and introduced the primary and secondary tools involved in these

82. Derek Tidball, *The Social Context of the New Testament: A Sociological Analysis* (Grand Rapids: Zondervan, 1984), 17; Thomas F. Best, "The Sociological Study of the New Testament: Promise and Peril of a New Discipline," *Scottish Journal of Theology* 36 (1987): 183.

practices,[83] the exegete is armed for a new task. As a lifestyle, the interpreter will want to continually seek the type of information that makes the student less of a tourist and more of a resident in the first-century Mediterranean world. But when an interpreter's general knowledge of the New Testament is not enough to bring clarity to a specific passage, it will be exceedingly helpful for the student of Scripture to consult material, including other portions of the Bible, in order to gain a clearer picture of how the words of Scripture were originally received. Much scholarship agrees about the features of the New Testament culture that clarify texts that seem otherwise bewildering to the contemporary hearer who "eavesdrops." It is these items that enjoy consensus among scholars, and yet remain little known by the majority of laypeople, that we as exegetes hope to discover and make relevant in the lives of those among whom we minister. Little by little, then, the New Testament world becomes a home for those who look to the Bible for answers to life's most pressing questions. As laypeople become more accustomed to the world of the New Testament, they will come to grips in their own study with the eternal message that is expressed concretely in the first-century Mediterranean culture, and they will be able to discern its timeless truth. Truth ultimately finds a way to express itself in action that becomes increasingly relevant to a watchful audience. God's people thus become God's witnesses, employing a language that is far from the New Testament world but close to the hearts of a contemporary audience, all of whom are potential new members of God's kingdom.

83. In addition to works already cited, see esp. Anthony J. Blasi, Jean Duhaime, and Paul-André Turcotte, eds., *Handbook of Early Christianity: Social-Science Approaches* (Walnut Creek, CA: Altamira Press, 2002); David G. Horrell, ed., *Social-Scientific Approaches to New Testament Interpretation* (Edinburgh: T&T Clark, 1999); and Philip F. Esler, ed., *The First Christians in Their Social Worlds: Social-Scientific Approaches to New Testament Interpretation* (London and New York: Routledge, 1994). For social-science commentaries on the various books of the New Testament, see Malina and Rohrbaugh, *Social-Science Commentary on the Synoptic Gospels*; Bruce J. Malina and Richard L. Rohrbaugh, *Social-Science Commentary on the Gospel of John* (Minneapolis: Fortress, 1998); Bruce J. Malina and John J. Pilch, *Social-Science Commentary on the Book of Acts* (Minneapolis: Fortress, 2008); idem, *Social-Science Commentary on the Letters of Paul* (Minneapolis: Fortress, 2006); and Bruce J. Malina, *Social-Science Commentary on the Book of Revelation* (Minneapolis: Fortress, 2000).

4

Literary Context

The visitor to the United States stared at the newspaper headline with a mixture of bewilderment and horror. "Holy Family Crushes Sacred Heart," it announced. What act of religious barbarism was this? Most Americans encountering such a headline off-guard would quickly note that it occurred in the sports pages, remember that two local Catholic high schools were named "Holy Family" and "Sacred Heart," and go on to observe that the article was about a lopsided defeat in some team sport. But without this literary context, the announcement can be baffling. Or consider this headline from 1968: "Catfish Hunter Gets Perfect Game." Plenty of Americans, even after noticing that they were looking at the sports pages, thought they were in the hunting and fishing section. You had to be a baseball fan to know that Jim Hunter, of the Oakland Athletics, had the nickname "Catfish" and that he had pitched a complete game in which he did not allow a single base runner (against the Minnesota Twins).

Here's another example: Jill didn't mean to eavesdrop, but as she walked across campus she heard a close friend end a conversation, shouting to someone who had apparently asked her a question, "Of course, she ran with it!" Here the ambiguity is even greater. Who is the "she"? What is the "it"? And what kind of running was involved? Is this also a reference to sports? Is this a long-distance runner using a pedometer to keep track of her mileage? Does it refer to carrying the ball in a girls' football game? Or is "it" an idea from a business meeting that this person quickly agreed to implement? Or did the speaker mean something else altogether?[1]

What these examples illustrate is the crucial role that the "literary" context of any communicative act (or the rhetorical context if that communication is oral rather than written) plays in correctly interpreting a speaker's or writer's meaning. When it comes to interpreting the Bible, as with any sizable anthology of related utterances, one must pay attention to multiple literary contexts. We may arrange these and think of them as a series of concentric circles becoming ever larger as one moves farther and farther away from the passage under scrutiny (see figure 4.1).[2]

Circles of Contextual Relationships

Within a Biblical Book

The first circle is *the immediate context*—the words or sentences immediately preceding and following the text to be interpreted. What does Jesus mean in John 4:26 when he declares, "I, the one speaking to you—I am he"? The only legitimate way to answer this question is to back up to verse 25 where a woman has just said to him, "'I know that Messiah' (called Christ) 'is coming.'" Jesus is thus declaring to this woman that he is the Messiah. What seems so straightforward an exegetical principle in a noncontroversial instance like this is often forgotten, however, when texts are quoted in isolation from their contexts in some theological controversy. Doesn't Romans 5:18 teach universalism—the doctrine that one day everyone will be saved regardless of their loyalties or behavior in this life? After all, it declares, "just as one trespass resulted in condemnation for all people, so also one righteous act resulted in justification and life for all." But all one has to do is read verses 17 and 19 to be disabused of this misconception. Verse 17b explains that "those who receive God's abundant provision of grace and of the gift of righteousness" are those who "reign in life through the one man, Jesus Christ." There has to be an appropriate response on our part to Christ's atoning death. And verse 19 switches from speaking about "all" to speaking about the "many" who "will be made righteous." Verse 18 must therefore refer to the *opportunity* for all humans to be justified before God and receive new life, rather than being a promise that everyone will automatically gain these blessings.[3]

1. The two examples in the first paragraph are real, the first from a local Denver area newspaper in the late 1990s or early 2000s, and the second from a Rock Island, IL, area newspaper when one of the authors was thirteen and in the prime years of his baseball "fandom." The third example here is entirely fictitious but very plausible.

2. Cf. Grant R. Osborne, *The Hermeneutical Spiral: A Comprehensive Introduction to Biblical Interpretation*, rev. ed. (Downers Grove, IL, and Leicester: InterVarsity, 2006), 39.

3. See further Douglas J. Moo, *The Epistle to the Romans* (Grand Rapids and Cambridge: Eerdmans, 1996), 339–46. The other possibility is that Paul's use of "all" in v. 18 is to refer

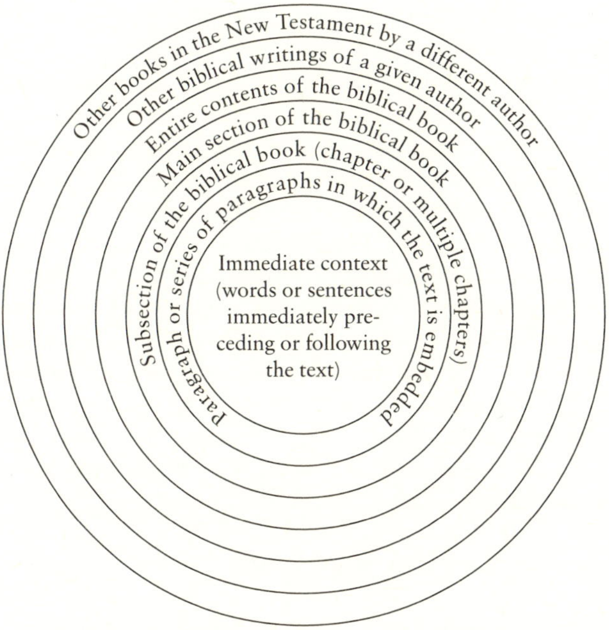

Figure 4.1: Concentric Layers of Literary Context

From the immediate context of the sentences just before and after a given text, we move to *the context of the whole paragraph* (if it is a large one) *or series of paragraphs* (if they are shorter) in which the text is embedded. If we wanted to know who the woman was to whom Jesus revealed his messianic identity, we wouldn't think twice about methodology but would just start proceeding backward through the text from John 4:25 until we got to verses 4–7 and learned that she was a Samaritan woman from the village of Sychar who had come to the town well to get water. En route, in verses 17–18, we would learn about her marital history as well. But again, when we turn to a more controversial issue or debated text, we often forget to look in the larger context. For example, did the household baptisms that Acts describes include babies or very small children, not yet old enough to believe for themselves? If so, was such baptism salvific? The one place in Acts where we receive a clear answer is the context of Acts 16:31, in which Paul and Silas proclaim to the Philippian jailer, "Believe in the Lord Jesus, and you will be saved—you and your household." Neither the immediately preceding nor the immediately following verse address the issue, but if we read on until verse 34 we discover

---

to all peoples or races of humanity. See, e.g., Robert Jewett, *Romans* (Minneapolis: Fortress, 2007), 385.

that the jailer "was filled with joy because he had come to believe in God—he and his whole household." It is belief, not baptism, that saves, and all who were baptized in this household, at least, were old enough to "come to believe in God."[4]

Sometimes the contextual clues to an exegetical crux appear even further removed yet are still within *the context of the same subsection of a biblical book*. The Sermon the Mount in Matthew 5–7 was surely intended to be taken as a unit. So when Matthew recounts that Jesus told his disciples and would-be followers, "Ask and it will be given to you; seek and you will find; knock and the door will be opened to you" (Matt. 7:7), he would have expected them to remember 6:10. There, in what we have come to call the Lord's Prayer, he enjoins them to pray, "Your kingdom come, your will be done, on earth as it is in heaven." All of our prayers should leave room for God's will to override ours, so 7:7 cannot be the "blank check" that it might at first appear to be. The asking, knocking, and seeking that Jesus commands recognizes that God knows better than we do what we truly need.[5]

From the context of an entire episode or subsection of a work of Scripture, we move further outward to *the context of a main section* in one of the biblical books. At this point, students should begin to form some opinions as to the author's flow of thought throughout the entire book from which their text comes. Outlines of books of the Bible often vary considerably from one commentator to the next, which leads to two contrasting corollaries. On the one hand, we must treat all proposed outlines of biblical books as tentative, though some much more than others, especially when we recall that ancient Jewish authors did not necessarily feel compelled to structure their writings in the linear fashion that came more to accompany Greek, Latin, and eventually Western compositions. On the other hand, rarely if ever do we sense that an inspired author had no structure in mind before beginning to write. Those parts of proposed outlines on which commentators more readily agree can be seen as most probable, and often we ourselves can perceive a flow of thought within one portion of a biblical book even if we are more uncertain about it elsewhere. In fact, one of the most rewarding parts of personal Bible study can be our own inductive work with the text, even before we consult reference

4. Cf. C. K. Barrett, *Acts: A Shorter Commentary* (Edinburgh: T&T Clark; New York: Continuum, 2002), 256. Everett Ferguson (*Baptism in the Early Church: History, Theology and Liturgy in the First Five Centuries* [Grand Rapids and Cambridge: Eerdmans, 2009], 166–85) makes the plausible case that the same is true for each of the passages in which households are baptized at one time.

5. "Jesus does not need to repeat the specific and legitimate objects for prayers, because he has already done that in the Lord's Prayer" (William W. Klein, *Become What You Are: Spiritual Formation according to the Sermon on the Mount* [Milton Keynes, UK, and Tyrone, GA: Authentic, 2006], 198). Or as David L. Turner (*Matthew* [Grand Rapids: Baker Academic, 2008], 209) puts it, "There are no exceptions—everyone who asks receives, albeit the Father determines how to answer the requests."

tools or see how scholars have outlined books, as we try to state in a sentence the main point of a paragraph, determine which paragraphs belong together in a larger subsection, which subsections go together to create a major section, and how the major sections move the author's flow of thought along.[6]

The fledgling theological student may find guidelines like Walter Kaiser's helpful in creating outlines of biblical writings:

1. "A repeated term, phrase, clause, or sentence" may indicate the beginning or the end of a section.
2. "Grammatical clues such as transitional conjunctions or adverbs" like "then, therefore, wherefore, but, nevertheless, meanwhile" may highlight a section break.
3. One or more rhetorical questions may start a new unit of material.
4. "A change in the time, location, or setting is a frequent device, especially in narrative contexts, to indicate a new theme and section."
5. Especially in letters, a vocative—a noun of direct address—may mark off a new section.
6. Changes in "tense, mood, or aspect of the verb, perhaps even with a change in the subject or object" may suggest a break.
7. Sometimes what we today would call topic sentences actually tip the writer's hand as to the theme or main point of a new section that is beginning.[7]

Acts 8, for example, contains the two vignettes involving Philip's ministry that Luke chooses to narrate. In verses 4–25, Philip preaches to Samaritans; in 26–39, to the Ethiopian eunuch. These passages are marked off by clear changes of location and characters. They belong together because Philip appears as the main character in both; nowhere else in the book is he mentioned more than in passing. Many difficult exegetical questions emerge from these stories. Why does the Holy Spirit not come upon the Samaritans when they believe and are baptized? What happened when the Holy Spirit did come upon them that enabled people to know this is what had happened? Does Simon the magician "get saved" and then forfeit his salvation? Does the eunuch's going "down into" and "up out of" water suggest immersion? Does it not matter that no one else besides Philip was around to witness the baptism? All these are legitimate questions, but they must not be allowed to

6. Particularly helpful in this respect is Grant R. Osborne and Stephen B. Woodward, *Handbook for Bible Study* (Grand Rapids: Baker, 1979), 24–49. Cf. also many of the techniques discussed for understanding the constituent elements of a biblical book in J. Scott Duvall and J. Daniel Hays, *Grasping God's Word: A Hands-On Approach to Reading, Interpreting, and Applying the Bible*, 2nd ed. (Grand Rapids: Zondervan, 2005), 28–82.

7. Walter C. Kaiser Jr., *Toward an Exegetical Theology: Biblical Exegesis for Preaching and Teaching* (Grand Rapids: Baker, 1981), 71–72.

overshadow the main point in each of the two vignettes: the gospel is moving ever further afield and people are coming to the Lord whom orthodox Jews would not have expected—Samaritans and a foreign eunuch![8] And the way we recognize these as the central points is by observing the overall structure of the book of Acts—successive sections in which the message of Jesus moves further outward, geographically as well as ethnically and culturally, from Jerusalem.[9]

The Overall Biblical Book

Being aware of *the entire contents of a given book* can also alert us to more or less probable interpretations of passages. In 1 John 3:6, we read, "No one who abides in Him sins; no one who sins has seen Him or knows Him" (NASB). Little wonder that some have concluded John is here teaching the possibility, even the necessity, of the believer attaining a state of sinless perfection in this life. Yet, even though he places them in a different major section of his letter, John has already penned two statements that declare, "if we claim to be without sin," or "if we claim we have not sinned," then "we deceive ourselves and the truth is not in us" and "we make [God] out to be a liar and his word is not in us" (1:8, 10). We usually give even uninspired writers the benefit of the doubt that they do not so flatly contradict themselves within the confines of one short document.[10] This is why translations like the ESV, NIV, NLT, and TNIV all understand the present tenses in 3:6 to indicate ongoing or repeated action, as they often do in Greek. Thus the NIV and TNIV translate, "No one who lives in him *keeps on* sinning. No one who *continues to* sin has either seen him or known him" (italics ours). There have been several other explanations of this incongruity, but this is one common way to resolve the problem.[11]

As we seek to outline an entire biblical book, or a major section or subsection, we must keep in mind that writers in the ancient Mediterranean world often utilized structures that are less common in the modern Western world. One of these is *chiasm(us)* or *inverted parallelism*. It was not at all uncommon for literary and nonliterary documents, papyri, and even

8. Keith H. Reeves, "The Ethiopian Eunuch: A Key Transition from Hellenist to Gentile Mission: Acts 8:26–40," in *Mission in Acts: Ancient Narratives in Contemporary Context*, ed. Robert L. Gallagher and Paul Hertig (Maryknoll, NY: Orbis, 2004), 114–22; John T. Squires, "The Function of Acts 8.4–12.25," *New Testament Studies* 44 (1998): 608–17.

9. See, e.g., Richard N. Longenecker, "Acts," in *Expositor's Bible Commentary*, ed. Tremper Longman III and David E. Garland, rev. ed. (Grand Rapids: Zondervan, 2005), 10:708–12.

10. Especially when the tension appears already in the more immediate context between 1 John 1:6 ("If we claim to have fellowship with him and yet walk in the darkness, we lie and do not live out the truth") and vv. 8 and 10.

11. For the full range of options, see Raymond E. Brown, *The Epistles of John* (Garden City, NY: Doubleday, 1983), 411–16. For this particular solution, see Marianne Meye Thompson, *1–3 John* (Leicester and Downers Grove, IL: InterVarsity, 1992), 82.

ostraca to contain writing that was structured in an ABBA or ABCBA or ABCDCBA (etc.) fashion. Not only was this a mnemonic device in a primarily oral culture, it also focused attention on the central element (at least in the extended chiasms of more than four parts) rather than on the end. While some scholars seem to have gotten carried away with the idea and claim to discern chiasms behind every bush, so to speak, there are enough instances that are sufficiently clear in Scripture that we must be open to each hypothesis of a chiastic structure and evaluate it on its own merits.[12] Second Corinthians 1:12–7:16 may reflect one such structure that spans a large portion of a New Testament document.[13]

Figure 4.2: Paul's Ministry with the Corinthian Church

Confidence in His Motives (1:12–22)   Confidence in the Corinthians (7:13b–16)

   Sorrow for Those Punished   Sorrow among the Corinthians
   (1:23–2:11)   (7:8–13a)

      Upcoming Travel Plans   Travel Plans Resumed
      (2:12–13)   (7:5–7)

         The Spirit vs. the Letter or   Christ vs. Belial or Belief vs.
         the New Covenant vs. the   Unbelief (6:11–7:4)
         Old (2:14–4:6)

            Present Afflictions vs.   Present Afflictions vs.
            Coming Glory (4:7–5:10)   Present Glory (6:1–10)

               Core of Ministry—Reconciliation (5:11–21).[14]

A second device is that of *chain-link* reasoning or association by *catchwords*. A key term or expression in one sentence or paragraph suggests a related concept, which then becomes the topic for the next sentence or paragraph. That concept spawns a third, which produces a fourth, and so on.[15] Much ancient Jewish scriptural commentary (midrash) proceeded along these lines, so we should not be surprised to find that a fair amount of the letter of James does so as well.[16] Thus "trials" in 1:2 lead to "testing" in verse 3, which produces "perseverance." "Perseverance" reappears in verse 4, so that we might not lack anything. But verse 5 explains what to do if we "lack" wisdom. We must "ask"

---

12. For a thorough treatment, see Craig Arnold Smith, "Criteria for Identifying Chiasm of Design in New Testament Literature" (PhD diss., University of Bristol, 2009).

13. For elaboration, see Craig L. Blomberg, "The Structure of 2 Corinthians 1–7," *Criswell Theological Review* 4 (1989): 3–20.

14. Craig L. Blomberg, *From Pentecost to Patmos: An Introduction to Acts through Revelation* (Nashville: B&H; Nottingham: Apollos, 2006), 211.

15. The fullest study is now Bruce W. Longenecker, *Rhetoric at the Boundaries: The Art and Theology of New Testament Chain-Link Transitions* (Waco: Baylor University Press, 2005).

16. See Craig L. Blomberg and Mariam J. Kamell, *James* (Grand Rapids: Zondervan, 2008), 23.

God, but asking God is repeated and qualified in verse 6. And so the patterns continue. It is also important to remember that one structuring device does not always preclude another. A series of catchwords could, for example, account for the sequence of topics in the first half of a chiasm, the second half of which would then be structured, by definition, by the same topics treated in reverse sequence.[17]

Outside a Biblical Book

By the time one reaches the analysis of the structure of an entire biblical book, one might think that has exhausted everything that could fairly be labeled "literary context." But the Bible is an anthology that Christians throughout history have typically believed contains many thematic unities. Put another way, while the Bible reflects varying perspectives on numerous topics, it never actually contradicts itself, at least if each passage is interpreted in context.[18] Even without any uniquely Christian convictions about the nature of the Bible, we might be inclined to suspect that the same biblical writer would demonstrate some consistency from one book to the next, especially when dealing with similar themes. The next context for consideration is thus *the other biblical writings of a given author.*

For example, when we recognize the overall similarities between the theology of Galatians and the teachings of Romans, and when we then come to brief, cryptic teachings in the first and shorter of those two epistles, we may turn to the later and longer work for elaboration. Thus Paul tantalizes us with Galatians 3:19: "What, then, was the purpose of the law? It was added because of transgressions until the Seed to whom the promise referred had come." What specifically does "because of transgressions" mean? At least a significant part of the answer appears in Romans 7:7–12. The law pointed out to what extent humanity violated God's perfectly righteous standards and thus showed their need for a Savior. But Paul may mean even more than that. Romans 5:20–21 explains that "the law was brought in so that the trespass might increase. But where sin increased, grace increased all the more, so that, just as sin reigned in death, so also grace might reign through righteousness to bring eternal life through Jesus Christ our Lord." "Trespass" is not any kind of sin but *conscious* transgression. Knowing God's standards more clearly meant that even the same amount of sin now contained a higher percentage of trespass. Moreover, like children who are

17. See further John Breck, *The Shape of Biblical Language: Chiasmus in the Scriptures and Beyond* (Crestwood, NY: St. Vladimir's Seminary Press, 1994).

18. For an introduction to the topic, see Craig L. Blomberg, "The Unity and Diversity of Scripture," in *New Dictionary of Biblical Theology*, ed. T. D. Alexander and Brian S. Rosner (Leicester and Downers Grove, IL: InterVarsity, 2000), 64–72. For a thorough discussion and demonstration, see C. H. H. Scobie, *The Ways of Our God: An Approach to Biblical Theology* (Grand Rapids and Cambridge: Eerdmans, 2003).

compliant until something is pronounced off limits to them and then they insist on doing it, humanity may have actually increased its total amount of sin in its rebellion against God. The unusual word for "because" in Galatians 3:19 can also be translated "in order to cause," and Paul may well be teaching that the law was intended to make it all the more clear how rebellious humanity was and thus make God's righteous judgment and provision for salvation that much clearer too.[19]

The next concentric circle outward after other books by the same author includes *other books in the New Testament by a different author*. Were we engaged in the study of a passage's historical background (see chap. 3) here, we would insist that *antecedent* Scripture (in time, not necessarily in the order of the canon), in either testament, can illuminate that passage.[20] But at the level of literary context, we begin to overlap with issues of systematic theology (see chap. 9). If all Scripture coheres, then at one level it *is* legitimate to interpret Scripture with Scripture anywhere in the canon, being sure we have studied each passage first in all its more immediate contexts. Similarly, there is then a proper time and place to allow a later book to help interpret an earlier book, say, using the Jewish Christianity disclosed in Matthew (written no earlier than the early 60s) to interpret the Jewish Christianity of James (possibly written as early as the late 40s), especially since there is no evidence of any seismic shifts in the nature or theology of that wing of the early church during those fifteen years or so in between.[21]

Or suppose we have become convinced on the basis of a broad cross section of New Testament books and texts of the recurrence of a particular principle but then come to one passage or author who at first glance seems to contradict it. It is only proper that we should analyze more carefully that minority voice to see if there might be good exegetical reasons to interpret it in a fashion consistent with everything else we have been perceiving. For example, we may read of Christ's promise in Matthew 28:20 to be with his followers forever, and his promise never to allow any of his people to be lost or snatched from his hand in John 6:39 and 10:29. We may observe Paul's ringing declarations that God will complete his good work in those he has started to transform (Phil. 1:6) and that nothing can separate us from his love which is in Christ Jesus (Rom. 8:38–39). We may note that 1 John 2:19 labels those who appeared to be believers but who left the church and became heretics as people who

19. For both of these options see, e.g., Ronald Y. K. Fung, *The Epistle to the Galatians* (Grand Rapids: Eerdmans, 1988), 159–60.

20. For appeal to Old Testament backgrounds in exegeting a New Testament passage, see pp. 190–93.

21. For an excellent survey of Jewish Christianity in Palestine from its inception to the time of the Bar Kokhba revolt in ca. AD 135, see Richard Bauckham, "James and the Jerusalem Community," in *Jewish Believers in Jesus: The Early Centuries*, ed. Oskar Skarsaune and Reidar Hvalvik (Peabody, MA: Hendrickson, 2007), 55–95.

were really "not of us." From these and similar passages, we may endorse the Reformers' doctrine of the perseverance of the saints—that those who have truly trusted in Christ as Savior and Lord cannot commit complete apostasy and be forever lost in eternity.[22]

But then we turn to the warning passages in Hebrews, especially 6:4–8, and it seems equally clear that the author of this letter is assuming such defection *is* possible. Reminding ourselves that we are scarcely the first people in history to have observed this tension, we become curious to see how Christians have dealt with it. One option, of course, is to understand the texts outside Hebrews in a different way, perhaps as promising that nothing external to a believer can ever jeopardize his or her salvation but that humans always have the freedom to "chuck it all" themselves. More probably, we may find clues within Hebrews itself to suggest that a passage like 6:4–6 is not actually teaching the loss of salvation for those who were full-fledged Christian believers.[23]

We have now discussed the successive steps of analyzing the literary context of a given passage all the way from its immediate context out to its context in the whole of the New Testament. We might be tempted to think that we have introduced every step possible in this undertaking. But we must also consider issues related to the literary *form* of the passage in question and of the *genre* of the book of the Bible in which it is embedded.

The Significance of Literary Forms and Genres

Not all New Testament books utilize the same genres. There are four major literary categories into which these works fall—gospels, an "acts," epistles, and an "apocalypse." Larger introductions to biblical interpretation, or hermeneutics, often devote lengthy sections to the diverse literary genres of Scripture; students wanting more information than we provide here should consult such works.[24] In a small handbook like this, we must be much briefer.

22. For an amazingly balanced and detailed treatment of this issue, see Thomas R. Schreiner and Ardel B. Caneday, *The Race Set before Us: A Biblical Theology of Perseverance and Assurance* (Downers Grove, IL, and Leicester: InterVarsity, 2001).

23. For a book-length treatment of these and related options, see Herbert W. Bateman IV, ed., *Four Views on the Warning Passages in Hebrews* (Grand Rapids: Kregel, 2007). For a concise treatment of six main approaches to Heb. 6:4–8 in particular, cf. George H. Guthrie, *Hebrews* (Grand Rapids: Zondervan, 1998), 226–32.

24. E.g., William W. Klein, Craig L. Blomberg, and Robert L. Hubbard Jr., *Introduction to Biblical Interpretation*, rev. ed. (Nashville: Nelson, 2004), 323–448; William W. Klein, *Handbook for Personal Bible Study: Enriching Your Experience with God's Word* (Colorado Springs: NavPress, 2008), 184–231; W. Randolph Tate, *Biblical Interpretation: An Integrated Approach*, rev. ed. (Peabody, MA: Hendrickson, 1997), 67–154; Duvall and Hays, *Grasping God's Word,*

Sidebar 4.1

Major New Testament Literary Genres and Examples of Forms within Each

Gospels	parables, proverbs, pronouncement stories, healing miracles, nature miracles, etc.
Acts	travel narratives, more miracles, speeches or sermons by early Christian leaders, etc.
Epistles	early Christian creeds or hymns, virtue and vice lists, diatribe, etc.
Apocalypse	early Christian hymnody, visions of the present and future in highly symbolic form, letters to seven churches, etc.

New Testament Genres

Gospels and Acts combine historical, theological, and literary features and purposes. In each instance, one should assume that the writers are narrating events they believed really happened, but the writers narrated those events based on the standards of history writing of their time, which do not necessarily match the greater levels of precision we often demand today. But the accounts were also selected, arranged, and recounted with the author's overall theological purposes particularly in view and, to varying degrees, with a measure of literary artistry.

So we should not be surprised that the Gospel parallels differ. All four Gospel writers offer basically the same story of Jesus's passion and death. But Matthew stresses the complicity of the Jewish leaders in Jesus's fate, Mark highlights Jesus's role as suffering servant, and Luke says less about the atonement than either Matthew or Mark but plays up Jesus's posture as a righteous and innocent victim/martyr. John, more than the three Synoptic Gospels, points out Jesus's authority over the events that transpire and the completely voluntary way in which he allowed others to mistreat and eventually execute him. None of these themes contradicts the others, but each focuses on different aspects of a multifaceted series of events. Without all four, our understanding of the events and their significance would be impoverished.[25]

So too when we read Acts 27, with Luke's account of Paul's ill-fated ship voyage with its passengers wintering on Malta, we see three complementary sets of features. First, the painstaking attention to nautical detail virtually requires that the author participated in the journey or relied on the accounts

---

216–90; and Gordon D. Fee and Douglas Stuart, *How to Read the Bible for All Its Worth*, 3rd ed. (Grand Rapids: Zondervan, 2003), 55–264.

25. On the first three Gospels, see further Robert H. Stein, "Interpreting the Synoptic Gospels," in *Interpreting the New Testament: Essays on Methods and Issues*, ed. David A. Black and David S. Dockery (Nashville: Broadman & Holman, 2001), 336–56. On the Fourth Gospel, see Gary M. Burge, "Interpreting the Gospel of John," in ibid., 357–90.

of someone who had. Second, the style of narration and selection of detail make clear Luke's belief in God's providential oversight of the journey, a central theological conviction throughout both Luke's Gospel and the Acts. Finally, Luke is an artistic writer, knowing how to craft a plot that builds suspense, has peaks and valleys, reaches a climax, and ends with a denouement.[26]

Regarding epistles, perhaps the most important general observation to make is that they are "occasional" literature. They were written in response to specific occasions—questions, settings, life situations of various groups of early Christians—and therefore are not comprehensive, detached theological textbooks. Thus it becomes crucial to reconstruct as much of the original context, purpose, and reception of each letter as the data permit (see pp. 70–72).

More important for an analysis of literary context, Hellenistic letters tended to fall into a five-part structure: opening greetings, thanksgiving prayer, information the author wished to convey, exhortations or instructions to be communicated, and closing greetings. Comparing the corresponding forms in New Testament letters with conventional Greco-Roman letters can help interpreters understand what was typical and therefore not necessarily stressed versus what would have stood out to the initial readers as unique and therefore distinctively Christian. One thinks, for example, of the conventional commands to slaves, children, and women to submit to those in authority over them as compared with the highly countercultural calls to masters, fathers, and husbands to love and serve those under them and to use their authority in a sacrificial, self-giving way. Also, the letter to the Galatians' lack of an opening thanksgiving or prayer highlights the urgency with which Paul felt he needed to address the problem of the Judaizers who were corrupting the churches in that Roman province.[27]

Epistles in the ancient Mediterranean world subdivided into nearly a couple dozen special forms. Recognition of Romans as an ambassadorial letter paving the way for Paul's hoped-for first visit to Rome, or of Philippians as a family letter (or letter of friendship), which accounts for the amount of attention devoted to seemingly incidental details, helps us to understand why the contents of each epistle appear as they do. The specific literary forms and rhetorical styles utilized are likewise illuminated.

The book of Revelation, finally, combines elements of three genres: epistolary, prophetic, and apocalyptic. Sent as a letter, containing seven letters to seven churches in Asia Minor (Rev. 2–3), it too addressed real people in very concrete situations, many of which are highly reconstructible. As prophecy, Revelation referred to real future events still to come. But as apocalyptic lit-

---

26. Cf. John B. Polhill, "Interpreting the Book of Acts," in Black and Dockery, *Interpreting the New Testament*, 391–411.

27. For an excellent introduction to the features of epistles that beginning exegetes most need to know, see John D. Grassmick, "Epistolary Genre: Reading Ancient Letters," in *Interpreting the New Testament Text: Introduction to the Art and Science of Exegesis*, ed. Darrell L. Bock and Buist M. Fanning (Wheaton: Crossway, 2006), 221–39.

erature, it often dressed those events in highly symbolic garb, requiring the interpreter to discern what its original readers could be most expected to have understood, with its visions of dragons and other beasts, locusts and horsemen, or gold and crystal.[28]

Constituent Literary Forms

The four main genres of New Testament books themselves contain multiple literary forms. The Gospels include discrete pericopes (passages) that narrate primarily Jesus's teaching or his mighty deeds. These in turn can be subdivided into parables, proverbs, pronouncement stories, miracles of healing, nature miracles, and so on. Different interpretive principles at times apply depending on these varying literary forms. We do not necessarily expect parables to present real people who actually lived, but their generally lifelike nature coupled with frequent surprise endings teach us about the nature of God's kingdom with striking impact as no simple set of propositions ever could. Proverbs encapsulate general truths but not didactic absolutes that apply to every situation without exception. Miracles are pointers to the in-breaking kingdom of God, so that if the kingdom is arriving, so too is the king. Their nature is not primarily anthropological (to meet human need, though they often do that) but christological (disclosing Jesus's messianic identity).

The Acts of the Apostles includes some of these same smaller literary forms but introduces new ones as well, most notably the speeches or sermons of the early Christian leaders. Sharing the central points of the gospel message, the speeches nevertheless contextualize that message in highly creative and relevant ways for their varying audiences, suggesting models for us to do the same today. The deeds of the first Christian preachers and missionaries often bear striking resemblance to what Jesus did during his mission, but with clear limits. (No one after Jesus ever again atones for the sins of the world!) Thus we can learn both the ways in which Christ's followers should expect to follow "in his steps" (1 Pet. 2:21) and the areas in which they should not.

The apostolic letters contain what may be preformed early Christian creeds or hymns—pointers to the high Christology emerging at a stunningly early period in the church's life (see esp. Phil. 2:6–11; Col. 1:15–20; and 1 Tim. 3:16). The letters contain virtue and vice lists, similar in form to many that were well known in other Jewish, Greek, or Roman circles. As already noted, we often learn far more from the ways in which these lists differed from their counterparts in other religious or cultural circles than from the ways in which

28. See further Richard Erickson, *A Beginner's Guide to New Testament Exegesis: Taking the Fear out of Critical Method* (Downers Grove, IL: InterVarsity, 2005), 179–203. For more on all four of these literary genres within the New Testament and their implications for interpretation, see also Craig L. Blomberg, "The Diversity of Literary Genres in the New Testament," in Black and Dockery, *Interpreting the New Testament*, 272–95, and the literature cited there.

they remained the same. Both Romans and James contain frequent use of the literary form known as diatribe (noticeably different from what we mean by the term today). Here letter writers raised potential questions placed in the mouths of real or hypothetical objectors and then replied to them. The book of Revelation, finally, is filled with early Christian hymnody, a key pointer to its purpose—to drive us to worship. And so the list could go on.[29]

Figures of Speech

More directly relevant for an exegetical handbook is the reminder that, in addition to diverse literary genres and forms, the New Testament is filled with all kinds of figurative speech. People who insist on interpreting the Bible literally, if they know what they are saying, mean that we should interpret Scripture according to its literary forms. To take a metaphor as the metaphor it was intended to be is to interpret, as the Reformers put it, according to the *sensus literalis* (literal sense). What they, like many in the history of the church, meant by interpreting literally was to avoid reading into the text allegorical or spiritual meanings never intended by the biblical authors.[30] But today, for some well-meaning but ill-informed individuals, treating a metaphor as if it were a straightforward fact is seemingly an interpretive virtue, when it actually guarantees that we will misinterpret the inspired author's intention.[31]

Metaphorical Language

Probably the most common place in the New Testament in which figurative language is misconstrued as literal language is in apocalyptic literature. Few

29. For a full treatment, see James L. Bailey and Lyle D. Vander Broek, *Literary Forms in the New Testament: A Handbook* (Louisville: Westminster John Knox, 1992). Cf. also, to varying degrees, all the works cited in nn. 24–28 above.

30. Cf. Kaiser, *Toward an Exegetical Theology*, 87–88. For a detailed treatment, see David S. Dockery, *Biblical Interpretation Then and Now: Contemporary Hermeneutics in the Light of the Early Church* (Grand Rapids: Baker, 1992).

31. One of us once used the example from Isa. 55:12—"the trees of the field will clap their hands"—to make this point in a local church setting, only to have an elderly man reply adamantly, "If the Bible says that the trees in Isaiah's day had hands, then I believe it." His wonderful piety was overwhelmed by his utter lack of understanding about hermeneutics. But the issue is no different, though far more subtle, when a majority of the Evangelical Theological Society voted to ask Robert H. Gundry to resign from membership twenty-five years ago because they believed he had denied inerrancy when he authored *Matthew: A Commentary on His Literary and Theological Art* (Grand Rapids: Eerdmans, 1982) and claimed that portions of this Gospel were unhistorical "midrash" on Mark and Luke. Gundry even included an appendix explaining why his view was consistent with inerrancy: once the correct genre of Matthew's Gospel was identified, then it inerrantly communicated the precise combination of historical and theological truth that Matthew intended. The proper response for those who disagreed should have been to argue persuasively against Gundry's identification of Matthew's genre, not to allege that he had violated the society's statement of faith.

people imagine that the portrayal of Satan as a dragon in Revelation 12 implies that dragons do exist after all, or that Satan is literally a beast with fangs, claws, a tail, and a scaly back. But flip back to chapter 9 and the imagery of two hundred million grotesque locusts emerging from the abyss, assembling for battle and killing a third of humanity, and far too many people follow Hal Lindsey in believing that these are literal descriptions of human warfare (armed helicopters complete with tail gunners), causing the physical death of human beings.[32] But of course, such an interpretation (inconsistently) has to ignore the fact that these locusts do not emerge from some earthly hangar but from the underworld home of Satan. This is most likely spiritual, quite possibly invisible, warfare, as demonic hordes seek to turn the earth's inhabitants away from God and to their eternal demise.[33]

Metaphorical language may be most common in apocalyptic literature but is scarcely limited to it. Jesus commands his disciples that if one of their eyes leads them to lust they should gouge it out (Matt. 5:29). But blind people report the ability to lust just as effectively as sighted ones, especially those who could once see and who have good memories of erotic sights. Clearly Jesus is using a vivid metaphor to tell his followers to take drastic action, if necessary, to remove themselves from the stimuli that trigger their lust.[34] Other contexts prove less clear. Matthew 17:27 (the coin in the fish's mouth) is a unique miracle on the pages of the Gospels, if it is in fact a miracle. On no other occasion is Christ said to have performed a miracle solely for the benefit of himself and his closest followers (here, to pay the tax for Peter and himself). Attention to the literary form may prove helpful: this is also the only passage usually included in lists of Jesus's miracles in which no narrative of the actual event occurs. All we read is a command to Peter to go to the Sea of Galilee, with the promise that he will find this fish with a coin in its mouth. Scavenger fishes (the *musht*) were common enough in the lake, and fishes with coins in their mouths have been caught there, so potentially the only miracle here is Jesus's foreknowledge of what would happen. But Matthew never tells us that Peter did as he was told; given his overall track record of obedience, it is hardly a foregone conclusion that he did. What we have here is not a narrative but a command. Perhaps Jesus intended something entirely metaphorical such as "cast your hook into the

32. Hal Lindsey, *The Apocalypse Code* (Palos Verdes, CA: Western Front, 1997), 42.

33. Cf. Ben Witherington III (*Revelation* [Cambridge: Cambridge University Press, 2003], 154): "John would no doubt have laughed at attempts to identify this horde with a group of human beings for he is talking about powers and principalities." David E. Aune (*Revelation 6–16* [Dallas: Word, 1998], 539) notes that twice in the Babylonian Talmud huge armies of destroying angels appear (*b. Shabbat* 88a; *b. Pesahim* 112b). In the second of these texts, "180 thousand angels of destruction go out every night" to wreak spiritual rather than physical havoc.

34. See, e.g., John Nolland, *The Gospel of Matthew* (Milton Keynes, UK: Paternoster; Grand Rapids: Eerdmans, 2005), 238–40.

sea, sell your catch, and pay the temple tax with the proceeds."[35] Perhaps he didn't. The point here is not to decide one way or the other but merely to alert readers to a wider array of legitimate interpretive options than they may have first considered.

The Most Common Figures of Speech

The number of specific kinds of figures of speech identifiable in Scripture is vast. E. W. Bullinger's thousand-page presentation has probably included many that may not actually qualify, but if even a quarter of his examples were on target (and probably more than that are), he has admirably proved the point.[36] Interpersonal communicative acts are laced with figures of speech, which is one of the significantly complicating factors in learning a foreign language. What indigenous speakers grow up learning, without much conscious reflection, baffles the nonnative. The coach "reads the riot act" to his players at halftime because they "blew it big time." "Hanging their tails between their legs," they return to the field. Soon, however, they are "pumped up," "jazzed," and "loaded for bear." It's time to "kick some butt," and they do. Their opponent's "swagger" disappears, their once raucous fans have to "eat crow," and the final score is a "blowout."[37] Need we continue? And for those who object that the Bible is much more elegant and poetic than ordinary idiomatic speech, just remember how filled with metaphors poetry is.[38]

---

35. Joachim Jeremias, *New Testament Theology*, vol. 1 (London: SCM; Philadelphia: Westminster, 1971), 87.

36. E. W. Bullinger, *Figures of Speech Used in the Bible: Explained and Illustrated* (1898; repr. Grand Rapids: Baker, 2003).

37. Gordon D. Fee and Mark L. Strauss (*How to Choose a Translation for All Its Worth* [Grand Rapids: Zondervan, 2007], 62) have a hilarious paragraph illustrating what they call "idiomania" (overdoing idioms) and invite readers to imagine trying to translate it meaningfully into a foreign language. Its first six sentences read: "My career had seen better days. I was skating on thin ice, scraping the bottom of the barrel, and ready to say uncle. The boss and I did not see eye to eye, and he told me to shape up or ship out. There was no silver bullet. It was a safe bet I was going to sink or swim. Nobody could save my bacon." They add that "a literal translation of this would be completely meaningless, since the story has nothing to do with skating, thin ice, barrels, uncles, eyes, bullets, bets, swimming, bacon, and so on."

38. Consider, e.g., all of the similes and metaphors Emily Dickinson uses to liken the conscious choice of love to believers' rather than infant baptism, in her poem "Love's Baptism":
I'm ceded, I've stopped being theirs; / The name they dropped upon my face / With water, in the country church, / Is finished using now, / And they can put it with my dolls, / My childhood, and the string of spools / I've finished threading too. / Baptized before without the choice, / But this time consciously, of grace / Unto supremest name, / Called to my full, the crescent dropped, / Existence's whole arc filled up / With one small diadem. / My second rank, too small the first, / Crowned, crowing on my father's breast, / A half unconscious queen; / But this time, adequate, erect, / With will to choose or to reject. / And I choose— just a throne.

This doesn't mean that every proposal to see in a passage a certain figure of speech is equally convincing, merely that we should take the possibility seriously and evaluate it against the alternatives rather than immediately dismissing it out of hand (oops, another idiom). Might a number of problematic passages where a tension appears between the literal meaning and what one would expect in its context be best explained as irony? Many interpreters suspect this is the case in Luke 22:35–38. Just before Jesus and the disciples leave the upper room for the garden of Gethsemane, he reminds them how they had previously traveled with very few provisions, dependent on others for support. Now, he tells them to be prepared to take money and supplies with them and to buy a sword if they don't have one. Does he really intend for them to fight the arresting party in the garden? When Peter acts as if he thought he was supposed to fight, Jesus rebukes him and heals the ear of the man Peter attacked (vv. 49–51). In verse 51 Jesus uses a figure of speech that most likely means "no more of this" (Ἐᾶτε ἕως τούτου).[39] Most likely Jesus was speaking equally figuratively in verse 38. We should probably hear a tone of frustration in his voice when he says, "That is enough," as if to imply, "Enough of this conversation. You just don't get it. You're not going to get it—yet."[40]

Likewise, when Paul replies to Ananias, after being unjustly struck on the mouth, he is rebuked for speaking to a high priest so harshly. Paul replies, "I did not realize that he was the high priest" (Acts 23:5). Interpreters remain puzzled over such a reply. Is it a retraction and implicit apology? Yet what Paul had said to Ananias about his unjust behavior and God's coming retribution was all true. And how could Paul not have known Ananias was the high priest? True, he had been away from Jerusalem for many years, and the hurried assembly of the Sanhedrin might have not given the high priest time to put on his official robes. But it would have been obvious to all who he was, dress or no dress, because he would have led the meeting. Although it has only occasionally been argued by commentators on this passage, an ironic interpretation works quite well here. We may imagine Paul speaking with an obviously sarcastic tone, as if to say, "I didn't know anyone who acted that way could possibly be God's true high priest." The reason most exegetes have not opted for this has to do with the way verse 5 ends: "for it is written, 'Do not speak evil about the ruler of your people.'" But this makes little sense as the conclusion to Paul's remarks if he is speaking ironically or even sarcastically. Here we may need to remember that there were no quotation marks in the original manuscripts, or for centuries afterward. Perhaps this is

39. Cf. I. Howard Marshall, *The Gospel of Luke* (Exeter: Paternoster; Grand Rapids: Eerdmans, 1978), 837. Virtually all modern translations agree. The NKJV, however, renders the idiom literally and therefore completely inverts the meaning ("permit even this"), based on the similarly implausible rendering of the KJV ("suffer [i.e., allow] ye thus far").

40. Ibid., 827. The HCSB brings this out nicely with its "Enough of that!" *The Message* gives the same rendering and clarifies even further by adding, "No more sword talk!"

Luke's explanatory aside to the reader; Luke certainly appends such remarks, especially to show where Scripture was being fulfilled, in many other places.[41] Again the point is not so much to insist that this is the correct interpretation of this passage as to illustrate the kinds of options to which thoughtful exegetes must be open.

Grant Osborne helpfully summarizes the range of figures of speech to which Bible readers must be alert under six basic headings. *Figures of comparison* include metaphor and simile, the latter making the comparison explicit by use of "like" or "as," with the former leaving the comparison without a specific comparative word (e.g., "Go tell that fox . . ." [Luke 13:32]). *Figures of addition or completion* include pleonasm, a form of verbal redundancy (someone "answered and said," without implying two separate actions); paronomasia, or plays on words ("faith without works doesn't work [lit., "is workless"—James 2:20]); epanadiplosis, or repetition for emphasis (e.g., Gal. 1:8 and 9); hyperbole, or rhetorical exaggeration (e.g., gouging out an eye if it offends you [Matt. 5:29]); and hendiadys, two mutually defining terms to express one concept (Saul breathes threats and murder [= murderous threats] in Acts 9:1).

Incomplete figures of speech include ellipsis (leaving out words that must be supplied [e.g., "Submit(ting) to one another out of reverence for Christ, wives . . . to your own husbands," in which the verb "submitting" has to be repeated—Eph. 5:21–22) and aposiopesis (when a portion of a sentence is omitted for emphasis [e.g., Luke 13:9 on the barren fig tree, which reads literally, "and if, on the one hand, it produces fruit in the coming (year). . . . But on the other hand if not, cut it down!" Translations typically complete the first sentence by adding a word like "good" or "fine"]).

Figures involving contrast or understatement include irony ("Fill up, then, the measure of the sin of your ancestors!" [Matt. 23:32]), litotes (a negative of the contrary—e.g., "no small city"), euphemisms (e.g., "sleep" for "death"), and antitheses ("You have heard it said of old, but I say to you," repeatedly in the Sermon on the Mount). Synecdoche (the part for the whole) and metonymy (one object substituted for a closely related one) form the two main examples of *figures centering on association or relation*. Luke's version of Jesus's command expressed as "be perfect" in Matthew 5:48 may employ synecdoche ("be merciful" [Luke 6:36]), while Philippians 1:17 speaks literally of the rival teachers as thinking they can create affliction for Paul's chains, metonymic for Paul in his imprisonment. Personification (e.g., "Where, O death, is your victory? Where, O death, is your sting?"—addressing death in 1 Cor. 15:55 as if it could hear and act) and apostrophe (addressing people not

---

41. See further Craig L. Blomberg, "The Christian and the Law of Moses," in *Witness to the Gospel: The Theology of Acts*, ed. I. Howard Marshall and David Peterson (Grand Rapids and Cambridge: Eerdmans, 1998), 414–15, and the literature cited there.

present to hear you [e.g., James 5:1]) are two key examples of *figures stressing the personal dimension of something*.[42]

Literary Criticism

Traditionally, literary criticism would not form a topic for inclusion in a handbook on exegesis, only in a broader introduction to hermeneutics (see the distinction discussed in our introduction). But because the boundaries between the two disciplines are easily blurred, and because literary criticism has blossomed into a huge discipline in contemporary biblical studies, it is worth making a few brief remarks here.

A bewildering variety of subdisciplines are often included under the heading of literary criticism.[43] In older works, items that today would form part of the historical analysis of a text (sources, settings, or redaction) were often classified as part of this topic. Philosophical issues such as the location of meaning (behind the text, in the text, in front of the text) and particularly the roles readers play in contributing to meaning dominate certain strands of what is labeled literary criticism. For those who are not focused on discerning any fixed meaning in texts themselves, reader-response criticism and deconstructionism have become thriving cottage industries. The former revels in the diverse number of creative yet coherent interpretations of a text that can be generated when one is not concerned with an author's original intent. The latter goes even further, showing how competing interpretations can be played off against one another and/or how different parts of a detailed text appear to be in conflict with one another, further destabilizing any supposed fixed meaning. In these instances, the exegetical task of leading out from the text what inheres in it is only marginally, if at all, in view.

Rhetorical Criticism

The branches of literary criticism that do merit further comment here are those that, like the study of genres and constituent subforms already discussed, stem from a close, careful reading of the actual text itself. One such branch is *rhetorical criticism*—the analysis of the kinds of rhetoric involved in a New Testament document.[44] On the one hand, not everything applicable to

42. Osborne, *Hermeneutical Spiral*, 121–30, with illustrations of each figure. For even more detail on a number of these, see esp. G. B. Caird, *The Language and Imagery of the Bible* (London: Duckworth, 1980), 131–97.

43. An excellent overview appears in Stanley E. Porter, "Literary Approaches to the New Testament: From Formalism to Deconstruction and Back," in *Approaches to New Testament Study*, ed. Stanley E. Porter and David Tombs (Sheffield: Sheffield Academic Press, 1995), 77–128.

44. The best introduction is now Ben Witherington III, *New Testament Rhetoric: An Introductory Guide to the Art of Persuasion in and of the New Testament* (Eugene, OR: Cascade, 2009). See also George A. Kennedy, *New Testament Interpretation through Rhetorical Criticism*

oral discourse and the rhetoric of speechmaking necessarily carried over to written documents. On the other hand, all the New Testament books were designed initially to be read aloud, so they would include various dimensions of rhetoric. Probably the two most useful features of rhetorical criticism for the beginning exegete are its possible impact on the outline of a letter and the identification of which of the three main "species" of rhetoric a given biblical book employs.

Commentaries (and other studies) today often consider the possibility that a given letter's structure is best discerned by following one of the *standard outlines of an ancient speech*.[45] Perhaps the most well-known proposal is Hans Dieter Betz's understanding of Galatians as an "apologetic" letter. In outline form, the structure he proposes appears as follows:

Epistolary Prescript (1:1–5)

Exordium—Statement of Problem (1:6–11)

Narratio—Thesis to be demonstrated and demonstration of facts (1:12–2:14)

Propositio—Summary of points of agreement and what remains contested (2:15–21)

Probatio—Proofs or support (3:1–4:31)

• Types of Arguments

    Logical

    Emotional

    Illustrative

    Figurative

Exhortatio—parenesis (5:1–6:10)

Epistolary Postscript (6:11–18)[46]

Most of the New Testament letters have been outlined according to these and similar categories, some more persuasively than others. The value for exegetes is identical to the value of any other plausible outline: enabling them to understand the author's flow of thought better and placing a passage in its appropriate place in the overall literary context.

The other main application of rhetorical criticism involves the *primary species of rhetoric* within a given book. Ancient rhetoricians thought in terms of

---

(Chapel Hill: University of North Carolina Press, 1984). Cf., more briefly, C. Clifton Black, "Rhetorical Criticism," in *Hearing the New Testament: Strategies for Interpretation*, ed. Joel B. Green (Grand Rapids: Eerdmans; Carlisle: Paternoster, 1995), 256–77.

45. See esp. the numerous "Socio-Rhetorical" commentaries authored by Ben Witherington III, published primarily by Eerdmans and InterVarsity.

46. Hans Dieter Betz, *Galatians* (Philadelphia: Fortress, 1979), 14–25.

three main divisions: forensic, deliberative, and epideictic. Judicial or forensic rhetoric argued for a certain understanding of an event and was often found in settings where the approach taken to a controversial issue was now being defended. Deliberative rhetoric could also seek to persuade but did so more indirectly, usually with reference to future events, perhaps considering the relative merits of several options; often this would take the form of raising key questions that listeners needed to decide how they would answer. Epideictic rhetoric praised or blamed an individual or group for their views or actions.[47]

Thus, one possible explanation of the noticeably different style of Ephesians, for example, when compared with the indisputably Pauline letters, especially in chapters 1–3, is that it is an encomium (one subcategory of epideictic rhetoric) lauding God as a benefactor of spiritual blessings, much like a rhetorician might publicly praise a well-to-do patron for generous financial provisions. This could also explain why Paul repeatedly lapses into the language of prayer and thanksgiving in these three chapters, rather than having a simple opening prayer and then an uninterrupted letter body.[48] While not as directly relevant to interpreting specific verses or sentences within Ephesians 1–3, such rhetorical analysis, when accurate, does add one more dimension to the literary context— an understanding of the document's narrative flow and an appreciation of why the author says certain things in certain ways or places.

Narrative Criticism

The other, potentially even more helpful subdiscipline of literary criticism, particularly for exegesis of the Gospels and Acts, is narrative criticism.[49] Narrative critics look at biblical books much like students do in Bible as Literature courses—examining plot, characterization, narrative time, peaking, and so on. For example, more so than with any of the other Gospels, Matthew builds relentlessly in his plot from Jesus's unmitigated early popularity with the Galilean populace to his growing rejection, first by most of the Jewish leaders but ultimately by a majority of his fellow Jews (frequently dubbed "this generation").[50] Where a given passage appears in this plot line may have ramifications for its interpretation. Thus, in Matthew 9:13, when Jesus justifies

47. In short, "deliberative oratory is either exhortation or dissuasion; judicial is either accusation or defense; epideictic is either praise or blame" (George A. Kennedy, "The Genres of Rhetoric," in *Handbook of Classical Rhetoric in the Hellenistic Period*, ed. Stanley E. Porter [Boston and Leiden: Brill, 2001], 44).

48. Holland Hendrix, "On the Form and Ethos of Ephesians," *Union Seminary Quarterly Review* 42 (1988): 3–15; more loosely, Charles H. Talbert, *Ephesians and Colossians* (Grand Rapids: Baker, 2007), 22–25.

49. See esp. Mark A. Powell, *What Is Narrative Criticism?* (Minneapolis: Fortress, 1990). Cf. also James L. Resseguie, *Narrative Criticism of the New Testament: An Introduction* (Grand Rapids: Baker Academic, 2005).

50. See throughout Jack D. Kingsbury, *Matthew as Story*, 2nd ed. (Philadelphia: Fortress, 1988).

his table fellowship with the notorious sinners of Jewish society against his Pharisaic critics, he declares, "For I have not come to call the righteous, but sinners." We need not lose a lot of sleep over how Jesus could be envisaging righteous Pharisees or insist that he is speaking ironically here about those who merely *think* they are righteous or who behave *self*-righteously. These are early days, according to Matthew's arrangement of the material, and opposition to Jesus's mission will only begin to emerge seriously in 9:32, and not for uninterrupted periods until much later in the Gospel.[51]

Or consider the characterization of Herod Antipas in Mark 6:14–29. Narrative critics identify three kinds of characters depicted in stories: round, flat, and stock. Round characters are multidimensional and the most lifelike of the three kinds. Flat characters are portrayed only as one-dimensional, while stock characters are exaggerated, stereotyped, or even caricatured, meant to remind readers of similar figures they have heard or read about in other narratives. Except for the main characters in a story, most people, if merely for economy of space, wind up being portrayed as at least flat, if not downright stock. So it is significant when Herod appears in Mark as having both attractive and repugnant features. On the one hand, Herod recognizes John the Baptist as someone special, thinking perhaps that he came back to life, after Herod had him beheaded, in the person of Jesus. Even while John was still alive but in prison, "Herod feared John and protected him, knowing him to be a righteous and holy man" (v. 20a). Herod didn't understand John well but found something about his message attractive (v. 20b). We have probably all known people who have similar vacillating responses to the gospel. On the other hand, despite his position of great strength as tetrarch over Galilee and Perea, Herod was too weak with respect to his wife's desires to do away with John and would not lose face in order to stand on principle in the company of honored guests when he rashly offered his stepdaughter up to half his kingdom and the request came back for John the Baptist's head. Herod is a very round character, especially in comparison to several other political leaders in the Gospels and Acts who are flatter or even stock, and especially in this passage in comparison to Herodias, the stock femme fatale.[52] Mark has disclosed both historical realism and literary artistry, and we are meant to empathize with Herod—up to a point—and then ask ourselves if we show any similar double-mindedness that we need to forgo.

---

51. Cf. R. T. France, *The Gospel according to Matthew* (Leicester: Inter-Varsity Press; Grand Rapids: Eerdmans, 1985), 168.

52. David M. Hoffeditz and Gary E. Yates, "*Femme Fatale* Redux: Intertextual Connection to the Elijah/Jezebel Narratives in Mark 6:14–29," *Bulletin for Biblical Research* 15 (2005): 199–221. Contra Abraham Smith, "Tyranny Exposed: Mark's Typological Characterization of Herod Antipas (Mark 6:14–29)," *Biblical Interpretation* 14 (2006): 259–93, who finds Herod to be a stock character too.

Conclusion

Many other examples of each of the forms of analyzing the literary context of a passage could be given. Hopefully these are enough to spur on the would-be exegete. Interpret every text in its immediate context, moving in concentric circles further outward from the text as necessary, but remember that the nearer the context to the text itself the more crucially relevant it will likely be for the passage. Identify the genre of the New Testament book in which your passage appears, as well as any particular literary form or subgenre in which your passage more narrowly falls. Determine if these genres and forms have any distinctive interpretive principles attached to them and proceed accordingly. Check for figures of speech that must not be interpreted literally. See if the kinds of rhetoric or techniques of narration employed shed any additional light. Most passages will not necessarily require performing all these tasks. Choose the tools from your tool box of methods that seem most likely to be of help with each text you exegete.

5

Word Studies

The arduous yet rewarding work of painting the larger pictures of historical and literary contexts paves the way for the exegete's next task of determining the original meaning of a biblical passage. Because contemporary students of Scripture are worlds apart in geography, time, and language, there exists the possibility of the meaning being lost in translation. It is not just variations in translation theory and objectives that make modern translations differ (see chap. 2); it is also the genuine differences among translators as to the most likely meaning of words in specific contexts. An interpreter can have abundant contextual information and still struggle with the meaning of various words and phrases as they appear in the New Testament. It is at this point that the interpreter will be interested in conducting a lexical analysis, also known as a word study.

The translation of a host language (in this case Greek) into a receptor language (here English) is not without its difficulties.[1] This is often encountered early on by students who find that a single Greek term takes an entire phrase in translation for the same idea to be intelligible to the modern reader.[2] Sometimes there simply is no corresponding word in English to express the concept from the original language. Confounding issues such as this one

1. On these and other important, commonly used terms, see Stanley E. Porter, "Studying Ancient Languages from a Modern Linguistic Perspective: Essential Terms and Terminology," *Filología Neotestamentaria* 2 (1989): 147–72.

2. The NIV renders ἱλαστήριον in Rom. 3:25 as "sacrifice of atonement," but then adds in a marginal footnote, "Or *as the one who would turn aside his wrath, taking away sin*"—twelve English words for one Greek word! The only English expression that really captures the meaning

are only the tip of the iceberg when it comes to considering words and their meanings. Still, difficulties in translation are far from insurmountable. With a working knowledge of how to study Greek words, a student can overcome many of the difficulties inherent in discerning original meaning.

In order to accurately translate the ideas of Scripture using appropriate terms in the receptor language, the student needs to master a certain set of skills. In response to this need, we will introduce a method for studying relevant words in a given passage. Before we venture into this new territory, it will be helpful to introduce some basic information about words as part of the larger construct of human language so that the student understands the nature of the object he or she is trying to define.[3] After laying such a foundation, we can then turn to guidelines that will enable the student to choose the most relevant words in a given context that warrant fuller study. Next, we will introduce the most useful tools or secondary literature for the word study process. Once familiar with these items, the student will be ready to explore the steps necessary to arrive at the original, context-specific meaning of the word under study. Because there are many potential hazards in this process, we will end our discussion with some general principles to embrace and others to avoid when defining theologically significant and/or problematic words. But first, some words about words and their meanings.

Meanings of Words

The very centrality of words to our communication process makes word study indispensable to understand meaning.[4] Although human communication is comprised of many other things besides words (e.g., gestures, posture, eye contact, and voice inflections), words prove key in expressing truth both orally and textually, and nonverbal communication often needs to be accompanied by words to make sense.[5] Most simply defined, a word is a verbal symbol (either written or spoken) that offers a way to refer to a concept.[6] As such, different

---

of this Greek term in a single word is "propitiation," but few twenty-first-century readers have any idea what that word means.

3. Perhaps the best introductory tool, overviewing the field for the serious student, is Moisés Silva, *Biblical Words and Their Meaning: An Introduction to Lexical Semantics*, rev. ed. (Grand Rapids: Zondervan, 1994). At a more technical level, see esp. Eugene A. Nida and Johannes P. Louw, *Lexical Semantics of the Greek New Testament* (Atlanta: Scholars Press, 1992).

4. See further Johannes P. Louw, "The Analysis of Meaning in Lexicography," *Filología Neotestamentaria* 6 (1993): 139–48.

5. See further Johannes P. Louw, "How Do Words Mean—If They Do?" *Filología Neotestamentaria* 4 (1991): 125–42.

6. These may in turn be subdivided into structure words and content words, depending on the kinds of concepts conveyed. See David A. Black, *Linguistics for Students of New Testament Greek: A Survey of Basic Concepts and Applications*, 2nd ed. (Grand Rapids: Baker, 2000), 97–100.

Sidebar 5.1

Determining Word Meanings

Here are a few basic but important concepts to keep in mind as you seek to determine the meaning of individual words and phrases in a given passage:

- A word is a verbal symbol (either written or spoken) that offers a way to refer to a concept; the goal of an exegete is to understand the concept conveyed in the host language and choose the appropriate word that will evoke as similar a concept as possible in the receptor language.
- Most words have a range of meaning, so that one word does double duty with regard to the concept it symbolizes. Word meanings can overlap with the meanings of other words.
- Word meanings change over time; therefore, it is the context rather than the original meaning of the term that must determine how the exegete will appropriately define and understand any given word.
- In addition to having denotative meaning (i.e., the meaning that a word has for most everyone who hears it in most contexts), words also have connotative value (i.e., special meaning for a particular person or group of people, perhaps only in certain contexts), which is why it's important to survey the literary and historical backgrounds of a passage before studying the words in that passage.
- Individual words function with the rest of the words in the context to express a larger set of concepts; they can rarely accomplish the feat of expressing a complete concept by themselves.
- The priority in determining word meaning should almost always go to the findings of synchronic (i.e., "with time") analysis of the word under study rather than those of diachronic (i.e., "through time") analysis.

---

languages employ different words to explain the same or similar concepts. There is sometimes profound disconnect when attempting to convey the same concept in different languages. To minimize confusion, the exegete must be interested in understanding the concept conveyed in the host language and choose the appropriate word that will evoke as similar a concept as possible in the receptor language.

Complicating the task even further is the fact that most words have a range of meaning, so that one word does double (sometimes even triple and quadruple) duty with regard to the concept it symbolizes. The English word "hand" offers a handy example (with the pun showing another way the word can be used by altering it to its cognate adjective). The hand of the human body is different from the hand on a clock or a hand of cards, or the measurement of the height of a horse. Even the entire the phrase "give them a hand" can be either a command to lend some help or to clap for someone, depending on

the context. While each of these uses undoubtedly finds its meaning in relation to the first definition of the human hand, the various examples all mean
something different. This phenomenon is not restricted to English; it occurs
in most all languages, including the Greek of the New Testament. Take, for
example, εἰρήνη, often translated "peace." The word can mean the external
absence of conflict in a statement such as, "The country is at peace with
its neighbors." It can also indicate internal tranquility as in, "I had a peace
about my decision." Absence of conflict is clearly intended by "peace" when
Matthew renders Jesus's words in 10:34, "Do not suppose that I have come to
bring peace to the earth. I did not come to bring peace, but a sword." Equally
clearly, internal tranquility is in mind with Paul's command to "let the peace
of Christ rule" in our hearts (Col. 3:15). But what of Luke 2:14, especially
in the KJV (and countless Christmas cards): "Glory to God in the highest,
and on earth peace, good will toward men"? Cease-fires on Christmas day
have halted numerous wars over the centuries because of a verse like this, yet
in light of Matthew 10:34, this is probably not the kind of peace the angels
had in mind.[7]

Word meanings can also overlap with the meanings of other words. A person could easily substitute the word "applause" for one of the meanings of "a
hand." This is because each meaning of a word exists as part of that word's
semantic domain, or range of meanings. Part of the semantic domain for the
word "hand" includes the idea of clapping, as does the semantic domain for
"applause." Because there is partial overlap of these domains, there are some
contexts in which the words are interchangeable, making them synonyms
(Greek σύν, "together" + ὄνομα, "name"—together naming the same reality).
Synonyms are rarely completely identical in semantic domains and thus not
always interchangeable. "Tired" and "sleepy" mean much the same thing in the
sentence, "I'm tired/sleepy, so I think I'll go to bed." But no one well schooled
in English ever says, "I'm sleepy of reading this book now." So before we assume that a biblical writer chose one word over a synonym because of some
precise nuance of meaning, we need to know that the other term was even
an option in the specific context at hand.[8] Some of the common generalizations about οἶδα versus γινώσκω (two words for "know") may fail to make
these distinctions.[9] Synonyms may also appear for stylistic variety as well as

---

7. But that does not mean we should abandon the quest to end or prevent as many wars as
possible. See further Erich Dinkler, "Eirēnē: The Early Christian Concept of Peace," in *The
Meaning of Peace*, ed. Perry B. Yoder and Willard M. Swartley (Louisville: Westminster John
Knox, 1992), 164–212.

8. See further Anthony C. Thiselton, "Semantics and New Testament Interpretation,"
in *New Testament Interpretation: Essays on Principles and Methods*, ed. I. Howard Marshall
(1977; repr. Eugene, OR: Wipf & Stock, 2006), esp. 90–93.

9. Silva, *Biblical Words and Their Meaning*, 164–69.

for emphasis and thus not always because there is necessarily any significant difference in shades of meaning.[10]

Another important feature of words to remember is that their meanings change over time. Because of this the study of etymology—a word's meaning as it first emerged in the history of a language—is often less than useful for determining how a word should be understood in a particular context centuries later. It would be difficult to find any English speaker today who uses the word "conversation" as a way to refer to conduct or a particular way of life, as in Elizabethan English, and thus as in the KJV of Philippians 1:27: "Only let your conversation be as it becometh the gospel of Christ." Contemporary translations use language that better captures the original idea in modern idiom, for example, "Only let your manner of life be worthy of the gospel of Christ" (ESV). "Conversation" in the current sense of the word is one small part of one's "conversation" in the Elizabethan sense, but not the main meaning Paul had in mind in this passage.[11] Therefore, it is the context rather than the original meaning of the term that must determine how the exegete will appropriately define and understand any given word while undertaking lexical studies.

So far, we have been concerned primarily with the *denotative* meaning of words. *Denotation* is the meaning that words have for most everyone who hears them in most contexts. For example, a dictionary definition of "child" could involve a description of a young human who has not yet reached adolescence. But depending on context, words also have *connotative* value. *Connotation* is the special meaning that a word has for a particular person or group of people, perhaps only in certain contexts.[12] To many mothers who speak of their children, the connotation of "child" is often that of a beloved dependent. But the same word can serve as a rebuke with negative connotations to a spouse or other adult in a statement such as, "Grow up! You are acting like a child!" Scripture too uses this very word with opposite connotations. Jesus encourages us to enter the kingdom like children (Matt. 18:4–5), connoting their recognition of their dependence on others and their frequent unswerving trust.[13] But in 1 Corinthians 14:20, Paul commands the church in Corinth to

10. Paul Ellingworth, "Translating Synonyms," *Bible Translator* 59 (2008): 18–26.

11. Even "manner of life" or "conduct" fails to capture the full sense of "living as a citizen" (in this case of God's colony rather than the Roman one established at Philippi) implied by the Greek πολιτεύεσθε. See John Reumann, *Philippians* (New Haven and London: Yale University Press, 2008), 284–86.

12. Cf. Peter Cotterell and Max Turner, *Linguistics and Biblical Interpretation* (Leicester and Downers Grove, IL: InterVarsity, 1989), 45–47.

13. Expositors often speak of children's subjective expression of humility, to which parents and youth workers may rightly protest that this is not a universal or ingrained trait of children at all. It is rather the objective state of dependence on the adult world, whether or not a given child appreciates it, that we must recognize as the main point of comparison. Michael Wilkins (*Matthew* [Grand Rapids: Zondervan, 2004], 612–13) refers to their vulnerability rather than

"stop thinking like children," connoting their immature thought processes. We must pay attention to the connotative as well as the denotative meaning of words. This is why it is important to survey the literary and historical backgrounds of a passage before studying the words in that passage. Connotative meaning is easily missed if the culture in which the writing originated has not been considered.[14]

By now the plaintive cry may arise, "Haven't commentators and translators considered the basic facts about words and done the work necessary to define difficult words in biblical passages?" The short answer is, "Yes, of course," but there still remain important disagreements over the results. Because we don't have the original authors to explain the concepts they intended to convey through particular words, the interpreters trying to define terms precisely may assess the evidence and come to different conclusions. As with textual criticism, when a variety of proposals exist, the exegete must be equipped to examine the data and form his or her own opinion. This way the student of Scripture can more confidently determine whether given scholars have responsibly done their "homework" by comparing others' claims to their own findings. It is empowering to realize that you are developing skills that enable you to evaluate competing views on the meanings of key words.

Broader Linguistic Considerations

The sprawling field of New Testament linguistics appropriately takes painstaking measures to use proper procedures in the study of human language. Word studies form a smaller subdiscipline of this much larger field. However, the student interested in studying the field of linguistics in greater depth should note that lexical study as a classical discipline has come under the scrutiny of New Testament exegetes. This is because linguists today unanimously recognize that when a word exists by itself, its meaning cannot be discerned with any amount of certainty. Meaning is discernible only as a word functions in a context that consists of at least a sentence or, even better, a discourse—that is, the structural segment of language of one or more paragraphs or their oral equivalent.[15]

The intense preoccupation with the study of individual words that began in the early twentieth century often removed words from their original contexts and gave a generic definition for a term that could supposedly be applied across the pages of Scripture. Rather than defining each word in its context,

---

their innocence and concludes, "The humility of a child consists of the inability to advance his or her own cause apart from the help and resources of a parent."

14. Definitions for both denotation and connotation come from Black, *Linguistics for Students of New Testament Greek*, 130–31.

15. The pioneering work here was that of James Barr, *The Semantics of Biblical Language* (1961; repr. Eugene, OR: Wipf & Stock, 2004).

"word studies" in this sense gave theological significance to individual words rather than to words in the contexts in which they appeared. Such studies failed to consider adequately how many different ways an author can use the same word and, even worse, did not sufficiently allow for different authors of Scripture, who wrote in different times to different audiences, to use the same word to express different concepts. In short, this methodology in word study confused a word for a concept. Individual words merely function with the rest of the words in a given context to express a larger set of concepts, and they can rarely accomplish the feat of expressing a complete concept by themselves. If a word appears to express theological meaning, it is only because the rest of the context has lent meaning and definition to that particular word. The word δίκαιος (upright, just, fair, righteous, equitable), for example, cannot be understood in one context without examining other contexts similar to the one at hand. In these similar contexts, other word such as ἀγαθός (useful, beneficial, good), ἅγιος (dedicated to God, holy, sacred), καθαρός (clean, pure, free), and καλός (beautiful, handsome, fine, good, useful) are used to express the same idea.[16] Therefore, any approach to word study that does not also take the presence or absence of such synonyms into account risks misunderstanding δίκαιος in the given context in which it appears.

To study a word and how it functions throughout time and across Scripture is to conduct *diachronic* (Greek διά, "through" + χρόνος, "time") analysis. To study a word in its immediate contexts (both literary and historical-cultural) is to conduct *synchronic* (Greek σύν, "with" + χρόνος, "time") analysis.[17] While we will discuss the potential benefits of diachronic analysis, the priority in determining word meaning should almost always go to the findings of synchronic analysis. How a word is generally used in 2010 is almost always more significant for interpreting any specific use of that word in 2010 than how it may have been used in years past, unless a writer is deliberately creating an archaic sound or appearance. Although we employ the term "word study" as a shorthand to refer to finding the meaning of a word in its particular context, we do not espouse a method that fails to consider that meaning is derived from context, which is responsible for accurately expressing a concept. Those negative connotations sometimes attached to the term "word study" in the broader field of linguistics, due to fears of atomistic analysis, should therefore not apply here.[18]

16. BDAG, 246–47, 3–4, 10–11, 489–90, 504–5.
17. Thiselton, "Semantics and New Testament Interpretation," 80–82; Silva, *Biblical Words and Their Meaning*, 35–38.
18. E.g., Gene L. Green ("Lexical Pragmatics and Biblical Interpretation," *Journal of the Evangelical Theological Society* 50 [2007]: 809) quotes "Kline [*sic*], Blomberg and Hubbard" on determining semantic range "as a first step in interpretation," with the interpreter then making "the appropriate selection." Green criticizes this approach as assuming "that there exists a stable set of concepts which are encoded and which may be neatly categorized." To

Where to Begin

The first step in conducting a good and informative word study is the proper selection of words to study. Certainly not every word in the text warrants in-depth analysis. As a general rule of thumb, any word that seems somewhat confusing to the contemporary reader of Scripture is good fodder for a word study. For example, there are a number of words that occur in even the most contemporary and reliable translations that may prove puzzling. Who among us in normal life often encounters words such as "phylacteries," "minas," or "millstone"? This category may be especially pertinent to someone who has not been around the church and its language for very long. Some words have come to be technical representations of certain broader theological concepts that make sense to those who have been active churchgoers for decades, but are fairly meaningless for those who are new to Christian culture. Think of words such as "justification," "righteous," "wrath," "save," and "redeem." In secular settings, the first thing that such terms may conjure up, respectively, are (1) the kinds of margins on a computer screen; (2) self-congratulatory, (3) arbitrary, hurtful outbursts of vindictiveness, (4) what a soccer or hockey goalie hopes to do, and (5) trading in coupons. Even those with a good working "Christian" vocabulary should not neglect the study of a word simply because they think they know what it means. If in doubt, study it!

Words that create trouble for the reader are not the only category that serve as good candidates for study. Any words that are theologically significant or on which the entire meaning of the passage seems to rest are also important (cf. "freedom" in Gal. 5, "reconciliation" in 2 Cor. 5:11–21, or "glory" in John 17:20–25). Sometimes an author will choose to repeat a key term a number of times. This repetition is a surefire clue that the word warrants study. Repeated words occur in passages such as Luke 12:22–31, in which "worry" occurs three times (in the context of material resources and God's provisions). Do commands not to worry really mean not to think about one's concerns, as in older translations? Do they mean not to have any anxiety, as in some newer ones? Or consider Paul's eleven remarkable uses of the word "law" in Romans 2:12–28.

---

this criticism we may reply, "Guilty as charged," unless his focus is particularly on the adverb "neatly." Such stability of meaning and categorizability (though not always neat) is precisely what makes a lexicon like Louw and Nida's based on semantic domains possible (Johannes P. Louw and Eugene A. Nida, *A Greek-English Lexicon of the New Testament Based on Semantic Domains*, 2 vols., 2nd ed. [New York: United Bible Societies, 1989]). But the burden of Green's article actually lies elsewhere, namely, that meaning is not *exhausted* by the selection of the best option from a lexicon for translating a given word. Ad hoc uses, additional nuances of meaning suggested by the immediate context, and what we have called "denotation" above may all add further dimensions to the meaning that must be taken into account. In fact, the entire section on word studies in William W. Klein, Craig L. Blomberg, and Robert L. Hubbard Jr., *Introduction to Biblical Interpretation*, rev. ed. (Nashville: Nelson, 2004), 240–57, contains nothing that contradicts Green's points and much that reinforces them.

Does he mean the Old Testament, the five books of Moses, legal principles in the Old Testament, obedience to the law in hopes of meriting God's favor, legal principles in the Greco-Roman world more broadly, or two or more of these usages depending on the verse? To understand such key words will inevitably clarify the meanings of these passages overall. Words that occur in a figure of speech that is no longer familiar in our language (e.g., "goads" in "it is hard for you to kick against the goads" [Acts 26:14]; recall above, chap. 2) would also be fertile ground for further study. Finally, using multiple English translations of a chosen passage will alert the interpreter to words that deserve in-depth analysis. Where the translations cannot decide on a single English word to render a given Greek word, students should consider additional analysis.[19] Οἰκονομία in Ephesians 3:2, for instance, is rendered "administration" (HCSB, [T]NIV), "stewardship" (ESV, NASB, NET), "dispensation" (KJV, NKJV), "commission" (NRSV), "special responsibility" (NLT), and "entrusted" (NJB). And not one of these words appears as a main definition in the most recent edition of the standard lexicon of the Greek of the New Testament (BDAG; see below), which instead itemizes "management, arrangement, order, plan and training."[20]

The Tools of the Trade

With a word in mind, the exegete is ready to employ the various tools available for conducting a word study. The major scholarly resources are best divided into three classes: lexica, theological dictionaries, and concordances. As the exegete moves through different tasks in the word study process, it will become evident that some tools are more suited to particular tasks than others. At the outset of the word study, the interpreter will need to limit the options for understanding the word to a particular range of meanings. Lexica, theological dictionaries, and concordances are all useful to this end.

Lexica

A reputable lexicon is a good place to begin the search for a word's meaning. The "heavy hitter" that enjoys scholarly consensus regarding its reliability and accuracy is the third edition of *A Greek-English Lexicon of the New Testament and Other Early Christian Literature*, which is conventionally abbreviated as BDAG (for its editors, Bauer, Danker, Arndt, and Gingrich). It can be used in much the same way that a person would use a dictionary in their own language, with several added bonuses to help clarify words and show

19. For similar criteria, see Neal Windham, *New Testament Greek for Preachers and Teachers: Five Areas of Application* (Lanham, MD, and London: University Press of America, 1991), 98–99.
20. BDAG, 697–98.

Sidebar 5.2

Scholarly Resources for Word Studies

Lexica

- Bauer, Danker, Arndt, and Gingrich's *Greek-English Lexicon of the New Testament and Other Early Christian Literature*
- Louw and Nida's *Greek-English Lexicon of the New Testament Based on Semantic Domains*
- Mounce's *Interlinear for the Rest of Us* and *Complete Expository Dictionary of Old and New Testament Words*

Theological Dictionaries

- Kittel and Friedrich's *Theological Dictionary of the New Testament*
- Brown's *New International Dictionary of New Testament Theology*
- Balz and Schneider's *Exegetical Dictionary of the New Testament*
- Spicq's *Theological Lexicon of the New Testament*

Concordances

- Moulton and Geden *Concordance to the Greek New Testament*
- *Greek-English Concordance to the New Testament*
- *Strong's Exhaustive Concordance of the Bible*
- *Young's Analytical Concordance to the Bible*

their contexts. When trying to access the meaning of a particular word, the interpreter needs first to determine its lexical form. The lexical form for nouns is the nominative singular, for adjectives the nominative singular masculine, and for verbs the present indicative active (or middle, if deponent) first-person singular. When a word is looked up, the lexicon presents various meanings as they occur throughout Scripture and other relevant early Christian literature. Listed behind those meanings are sample references where the word in context takes on that particular definition. This structure is helpful not only for seeing the possible range of meaning for a word, but also for seeing how the word occurs in context, which proves crucial.

The second most important lexicon is Louw and Nida's.[21] One volume indexes all the Greek words of the New Testament in alphabetical order by lexical form just like BDAG. But then it points the user to relevant sections in the larger, second volume, in which these same words are arranged according to their semantic domains. Ninety-three semantic domains include such topics as "Geographical Objects and Features," "Natural Substances," "Plants,"

---

21. Louw and Nida, *Greek-English Lexicon of the New Testament*.

"Artifacts," "Kinship Terms," "People," "Household Activities," "Proper, Improper," "Weight," "Discourse Markers," and so on. Each domain is then divided into subdomains. For example, "Courts and Legal Procedures" is subdivided into "Court of Justice," "Lawsuit, Case," "Accusation," "Judicial Hearing, Inquiry," "Judge, Condemn, Acquit," "Obtain Justice," "Attorney, Lawyer," and "Lead Off to Punishment." The relevant Greek terms that fall into each subdomain are then listed in a logical rather than an alphabetical sequence so that the closest synonyms to a given word will appear in close proximity to that word. Definitions are then frequently given in terms of explanatory phrases, as well as single words, and footnotes often explicitly discuss the similarities and differences among synonyms. A handful of key New Testament uses are highlighted under each word along with its definitions. Words that have two or more quite different meanings appear in multiple semantic domains so that they can be compared with their synonyms for each major usage.

For students without Greek, various English concordances (see below, pp. 129–30), along with tools like William D. Mounce's *Interlinear for the Rest of Us: The Reverse Interlinear for New Testament Word Studies*,[22] key their entries to the relevant page numbers in one of the major lexica or theological dictionaries. So too, Mounce's *Complete Expository Dictionary of Old and New Testament Words* cross-references locations in key concordances and also doubles as an abbreviated theological dictionary, with brief entries (and longer ones for more theologically significant words) on many important biblical terms in English.[23] But the entries are then broken down, section by section, according to the Hebrew or Greek terms translated by those words throughout the Old and New Testaments. So for students who have never studied Greek and are unable to look up a Greek word that they see on a page in an alphabetical lexicon, using Mounce's *Interlinear* to get a numerical code for that word to look it up in his dictionary is the next best approach. The same can be done with tools like Strong's concordance, which contains both Greek and Hebrew lexica in its back.[24] But short lists of word meanings like these, or those that frequently come with computer programs (often appearing when the cursor pauses over a word in the biblical text), are inadequate substitutes for a full-orbed reference work like BDAG or Louw and Nida for those who want both thorough and linguistically cutting-edge analyses of New Testament words.

22. William D. Mounce, *Interlinear for the Rest of Us: The Reverse Interlinear for New Testament Word Studies* (Grand Rapids: Zondervan, 2006).
23. William D. Mounce, *Complete Expository Dictionary of Old and New Testament Words* (Grand Rapids: Zondervan, 2006).
24. James Strong, John R. Kohlenberger, and James A. Swanson, *The Strongest Strong's Exhaustive Concordance of the Bible*, rev. ed. (Grand Rapids: Zondervan, 2001).

Theological Dictionaries

Theological dictionaries also offer considerable help with the interpretive task. They go above and beyond the typical English dictionary or Greek lexicon and offer usually short discourses on particular aspects of a word's usage as it occurs in classical Greek works, the Septuagint (the Greek version of the Old Testament), and/or the New Testament, and sometimes even a word's usage in particular genres or in a specific New Testament author's writing. In addition to these discussions, the opening section of material on a particular word usually lists synonyms and gives a good idea of the word's semantic domain (i.e., the range of possibilities for the word, given its use in both biblical and extrabiblical Greek material).

The most comprehensive theological dictionary is the ten-volume set edited by Gerhard Kittel and Gerhard Friedrich, titled *Theological Dictionary of the New Testament*, often referred to simply as Kittel (or *TDNT*). A wide selection of important Greek words appears, in alphabetical order, often with lengthy and substantial articles about them. Because the German originals began to be produced as early as the 1930s, there is a broad variety of quality in the articles, hints here and there of anti-Semitism, and lack of awareness of a virtual revolution in the field of linguistics during the past sixty years or so.[25] The best and most enduring insights of Kittel were preserved and abridged, with focus mostly on New Testament usage, in the one-volume edition produced by Geoffrey W. Bromiley in 1985.[26]

For most purposes, students and pastors will find more than enough reliable information in the *New International Dictionary of New Testament Theology*, edited by Colin Brown and completed in 1978.[27] Again, because of the length of the title, this series is often more simply referred to as "Colin Brown" or just "Brown," after the name of its editor (or just *NIDNTT*). The work was another translation from German, so that Brown often expanded individual articles and included editorial notes to update them. The result is also a more uniformly evangelical resource. Another advantage of Brown over Kittel is that students not familiar with Greek are able to look up New Testament words and concepts using their English equivalents, while an index of Greek words in transliteration is available for even easier access for students who know the words in the original language. A one-volume abridgment of *NIDNTT* has been produced by Verlyn Verbrugge.[28]

---

25. See esp. Barr, *Semantics of Biblical Language*; and, more recently, John A. Lee, *A History of New Testament Lexicography* (New York: Peter Lang, 2003).

26. Geoffrey W. Bromiley, ed., *Theological Dictionary of the New Testament: Abridged in One Volume* (Grand Rapids: Eerdmans, 1985).

27. The index, originally a large part of vol. 3, was later published separately as vol. 4.

28. Verlyn Verbrugge, ed., *New International Dictionary of New Testament Theology: Abridged Edition* (Grand Rapids: Zondervan, 2003).

A third important theological dictionary for New Testament word studies is Horst Balz and Gerhard Schneider's *Exegetical Dictionary of the New Testament*.[29] Its articles are noticeably shorter even than Brown's because it includes entries, many of them just a paragraph or less in length, on every word in the New Testament, not merely theologically important ones. About the same size but much more selective in the words it studies, and therefore including more substantial entries, is Ceslas Spicq's *Theological Lexicon of the New Testament*, a translation of an older French classic, edited and revised by James D. Ernest.[30]

Concordances

The busy pastor may sometimes have to resort to a quick check in a lexicon and/or theological dictionary for greater understanding of important words. But students honing their skills in word studies should first practice a more detailed and reliable method. Because no reference tool is flawless in its analysis, researchers should begin to form their own opinions about a word by consulting a concordance before turning to the expert opinions offered in the kinds of resources discussed thus far. An exhaustive concordance will offer all other occurrences of the word across the entire canon of Scripture so one can see its usage in every context, something the tools already introduced are able to do only for rare terms. Students who can look up words in Greek will find Moulton and Geden's *Concordance to the Greek New Testament* especially helpful in locating and providing in canonical sequence the Scripture references for all usages of that word, along with a snippet of the Greek text itself that includes the chosen word.[31]

Requiring less familiarity with Greek are concordances that still arrange their words in the alphabetical sequence of the Greek terms but provide the context for each usage of those terms in English. *The Greek-English Concordance to the New Testament*, which uses the NIV for its translations, is an ideal example of this exegetical tool.[32] Finally, for those who can't manage much Greek, there are the standard concordances that arrange words according to their English translation in a designated version of the Bible, as well as giving the surrounding snippet of text in each case. Even then, however, many will

29. Horst Balz and Gerhard Schneider, eds., *Exegetical Dictionary of the New Testament*, 3 vols. (Grand Rapids: Eerdmans, 1990–93).

30. Ceslas Spicq, *Theological Lexicon of the New Testament*, ed. and trans. James D. Ernest, 3 vols. (Peabody, MA: Hendrickson, 1994).

31. The best edition of which is I. Howard Marshall, ed., *Moulton and Geden Concordance to the Greek New Testament*, 6th ed. (London and New York: T&T Clark, 2002).

32. John R. Kohlenberger III, Edward W. Goodrick, and James A. Swanson, *The Greek-English Concordance to the New Testament, with the New International Version* (Grand Rapids: Zondervan, 1997). An older standard, still useful, is George V. Wigram, *The New Englishman's Greek Concordance and Lexicon*, rev. Jay P. Green (Peabody, MA: Hendrickson, 1982).

use some sort of cross-referencing device that can enable students to determine the Greek word underlying the English and to learn at least a little more about it. The best known of these concordances, created originally for use with the KJV, are Strong's and Young's.[33] But beware of using their Greek and Hebrew dictionaries as the final authorities on word meanings—they are both very dated and very truncated. The same is true of most abbreviated definitions of words available on computer software, unless the given program indicates that it is reproducing BDAG, Louw and Nida, or one of the other tools already discussed above.[34] Some computer programs, most notably those produced by Logos and BibleWorks, however, do have excellent word-search engines, which can replace looking up words in hard-copy concordances.

What Does It All Mean? Steps in Word Study

With a word in mind, and familiarity with the most important reference works, the exegete is now ready for the work of analysis. We are interested in the following areas of analysis only insofar as they yield meaning for the text. It is never the interpreter's intention to engage analytical processes simply for the sake of the individual components. Taking seriously the beatitude in James 1:25, which teaches that we are blessed in the doing rather than in the hearing of God's Word, we are interested in disassembling the text only to reassemble it with greater clarity for better application. The ends, not the means, are the appropriate reward in word studies. With this in mind, we can progress through the individual steps with confidence that in this case the end will indeed justify the means.

Determining the Range of Meaning

Words have a range of meaning outside of any context, but a more precise meaning determined by individual contexts. (Recall our example of the word "hand" earlier in this chapter.) A good place to start in determining how an

33. Strong, Kohlenberger, and Swanson, *Strongest Strong's Exhaustive Concordance*. Cf. Robert Young, *Young's Analytical Concordance to the Bible*, rev. ed. (Nashville: Thomas Nelson, 1982). For other translations of the Bible, see William D. Mounce, *The Crossway Comprehensive Concordance of the Holy Bible: English Standard Version* (Wheaton: Crossway, 2002); Richard E. Whitaker, *The Analytical Concordance to the New Revised Standard Version of the New Testament* (New York: Oxford University Press; Grand Rapids: Eerdmans, 2000); *The Strongest NASB Exhaustive Concordance* (Grand Rapids: Zondervan, 2004); Edward W. Goodrick, John R. Kohlenberger, and James A. Swanson, *The NIV Exhaustive Concordance* (Grand Rapids: Zondervan, 1999); and James A. Swanson, *New Living Translation Complete Concordance* (Wheaton: Tyndale, 1996).

34. Of the standard program packages equally usable on all major computers, the best may well be Michael S. Bushell, Michael D. Tan, and Glenn L. Weaver, "BibleWorks" (Norfolk, VA: BibleWorks).

author is using a word in a specific text is to gather information that establishes the word's range of meaning. So we turn to the reputable lexica and theological dictionaries and create a list of possible meanings. For example, suppose we want to know more precisely what is and isn't included in the word the (T)NIV frequently translates as "repent," including in the headline verses over Jesus's public ministry in Mark 1:14–15, in which Jesus calls people to "repent and believe the good news" (v. 15). Whether by reading the Greek, locating the word in an interlinear, or looking up the English word in a concordance or dictionary that then points us to the corresponding Greek word, we learn that its Greek equivalent is the verb μετανοέω.

The range of possible meanings, then, is determined by looking at a word's usage throughout history and across the New Testament canon. By considering its diachronic usage (that is, its appearances at various times throughout history), the interpreter gathers the different options for the word's synchronic usage (that is, the definition as it appears in the particular text under study). When determining the use of a puzzling or uncertain New Testament word throughout its historical development, the exegete is especially interested in its etymology, its use in classical Greek if that differs from the etymology, its meaning(s) in the Septuagint, and its contemporary use(s) in both nonbiblical and biblical contexts. Knowledge of the word across this broad sweep of history gives us a list of potential options for definition, since a word will almost certainly not mean something that it has never meant before.[35] While a diachronic study may show some distinct changes in a word throughout its historical development, the exegete can usually determine how one usage of a word morphed into a different meaning at each new stage of its history.

Although compiling a list of potential definitions is a significant step toward identifying a word's original meaning, it will not do to have *only* a list, especially for words with a wide range of meaning. Therefore, after surveying the options, the interpreter is left to determine whether the word in context reflects one or more of its classical, Septuagintal, or contemporary meanings, or some combination of one or more of the above. With that as our end goal, let us turn to the remaining component parts of word study, beginning with a word's classical usage.

Classical Greek Background

The standard, authoritative Greek-English lexica of classical Greek, particularly in its heyday in fourth- and fifth-century BC Athens, are by Liddell, Scott, and Jones. They come in three sizes, affectionately dubbed the "little

---

35. Unless, of course, an author coins a new word, in which case etymology and immediate literary context are the only helps. Δίψυχος ("double-souled" or "double-minded") in James 1:8 and 4:8 may be just such a word. See Stanley E. Porter, "Is Δίψυχος (James 1:8; 4:8) a 'Christian' Word?" *Biblica* 41 (1990): 469–98.

Liddell," the "middle Liddell," and the "great Scott."[36] These reference works provide basic definitions from the more upper-class Greek of the pre-Christian, pre-Hellenistic age, but often more can be learned by consulting either Kittel's or Brown's theological dictionaries under the relevant sections on classical Greek backgrounds. For μετανοέω, Liddell, Scott, and Jones give as the main meanings "to perceive afterwards or too late" and "to change one's mind or opinion."[37] These definitions make good sense in light of the etymology of μετανοέω—from the preposition μετά, "with" or "after," and the verb νοέω, "to think."

For additional lexical information, from the nonliterary papyri of the ancient Greek world, James H. Moulton and George Milligan's early twentieth-century work, *The Vocabulary of the Greek New Testament*, remains the standard, though it must now be supplemented with the ongoing publications by G. H. H. Horsley in the series *New Documents Illustrating Early Christianity*.[38]

Septuagintal Usage

Given the Jewish worldview of most New Testament authors, it is important to consider the Old Testament usage of significant New Testament words to determine the words' intended meanings. Yet, however steeped in the Hebrew Scriptures these writers may have been, they were equally products of their first-century Hellenized culture and were therefore comfortable with the Septuagint, using it and quoting it freely as often as it illustrated or provided a foundation for their theological arguments. The Septuagint (LXX), as the Greek translation of the Hebrew Old Testament, thus gives the interpreter an even greater edge in understanding the nuance of puzzling New Testament Greek words. So influential is Septuagintal word usage that some scholars recommend that if a word encountered in the New Testament has one primary meaning in the rest of the Greek language and a different primary meaning in the LXX, the interpreter should give priority to the LXX.[39] Of course, the meaning still has to make sense in its immediate context, but this methodology may help unveil theological and religious meanings of an author's chosen word.

36. Respectively, H. G. Liddell and Robert Scott, *A Lexicon Abridged from Liddell and Scott's Greek-English Lexicon* (1963; repr. Oxford: Clarendon, 1980); idem, *An Intermediate Greek-English Lexicon* (1963; repr. Oxford: Clarendon, 1992); H. G. Liddell, Robert Scott, Henry S. Jones, and Roderick McKenzie, *A Greek-English Lexicon*, 9th ed. (Oxford: Clarendon, 1996). I owe these nicknames to Mariam J. Kamell.

37. Liddell and Scott, *Lexicon Abridged*, 439.

38. James H. Moulton and George Milligan, *The Vocabulary of the Greek New Testament* (1930; repr. Peabody, MA: Hendrickson, 1997); G. H. H. Horsley and S. R. Llewelyn, eds., *New Documents Illustrating Early Christianity*, 9 vols. (Grand Rapids: Eerdmans, 1997–2002).

39. Stanley D. Toussaint, "A Method of Making a New Testament Word Study," *Bibliotheca Sacra* 120 (1963): 39.

A concordance to the LXX is an excellent tool for conducting this step in the word study process. The main Greek concordance is that of Hatch and Redpath, but for students who need an English equivalent, George Morrish's *A Concordance of the Septuagint* can also prove useful.[40] In addition to looking for meanings in the Greek of the LXX, one can also see what Hebrew words the Greek word translates and then look at any further insights that might be gained from the term in Hebrew.[41] Shortcuts for this process, as noted earlier, involve looking up the relevant sections of Kittel or Brown that deal with Septuagintal usage.

If the word's meaning seems consistent in the underlying Hebrew, the LXX, and classical Greek, there is a good chance that the New Testament will reflect the same meaning. If the meanings vary considerably, then the immediate New Testament context will be all the more determinative. In the case of μετανοέω, this is exactly what we find. Because in the LXX it sometimes translates the Hebrew שׁוּב (though this is even more often rendered by the Greek ἐπιστρέφω), which means an about-face in behavior or change of action (not what we found typically in classical Greek), and in light of the nature of Jesus's ethical teachings more generally, it seems likely that his call to repentance focuses even more on transformed living than merely a change in thinking.[42]

Incorporating Nonbiblical Contemporary Greek Usage

The Classical Greek period spans the centuries from 900 BC to 330 BC, and the Hellenistic Greek period from 330 BC to AD 330.[43] The latter is the period in which Greek dominated not just in the peninsula we think of as Greece but throughout the eastern half of the Mediterranean world, especially after Alexander the Great's major conquests. Because Hellenistic Greek evolved in many ways into a simpler form of language, even while the minority of highly educated and literate Greeks preserved more complex, classical forms, the Greek of the New Testament period is also often called Koine, from the Greek word κοινή, or "common." Classical Greek in most cases influenced the

---

40. Edwin Hatch and Henry A. Redpath, *A Concordance to the Septuagint*, 2nd ed. (Grand Rapids: Baker, 1998); George Morrish, *A Concordance of the Septuagint* (Grand Rapids: Zondervan, 1981).

41. Standard word study tools for Hebrew include G. Johannes Botterweck, Helmut Ringgren, and Heinz-Josef Fabry, eds., *Theological Dictionary of the Old Testament*, 15 vols. (Grand Rapids: Eerdmans, 1974–2006); Willem A. VanGemeren, *New International Dictionary of Old Testament Theology and Exegesis*, 5 vols. (Grand Rapids: Zondervan, 1997); F. Brown, S. Driver, and C. Briggs, *The Brown-Driver-Briggs Hebrew-English Lexicon* (1906; repr. Peabody, MA: Hendrickson, 1996); and Ludwig Köhler and Walter Baumgartner, *The Hebrew and Aramaic Lexicon of the Old Testament*, rev. ed., 5 vols. (Leiden: Brill, 1994–2000).

42. Cf. Mounce, *Complete Expository Dictionary*, 580–81.

43. Such dates are always approximate. These follow Darrell L. Bock, "Lexical Analysis: Studies in Words," in *Interpreting the New Testament Text: Introduction to the Art and Science of Exegesis*, ed. Darrell L. Bock and Buist M. Fanning (Wheaton: Crossway, 2006), 144.

Koine Greek meaning of a word, but it is the Koine usage that will provide the greatest insight to everyday meaning of the term, the one that was probably most on the mind of the New Testament author.[44]

In other words, interpreters must not assume that biblical language *often* adopted meanings for words other than what they meant to the culture at large. While some key terms are obviously religiously loaded and used in a way the culture might not readily use them, like our example with "repent" above, this is not the case for most words. If a biblical author used a term with a technical theological meaning not pervasive in the culture, he knew his audience would be familiar with its implications through previous communication with them, either by the author's intentional explanation of the term or by virtue of shared Jewish and/or some distinctive Greco-Roman background. Therefore, where these issues do not come into play, the exegete is wise to assume that the ordinary, nonbiblical Greek usage of the day will shed light on the term's meaning. Again, for the pastor or student interested in utilizing sources that have already compiled the significant data, theological dictionaries like Kittel and Brown offer the most helpful insights.

Assessing New Testament Usage

The final step in gathering potential definitions for a chosen word is synchronic. It involves assessing the meaning of a word in other New Testament writings. The student will first want to consider uses of the word in the same biblical book or in other works by the same author. These usually take precedence over the use of the same word by other New Testament authors. For example, Paul is more likely to mean the same thing by the word ἔργα (works) in Romans as he did in Galatians than to reflect the meaning of the word in James's epistle. Therefore, if a student comes to Romans 3 and wonders what exactly Paul has in mind when he talks about works, Galatians 2:16 provides a good backdrop, because it likewise speaks of works of the law or torah. James 2:18–26 is not out of the picture, since it reveals a wider range available to the author (Christian deeds of mercy), but when it comes to determining a precise meaning for Paul, Galatians proves far more helpful than James. This step in the process balances our statement about many of the words chosen by biblical authors having resonance with contemporary extrabiblical definitions. While this is the case most of the time, the places where biblical writers

44. By far the most important, recent study by a New Testament scholar of the history of the Greek language, down to the present day, available in English is Chrys C. Caragounis, *The Development of Greek and the New Testament: Morphology, Syntax, Phonology, and Textual Transmission* (Tübingen: Mohr Siebeck, 2004; Grand Rapids: Baker, 2006). Caragounis goes so far as to argue that changes from classical to Hellenistic Greek, combined with parallels in grammatical forms and word meanings between the Hellenistic period and contemporary Greek today, make observations from modern Greek at times more relevant to understanding the Greek of the New Testament than insights from classical Greek.

differ from the surrounding cultures usually involve key theological terms, the very ones that will likely be the subject of many word studies. These are often more distinctive to the biblical writers when compared to usage in surrounding culture.[45]

For this first step in studying a given word's usage elsewhere in the New Testament, a student needs only a concordance. He or she can see the word appear across various contexts and then determine a range of meanings for its New Testament usage. These results can be recorded along with the results of the study of extrabiblical Greek and Septuagintal usage. It is wise always to note where the word occurs, looking for possibly distinctive meanings in specific genres, authors, and books. This will help to determine, for example, whether a word is specially nuanced in the Gospels in a way that it is not in the Pauline Epistles, or if James uses a word differently than John. Even the same author may well use a word differently in two quite different books. While terms in Romans and Galatians tend to match each other in usage, terms in both works are often used somewhat differently than in, say, Ephesians or Colossians, one of the very reasons some scholars doubt the Pauline authorship of one or both of those books. With all this information collated, a word can be observed in the chronological sequence of its occurrences, if one wants to see if a term or theological concept has developed or changed in its meaning across the New Testament canon.

"Heads Up" on the Down Side of Word Study

After engaging the different steps of word study, the interpreter has a fairly comprehensive list of potential meanings for the word at hand. Some general rules are necessary to help the interpreter wisely discern the best meaning from among the options. Failure to give the immediate literary context its proper preeminence when determining word meaning has the potential to derail even the most committed student of the New Testament. There are several pitfalls to avoid when coming to this point in one's lexical analysis. D. A. Carson offers a detailed list and explanation of sixteen fallacies that plague the word-study process.[46] We will treat briefly only the most common errors. Mistakes occur for two main reasons: (1) a legitimate definition from a word's history is not appropriate to the context of the time period in which the text under study appears (*anachronistic* fallacies); (2) an illegitimate definition is chosen and applied (*definitional* fallacies).

---

45. Silva, *Biblical Words and Their Meaning*, 75. For the principle of concentric circles of contexts decreasingly relevant for the meaning as one moves outward from the immediate context of that word, see above, pp. 94–102; cf. Klein, Blomberg, and Hubbard, *Introduction to Biblical Interpretation*, 219–29.

46. D. A. Carson, *Exegetical Fallacies*, 2nd ed. (Grand Rapids: Baker, 1996).

Sidebar 5.3

Common Errors in the Word Study Process

Anachronistic Fallacies

- Granting more interpretive weight to the etymology of a word than is appropriate (etymological or root fallacy)
- Assuming that a word in the text takes on a meaning that was not yet present in the time of the author
- Supplying a word's meaning with a definition that preceded the author but that had fallen out of popular usage by the time of the author (semantic obsolescence fallacy)

Definitional Fallacies

- Making an appeal to an unknown or unlikely meaning of a word, due to either the interpreter's theological presuppositions or reliance on out-of-date or idiosyncratic secondary literature
- Assuming that a word carries several or all of its possible meanings in each of its appearances when in fact the most probable meaning of any word is that which contributes the least amount of new information to the overall context (illegitimate totality transfer)
- Assuming that if a word in the New Testament means something in the majority of its appearances, it must also take on that meaning in *any* context in Scripture where it appears (prescriptive fallacy)

Anachronistic Fallacies

The most common anachronistic fallacy in lexical analysis is to grant more interpretive weight to the etymology of a word than is appropriate. The *etymological* or *root fallacy* makes the faulty assumption that a word always carries the meaning of its original root. For example, because ἐκκλησία, the noun used throughout the New Testament to designate the "church," shares a root with the verb καλέω (I call), while the preposition ἐκ (out) is a prefix, there is faulty emphasis in some preaching and teaching on the church being "a called-out group." Classical and contemporary Greek usage had come to use this term for many forms of assemblies. In the LXX ἐκκλησία regularly translates the Hebrew קָהָל, the standard term for the congregation of Israel. And the contextual usage of ἐκκλησία throughout the New Testament consistently refers just to the gathered followers of Jesus in local churches. There is thus no reason to imagine that people often thought of the etymology of the term when they used it any more than English speakers regularly muse on the etymology of "butterfly" (as a piece of butter flying by) when they speak of the insects so named, especially if the butterflies are not yellow. Perhaps one can build a case theologically that the church is called out by God, but if so it will have to be on grounds other than the etymology of the Greek word for "church."[47]

To give a second analogy, to insist that the church should be understood as a called-out group each time the word appears is akin to arguing that that Christians who select godparents for their children imagine that they might function as substitute gods. The one exception to this generalization is if contextual material suggests the author may be deliberately exploiting a word's etymology. For example, ἁμαρτάνω, the most common Greek verb for "sin," originally meant "to miss the mark." Such a meaning is probably not consciously in each author's mind with every New Testament appearance of the verb, but when Paul in Romans 3:23 declares that "all have sinned *and fall short* of the glory of God" (italics ours), the accompanying verb of "falling short" does suggest the metaphor of the arrow that doesn't reach its target. In this instance, Paul may well have had the root meaning of ἁμαρτάνω in mind.[48]

The next most common form of the *anachronistic fallacy* (sometimes the only one implied by this expression, when it is used more narrowly) assumes that a word in the text takes on a meaning that was not yet present in the time of the author. For example, in Romans 1:16 Paul calls the gospel of Jesus Christ the δύναμις (power) of God's salvation. It is tempting to take the English transliteration of δύναμις, from which we get the word "dynamite," and assert that Paul means to say that the gospel is the dynamite of God. It has explosive power to transform one's entire landscape! However, since Paul predates dynamite by almost two millennia, it is impossible that this was what he intended.[49] The same is true when speakers appeal to 2 Corinthians 9:7 ("God loves a cheerful giver") and point out that the word for "cheerful" is ἱλαρός, from which we get our English "hilarious." Then the conclusion is drawn that we should be so joyful in giving to the Lord's work that it is as if we are laughing. But meanings of words change significantly over time, and "hilarious" is not one of the attested meanings anywhere close to the first-century for ἱλαρός,[50] so the most that can be said is that the interpretation itself is hilarious!

One final, frequent anachronistic mistake involves supplying a word's meaning with a definition that preceded the author but by the time of the author had fallen out of popular usage. It is the opposite of the anachronistic fallacy and called the *semantic obsolescence fallacy*. A good example would involve how κόσμος (world) meant "adornment" in classical Greek but rarely in Hel-

---

47. Cf. Silva, *Biblical Words and Their Meaning*, 45.
48. Ibid., 50.
49. Carson, *Exegetical Fallacies*, 33–34.
50. Ibid., 34.

lenistic Greek. Moreover, it would make no contextual sense in the 183 uses of κόσμος in the New Testament where the term consistently means either the earth/planet/universe or fallen, unregenerate humanity. But in the lone instance of 1 Peter 3:3, it is important to learn about this older, largely archaic usage, because it is the *only* one that makes sense of Peter's command that women's beauty should not come from some outward κόσμος. Understanding that for ancient Greek philosophers, the earth, as the one known inhabited planet, was considered the adornment of the universe helps to explain not only how the one meaning evolved from the other but actually comes into play in exactly one scriptural text. But it would be unlikely that in any other contexts in the New Testament the notion of the earth as the universe's adornment was in anyone's mind when the word κόσμος appears.[51]

Definitional Fallacies

The previous mistakes are a result of relying too heavily on diachronic word study. The following fallacies come from errors in meaning, mainly by unduly restricting or expanding the possible semantic domain of a word in any given text. One common error to which interpreters seem overly prone happens when an *appeal to an unknown or unlikely meaning of a word* is made. In most cases, the interpreter comes to the text with a given set of theological presuppositions. These convictions drive exegesis, so that if there is an available meaning for a word that better serves the researcher's own theological paradigm, that person favors the more obscure definition over the common definition. The mistake could also result from the less blatant error of dependence on out-of-date or idiosyncratic secondary literature[52] without conducting a word study first. Either way, the interpreter must be aware of the dangers of using a meaning that was most likely unintended by the original author.

The debate surrounding the meaning of the New Testament word for "head" (κεφαλή), especially as it touches the issue of gender roles, illustrates the point well.[53] Though many interpretations have indicated that in its New Testament metaphorical uses the word can mean "source" without simultaneously implying some form of "authority," such a meaning is extremely rare in the available ancient literature. Some scholars would deny that it ever occurs.[54] There are,

51. Cf. W. Mundle, "Κόσμος," in *NIDNTT*, 1:524. Mundle refers to 185 total uses in the New Testament, presumably including Mark 16:15, which we have omitted since it is almost certainly not part of Mark's original text.

52. Most free computer shareware falls into this category, which is why it is made available free of charge! See also the older reference tools noted below, p. 142n66.

53. Among the most important New Testament appearances of κεφαλή for understanding it as a metaphor are 1 Cor. 11:2–16; Eph. 1:22; 4:15; 5:23; and Col. 1:18; 2:10, 19.

54. See Wayne Grudem in numerous writings and esp. his "Does Κεφαλή ('Head') Mean 'Source' or 'Authority Over' in Greek Literature? A Survey of 2,336 Examples," *Trinity Journal* 6 (1985): 38–59; idem, "The Meaning of Κεφαλή ('Head'): An Evaluation of New Evidence, Real

however, plenty of examples in ancient literature close in time to the biblical writings that show κεφαλή is better understood as "authority." What that authority means is radically qualified in texts like Ephesians 5:21–33, so that it is far from a ticket for men to lead autocratically, but "authority" rather than (or at least in addition to) "source" is indicated nonetheless. While κεφαλή can be interpreted as "source" in some New Testament texts, none of the occurrences demands it, and the better attested "authority" works well in each of these cases also. The appeal to the less common and less likely meaning could stem from the solitary Liddell, Scott, and Jones reference to κεφαλή as source, which has been picked up by other scholars and used for the purpose of making gender roles interchangeable, and thus birthing a new idea that interpreters continue to reference.[55] Sadly, in the vast majority of the literature on both sides of the debate, it is clear that definitions are adopted because they say what the interpreters want them to mean.

Perhaps even more prevalent among definitional fallacies is a phenomenon called *illegitimate totality transfer*.[56] Here the interpreter makes the mistake of assuming that a word carries several or all of its possible meanings in each of its appearances, even though linguists agree that the most probable meaning of any word is that which contributes the least amount of new information to the overall context.[57] Again, we stress the necessity of interpreting words primarily by their immediate context. Therefore, James's use of the word θλῖψις (distress) in regard to the plight of orphans and widows (James 1:27) need not carry the apocalyptic sense of end-time "tribulation" of Jesus's words in Matthew 24:21 or John's in Revelation 7:14.[58] Conversely, when talking about the "Great Tribulation," one should not assume that because James uses θλῖψις with poverty in view that Jesus or John are using it to stress financial suffering as a chief part of the Great Tribulation.[59] Even more egregious is to teach on

---

and Alleged," *Journal of the Evangelical Theological Society* 44 (2001): 25–65. For an excellent synopsis of the debate early on, see Cotterell and Turner, *Linguistics for Biblical Interpretation*, 141–45. For an update, with reference to the most relevant related issues and secondary literature, see Craig L. Blomberg, "Women in Ministry: A Complementarian Perspective," in *Two Views on Women in Ministry*, ed. James R. Beck, rev. ed. (Grand Rapids: Zondervan, 2005), esp. 155–78.

55. See Steven Bedale, "The Meaning of Κεφαλή in the Pauline Epistles," *Journal of Theological Studies* 5 (1954): 211–15, for the first argument for κεφαλή as source. But what many who cite Bedale fail to observe is that he does not assert that the word ever means "source" or "origin" without simultaneously implying some kind of authority (see esp. p. 214). See Joseph A. Fitzmyer, "*Kephalē* in 1 Corinthians 11:3," *Interpretation* 47 (1993): 53–59, for an excellent defense of κεφαλή as "authority."

56. The phrase was coined by Barr, *Semantics of Biblical Language*, 218.

57. Cf. esp. Silva, *Biblical Words and Their Meaning*, 153–55.

58. So most commentators. Ralph P. Martin (*James* [Waco: Word, 1986], 53), however, suspects that "the 'affliction' spoken of in the term θλῖψις may anticipate the eschatological woes preceding the end time."

59. That theme appears in Rev. 13 and 18, but not by means of this particular word.

Jesus's description of the disciples as "the salt of the earth" by discovering as many possible things as salt connoted in their world and read them all into the one metaphor.[60] These kinds of interpretations illegitimately transfer more of the total range of the word's meaning into every context and overinterpret the meaning of the passage. Only when context indicates that an author most likely intended a double entendre is it wise to select an interpretation that adopts multiple nuances for a single word. Thus it *is* probable that John's translation of Jesus's discourse to Nicodemus in John 3:3, 7 intends the Greek ἄνωθεν to mean both "from above" and "again," so that the idea of rebirth is understood as a heavenly gift from God.[61] Such examples are relatively few, however, compared to the number of times that a single meaning for a single word is intended.[62]

Finally, beginning students are often sidetracked from good exegesis when they commit the *prescriptive fallacy*. It is generated from the faulty assumption that if a word in the New Testament means something in the majority of its appearances, it must also take on that meaning in any context in Scripture where it appears.[63] Applied to κόσμος in 1 Peter 3:3, it would leave the interpreter without any meaningful translation of the verse: "Let a woman's beauty not be that of an outward planet." An example where the standard meaning of a word does make sense in an unusual context but then yields an internal contradiction is Paul's use of φύσις in 1 Corinthians 11:14. In every other instance in Paul, this word means "nature," in the sense of the way God created and ordained things to be. But when Paul asks, literally, "Does not nature itself teach you that if a man has long hair it is a dishonor to him?" he does not likely mean that God always expects men in all situations to have short hair. After all, as a devout Jew before he became a Christian, he knows about the Nazirites, who let their hair grow long as an act of obedience to God and a sign of special piety (see Num. 6). So in this context φύσις must mean something like the general custom of the first-century Greco-Roman world.[64] If synchrony always trumps diachrony when the two conflict, then immediate context always trumps everything else even in synchronic analysis.[65]

60. For a list of eleven main possibilities, see W. D. Davies and Dale C. Allison Jr., *A Critical and Exegetical Commentary on the Gospel according to Saint Matthew*, vol. 1 (Edinburgh: T&T Clark, 1988), 472–73.

61. D. A. Carson, *The Gospel according to John* (Grand Rapids: Eerdmans; Leicester: Apollos, 1991), 189.

62. Cf. esp. Walter C. Kaiser Jr., *Toward an Exegetical Theology: Biblical Exegesis for Preaching and Teaching* (Grand Rapids: Baker, 1981), 105–29.

63. Bock, "Lexical Analysis," 151.

64. Cf. Anthony C. Thiselton, *The First Epistle to the Corinthians* (Carlisle: Paternoster; Grand Rapids: Eerdmans, 2000), 844–46. After all, the "natural" thing for hair to do is to grow long if it is not cut. Thus K.-K. Yeo, "Differentiation and Mutuality of Male-Female Relations in 1 Corinthians 11:2–16," *Biblical Research* 43 (1998): 20.

65. Cf. Thiselton, "Semantics and New Testament Interpretation," 80–85.

"And the Winner Is . . ." (Choosing Meaning from among the Options)

The repeated emphasis on context's preeminent role in determining a word's meaning leaves the door wide open for incorporating information found in the analyses of literary context and historical-cultural context. Is there one meaning that does more justice to the historical-cultural context of the writing in which the word appears? Does one meaning show itself more appropriate in light of literary context or structure? These considerations become crucial in this final stage of the process. Because both literary context and historical-cultural context have preceded this stage of the exegetical process, the interpreter has likely, even if unconsciously, incorporated the findings of previous exegetical steps into determining the most likely meaning. It is important to make the comparisons explicitly. If one of the meanings fits both historical and literary contexts, and to the best of the interpreter's reckoning does not reflect any of the exegetical fallacies mentioned in the previous section, then the probable meaning of the word is at hand.

Still, no matter how seasoned an exegete may be, word study fallacies are inevitable from time to time. Therefore, after reaching a conclusion about the most probable meaning, the interpreter needs to interact with the reference works pertinent to word study. BDAG, Brown (*NIDNTT*), Kittel (*TDNT*), and their abridgments, along with Louw and Nida, are the best resources to use to corroborate or call into question one's personal study. Consulting at least two of these sources will likely bring to light any of the interpreter's accidental lexical fallacies. For the interpreter who has neither time for nor access to even these basic helps, at least consulting several major modern-language translations, especially several with differing philosophies and objectives of translation, can alert one to possible meanings or nuances of meaning that might well be overlooked otherwise.

Conclusion

A retired local pastor recently explained to one of us how he faithfully used his word study tools for several years after he graduated from seminary as he prepared weekly sermons. Then it dawned on him, as he put it, that there were people who had already done this, namely the committee responsible for translating one of the well-known contemporary English versions of the Bible, so he simply relied on that translation from then on. If it did not become clear from our chapter on translations how inadequate this philosophy is, let us state it plainly here. There is no translator or translation committee of any version of the Bible that has ever done formal word studies of more than a tiny fraction of the most important and controversial words in either testament. Had they done so, they would be working still, and we would not have the published fruit of their labor. There are specialized monographs and journal articles that *have* undertaken the task for individual words or clusters of related terms in even more detail than the tools surveyed in this chapter, but those studies encompass even fewer of the biblical words worthy of lexical analysis than the translators or translation committees have investigated.

We are in a much better position than we were forty years ago, when only Kittel and the original edition of Bauer (now BDAG), among the resources surveyed in this chapter, were available. To be sure there were older tools, many of them still in print or available for free as shareware online: word studies by such scholars of other generations as Vine, Wuest, Vincent, Robertson, and Trench.[66] Each still contains much valuable and accurate information. But, given the veritable revolution in linguistics that has occurred in the last half-century and given the current ease of access through computer search engines to study huge volumes of Greek documents from a half-millennium before the time of the New Testament to a half-millennium afterward, it is unwise in the extreme to rely solely on such older volumes. Few pastors or students have the specialized understanding of modern linguistics to determine where the information in such books will mislead rather than illuminate.

It is thus much truer today than when our retired pastor friend began his ministry that one may well choose to rely on two or three major word study tools rather than performing full-length word studies from scratch. But even today, no single translation can ever substitute for that kind of study, and for less frequent words—the very kind for which it is not at all time consuming to look up all of the New Testament's usages of the word—there is not now or ever will be a substitute for working through the relevant material for oneself. Even if the results merely confirm what you can read in a reference work, you will be able to preach and teach with the confidence of knowing you have "checked out" the so-called authorities and not just accepted them at their word. Because even the "greatest" authorities disagree with each other at times, there has to be some mechanism enabling individual sermon or lecture writers, to say nothing of ordinary Bible readers, to decide for themselves what a given word means in a specific context. This chapter has provided an explanation of that mechanism.

---

66. W. E. Vine, *Vine's Complete Expository Dictionary of Old and New Testament Words* (Nashville: Thomas Nelson, 1996); Kenneth S. Wuest, *Word Studies in the Greek New Testament*, 4 vols. (1944–73; repr. Grand Rapids: Eerdmans, 1980); Marvin R. Vincent, *Vincent's Word Studies in the New Testament*, 4 vols. (1887; repr. Peabody, MA: Hendrickson, 1985); A. T. Robertson, *Word Pictures in the New Testament*, 6 vols. (1932–33; repr. Nashville: Broadman, 1980); R. C. Trench, *Synonyms of the New Testament* (1894; repr. Peabody, MA: Hendrickson, 2005). All of these are still kept in print and sometimes much more highly touted than is merited today, given the newer, more accurate resources now available.

6

Grammar

By now, students who have worked through the preceding steps of exegesis with a particular passage should have a good grasp of its contents and meaning. They will have established, as best as possible, the correct text and a reliable translation. They will have identified the author's flow of thought throughout the book, and especially in the immediate context, and they will have noted any other literary devices that shed light on the passage at hand. They will understand the historical background, both to the passage itself and to the overall biblical book in which it appears. Finally, they will have focused on key words, clarifying their meaning in context as precisely as possible. There can't be much left to do, right?

For some passages this may be true. But we are only halfway through the ten chapters of this book. What could possibly be left? The five main answers to that question set the stage for the second half of this handbook. (1) There may be intricacies of *grammar* that help us fine-tune our understanding of the text. (2) There may be broader, more complex, synthetic issues of *interpretation* that the discrete steps employed thus far have not solved. (3) The detailed *outline* or structure of the passage may disclose still further insights. (4) We will want to evaluate our interpretation in light of Scripture's *theology* overall as well as understand how our text contributes to that theology. (5) We need to *apply the text* and its themes in a valid way to contemporary life. This chapter takes up the first of these remaining tasks, the analysis of a passage's grammar.

The Connective Tissue of a Text

Dealing with the grammar of a scriptural passage often feels like the hardest task for students who have not studied the biblical languages. It can still be somewhat daunting for those who have. One of the most straightforward tasks that anyone can tackle, however, is to look in one of the formally equivalent translations of the Bible (on which, see chap. 2) and determine how the sentences and clauses of a passage fit together. An interlinear Greek-English New Testament can help one, even the student who cannot read the Greek, to see where the standard editions of the Greek New Testament have determined that the various kinds of punctuation most likely belong.[1] Bible readers can then see how many independent clauses or sentences there probably were in the original manuscripts and verify for themselves exactly where connective words did and did not appear between them.

Thus, much as in English, one can identify where two or more independent clauses are linked together—by "or," "and," or "but," creating two or more balanced, main units of thought—balanced by *alternation, addition,* or *antithesis,* respectively. Alternation between pairs of concepts can also be shown by "either . . . or" and negated by "neither . . . nor." Additive pairs can be highlighted via "both . . . and." Antithesis generates opposites—"not this . . . but that." Where independent clauses are this tightly connected together, we typically find one sentence containing the multiple clauses. These are known as *compound* sentences. Sentences with one independent and one or more dependent clauses are called *complex*; sentences with more than one independent clause and one or more dependent clauses are *compound-complex*.

In other cases, linkage between consecutive independent thoughts is not as tight and we create separate sentences. But if a number of sentences appear to belong together as a discrete paragraph, we still want to ask how they are related. Introductory words, in both Greek and English, again prove useful. Perhaps one complete thought will lead to one or more *inferences* as tipped off by a "therefore." Perhaps a second sentence will reinforce the previous one, creating *emphasis* on a thought, often highlighted by words like "certainly," "even," or "indeed." Perhaps one or more follow-up sentences to an original sentence will provide *illustrations*, sometimes indicated by "thus," "for example," or "namely."

---

1. Many such interlinears exist. The state-of-the-art edition is now William D. Mounce and Robert H. Mounce, eds., *The Zondervan Greek and English Interlinear New Testament* (Grand Rapids: Zondervan, 2008). Also very helpful for people who want to find the Greek word or words behind a particular English term is William D. Mounce, *Interlinear for the Rest of Us: The Reverse Interlinear for New Testament Word Studies* (Grand Rapids: Zondervan, 2006). Instead of a woodenly literal English translation word by word underneath the Greek as in standard interlinears, a reverse interlinear places the corresponding Greek words underneath one of the standard English translations of the New Testament.

One can also discover where dependent clauses appear, particularly adverbial ones. *Temporal* clauses will be introduced by words like "while," "during," "when," "after," and "before." *Causal* clauses will typically begin with "because" or "since." *Modal* and *instrumental* clauses will start with "with," "by," "by means of," and synonyms (in English; in Greek these may be represented by certain case endings). *Comparative* clauses will utilize "as," "so," "like," or "just as." *Local* clauses are often triggered by "where"; purpose clauses by "in order that," or "so that"; and *result* clauses by "with the result that," "resulting in," or "so that." *Conditional* clauses are indicated by "if"; *concessive* clauses by "although." Dependent clauses that are adjectival are predominantly introduced by *relative* pronouns ("which," "who," "that") modifying nouns. Still other dependent clauses function like direct objects, often introduced with a "that" following verbs of speech: "Someone said that . . ." where what follows "that" is the *content* of that person's speech.[2]

Depending on how detailed an analysis one wants to perform, one can eventually identify any or every clause and phrase in a passage according to the following classification system. Independent clauses can function as *assertions, descriptions of events or actions, rhetorical questions, desires, exclamations, exhortations, warnings, promises, problems (with or without their resolutions),* or *entreaties.* Such "foundational expressions" when dealing with events can in turn be preceded or followed by independent or dependent clauses or phrases that relate to them temporally, denoting time, including *simultaneity, sequence,* or *progression;* locally, indicating *place, sphere, source,* or *separation;* or in a variety of other ways, especially *measure, circumstance, object, cause, result, purpose, means, manner, agency, reference, advantage or disadvantage, association, relationship,* or *possession.* The same foundational expressions in arguments or discussions can be associated with sentences or sentence parts that link together logically, showing a *basis, inference, condition, concession or contra-expectation, contrast or comparison,* or *a move from general to specific or vice versa.* They can also link together to clarify, especially by means of *restatement, description, identification, illustration, apposition, explanation, expansion, alternation, question and answer,* or *content and verification.*[3] In most instances, however, it suffices merely to know how to reference such lists if it is puzzling how sentence parts relate and one senses the need to consider options that haven't yet come to mind.

---

2. For a very succinct overview of the grammar of Greek clauses, see David A. Black, *It's Still Greek to Me: An Easy-to-Understand Guide to Intermediate Greek* (Grand Rapids: Baker, 1998), 141–46. For nearly comprehensive detail, cf. Daniel B. Wallace, *Greek Grammar Beyond the Basics: An Exegetical Syntax of the New Testament* (Grand Rapids: Zondervan, 1996), 656–712.

3. The lists of usages in this paragraph come from George H. Guthrie and J. Scott Duvall, *Biblical Greek Exegesis* (Grand Rapids: Zondervan, 1998), 43–53, which also includes definitions and illustrations of each.

Unless the exegete consults the Greek New Testament, an interlinear Greek-English text, or a commentary or other resource book that specifies the explicit connective words used by the original authors, it is easy to be unsure (or at times actually in error) as to how parts of a passage relate to each other. Even the most formally equivalent modern translations sooner or later find the number of connectives in the Greek excessive for acceptable English style. The mediating translations along with the completely functionally equivalent translations regularly omit what often appear to be superfluous connectives for the sake of smoother English style. The NIV, for example, has been criticized for leaving out a lot of connective words within paragraphs when the sense was reasonably clear without them.[4] But not all readers find every implicit connection equally obvious. Even when the flow of thought can appear straightforward, students will usually prefer to be able to confirm their hunches (or inferences). Sometimes, even the Greek may not contain a connective word between statements where we might wonder if one should be inferred.

James 1:5–8

We have proceeded longer than normal without an illustration from Scripture. Consider James 1:5–8. The ESV (one of our recommended formally equivalent translations) reads:

> [5]If any of you lacks wisdom, let him ask God, who gives generously to all without reproach, and it will be given him. [6]But let him ask in faith, with no doubting, for the one who doubts is like a wave of the sea that is driven and tossed by the wind. [7]For that person must not suppose that he will receive anything from the Lord; [8]he is a double-minded man, unstable in all his ways.

The first sentence begins with a conditional clause: "*If* any of you lacks wisdom." It proceeds to the main clause of the first sentence—a third-person imperative or exhortation for which we have no exact English equivalent (but see below)—"let him ask God," meaning people *should* ask God. It continues with a relative clause, describing more about God ("*who* gives generously to all without reproach") and ends with an additive clause denoting the *result* ("*and* it will be given him"). Technically, the last of these four clauses forms a complete sentence by itself, so it could have been punctuated as a separate sentence. Yet it is obviously bound up closely with the three-part sentence that precedes it, and by itself it is quite short, so it is natural to keep it together with the rest of verse 5. The two conceptually balanced main clauses of this compound sentence are thus "let him ask God" and "it will be given him."

4. Barclay M. Newman, "Readability and the New International Version of the New Testament," *Bible Translator* 31 (1980): 328.

Verse 6 clearly begins a new thought, with a mild but not a complete contrast (δέ). The sense of the "but" here is "but don't imagine this is an automatic guarantee; faith must be involved." One could also translate δέ as "and" or "now," treating it as continuative and an *expansion* of the previous verse. Asking "in faith" and "with no doubting" are flip sides of the same qualification as to the *manner or mode* of asking. Why introduce these specific qualifications? The rest of the passage potentially offers three parallel reasons that most English translations mask to some degree.

The first is "*for* [γάρ] the one who doubts is like a wave of the sea that is driven and tossed by the wind." This use of "for" is more *illustrative* than causal, giving an example of what a doubter is like. But there is still a sense in which it provides a reason for James's command to ask in faith. If a person is vacillating between allegiance to God and loyalty to someone or something else, what that person wants one day may not be what he or she wants the next. Why should God grant the petitions of someone that fickle? The second reason emerges as verse 7 and provides the basis for James's command: "*For* [γάρ] that person must not suppose that he will receive anything from the Lord." In other words, ask in faith because otherwise you certainly won't get what you want from God. Because English translations often keep verse 6b together with verse 6a in the same sentence but punctuate verse 7 as a separate sentence, even when they use "for" to begin both clauses, the parallelism is not always as obvious as in the Greek. Verse 8, finally, begins asyndetically, that is, without any word connecting to what comes before. In context, though, it appears that James is giving a third reason for his exhortation, one that expands on the nature of the doubting to be avoided: "he is a double-minded man, unstable in all his ways." One could supply a γάρ, understanding James to have been employing the figure of speech of ellipsis (recall above, p. 110). In some respects this third reason matches the first one—it is the doubter's instability that makes it inappropriate for God to answer prayers as framed. The NAB takes this tack and inserts "*since* he is a man of two minds, unstable in all his ways." Likewise the NET reads, "*since* he is a double-minded individual, unstable in all his ways." But by changing from "for" to "since," no doubt for the stylistic variation that improves English translations, the reader without Greek won't know whether the same concept is implied as in the previous two verses.[5]

Such grammatical analysis has direct bearing on how one outlines the passage (see chap. 8), so we will return to this example. Anticipating that discussion, we may note here that a sermon, lesson, or talk on verses 6–8 has now fallen into place with its three main points unpacking what James means by and what rationale he gives for asking God for things "in faith, with no doubt-

---

5. For more on the grammar related to James 1:5–8, see Craig L. Blomberg and Mariam J. Kamell, *James* (Grand Rapids: Zondervan, 2008), 45–47, 50–54, and the literature cited there.

ing." First, it means avoiding the kind of doubt that can't even decide on what one wants and keeping one's mind made up. Second, such a person cannot expect to have God answer his or her prayers. Third, we are talking not about a kind of doubt that is unsure of God's will but about one that is unsure of which "god" one serves. The grammatical analysis can seem like drudgery, but the end result may be as life-changing as rejecting the "name it and claim it" movement that insists we have to know God's will for our lives in every detail and demand it of him, demonstrating our confidence that he has granted our requests even when present circumstances appear to contradict that. Such an attitude or behavior is not faith but manipulation. It is common in pagan ritual but anathema to the sovereign God of the Bible (cf. James 4:15).[6]

Mark 1:9–13

Or consider a narrative portion of the New Testament. Take Mark 1:9–13, for example. After a brief introduction to the ministry of John the Baptist, Mark writes:

> [9]In those days Jesus came from Nazareth in Galilee and was baptized by John in the Jordan. [10]Immediately coming up out of the water, He saw the heavens opening, and the Spirit like a dove descending upon Him; [11]and a voice came out of the heavens: "You are My beloved Son, in You I am well-pleased."
>
> [12]Immediately the Spirit impelled* Him *to go* out into the wilderness. [13]And He was in the wilderness forty days being tempted by Satan; and He was with the wild beasts, and the angels were ministering to Him.

This time we have cited the NASB updated version of 1997, another highly formally equivalent translation. The actual printed format makes it look like each verse starts a new paragraph, but boldface Bible verse numbers indicate where the editors think a new paragraph should start. So we have reformatted the text to make it look like traditional paragraphing for clarity's sake.

How many discrete events is Mark intending to itemize here? Are some of the independent clauses conceptually even if not grammatically subordinate to others? Mark is notorious for his paratactic style, simply juxtaposing seemingly endless independent clauses together with no other connectives except "and" (καί).[7] Even as literal a translation as the NASB cannot tolerate, stylistically, as many "ands" as Mark regularly includes. Here it has omitted them at the beginning of verses 9a, 10, and 12, leaving them intact at the beginning of verses 9b, 11, 13a, 13b, and 13c. (There is also a καί in the middle of verse 10, but it does not link independent clauses together.) The resulting NASB

---

6. See further ibid., 61–63, 208–13, and the literature cited there.

7. Cf. F. Blass and A. Debrunner, *A Greek Grammar of the New Testament and Other Early Christian Literature*, rev. Robert W. Funk (Chicago and London: University of Chicago Press, 1961), 239, s.v. §458.

punctuation creates two main subdivisions of verses 9–11 on Jesus's baptism: verse 9, which states the two simple facts of Jesus's arrival at the Jordan River from Nazareth and his baptism, and verses 10–11, which describe the two parts to the immediate aftermath of that baptism—the coming of the Holy Spirit and the heavenly voice testifying to Jesus's identity. Verses 12–13 proceed to offer a very succinct account of Jesus's subsequent temptation in the wilderness. The NASB creates two discrete sentences here, one per verse. Verse 12 declares the basic fact of Jesus's temptation, while verse 13 specifies three key details—its length, the presence of danger during that time (wild animals), and the appearance of an important protecting agency (the angels).

Were we trying to understand Mark's narrative flow merely from the Greek, making each independent clause of equal significance, we would have an eight-part structure that proceeded in sequence (a) from Jesus's travel, (b) to his baptism, (c) to his vision of the dove, (d) to the words of the voice, (e) to the Spirit's driving him into the desert, (f) to his temptation by Satan, (g) to his living among the beasts, (h) to the ministry of the angels. We might miss the fact that (c) and (d) could easily have overlapped and that (f), (g), and (h) almost certainly did, as demonstrated by the parallel imperfect tense verbs (ongoing past action) immediately following a historical present tense verb (vividly describing past action as if it were occurring in the present, often used for topic sentences and/or scene changes in historical narrative).[8] The NASB comes as close as any translation to tipping the reader off to each of these phenomena by translating the four relevant verbs as "impelled" (with an asterisk to denote the historical present), "was [in]," "was [with]," and "were ministering." The NASB's segmentation into plausible sentences marked off with periods, and into the constituent independent clauses within compound sentences by means of semicolons, helps the reader understand the structure that Mark likely intended but that his paratactic style in part blurred. In this instance, a carefully structured and well-thought-out English translation may well provide more help than the original Greek, at least for us who are two millennia and several cultures (including the linguistic culture) removed. But we still need to remember that the flow of thought suggested by the punctuation in any later version remains the work of translators and not part of the inspired originals. We are certainly free to propose our own alternatives if we think that the Greek text suggests them.

Categories of Grammatical Forms

The comments on verb tenses in the second illustration above foreshadow the next major contribution of grammatical analysis. We already mentioned in our chapter

8. Cf. further Robert H. Gundry, *Mark: A Commentary on His Apology for the Cross* (Grand Rapids: Eerdmans, 1993), 54; Stanley E. Porter, *Verbal Aspect in the Greek of the New Testament, with Reference to Tense and Mood* (New York: Peter Lang, 1989), 195–96.

on translation (chap. 2) that many judgment calls have to be made in categorizing grammatical forms, more with certain parts of speech and their morphological forms than with others. English has only one past tense; Greek (like Spanish) has two. English nouns don't have case endings; Greek (like German) nouns do, so that they can be nominative, genitive, dative, or accusative (and occasionally vocative).[9] In English, we don't change suffixes on adjectives to make them agree with the nouns they modify; Greek (like both Spanish and German) does. These and similar phenomena enable a higher degree of precision in meaning in some instances, but open up new options for interpretation in others.

Students who are acquainted with intermediate Greek grammar will understand in detail what we mean. Probably the most important role for grammatical analysis of a passage is to assess—when it makes a difference for interpreting a passage—what kind of usage a given case, tense, mood, voice, and so on, reflects. *Particularly crucial* are the analyses of genitive and dative nouns, the uses and omissions of the article, the reasons for the middle voice, differentiation between the three verbal aspects (especially aorist vs. imperfective), further subcategorization of participles and imperatives, and identification of the classes of conditional clauses.[10] *Frequently important* also are the uses of accusative cases, the categorization of adjectives, identifying what words prepositional phrases modify, specific uses of pronouns, specific uses of the five main Greek tenses (present, future, imperfect, aorist, and perfect), further categorization of subjunctive moods, and distinguishing between questions requiring an affirmative and those demanding a negative reply (based on the use of οὐ vs. μή).[11] These are the kinds of grammatical

9. An older eight-case system, analogous to what exists in Latin, is no longer utilized by many contemporary linguists. Ablatives, which in Greek never differ in form from genitives, are best viewed as a subcategory of genitive (often called a genitive of source or origin). Locatives and instrumentals, which never differ in form from datives, are best viewed as subcategories of datives.

10. Scot McKnight (editor's preface to *Introducing New Testament Interpretation*, ed. Scot McKnight [Grand Rapids: Baker, 1989], 10) notes that his seminary Greek teacher declared "that exegesis is essentially understanding the genitive case, the article, and the aorist tense." McKnight continues, "Perhaps this is an overstatement; but from my own teaching experience I can say that if the student comes to terms with these features of the Greek sentence, that student will reap abundant harvests." In his "New Testament Greek Grammatical Analysis," in ibid., 78–89, McKnight treats the genitive, the article, voice, and tense, especially the aorist, as his major examples of the payoff that syntactical analysis can provide.

11. See any intermediate grammar for the numbers of subdivisions each of these grammatical categories contains, which enhances both their complexity and their importance. For medium-length detail, in between Black, *It's Still Greek to Me*, and Wallace, *Greek Grammar Beyond the Basics*, see esp. Richard A. Young, *Intermediate New Testament Greek: A Linguistic and Exegetical Approach* (Nashville: Broadman & Holman, 1994); and Stanley E. Porter, *Idioms of the Greek New Testament* (Sheffield: Sheffield Academic Press, 1992). For another listing of the reasonably important categories for exegesis, with illustrations, see William J. Larkin, *Greek Is Great Gain: A Method for Exegesis and Exposition* (Eugene, OR: Wipf & Stock, 2008), 140–51.

Sidebar 6.1

Important Tasks in Grammatical Analysis

The *most important* task in grammatical analysis is to assess—when it makes a difference for interpreting a passage—what kind of usage a given case, tense, mood, voice, and so on, reflects.

Particularly important tasks include:

- analysis of genitive and dative nouns
- analysis of the uses and omissions of the article
- analysis of the reasons for the middle voice
- differentiation between the three verbal aspects (especially aoristic vs. imperfective)
- further subcategorization of participles and imperatives
- identification of the classes of conditional clauses

Frequently important tasks are:

- understanding the uses of accusative cases
- understanding the categorization of adjectives
- identifying what words prepositional phrases modify
- identifying specific uses of pronouns
- identifying specific uses of the five main Greek tenses (present, future, imperfect, aorist, and perfect)
- further categorization of subjunctive moods
- distinguishing between questions requiring an affirmative and those demanding a negative reply (based on the use of οὐ vs. μή)

---

issues that often make Bible translators, especially when they are turning the Greek into non-Western languages, grow prematurely gray![12]

Exegetes who have not studied Greek, and especially those who have limited facility in foreign languages or English grammar skills, may feel inadequate to analyze Greek grammar. There is probably no other area of exegesis that better demonstrates how crucial the study of the original languages is. Still, there are tools that everyone can use to understand the original grammar better. An excellent, succinct overview of those portions of English grammar most relevant for understanding the Greek of the New Testament appears in Jeremy Duff's revision of John Wenham's classic first-year Greek textbook.[13] William

---

12. For excellent help, see John Beekman and John Callow, *Translating the Word of God* (Grand Rapids: Zondervan, 1974), 212–66; and Mildred Larson, *A Manual for Problem Solving in Bible Translation* (Grand Rapids: Zondervan, 1975), 115–56.

13. Jeremy Duff, *The Elements of New Testament Greek*, 3rd ed. (Cambridge: Cambridge University Press, 2005), 240–49.

Mounce's widely used first-year grammar also includes analogous information, but interspersed throughout his text, as he typically introduces each new topic by comparing the way English and Greek function.[14] For those who think they may need an entire small, book-length review, Samuel Lamerson's *English Grammar to Ace New Testament Greek* proves ideal.[15]

Where terminology and concepts in English and Greek grammar remain reasonably parallel, students without Greek can still utilize with great profit commentaries and other reference works that identify (or give their opinion on) important forms. Pride of place among the reference works that suggest classification of forms for the greatest number of New Testament words or constructions goes to the father-son team of Cleon Rogers Jr. and Cleon Rogers III. Their book, *The New Linguistic and Exegetical Key to the Greek New Testament*, proceeds through the New Testament book by book, chapter by chapter, and verse by verse, parsing and analyzing key words, including selected grammatical categorizations, along with brief exegetical comments on particularly important matters of content.[16] A slightly older work of the identical format, Robert Hanna's *A Grammatical Aid to the Greek New Testament*, focuses only on grammatical issues and selects excerpts from the eight main advanced grammars of the Greek of the New Testament in print when it was published in 1983.[17] Checking the extensive Scripture indexes of Porter's, Fanning's, and Wallace's more recent grammars to see if they make comments about a given passage being studied can nicely substitute for or supplement the use of Hanna.[18] An older and shorter complement to these various works, but still very insightful, is Maximilian Zerwick's *Biblical Greek: Illustrated by Examples*.[19]

14. William D. Mounce, *Basics of Biblical Greek Grammar*, 2nd ed. (Grand Rapids: Zondervan, 2003).

15. Samuel Lamerson, *English Grammar to Ace New Testament Greek* (Grand Rapids: Zondervan, 2004).

16. Cleon Rogers Jr. and Cleon Rogers III, *The New Linguistic and Exegetical Key to the Greek New Testament* (Grand Rapids: Zondervan, 1998). Again, remember that some of the grammatical classifications are judgment calls and there may be other viable options. A less user-friendly equivalent, minus the exegetical commentary, but still very helpful, is Max Zerwick and Mary Grosvenor, *A Grammatical Analysis of the Greek New Testament*, 5th rev. ed. (Chicago: Loyola University Press, 1996).

17. Robert Hanna, *A Grammatical Aid to the Greek New Testament* (Grand Rapids: Baker, 1983). The grammars from which Hanna selects are themselves valuable too, if one can acquire them—esp. Blass, Debrunner, and Funk, *Greek Grammar of the New Testament*; A. T. Robertson, *Grammar of the Greek New Testament in the Light of Historical Research*, 4th ed. (Nashville: Broadman, 1934); and J. H. Moulton, W. F. Howard, and N. Turner, *A Grammar of New Testament Greek*, 4 vols. (Edinburgh: T&T Clark, 1908–76)—even if to some degree superseded by more recent work.

18. Porter, *Verbal Aspect*; Buist M. Fanning, *Verbal Aspect in New Testament Greek* (Oxford: Clarendon, 1990); Wallace, *Greek Grammar Beyond the Basics*.

19. Maximilian Zerwick, *Biblical Greek: Illustrated by Examples* (Rome: Biblical Institute Press, 1963).

Where terminology or concepts in Greek grammar are sufficiently different from English to remain indecipherable to the reader who has not studied Greek, detailed commentaries on the New Testament book at hand often prove most useful. Especially among the more recent series, authors are increasingly including English translations of all Greek words and expressions cited and explaining, even if by means of paraphrasing their translations, many of the classifications of forms they adopt.[20] Those who preach regularly but have not had Greek may wish to take the time to work through *Greek for Preachers* by Joseph M. Webb and Robert Kysar to learn the basics about those forms where Greek and English do differ the most (without having to master an entire Greek grammar) and to see all kinds of illustrations and applications of how busy preachers can responsibly use these grammatical insights.[21] A shorter booklet with the same goal, which is eminently readable, is Kendell H. Easley's *User-Friendly Greek: A Common Sense Approach to the Greek New Testament.*[22] Enticing the reader with the potential value of Greek grammar, though occasionally idiosyncratic in its conclusions, is Nigel Turner's *Grammatical Insights into the New Testament.*[23]

Examples of How Greek Grammar Makes a Difference

Without duplicating Turner's collection of illustrations, we may present a select group of examples where even just a little knowledge of Greek grammar yields exegetical fruit not readily attainable otherwise. For example, formally equivalent translations of Matthew 1:16 typically bring Jesus's genealogy to a conclusion by saying, "and Jacob the father of Joseph the husband of Mary, of whom Jesus was born, who is called Christ" (ESV), making the reader wonder if Matthew thought Jesus was born from both Joseph and Mary. A quick look at the Greek shows that "of whom" is a genitive feminine singular relative pronoun that can have only Mary for its antecedent. Thus a translation like the TNIV is actually more faithful to the Greek *meaning* if not wording when it renders this verse as "and Jacob the father of Joseph, the husband of Mary, and Mary was the mother of Jesus who is called the Messiah." Capturing the

20. See esp. the Baker Exegetical Commentary on the New Testament series, the New International Commentary on the New Testament series, and the Word Biblical Commentary series.
21. Joseph M. Webb and Robert Kysar, *Greek for Preachers* (St. Louis: Chalice, 2002). A shorter, though not quite as fruitful, exercise would involve working through chap. 6 on "Syntax: Analyzing Meaningful Units of Thought," in Neal Windham, *New Testament Greek for Preachers and Teachers: Five Areas of Application* (Lanham, MD: University Press of America, 1991), 147–95.
22. Kendell H. Easley, *User-Friendly Greek: A Common Sense Approach to the Greek New Testament* (Nashville: Broadman & Holman, 1994).
23. Nigel Turner, *Grammatical Insights into the New Testament* (Edinburgh: T&T Clark, 1965).

best of both approaches is the NAB: "Jacob the father of Joseph, the husband of Mary. Of her was born Jesus who is called the Messiah." Matthew alludes to the virginal conception of Jesus even before he actually narrates it.[24]

Ephesians 4:11, in some translations (e.g., NKJV, NRSV; cf. NIV, NASB), speaks of God giving spiritual gifts so that some of his people are "apostles, some prophets, some evangelists, some pastors and teachers." The English replicates the appearance of the article (or at least the adjective "some") before each of the first four categories of gifted individuals but not before "teachers." What is the significance of this grammatical anomaly? Granville Sharp's rule, as popularly presented, is said to show that when the article is used to introduce a pair of nouns separated by an "and," the Greek speaker or writer is equating the two nouns. Thus pastors and teachers are one and the same. This analysis is not quite accurate. Granville Sharp's rule declares that two nouns in this kind of construction refer to the same entity if they are singular, personal, and nonproper.[25] Ephesians 4:11 satisfies two of the three criteria—"pastors and teachers" do refer to persons and they are not proper nouns (i.e., personal names). But they are plural in number rather than singular. Nevertheless, follow-up studies to Sharp's have shown that even in the plural such constructions normally relate the two nouns closely to each other.[26] So while it remains appropriate to distinguish pastors and teachers, it is probably equally important to recognize that Paul believed that pastors would have a significant teaching component to their ministries and that teachers needed to exercise a kind of pastoral oversight and care for their students.

Galatians 5:4 in the KJV proclaims, "Christ is become of no effect unto you, whosoever of you are justified by the law; ye are fallen from grace." But who can ever be justified by the law? Central to all of Paul's teaching, indeed to all of Scripture, is that no one is ever made right with God by the works of the law (see, e.g., Rom. 3:20). The NKJV recognizes the problem and adds, in italics, "you who *attempt* to be justified by law." Most modern translations don't even bother with italics. The TNIV writes, "you who are trying to be justified by the law;" the NRSV, "you who want to be justified by the law;" and the ESV, "you who would be justified by the law." But the Greek has no word corresponding to "attempt," "try," "want," or "would." It reads simply, οἵτινες ἐν νόμῳ δικαιοῦσθε. What is going on here? One usage of the present tense (and also of the imperfect) is the *conative* or *tendential* use, in which someone tries (or was trying) or wants (or was wanting) to do something but in fact did not accomplish their objectives. That usage fits perfectly here and is almost certainly what Paul intended.[27]

---

24. Cf., e.g., Donald A. Hagner, *Matthew 1–13* (Dallas: Word, 1993), 8, 12.

25. Wallace, *Greek Grammar beyond the Basics*, 271.

26. Ibid., 277–78.

27. Cf. F. F. Bruce, *The Epistle to the Galatians* (Exeter: Paternoster; Grand Rapids: Eerdmans, 1982), 231.

Revelation 20:4 is a long, crucial verse for understanding eschatology. The TNIV (cf. NIV) reads:

I saw thrones on which were seated those who had been given authority to judge. And I saw the souls of those who had been beheaded because of their testimony about Jesus and because of the word of God. They had not worshiped the beast or his image and had not received his mark on their foreheads or their hands. They came to life and reigned with Christ a thousand years.

Almost all modern translations agree in rendering the first verb in this last sentence as "they came to life." But the Greek has just an aorist, ἔζησαν ("they lived"—[N]KJV). In an era in which amillennialism dominated the Christian world, this verse was routinely applied to Christ's first coming, and believers' living and reigning with Christ was seen as occurring in this current age. There would have been no reason for the translators to consider any other option. But a common use of the aorist (and the imperfect) is its *ingressive* (or *inceptive*) use, in which the beginning point of an action in the past is highlighted. "Came to life" captures this option well and allows for a premillennial interpretation as well as an amillennial one. Indeed, if this is resurrection at the beginning of a millennium that Christ's return inaugurates, one has to be able to appeal to such a grammatical category.[28] But the (T)NIV makes it sound like only those beheaded for their faith come to life. Perhaps beheading is synecdoche for all Christian martyrs, but don't *all* believers come to life at the beginning of the millennium, whether it is the amillennialist's spiritual life at the beginning of the church age or the premillennialist's physical life after Christ's return? In its desire to break up a long, complex sentence in translation, the (T)NIV has left out a crucial "and." After referring to those John saw who had been beheaded for their faith, the Greek adds, καὶ οἵτινες οὐ προσεκύνησαν τὸ θηρίον ("and those who had not worshiped the beast"—i.e., all true Christians). Specifically, it employs the indefinite relative pronoun οἵτινες, meaning "those who are of such nature." The (T)NIV misses both the conjunction and the distinctive nuances of the pronoun.[29]

Longtime churchgoers have most likely heard some speaker try to explain the original Greek of the Great Commission (Matt. 28:19–20). Usually, the observation is made that there is only one main verb, the command to "disciple" (or "make disciples"), so that what sounds like a parallel command in English

28. See further George E. Ladd, "Historic Premillennialism," in *The Meaning of the Millennium: Four Views*, ed. Robert G. Clouse (Downers Grove, IL: InterVarsity, 1977), 32–38.

29. See further Stephen S. Smalley, *The Revelation to John* (London: SPCK; Downers Grove, IL: InterVarsity, 2005), 507: "The introductory expression at this point, καὶ οἵτινες (*kai hoitines*, 'and others', lit. 'and whoever'), uses the nominative plural, rather than the accusative which might be expected after the opening verb in verse 4, εἶδον (*eidon*, 'I saw'); cf. the earlier ψυχάς (*psychas*, 'souls'). This suggests that John is referring here to a different assembly of Christian saints in general."

("*go* . . . and make disciples") is actually subordinate ("when you go . . . make disciples"). Thus the focus isn't on going (the classic missionary appeal) but on making disciples, wherever one goes, whether that is across the world or next door or to one's own family. All this is accurate enough, but why then do all the major English translations still preserve the reading, "Go . . . and make . . ."?[30] The answer has to do with categorizing the participle πορευθέντες (lit., "having gone") with which verse 19 begins. Matthew frequently uses aorist adverbial participles at the beginnings of clauses as participles of attendant circumstances.[31] Such circumstantial participles are grammatically subordinate to the main verbs they modify but are conceptually coordinate. Participles also take on something of the mood of those main verbs. Thus any imperative-mood verb (a command), like μαθητεύσατε (make disciples) here, that is modified by participles will convey some imperative sense to those participles.[32] Combine these two grammatical observations and one can understand why πορευθέντες is translated as if it were a main verb itself, and a command to boot. The translators are right, and the exegetes are right. Neither need cast stones at the other; both perspectives are necessary to say everything that should be said about the clause.

Examples of How Greek Grammar Makes a *Big* Difference

As in any academic discipline, much of the work in mastering grammar and applying it to biblical passages involves a fair amount of tedium and slogging. The times when one suddenly discovers a possible solution to an exegetical crux or a new way of translating a text that didn't make sense more than compensates for all the time and effort expended. If the examples in the last section aren't sufficiently convincing, let's consider a cross section of passages in which correct identification of grammatical forms makes a huge difference in interpretation. Hopefully, between these two sections your appetite will be sufficiently whetted so that you will want to study grammar, in English and/ or Greek, in order to take your skills to the next level.

Philemon 6

The NIV of Philemon 6 reads, "I pray that you may be active in sharing your faith, so that you will have a full understanding of every good thing we have in Christ." The ESV similarly declares, "I pray that the sharing of your faith may become effective . . ." In the last thirty years, since the completion of the NIV, this verse has become a premier proof text in many circles for the

30. The easy-to-read, dynamically equivalent *God's Word to the Nations* is a rare exception: "So wherever you go, make disciples of all nations."
31. See further Wallace, *Greek Grammar Beyond the Basics*, 640–45.
32. Donald A. Hagner, *Matthew 14–28* (Dallas: Word, 1995), 886.

importance of evangelism. But the Greek behind the first clause reads, ὅπως ἡ κοινωνία τῆς πίστεώς σου ἐνεργὴς γένηται—literally, "so that the fellowship of your faith might become effective [or powerful, or active]." The NASB reads almost identically: "*I pray* that the fellowship of your faith may become effective." Is πίστεως (of faith) here an objective or a subjective genitive?[33]

To read πίστεως as an objective genitive, as in the NIV, would mean that κοινωνία is treated as a verbal noun (the activity involved in "fellowship," hence, "sharing"), with "faith" as its direct *object*: Paul wants Philemon to share his faith with others. To read πίστεως as a subjective genitive would mean that the activity involved in fellowship (in context, the love Philemon regularly shows to others [v. 5]) was produced by faith or had faith for its *subject*: Paul wants Philemon's generosity to overflow even to his runaway slave, Onesimus. The TNIV reflects this interpretation ("I pray that your partnership with us in the faith may be effective") and the NLT makes it crystal clear ("And I am praying that you will put into action the generosity that comes from your faith"). Given that Paul regularly prefers the subjective genitive with paired sets of abstract nouns analogous to his construction here, and that in the context of the whole letter the only evangelism that occurs has already happened when Onesimus came to Christ, the TNIV/NLT interpretation is much to be preferred.[34] Paul certainly believes in evangelism, but it does not appear likely that Philemon 6 is talking about that topic.

Romans 8:28

A tragedy has just struck you or someone close to you. How are people to make sense of it? Well-meaning Christians typically cite Romans 8:28 in the KJV, even those who never read that version, because they have heard others quote it, or know a version quite like it (like the NRSV, ESV, HCSB, or NET): "And we know that all things work together for good to them that love God, to them who are called according to his purpose." *All things* work together for good? Really? Cold-blooded murder, callous adultery and divorce, tsunamis that kill hundreds of thousands, a child's suicide—all these things work together for good? And wouldn't that be pantheism anyway, as if inanimate objects or abstract events had intentions and the ability to carry out plans? Is that what the Greek text actually says?

No, it probably isn't. The most textually secure original reads, in the relevant part of the verse, πάντα συνεργεῖ εἰς ἀγαθόν.[35] The neuter plural form πάντα

---

33. Translating Greek nouns in the genitive case into other languages regularly poses special problems. See, e.g., Gordon D. Fee and Mark L. Strauss, *How to Choose a Translation for All Its Worth* (Grand Rapids: Zondervan, 2007), 77–83.

34. See esp. Douglas J. Moo, *The Letters to the Colossians and to Philemon* (Grand Rapids and Cambridge: Eerdmans; Nottingham: Apollos, 2008), 389–94.

35. Bruce M. Metzger, *A Textual Commentary on the Greek New Testament*, 2nd ed. (Stuttgart: Deutsche Bibelgesellschaft/German Bible Society, 1994), 458.

(all things) could be either nominative or accusative. If nominative, the clause would indeed mean "all things work together for good." But many manuscripts add ὁ θεός (God) before συνεργεῖ (works together), creating, "All things God works together for good" or, in more standard English word order, "God works all things together for good."[36] Even if not original, this textual variant reflects the oldest interpretive tradition and probably just spells out what Paul thought was implicit already, because he has just referred to God and God's will in the last clause of verse 27.[37]

But now we encounter a new grammatical problem. We may have saved the text from pantheism, but συνεργέω is usually an intransitive verb (one doesn't "work together" someone or something).[38] It does not take a direct object. How then is πάντα functioning? It is not the subject of the verb, if θεός is understood as the subject (implicitly or explicitly), so it would not be nominative. It is not the direct object of the verb, which is the main use of the accusative. The only remaining possibility in this context is that it is an *adverbial* accusative, directly modifying the verb, in this case describing where or how God does this working together. The (T)NIV has it exactly right: "in all things God works for the good." Evil things do not by themselves work together for good. That view is grammatically possible, but theologically objectionable. Nor does God work everything together for good. That view is theologically possible, but grammatically objectionable. Rather, God is present *in the midst of all circumstances*, good and evil, working out his good purposes for his people.[39] How we counsel our friends and how we make sense of hard times ourselves clearly changes based on this grammatical identification.

John 1:1

The NWT, produced by the Jehovah's Witnesses, translates John 1:1, "In [the] beginning the Word was, and the Word was with God, and the Word was a god." This fits their modern-day Arianism, with its belief that Jesus was the first and most exalted of all the beings God created, rather than a coequal part of the uncreated Trinity from all eternity, as in orthodox Christian theology.[40] How do they justify this translation of a verse that almost everyone else knows

36. Cf. the NASB: "God causes all things to work together for good." The NLT reads similarly.

37. Ben Witherington III with Darlene Hyatt, *Paul's Letter to the Romans: A Socio-Rhetorical Commentary* (Grand Rapids and Cambridge: Eerdmans, 2004), 226.

38. For the line of interpretation developed here, see esp. Carroll D. Osburn, "The Interpretation of Romans 8:28," *Westminster Theological Journal* 44 (1982): 99–109. On συνεργέω, cf. C. H. Talbert, *Romans* (Macon, GA: Smyth & Helwys, 2002), 223.

39. Cf. BDAG, 969. Others prefer to translate, "[God] works together with all things," but the accusative remains adverbial, often then identified as an accusative of respect.

40. For a concise introduction to Jehovah's Witnesses' distinctive beliefs, esp. in the area of Christology, see Ron Rhodes, "Jehovah's Witnesses," in *A Guide to New Religious Movements*, ed. Ron Enroth (Downers Grove, IL: InterVarsity, 2005), 26–41. For more detail, cf. George W.

as, "In the beginning was the Word, and the Word was with God, and the Word was God" (KJV, NKJV, RSV, NRSV, NAB, NIV, TNIV, HCSB, ESV)? They appeal to a "literal" translation of the Greek, which reads, Ἐν ἀρχῇ ἦν ὁ λόγος, καὶ ὁ λόγος ἦν πρὸς τὸν θεόν, καὶ θεὸς ἦν ὁ λόγος. An interlinear rendering of the Greek, word by word, without adding any capital letters in English except at the beginning of the sentence, would read, "In beginning was the word, and the word was with the god, and god was the word."

The NWT translators recognized that we don't say "in beginning" in English, so they have added "the" in brackets. Like the more reputable translations they put the three independent clauses into more normal English word order, with subjects preceding predicates. But their treatment of the use and the nonuse of the article in the second two clauses is grammatically unjustified. Sometimes Jehovah's Witnesses have claimed that the NWT is superior to other translation because it consistently introduces a definite article ("the") when the article appears in the Greek and not when it doesn't. In fact, this is true only about 50 percent of the time.[41] The translators obviously realized that "God" in the second clause of John 1:1 referred to God the Father—Jehovah, as the Jehovah's Witnesses prefer to call him—and that employing the translation "the Word was the God" could mislead. But they insisted that it was appropriate to insert the English indefinite article (which has no counterpart in Greek) into the third clause, making God "a god" when speaking of Jesus (the Word), because the article is absent in Greek.[42]

In fact, the grammatical issues here are far more complex. Colwell's rule, which applies 87 percent of the time in the New Testament, teaches that "definite predicate nouns which precede the verb usually lack the article."[43] Unpacking this rule, what this means is that in a sentence of the form "x is y" (or with any other form of the verb "to be" joining x and y), where x and y are nouns, if Greek writers wanted to distinguish which noun was the subject, and especially when ẏ was the subject, they would use the article with the subject and not with the predicate complement. It is not word order, as in English, that determines which is which. Now, this rule comes into play only when there is already good reason to believe that the predicate noun (the complement) is definite, but "God" is clearly definite in the second clause of John 1:1, and there is no reason (prior to actually translating the verse) to suspect John would be

---

Braswell, Jr., *Understanding Sectarian Groups in America*, rev. ed. (Nashville: Broadman & Holman, 1994), 55–95.

41. See further Robert H. Countess, *The Jehovah's Witnesses' New Testament: A Critical Analysis of the New World Translation of the Christian Greek Scriptures* (Phillipsburg, NJ: P&R, 1982), 70–74.

42. See further ibid., 41–58.

43. E. C. Colwell, "A Definite Rule for the Use of the Article in the Greek New Testament," *Journal of Biblical Literature* 52 (1933): 20.

using it in a different way in the third clause.[44] Thus, the Jehovah's Witnesses have a 13 percent chance, on sheer statistical grounds alone, of being right in their translation of this verse; historic Christianity has an 87 percent chance. Readers can choose on whom they want to bet.[45]

1 Corinthians 13:8

"Love never ends. But as for prophecies, they will come to an end; as for languages, they will cease; as for knowledge, it will come to an end" (1 Cor. 13:8 HCSB). Tucked into Paul's beautiful love chapter is this affirmation of the eternality of love. To highlight the point, Paul refers to three spiritual gifts that are not eternal. Is he singling these out over against other gifts? Is it significant that he uses the same verb (καταργέω, "come to an end") with prophecies and knowledge, but a different one (παύω, "cease") with tongues? What about the use of the middle voice with παύω rather than the passive voice with the two uses of καταργέω? Cessationists, who believe that the charismatic gifts ended with the close of the apostolic age, often appeal to the middle form παύσονται (arguably, "they will cease by themselves"[46]) to claim that Paul is teaching that tongues will go away on their own long before the end of the church age.[47]

While there are some tenses in which middle and passive voice forms are identical, that is not the case with the future tense. Therefore καταργηθήσονται must be passive; prophecies and knowledge will *be* abolished (or destroyed, done away with, ended, etc.), presumably by God. Παύσονται can be only a middle form, and the three main subdivisions of the pure middle in classical Greek were the reciprocal (here, "they will cease each other," which makes no sense), the reflexive ("they will cease themselves"—as if "cease" were a transitive verb that could act on oneself, like "they will hit themselves"), and the indirect ("they will cease to/for/by themselves").[48] Only the last of these works with this verb, and in this context, it works well.

---

44. D. A. Carson, *Exegetical Fallacies*, 2nd ed. (Grand Rapids: Baker, 1996), 82–84.

45. Daniel Wallace (*Greek Grammar Beyond the Basics*, 266–29) argues, slightly differently, that θεός lacks the article because it is the qualitative aspect of the noun that is being stressed—a common use for the anarthrous (nonarticular) form. Thus, the sense is "the Word was divine" (not in the reduced sense we sometimes use the word for this-worldly entities but in the sense of that which can apply only to true deity). This is another very legitimate potential explanation of John 1:1, also with a much higher degree of probability than the Jehovah's Witnesses' explanation.

46. See, e.g., James A. Brooks and Carlton L. Winbery, *Syntax of New Testament Greek* (Lanham, MD: University Press of America, 1979), 101.

47. E.g., John F. MacArthur, *1 Corinthians* (Chicago: Moody, 1984), 359.

48. On these uses of the middle voice, see traditionally most any first-year Greek grammar. Recently, this is beginning to change, in light of the observations made in the next paragraph. See esp. Mounce, *Basics of Biblical Greek Grammar*, 230–32; Duff, *Elements of New Testament Greek*, 172–74.

Nevertheless, considerably fewer than half of all middle-voice verbs in the New Testament appear to be pure middles.[49] Many are either deponent (the active forms have dropped out in the development of the language, so that middle forms do double duty for both middle and active *meanings*), or else they have a different meaning than they do in the active voice, while remaining active in *function*. Barclay Newman's Greek-English dictionary of New Testament words and forms, often bound together with the UBS Greek New Testament, is particularly helpful here, because if a verb is deponent in all of its uses in the New Testament, even if it still preserves active forms in some other branches of Greek, Newman will give the middle voice (usually ending in -ομαι) as the lexical form or dictionary entry. He also indicates whenever words have different meanings in the middle voice than in the active.

If, therefore, Newman's dictionary were to list παύομαι instead of παύω, we would know that the verb was deponent, at least in the New Testament, and that it most likely meant nothing more in 1 Corinthians 13:8 than "[tongues] will cease" without any implications of in what manner. But, as it turns out, the dictionary lists παύω, the active voice form, as its lexical entry. More precisely, the entire entry reads, "**παύω** *stop, keep from* (1 Pet. 3.10); midd. *stop, cease; cease from, be done with.*"[50] Obviously, there is little if any difference in meaning between the word in its active and middle forms, and the lexical form demonstrates that there is at least one if not several places in the New Testament in which the active forms remain, different from the middle forms. So far this evidence appears to reinforce the cessationist argument.

Still, it would be interesting to know how often the active form occurs in the New Testament. A Greek concordance enables us to look up παύω and see how often and where it occurs. There are only fifteen uses of the verb. Excluding 1 Corinthians 13:8, thirteen of the remaining fourteen uses have middle or middle/passive endings.[51] Every one of these makes good sense if one translates them as active in meaning and, indeed, ten of them *must* be taken that way because they have direct objects, usually in participial form (someone ceased *doing* something).[52] What is the lone exception that kept Newman from using παύομαι as the lexical form and that appears to keep us from identifying the verb as strictly deponent in New Testament usage? It is 1 Peter 3:10. Now we know why Newman listed it in his entry: it was the *only* active form. When we look this verse up, we discover it is a quotation from the LXX, the Greek translation of the Hebrew Scriptures, of Psalm 34:12–13

---

49. Porter, *Idioms of the Greek New Testament*, 71.

50. Barclay M. Newman Jr., *A Concise Greek-English Dictionary of the New Testament* (Stuttgart and New York: United Bible Societies, 1971), 137.

51. Luke 5:4; 8:24; 11:1; Acts 5:42; 6:13; 13:10; 20:1, 31; 21:32; Eph. 1:16; Col. 1:9; Heb. 10:2; 1 Pet. 4:1.

52. Luke 5:4; Acts 5:42; 6:13; 13:10; 20:31; 21:32; Eph. 1:16, Col. 1:9, Heb. 10:2, 1 Pet. 4:1 (the lone instance of the direct object being a noun rather than a participle).

(33:13–14 LXX). But the Septuagint was completed at least two centuries before the composition of 1 Peter. One active voice form in it, quoted in the New Testament, tells us nothing about the state of the Greek language in the mid-first century AD.[53] All other forms of παύω in the New Testament appear to be deponent.[54] This does not prove that 1 Corinthians 13:8 has to be taken in the same way, but it does mean that those who argue that the middle voice in this one verse *must* mean "cease by themselves" must give much stronger lexical and contextual evidence to support their view. As it stands, for their view to be right 1 Corinthians 13:8 would have to be the lone first-century exception in the New Testament to the grammatical pattern just observed.[55]

Romans 9:22–23

Does God predestine people to salvation and/or to damnation? Romans 9 is a key chapter to exegete for anyone who would tackle this question. Verses 22–23 prove particularly crucial. In the updated NASB they read:

> [22]What if God, although willing to demonstrate His wrath and make His power known, endured with much patience vessels of wrath prepared for destruction?
> [23]And *He did so* to make known the riches of His glory upon vessels of mercy, which He prepared beforehand for glory . . ."

One can quickly see how reading these two verses could suggest the doctrine of double predestination: God chooses, in advance of anything a human being does, who will go to heaven and who will go to hell.[56] One might

53. To be precise, the LXX uses the second-person singular aorist active imperative, whereas Peter uses the third-person aorist active imperative. What is a direct command in the LXX becomes rhetorically more indirect. The New Testament writers regularly adapt Old Testament quotations in a variety of ways; this should cause us no surprise. But then it is equally natural that they would preserve an archaic use of the word at the same time (in this case its voice) to make it sound "like the Bible."

54. Cf. D. A. Carson, *Showing the Spirit: A Theological Exposition of 1 Corinthians 12–14* (Grand Rapids: Baker, 1987), 66–67; idem, *Exegetical Fallacies*, 76–77. Wallace (*Greek Grammar beyond the Basics*, 422–23) objects on the basis that the active form does occur frequently in Hellenistic Greek outside the New Testament and that the Greek of the New Testament is not a separate dialect. Both points are accurate, but this ignores numerous ways in which small points of style and grammar, hardly sufficient to constitute a separate dialect, *do* distinguish the Greek of the New Testament from Hellenistic Greek more generally. But Wallace and we agree that the main point is simply that one can't argue for cessationism just from the parsing of this one verb in this verse.

55. For a good overview of four major perspectives on the debate, see Wayne A. Grudem, ed., *Are Miraculous Gifts for Today?* (Grand Rapids: Zondervan, 1996). For a thorough, persuasive exegesis of 1 Cor. 13:8–13, see Anthony C. Thiselton, *The First Epistle to the Corinthians* (Carlisle: Paternoster; Grand Rapids: Eerdmans, 2000), 1060–74.

56. See esp. John Piper, *The Justification of God: An Exegetical and Theological Study of Romans 9:1–23* (Grand Rapids: Baker, 1983).

wonder, nevertheless, about the difference between Paul's grammar for the vessels (i.e., people) of wrath "prepared for destruction" (v. 22) and those "prepared in advance for glory" (v. 23). Is it significant that "beforehand" appears only in the second instance, with the vessels of mercy? Lutheran theologians have traditionally held to "single predestination"—the doctrine that God chooses in advance those who will be saved but does not choose those who will be lost. This coheres with the biblical testimony that eternal salvation is always by God's grace at his initiative and that eternal judgment is always according to our works and based on our initiative to rebel against God.[57]

An inspection of the Greek text discloses a second feature that is *not* identical with respect to the saved and the lost. In verse 22 the word translated "prepared" is κατηρτισμένα; in verse 23, it is προητοίμασεν. The phrase "in advance" actually renders just the prefix προ- added to the root verb ἑτοιμάζω. Now ἑτοιμάζω and καταρτίζω are sufficiently synonymous that there is no great difference between the two root verbs. But προητοίμασεν is an *active*-voice verb, whereas κατηρτισμένα is either middle or passive (in the perfect tense the forms are identical for both voices). Whereas in verse 23 God is the subject of the active voice "prepared in advance [for glory]," there is no expressed agent for the middle or passive voice "prepared [for destruction]." If the expression is middle, the reflexive sense fits best in this context: the vessels of wrath "prepared themselves" for destruction through their sins and rejection of God. If the expression is passive, then the sense is "having *been* prepared," and it could be a divine passive (in which God as agent is left unexpressed, hence, "having been prepared by God"). The former would support single predestination; the latter, double predestination.[58]

As with our last example from 1 Corinthians, we should combine our grammatical analysis with some lexical study. It is also important to pay attention to the literary context. The immediate context, to which we should turn first, is notoriously ambiguous. Verses 19–21 justify God's right to make two kinds of pottery, because he is the potter, some for noble and some for ignoble use (or "for honor" and "for dishonor"). But it is not clear whether Paul is making an exact analogy to the saved and the lost, whom he will introduce in verses 22–23, or simply making the point that God can do as he pleases in fashioning contrasting creations. After all, both vessels have a use, the latter perhaps for the disposal of refuse (TNIV). But that is not necessarily the same as saying the vessels themselves will be disposed of. Verses 16–18 speak more

57. David P. Scaer, "The Doctrine of Election: A Lutheran Note," in *Perspectives on Evangelical Theology*, eds. Kenneth S. Kantzer and Stanley N. Gundry (Grand Rapids: Baker, 1979), 105–15.

58. For the single predestinarian approach, in the context of these two verses, see C. E. B. Cranfield, *A Critical and Exegetical Commentary on the Epistle to the Romans*, vol. 2 (Edinburgh: T&T Clark, 1979), 495–96.

clearly of God's authority to show mercy on whom he wants and to harden whom he wants, with Pharaoh as the classic example of the latter. But here Paul is using Old Testament illustrations, as throughout verses 7–18, which may refer only to temporal rather than eternal election, that is, election to God's purposes for them in this world irrespective of their final spiritual status. If we look to the other side of verses 22–23, all of verses 24–29 are about those chosen for salvation. When Paul returns to the lost in verses 30–33, he places the blame squarely on the shoulders of the people who refused to pursue righteousness by faith rather than by works, even while acknowledging that God placed in Zion the stumbling stone (Christ) over which they (but not the saved) stumbled.[59]

There is another passage in the Pauline corpus, however, that may be relevant. The only other place in all thirteen Pauline Epistles where the words and imagery of "vessels," "honor," and "dishonor" occur together is 2 Timothy 2. But there Paul makes perfectly clear that it is possible for "vessels of dishonor" to "cleanse themselves" and become instruments for noble or honorable purposes. Of course, this is not through meritorious works but by trusting in Christ, but the point is that "vessels of dishonor" are not people irrevocably elected to damnation. It seems unlikely that they are in Romans 9 either, and that therefore κατηρτισμένα must be in the middle rather than the passive voice. Those who are on their way to destruction have prepared themselves for that fate, but they can always change as long as the breath of life remains in them, and Paul desperately hopes that they will.[60]

---

59. For this whole line of reasoning, see further William W. Klein, *The New Chosen People: A Corporate View of Election* (Grand Rapids: Zondervan, 1990), 166–67, 174–75. Klein sees *only* corporate election, even beyond verse 18, where we would see individual, eternal election coming into play as well.

60. Cf. further I. Howard Marshall with Philip H. Towner, *A Critical and Exegetical Commentary on the Pastoral Epistles* (Edinburgh: T&T Clark, 1999), 763. Wallace (*Greek Grammar Beyond the Basics*, 417–18) finds this view unlikely because of the infrequency of the direct middle. But subdivisions of tense and voice typically apply primarily to indicative-mood verbs, whereas here we have a participle, so such generalizations are largely irrelevant. Wallace also observes that καταρτίζω in the middle-passive "is always to be taken as a passive in the NT." But there are only three other such occurrences. Two of them are in periphrastic constructions that require the passive sense (Luke 6:40; 1 Cor. 1:10), while the other has an express statement of agency that makes the voice equally unambiguous (Heb. 11:3). None of the three texts, therefore, sheds any light on the construction at hand. In addition, Wallace argues from the perfect tense that this verb represents a "done deal," but this is to overinterpret the stative aspect (see Porter, *Idioms of the Greek New Testament*, 22–24, 40–42). Finally, Wallace argues from the immediate context of Rom. 9, but we have already addressed that above. In the final analysis, though, our point is not to insist on our theological conclusions but to illustrate the kinds of issues on which grammar comes to bear and to show the complexity and interconnectedness of the various exegetical decisions that have to be made.

Conclusion

Examples could be multiplied considerably. This chapter cannot substitute for actually studying Greek grammar, but it has hopefully encouraged students to recognize the importance of grammar. Reference works can go a long way toward helping students who have no facility in Greek, but unless somewhere one picks up the meaning of an aorist rather than an imperfect tense, a present rather than an aorist imperative, and so on, all the reference tools in the world will get a person only so far. As we saw in our chapter on translations (chap. 2), there is no single version of the Bible that will do everything students without Greek often want a Bible translation to do. At the very least, they will need to consult several translations, hopefully with study notes. Better still, serious theological students need to begin acquiring a library of good commentaries, first on the whole Bible and then on individual biblical books. Many detailed commentaries, though, cover almost everything readers could want to investigate *except* grammar. Therefore, tools like Rogers and Rogers or Zerwick become important also.[61] But little in exegesis replaces the thrill and satisfaction of mastering enough Greek vocabulary and grammar to be able to read the Greek New Testament for yourself, come up with your own exegetical insights, and then have them confirmed by the secondary literature (or, on occasion, challenged). You will no longer feel dependent on "guessing" correctly as to which scholar or authority is most trustworthy on particularly debated issues, especially since no commentator is ever inerrant. You can then understand the debate firsthand and make informed decisions for yourself.

---

61. Rogers and Rogers, *New Linguistic and Exegetical Key to the Greek New Testament*; Zerwick, *Biblical Greek*.

7

Interpretive Problems

In the exegetical process, the interpreter sometimes arrives at a crossroads. There are times when difficult questions about the meaning of the text cannot be answered by employing just one method from the various exegetical steps discussed so far. Such questions may be treated in a "catch-all-that's-left" category of interpretive problems. They must be approached synthetically, often requiring that the interpreter combine two or more of the exegetical steps in order to come to a sustainable conclusion about the tenuous issue. Sometimes the issues are unclear enough that even synthetic application of appropriate hermeneutics yields multiple conclusions, each defensible by those who hold the respective views. We will see in later examples of interpretive problems how opposite sides of debates can use the very same verses to defend their own arguments. However, the interpreter need not despair that the interpretive process is useless. Just because there are interpretive issues that cannot be fully resolved does not excuse students of the Bible from trying to gather enough evidence to make a responsible and educated inference as to the most probable meaning. By and large, seemingly difficult issues become much clearer if the interpreter will take the time and do the homework required. Here, we are concerned with those issues where the interpreter has done these things but there is still no clear-cut answer.

Even while we approach these difficult issues, let us recall our opening chapter on textual criticism and how the reliability of the vast majority of the New Testament text can be established beyond any reasonable doubt. An analogous situation exists here: issues in interpretation that are completely beyond final resolution are the exception and not the norm in the New Testament. If you consult two or more responsible, recent commentators on any passage, you will likely be surprised at the number of points on which they agree. It is certainly the disagreements that enjoy the limelight, but this is largely because they are more distinctive than dominant.[1] Much of what we read on the pages of Scripture is understandable and therefore we know how to live by it, without having to spend all our days in exegetical quandaries.

Because of the synthetic nature of solving the interpretive problems discussed in this chapter, it will quickly become apparent that this part of the exegetical process defies a simple, step-by-step methodology like many of our other chapters suggest. For this reason, instead of proposing a multistep process, we will here offer advice on how to move beyond dependence on commentaries and recognize the issues involved in complex interpretive problems. Next, we will illustrate the various tasks that are relevant to the sample problems mentioned and offer viable positions for the curious interpreter. If solving these interpretive problems seems difficult, that is because it is. It requires familiarity with all the steps and the tools thus far surveyed. However, while pastors and teachers often must take a tentative stand on how to deal with these issues for those within their spheres of influence, they can exonerate themselves of the pressure to resolve these problems beyond a shadow of a doubt. The odds are good that if the problem has existed throughout church history, we will not solve it here. We must be aware of the conversation, however, and decide which approach makes the best sense based on sound exegetical method.[2]

Houston, How Do We Know We Have a Problem?

For the beginning interpreter, commentaries will be the first place to turn in order to identify interpretive problems, if such problems haven't already suggested themselves. Commentators will approach interpretive difficulties in a variety of ways. One writer may solve an interpretive problem simply without mentioning that there is any alternative position. This will become obvious to the interpreter who reads multiple commentaries side by side. Even if a writer does not mention each possible position, the student can construct the various sides of the argument by reading widely on the problematic passage. When the options and arguments start to sound familiar and repetitious to the student, and he or she is able to describe the varying positions with encountering anything new, that usually means the student has conducted enough research.

1. Of course, the more the commentators differ in initial presuppositions (evangelical vs. liberal, dispensational vs. covenantal, Calvinist vs. Arminian, etc.), the more we can expect differences on those texts whose interpretation varies according to the given presuppositions.

2. There is some overlap here with the most conservative forms of "reader-response" criticism; see William W. Klein, Craig L. Blomberg, and Robert L. Hubbard Jr., *Introduction to Biblical Interpretation*, rev. ed. (Nashville: Nelson, 2004), 192–201.

Often commentators will treat an interpretive problem in its entirety, mentioning opposing viewpoints, and some will even construct the argument they deem most probable, refuting the rival positions by highlighting weaker points of diverging arguments.[3] It is characteristic for some writers to lay out the arguments and leave the students to come to their own conclusions. It is tempting in many of these cases to do the same for our own audiences. While it is permissible and even admirable to let those we teach know that interpretive options are available to them in these areas of Scripture, we may still be asked to offer a conclusion on which option we think is best and why. Remember as you make statements on which option seems best to do so humbly, recognizing that there are other viable conclusions, even if you do not favor them. You should also do so with the measure of tentativeness appropriate to your amount of study, familiarity with the issue, and Christian experience, leaving room to change your mind as your life and ministry continue. This will help you keep from unnecessarily alienating those who have done similar work and yet have come to differing conclusions. Of course, these principles apply only where you are dealing with opposing interpretations within the boundaries of Christian orthodoxy. This is not a concession to let any or all interpretations, however heretical or improbable, carry equal clout. And how will you know if opposing viewpoints are orthodox? Only by reading widely and researching thoroughly on the given topic or passage, along with, of course, having a familiarity with systematic and historical theology.[4]

Not even novices, though, should be content to let commentaries do all the work for them. There are a variety of additional ways to identify key interpretive problems in a given passage. The first and easiest way is to consult a number of translations for the text being studied.[5] Any verse, or section of a verse,

3. The more detailed and scholarly commentary series that often include full arguments and conclusions include the International Critical Commentary, Baker Exegetical Commentary on the New Testament, New International Greek Testament Commentary, Word Biblical Commentary, Anchor Bible, New Testament Library, Hermeneia, Pillar, and the New International Commentary on the New Testament.

4. For systematic theology, see esp. Millard Erickson, *Christian Theology*, 2nd ed. (Grand Rapids: Baker Academic, 1998); Gordon R. Lewis and Bruce A. Demarest, *Integrative Theology*, 3 vols. in 1 (Grand Rapids: Zondervan, 1996); Stanley J. Grenz, *Theology for the Community of God* (1994; repr. Grand Rapids: Eerdmans; Vancouver: Regent College Publishing, 2000); or Daniel L. Akin, ed., *A Theology for the Church* (Nashville: B&H, 2007). For historical theology, see esp. Louis Berkhof, *The History of Christian Doctrines*, rev. ed. (1937; repr. London: Banner of Truth, 1969); Geoffrey Bromiley, *Historical Theology: An Introduction* (1978; repr. Eugene, OR: Wipf & Stock, 1998); Alister E. McGrath, *Christian Theology: An Introduction* (Oxford and Cambridge, MA: Blackwell, 1994); idem, *The Christian Theology Reader* (Oxford and Cambridge, MA: Blackwell, 1995); or Roger E. Olson, *The Story of Christian Theology: Twenty Centuries of Tradition and Reform* (Downers Grove, IL: InterVarsity, 1999).

5. One helpful tool that lays out some of the best translations in one volume is John Kohlenberger III, *The Contemporary Parallel New Testament* (New York: Oxford University Press, 1997). This volume includes the following translations: King James Version, New American

Sidebar 7.1

Common Indicators of Interpretive Problems

- Nontrivial differences among the major translations of a given text
- A passage of Scripture that seems to disagree with something the author has said elsewhere
- Apparent disagreement between the author and what other inspired authors of Scripture say about the same topic
- A single text that has spawned multiple, complex debates
- A text whose meaning is hardly debated today but whose background indicates a diverse history of interpretation
- Places in the New Testament that use a quotation from the Old Testament in a way that does not seem consonant with the meaning of the verse in the original context

that has nontrivial differences among the major translations (i.e., differences that go beyond a single word or grammatical construction) likely contains an interpretive problem. Students who have studied Greek can compare the original language with the divergent English translations and hypothesize why each version chose as it did. They can then consult commentaries that are based on those translations to validate, supplement, or correct their hypotheses.[6]

As students become increasingly familiar with Scripture, they will be able to recognize other interpretive issues, even where the translations do not betray differences in interpretation. First, wherever any passage of Scripture seems to disagree with something the author has said elsewhere, there is an interpretive problem to be solved. For example, after the Pentecostal events of Acts 2, belief, baptism, and the gift of the Holy Spirit are presented as a closely knit package throughout Acts and Paul's epistles in all but two peculiar instances: Acts 8:15–25, where the Samaritans receive baptism and yet do not receive the Holy Spirit; and Acts 10:44–48, in which Cornelius and his household

---

Standard Bible (updated edition), New International Version, New Living Translation, New Century Version, Contemporary English Version, New King James Version, and *The Message*. To see the Greek text, King James Version, Rheims New Testament, Amplified Bible, New International Version, New Revised Standard Version, New American Bible, and New American Standard Bible side by side, consult idem, *The Precise Parallel New Testament* (New York: Oxford University Press, 1995). Software packages like BibleWorks also allow for many modern translations of Scripture to be compared quickly. An outstanding online equivalent may be found at www.biblegateway.com.

6. E.g., readers of the New Living Translation will want to consult the Cornerstone Commentaries, aficionados of the New Revised Standard Version will glean much from Black's New Testament Commentaries, while fans of the New International Version can take their pick from several series (e.g., the Pillar New Testament Commentaries and the New International Commentary on the New Testament). In other cases, series or authors produce their own translations.

receive the Holy Spirit prior to baptism.[7] Neither of these would seem quite so remarkable if Luke had not spent significant time on Peter's message, culminating in Acts 2:38, establishing the connections between belief, baptism, and the gift of the Spirit. Even the Messiah himself in Luke's Gospel has the Spirit come upon him at his baptism in the Jordan (Luke 3:21–22).[8] How do we reconcile the differences between what Luke tries to establish in one place, yet seems to undo in another? Or consider 1 Corinthians 10:23, where Paul makes the statement, "Everything is permissible" (NIV), after spending much of the letter lamenting and correcting the blatant sin of some in the Corinthian congregation. Unless the authors are unintentionally contradicting themselves (and we usually give the benefit of the doubt even to uninspired authors that they are not doing so before we accuse them of such), we must try to solve these interpretive mysteries.[9]

Second, even when an author is consistent on a given topic, interpretive problems may still exist where that writer seems to disagree with other inspired authors of Scripture about the same issue. For example, there seems to be a marked difference between what the letter to the Hebrews says about "eternal security" and other statements in Scripture about the surety of a believer's eternal salvation.[10] John 3:36 and 6:47 affirm that the believer already *has* (not *will have*) eternal life. Can it rightly be called eternal life if there is a chance of it ending in the future? Reading further along in John, 10:28–29 reminds believers that no one who belongs to God can be snatched out of his hand. First Peter 1:4–5 and Jude 1 make the statement that believers are kept safe by the power of God. Hebrews 6:4–6, however, reads, "It is impossible for those who have once been enlightened, who have tasted the heavenly gift, who have shared in the Holy Spirit, who have tasted the goodness of the word of God and the powers of the coming age, and who have fallen away, to be brought back to repentance. To their loss they are crucifying the Son of God all over again and subjecting him to public disgrace." There is certainly an interpre-

---

7. One could add Acts 19:1–7 to the list, in which some disciples of John have yet to be baptized in the Holy Spirit and, indeed, have not even heard of the Holy Spirit. But for that very reason, their knowledge of Christian truth seems so truncated that it is hard to imagine they were ever true believers prior to their encounter with Paul.

8. Cf. David A. Handy, "Acts 8:14–25," *Interpretation* 47 (1993): 291.

9. This latter problem in 1 Corinthians is much more quickly solved than the issue in Acts. First Cor. 10:23 continues, "but not everything is beneficial" ([T]NIV). Because Christians are no longer under the Mosaic law, there is a sense in which everything is permissible. But that scarcely means Jesus or the apostles were antinomian; many things still harm an individual and therefore should be avoided. It is also quite likely that the first part of this verse was a Corinthian slogan, perhaps based on a misinterpretation of Paul's law-free gospel, which he has to qualify (hence, the TNIV: "'I have the right to do anything,' you say"). See, e.g., Gordon D. Fee, *The First Epistle to the Corinthians* (Grand Rapids: Eerdmans, 1987), 478–79.

10. The author of Hebrews makes the most pronounced statements about the threat of apostasy, particularly in the warning passages (Heb. 2:1–4; 3:7–4:13; 5:11–6:12; 10:19–39; 12:14–29). Of these, Heb. 6:4–6 and 10:26–31 are the strongest.

tive problem here that must be dealt with in order to make a statement on the perseverance of the saints in a way that maintains the unity of Scripture.[11] We will have more to say about this kind of intracanonical witness in our chapter on theology (pp. 234–36).

A third type of problem occurs whenever interpreters have difficulty making sense of a text that has spawned multiple, complex debates. A quick read in the Greek of James 4:5–6 indicates a number of thorny problems. First of all, it is difficult to determine how to translate the quotation that comes after the introduction, "Or do you think Scripture says without reason, '. . .'?" A grammatical issue must be tackled to determine the subject of the direct quotation that James introduces from Scripture. Even after one wrestles with the grammatical issue, none of the renderings can be found in the Old Testament.[12] Here, the responsible interpreter has more to research in order to determine the intended meaning of the text.

Fourth, there are some texts whose meanings are hardly debated today, but a glance at the history of the text's reception reveals that it has diverse interpretations. As one example, in recent scholarship most writers have strongly affirmed that the mention of water in John 3:5, in Jesus's statement to Nicodemus that he must be born of water and the Spirit, is not a reference to the Christian rite of baptism.[13] Although modern interpreters do not always agree on what the verse *does* mean, they have largely ruled out baptismal regeneration as one of its potential original meanings, not least because distinctively Christian baptism was not instituted until after Jesus's death. However, many of the earliest church fathers interpreted the passage as though Jesus's words directly referred to Christian baptism.[14] For example, Tertullian remarks, "'Unless one has been reborn of water and the Spirit, he shall not enter into the kingdom of the heavens,' has tied faith to the necessity of baptism." Ambrose writes, "Who is the one who is born of the spirit and is made spirit but he who is renewed in the spirit of his mind?

11. For representative perspectives on perseverance, see J. Matthew Pinson, ed., *Four Views on Eternal Security* (Grand Rapids: Zondervan, 2002); for the main approaches to the warning passages in Hebrews, see Herbert W. Bateman IV, ed., *Four Views on the Warning Passages in Hebrews* (Grand Rapids: Kregel, 2007).

12. Almost every time ἡ γραφή is used in the New Testament, it introduces a direct quotation from Scripture; if the text that James quotes is not scriptural, this instance of ἡ γραφή becomes a rare exception, making it difficult to interpret what James might have meant by introducing the quotation in this way.

13. See, e.g., Gerald L. Borchert, *John 1–11* (Nashville: Broadman & Holman, 1996), 173–76; Craig S. Keener, *The Gospel of John: A Commentary*, 2 vols. (Peabody, MA: Hendrickson, 2003), 1:550–52; Andreas Köstenberger, *John* (Grand Rapids: Baker, 2004), 123–24; and A. T. Lincoln, *The Gospel according to Saint John* (London: Continuum; Peabody, MA: Hendrickson, 2005), 150–51.

14. Sometimes the patristic writers differ from modern exegetes because they are applying a text to their settings rather than seeking its original meaning, but that does not appear to be the case in this instance.

This certainly is he who is regenerated by water and the Holy Spirit, since we receive the hope of eternal life through the laver of regeneration and renewing of the Holy Spirit." Consider also the musings of Gregory of Nazianzus on John 3:4: "We are a compound of both body and soul. The one part is visible, the other invisible. In the same way, our cleansing also is two-fold, that is, by water and the Spirit. The one is received visibly in the body, the other concurs with it invisibly and apart from the body. . . . The virtue of baptism is to be understood as a covenant with God for a second life and a purer conversation."[15] Each of these comments clearly ties baptism to the understanding of this verse. Who is correct in their interpretation, these church fathers or most contemporary scholars? Some entire denominations have tied baptism inexorably to salvation because of this passage. Others refuse to do so. Clearly, an interpretive problem is present where there is a history of divergent interpretation.

Finally, places in the New Testament that use a quotation from the Old Testament in a way that does not seem consonant with the meaning of the verse in the original context tend to create areas for interpretive strife. Matthew 2:15 quotes Hosea 11:1, using it to show that Joseph and Mary's flight to and return from Egypt in the wake of Herod's infanticide was a fulfillment of Old Testament prophecy. But Matthew seems to make sense only if one completely disregards the original context of Hosea, which speaks about God calling Israel out of captivity in Egypt. In fact, in context, the statement in Hosea 11:1 is not even a prediction at all, but rather an affirmation of God's loving care and election of Israel. Many of the Old Testament quotations in the New Testament appear to be used by the New Testament author for distinctive purposes, with little regard for their meaning in their Old Testament contexts.[16] The New Testament authors' use of Old Testament Scripture in such ways raises significant hermeneutical questions for contemporary expositors of Scripture. Because New Testament authors often used Old Testament texts to support their arguments in ways that don't necessarily concern themselves with preserving those texts' original meaning, may we as Christians do the same with the Old Testament today? May we use the *New* Testament in these manners? While these questions open the proverbial can of worms with regard

---

15. Tertullian, *On Baptism* 13; Ambrose, *On the Holy Spirit* 3.10.64; Gregory of Nazianzus, *On Holy Baptism,* Oration 40.8. All three quotations come from Joel C. Elowsky, ed., *John 1–10,* Ancient Christian Commentary on Scripture: New Testament (Downers Grove, IL: InterVarsity, 2006), 110–13. This series, covering both testaments, is an invaluable resource for determining representative interpretations of any passage of Scripture by the first five hundred years of orthodox Christian writers. A similar series is now being prepared for Reformation-era commentary.

16. Just in Matthew alone, cf. the various uses of the Old Testament identified in Craig L. Blomberg, "Interpreting Old Testament Prophetic Literature in Matthew: Double Fulfillment," *Trinity Journal* 23 (2002): 17–33.

to principles of biblical interpretation, they also impinge on significant issues within individual texts and cannot be sidestepped.[17]

After using your own theological know-how to identify possible interpretive problems, it is wise to turn to the scholarly literature to confirm whether your hunches cover the most significant interpretive problems presented by a given text. In addition to commentaries, look for significant monographs on your passage, book, or theme, as well as recent journal articles. Once you have identified the most significant interpretive problems, it is time to put together all of the exegetical steps we have discussed thus far, as each problem dictates. When dealing with complex interpretive issues, there are no principles or concrete methods apart from what we have already discussed. When attempting to solve an interpretive problem, the exegete will want to consider each step of exegesis (from textual criticism on through the list to grammatical issues) and decide which elements are most pertinent to shed light on the issue at hand. The only thing remotely resembling a formula is to *look for the non-negotiables*. If there are five problems in a passage and four of them can be resolved in more than one plausible way but the fifth makes good sense in only one way, then begin with that clearest piece of the process. Perhaps it will help you exclude certain options for the more ambiguous issues. Or if certain problems in a text can be resolved with a higher degree of probability, begin with them and work toward the more uncertain ones. Perhaps the best way to explain this is simply to illustrate it. In the following section, therefore, we will walk through sample texts, factoring in and discussing the relevant elements of the exegetical methods and then show how we distinguish the best interpretations from the options available.

"Fixing" the Problems

As we warned earlier, there are difficult passages in Scripture on which interpreters can make only reasonable conjectures; so when we talk about fixing the problems, we do so recognizing that not all can be solved with equal probability.

Acts 8:9–25 and Acts 10:44–48

Given that Luke establishes the close chronological connections between conversion and water baptism on the one hand, and between conversion and the gift of the Holy Spirit on the other (Acts 2:38; 8:36–38; 9:17; 15:8; 16:15, 31–33; 19:4–6; 22:16),[18] how does the interpreter understand the seemingly

---

17. Cf. Kenneth Berding and Jonathan Lunde, eds., *Three Views on the New Testament Use of the Old Testament* (Grand Rapids: Zondervan, 2007).

18. On which, see esp. Max Turner, *Power from on High: The Spirit in Israel's Restoration and Witness in Luke-Acts* (Sheffield: Sheffield Academic Press, 1996).

incongruent accounts found in Acts 8:9–25 and 10:44–48?[19] In other words, belief, baptism, and reception of the Holy Spirit are presented as a "package deal," particularly in Acts 2:38 at Pentecost, so that we can refer to this cluster of events as the "Pentecostal package." Acts 8, however, depicts a group of Samaritans who believe and are baptized but then experience a significant delay before the coming of the Spirit, while Acts 10 shows the Spirit arriving prior to baptism and does not mention belief at all. If there were no larger pattern from which these two texts diverged, we could conclude that the Spirit comes and goes as he sovereignly pleases, as clearly happened in Old Testament times.[20]

One significant principle to be drawn from narrative is to look for positive patterns that remain throughout a book (or even the entire New Testament), even while contexts vary. These patterns are likely normative for Christians today. The elements that vary from context to context, unless otherwise indicated by the author, were likely situation-specific events dictated by the contexts in which we find them in the New Testament. For example, Acts 2:43–47; 6:1–7; and 11:27–30 give three very different models for helping the poor, none of which needs be absolutized, but all of which may prove useful in various circumstances.[21] This principle enables us to take one significant step toward resolving the differences among Luke's theological statements on the relationship between belief, baptism, and the Holy Spirit. The two accounts that differ from the majority in the order or presence of the elements are probably not as normative as are those texts that record the three elements together. Yet, exegetically, it is not enough to dismiss these two exceptional episodes. The author has some important theological lessons in mind with their inclusion, and so the interpreter must discern what the author is emphasizing through the subtle nuances of the different texts.

Acts 10:44–48

Dealing first with the text that is a bit easier to reconcile, let us consider the literary context of Acts 10:44–48. If Acts 1:8 is taken as a miniature outline for the rest of the book, which plots the progress of the gospel to increasingly far-away regions, by the time we reach Acts 10:44 the gospel has moved beyond Jerusalem, Judea, and Samaria to a Gentile in the coastal plains of Sharon where the Gentile (Roman) governor resided. Cornelius, a Hellenistic commander of up to one hundred troops, along with his family, culturally and ethnically (even if not geographically) represented what 1:8 calls the ends

---

19. Romans 8:9 also displays Paul teaching that those without the Holy Spirit are not Christian.

20. See esp. Robert P. Menzies, *Empowered for Witness: The Spirit in Luke-Acts* (Sheffield: Sheffield Academic Press, 1994).

21. See further Walter L. Liefeld, *Interpreting the Book of Acts* (Grand Rapids: Baker, 1995), 113–27.

of the earth.[22] In even closer proximity, in the passage immediately preceding the text (10:9–23), Peter has been given a vision from God that posits the cleanliness of all foods, even nonkosher foods previously forbidden by Jewish law. The immediate arrival of the messenger with the request that Peter accompany him to the house of a Gentile extends the message expressed in the vision. If all foods are now declared clean by God, by extension so are all people. The gospel can freely move to people who were previously excluded from God's community.

In the encounter that Peter has with Cornelius (10:24–48), the apostle begins to preach the gospel when, in surprising order, prior to repentance and baptism, the Spirit falls on these Gentiles in a way that is reminiscent of Pentecost, complete with the Gentiles speaking in tongues and praising God. Peter, seeing that the Gentiles have received the Spirit in the same way the apostles had, immediately recommends baptism, which they receive with all haste. Although not mentioned explicitly, belief on the part of the Gentiles who receive the Spirit can be assumed by the combination of the message Peter is preaching—about repentance—at the time of their encounter with the Spirit (10:34–44) and the Gentiles' subsequent praise to God (v. 46). The reversal of the usual order of baptism and the reception of the Spirit does not present a big interpretive problem unless one shares some denominations' doctrinal commitment to baptism as a necessary precursor to salvation and the arrival of the Spirit.[23] For our purposes, we are content to say that, based on context, all necessary elements of the Pentecostal package are present in this conversion experience.

While the reversal in the order of events is not a lasting exegetical problem, it is worth highlighting because it points to Luke's larger purpose in the narrative itself. God confirms the legitimacy of the Gentiles' conversion in a dramatic way by sending the Spirit. It surprises Peter and leads him to the exclamation that

22. This is especially true given their association with Rome, the capital and heart of the empire that spanned most of the known world for first-century Israelites. Cf. E. Earle Ellis, "'The End of the Earth' (Acts 1:8)," *Bulletin for Biblical Research* 1 (1991): 123–32.

23. Such a commitment is based on the statement by Peter in Acts 2:38: "Repent and be baptized, every one of you, in the name of Jesus Christ for the forgiveness of your sins. And you will receive the gift of the Holy Spirit." The text clearly proceeds in this order, making it seem that repentance and baptism logically predicate the forgiveness of sins and reception of the Holy Spirit. However, a good literary argument can be made for Acts 2:38 as a chiasm (ABBA structure), so that repentance is linked to the forgiveness of sin and baptism is done in the name of Jesus Christ. Additionally, the shift in the second-person plural "repent" to the third-person singular "be baptized" indicates that the verbs are being treated differently, which becomes all the more noteworthy when one considers the sermon in 3:12–26, where Peter demands repentance but baptism is not mentioned. In 2:38 the reception of the Holy Spirit does not need to be a result of the previous actions, but something that is part of this conversion package. That all elements are present in close succession is what matters to Luke when he recounts incidents of authentic conversion. Cf. further Luther McIntyre, "Baptism and Forgiveness in Acts 2:38," *Bibliotheca Sacra* 153 (1996): 53–62.

Gentiles have received the Spirit just as the apostles had at Pentecost. Peter's affirmation is a "bigger deal" than a contemporary audience may recognize at first (cf. 10:45, 47). Consider the historical-cultural background of the episode. Jew-Gentile relationships were as tenuous as any ethnic tensions we have today. Jews reviled Gentiles, for it was the Gentile Romans who kept them captive, preventing God's promise of land to Israel from becoming a reality again. A survey of the Pauline Epistles will reveal that the consistent theme of Jew-Gentile unity in Christ emerges in numerous, distinct settings. Even more pointedly, here in Acts Cornelius is a centurion, a commander in the hostile, occupying army. A first-century audience would have read this story with all this in mind, and in this light the picture of Gentiles here becomes remarkable. Peter concludes that God's cleansing of all foods implies his cleansing of all peoples (vv. 34–35).[24] The order of events in Acts 10 serves as an exclamation point to a larger Lukan theme—Gentiles are welcomed into the kingdom of God in a way they had not previously known, not by acceptance of Jewish ritual law but by God sending his Spirit. Jews must therefore respond to Gentiles with the same acceptance that God has now shown them.

ACTS 8:9–25

Acts 8:12–17 are the crucial verses that pose the biggest interpretive problem on this topic in Acts, in the larger context of 8:9–25. Here, after hearing Philip preach, the Samaritans believe him and are baptized (v. 12). However, later, when the apostles arrive, they find that they have not yet received the Spirit. With Acts 10 we were able to adequately solve the issue with a bit of literary and historical context work. This passage will require our fuller exegetical arsenal, incorporating word studies, grammatical studies, literary context, and historical-cultural background. The results of our exegesis are of no small consequence. It is on the interpretation of this passage that many Pentecostal theologies hang their hat, claiming that in addition to conversion and water baptism there is a subsequent "baptism of the Holy Spirit" that marks a mature believer, or in some cases that makes one a Christian altogether.[25] Roman Catholic and some mainline Protestant traditions have deduced that the subsequent reception of the Spirit is akin to the later Christian ceremony of confirmation, which then remains normative for believers today.[26] Still oth-

---

24. Cf. Charles E. Van Engen, "Peter's Conversion: A Culinary Disaster Launches the Gentile Mission: Acts 10:1–11:18," in *Mission in Acts: Ancient Narratives in Contemporary Context*, ed. Robert L Gallagher and Paul Hertig (Maryknoll, NY: Orbis, 2004), 133–43.

25. For a full-length treatment of the key passages from a thoroughgoing Pentecostal perspective that advocates a "second blessing," see Howard M. Ervin, *Conversion-Initiation and the Baptism in the Holy Spirit* (Peabody, MA: Hendrickson, 1985).

26. Calvin's *Institutes of the Christian Religion*, II.19.4–13 discusses, with some contempt, the Catholic and Anglican rite of confirmation as a sacrament but concludes with Calvin's preference for the continuation of the ceremony in a nonsacramental sense. Acts 8:15–17 remains a key textual linchpin (sec. 6).

ers, based on the larger testimony of Luke and Acts, are firmly committed to making all elements of the Pentecostal package normative in every conversion, so that the delay of the Holy Spirit in Acts 8 is grounds enough to question the genuineness of the Samaritans' belief.[27] We will invoke the full range of exegetical tools in order to come to the most appropriate conclusion. Interestingly, some options among the differing conclusions seem equally viable enough that each of the authors of this book comes to different conclusions. This passage, therefore, affords an excellent exercise in weighing the various options and then ranking them, rather than holding to one so tenaciously that other viable interpretations are dismissed entirely.

Literary Context Analysis

We will begin with literary context analysis of the passage. As was important in our brief treatment of Acts 10, we must consider the overall outward movement of the gospel from Jerusalem to Judea and Samaria, and then to the ends of the earth. Acts 8 is located in the gospel's movement outward from the apostolic center of Jerusalem to neighboring Samaria. Throughout Luke and Acts, Samaria serves as a bridge between Jerusalem and the Gentiles, and the same is true in this instance.[28] Additionally, considering the entire literary composition of Luke-Acts together, the Acts 8 episode of Samaritan faith and subsequent confirmation by Peter and John dramatically invert the account in Luke 9:52–56, where Jesus is denied entry into a Samaritan village and James and John offer to call down fire from heaven and destroy it. In Acts 8, however, the Samaritans receive the message of Jesus through Philip and the apostles, two of whom previously wanted to see the city annihilated for its rejection of Jesus, as they arrive and confirm the faith of these new converts.[29]

In Acts 8:1–3, Luke recounts the scattering of all but the apostles from Jerusalem after the stoning of Stephen and the subsequent persecution of the church by zealous Jews such as Saul of Tarsus. Philip, one of the seven Hellenistic Jews (i.e., Greek-speaking from outside Israel) including Stephen chosen to serve as a "deacon" in Jerusalem (6:5), appears among these scattered Christians.[30] Luke makes the statement in 8:4 that all who scattered preached the word wherever they went. Then he hones in on the travels of Philip, who fled to Samaria.

The entire account covers 8:4–25 and intertwines the stories of Simon the Sorcerer and the Samaritan people. Philip captures the attention of the crowds (the action being expressed by the verb προσέχω) with his proclamation

---

27. See esp. James D. G. Dunn, *Baptism in the Holy Spirit* (London: SCM; Philadelphia: Westminster, 1970).

28. John T. Squires, "The Function of Acts 8.4–12.25," *New Testament Studies* 44 (1998): 608–17.

29. See further F. Scott Spencer, *Acts* (Sheffield: Sheffield Academic Press, 1997), 86.

30. It is a short step from geographical and linguistic differences to cultural ones as well, although this is debated.

about the Messiah, which is paired with various signs, including exorcisms and physical healings (8:6). Simon, who had practiced sorcery and boasted that he was someone great, and who was used to having the attention (again using a form of προσέχω [vv. 10, 11]) and affections that were now given to Philip, is astonished at the accompanying signs. The Samaritans respond to Philip's new message and signs with belief and baptism; so too does Simon, who "believed and was baptized" (v. 13). In drastic departure from the Lukan norm with regard to conversion experience, the reception of the Holy Spirit is not mentioned at the time of the Samaritans' belief and baptism. It is not until the apostles from Jerusalem arrive and lay hands on the Samaritans that they receive this gift.

Literarily, it is worth noting that the narrative alternates between Simon and the Samaritans throughout. Commentators disagree about what is to be made of the parallelism. Some say Simon is the foil for the right belief of the Samaritans. While both Simon and the Samaritans believe and are baptized, the Samaritans get it right by receiving the Spirit, while Simon gets it wrong by greedily desiring to purchase the Spirit so that power such as Philip's will be at his beck and call. Other scholars posit that Simon and the Samaritans are mutually interpreting characters. Since Simon proves his belief and baptism inauthentic by his later behavior of trying to purchase the Spirit, it can also be assumed that the same words used of the Samaritans' conversion (belief and baptism) must be interpreted as counterfeit faith by virtue of the close proximity of Simon's decidedly unchristian actions.[31] We will need to use other interpretive tools to make a final decision.

Immediately following this passage, Philip is once again on the move, this time at the behest of an angel, and he meets an Ethiopian eunuch. Without ruining the conclusions that historical-cultural background analysis will yield for this passage, it will suffice to say that an Ethiopian eunuch represents a quintessential Gentile, both in his ethnicity and in his ritual defilement. Philip helps the Ethiopian interpret Isaiah, by showing him how it points to Jesus as the Messiah. The man believes, asks to be baptized, and then the Holy Spirit arrives and takes Philip away, leaving the Ethiopian behind rejoicing at the good news he has heard and received.[32]

Our literary context analysis presents two pertinent points. First, this narrative fits purposefully into Luke's overarching emphasis on the outward movement of the gospel, as a bridge between the Christian movement in Jerusalem and the gospel's advances to the far reaches of Gentile territory. Therefore, it

31. For a thorough analysis of the biblical and extrabiblical material about Simon Magus traditions and a demonstration of the theological ambiguities surrounding them, see Stephen Haar, *Simon Magus: The First Gnostic?* (Berlin and New York: de Gruyter, 2003).

32. Cf. Keith H. Reeves, "The Ethiopian Eunuch: A Key Transition from Hellenist to Gentile Mission: Acts 8:26–40," in *Mission in Acts: Ancient Narratives in Contemporary Context*, ed. Robert L. Gallagher and Paul Hertig (Maryknoll, NY: Orbis, 2004), 114–22.

is not intended to be a free-standing systematic statement on how all people ought to experience conversion and subsequent Spirit reception. A thorough literary context analysis allows us to dismiss the claim that this text is intended to be normative for Christian believers in all times and places. Based on the hermeneutic for narrative described earlier, which recognizes patterns repeated in various contexts as prescriptive for Christian living and departures from that pattern as merely descriptive, we reject any position that *requires* a subsequent experience of the Holy Spirit after initial reception at conversion.[33] Second, the passage's structure of alternating between Simon and the Samaritans indicates an interpretive relationship between the two, though from literary context alone it cannot be determined what that relationship is.

Historical-Cultural Background Analysis

The same kind of information considered for Acts 10 is pertinent here. We do not need to look much further than New Testament accounts to determine how strained Jewish-Samaritan relationships were in the first-century historical-cultural milieu. Luke often uses the Samaritans to display right behavior where Israel gets it wrong. What makes this so effective is that Luke plays on sentiments in his audience that would leave them scandalized that he would use a despised people group as a foil for God's chosen people, showing the outcast to be right where the chosen have failed. Jewish characters in the Gospels often avoid Samaria altogether, taking much longer routes around it, because of the Jewish-Samaritan disdain for each other. Extrabiblically, Josephus confirms the contempt the Jews had for Samaritans, whom they considered half-breeds and unorthodox worshipers.[34]

How does this contribute to our understanding of the passage at hand? It alerts us to what Luke's audience would have sensed immediately, namely that the Samaritans, whom they would have expected to receive condemnation from the author, are now welcomed into the fold of God's kingdom. Something unique and drastically different is happening. The subsequent events are fittingly drastic also as the kingdom dawns in new and highly unexpected places.

Word Study and Grammar Analysis

The most debated word in this section of Acts 8, πιστεύω, translates into English as the verb "believe." Luke announces in this passage that the Samari-

33. For a full exegetical refutation of this doctrine, incorporating all the canonical data, see Gordon D. Fee, "Baptism in the Holy Spirit: The Issue of Separability and Subsequence," *Pneuma* 7.2 (1985): 87–99.

34. For a brief history of the events in ancient Israel and a discussion of Old Testament texts that explain the Samaritan origins that led to the volatile relationship between the Jews and Samaritans, and which also surveys Samaritan belief compared to Judaism, see H. G. M. Williamson and C. A. Evans, "Samaritans," in *The Dictionary of New Testament Background*, ed. Craig A. Evans and Stanley E. Porter (Leicester and Downers Grove, IL: InterVarsity, 2000), 1057–60.

tans "believed Philip as he proclaimed the good news of the kingdom of God and the name of Jesus Christ" (8:12). In the very next verse, "Simon himself believed and was baptized." In Acts, Luke often uses πιστεύω to indicate that a person has become a believer, that is, a genuine follower of Jesus (e.g., 2:44; 4:4; 13:48; 16:31). In fact, the term does not imply false belief in any of its other uses in Acts. So how do those who hold the view that this is inadequate belief here have a leg to stand on? For one thing, they stand on context. In the passage, Simon's later actions indicate that whatever he believed previously was obviously not sufficient to save him from the blunder of trying to buy the power of the Spirit. Indeed, this error is so serious that Peter's reply can be literally translated, "May you and your money go to hell" (v. 20; cf. J. B. Phillips's translation). If Simon's belief and baptism prove inadequate,[35] so too may the Samaritans' belief.

At this point in the argument, those who posit that the Samaritans' belief is artificial by its association with Simon also invoke a grammatical argument. Very rarely will one find the verb πιστεύω followed by an object other than Jesus or God (e.g., 5:14; 9:42; 16:34). That the preacher Philip is the object of belief makes one question whether it is the right kind of faith. Is it mere mental assent rather than wholehearted commitment to God? Is it superstitious loyalty to a human preacher? Furthermore, the Samaritans "paid close attention" (v. 6; from προσέχω) to Philip, just as they had reportedly given their attention to Simon before Philip arrived (v. 10). They had previously been "amazed" by Simon (v. 9), just as Simon was "astonished" by Philip (v. 13); in both verses the Greek verb is a form of ἐξίστημι. By these associations, the Samaritans' faith, based on signs and wonders alone, could have been like the inadequate "faith" Jesus had repeatedly rebuked throughout his own ministry (e.g., John 2:23–25; Matt. 16:1–4). Those who argue it is inadequate further assert that the deficiencies in this "faith" are confirmed by the delay of the Spirit, who arrives only after the apostles arrive, to complete their incomplete experience.[36]

Proponents of the other side of the debate will quickly counter with additional contextual evidence. The text does not report only that the Samaritans believed Philip. There is more. They believed Philip "as he proclaimed the good news of the kingdom of God and the name of Jesus Christ" (8:12). It seems that the content of Philip's message is the gospel, namely, the message of the kingdom of God as it has been mediated through Jesus Christ. It does not seem that Philip's preaching is inadequate if this is the content.[37] But if

---

35. See 8:20b–21 where Peter's strong rebuke of Simon continues with "you thought you could buy the gift of God with money! You have no part or share in this ministry, because your heart is not right before God."

36. See Dunn, *Baptism in the Holy Spirit*, 64–68, for a full word study and grammatical discussion.

37. So, e.g., David G. Peterson, *The Acts of the Apostles* (Grand Rapids and Cambridge: Eerdmans; Nottingham: Apollos, 2009), 283–87.

Philip is able adequately to preach the orthodox gospel on his own, why do the apostles also arrive on the scene? The most common answer has been that it is to bridge the historical chasm between Samaritan and Jewish Christians. Judea and Samaria were suddenly joined under a radical message that brought unity in ways that seemed previously impossible. It was no doubt remarkable to be baptized by a freelance Hellenistic-Jewish preacher like Philip, but it was staggering for the Hebraic-Jewish apostles to display the type of solidarity that comes with the laying on of hands. This is followed by the arrival of the Spirit, with both actions indicating that the Samaritans were now full-fledged members of the ever-expanding community of God.[38] Luke understands God to have varied the Pentecostal package to emphasize this lesson, a literary exclamation point of sorts.

However, this text is not necessary to confirm the overarching Lukan theme of the gospel reaching new people groups in various ways. If the conclusion just described is in error, the Lukan theme remains strong elsewhere. While both of us reject the doctrine of a unique, second experience of the Holy Spirit, subsequent to conversion and water baptism, as a necessary part of Christian living, we remain split on what to make of the Pentecostal package variation. One of us questions the genuineness of the Samaritans' belief and considers this the reason for the delay of the Spirit until the apostles arrive to give further instruction and instill true faith. The other one believes the initial experience was genuine and that God withheld his Spirit in order to confirm the new converts in a dramatic way that reinforced ethnic unity among Christians. We have here a perfect example of the ambiguity in interpretation that is sometimes present in such a way that those who share the same interpretive principles arrive at differing conclusions. We both agree that something must be done with the two accounts in Acts where belief, baptism, and reception of the Spirit vary from the usual pattern, and we both share the commitment to use sound exegetical method to come up with the best interpretation of the biblical author's variation. But much of our disagreement hinges on how much each of us is willing to live with a solitary exception to an otherwise consistent pattern and how much each of us is willing to invest small textual details with great significance for the sake of producing complete consistency. Which feature is less "negotiable" winds up determining our conclusions as to which exegetical arguments we find more persuasive.

James 4:5–6

The difficulty with the texts addressed above was that the passage seemed at first glance to be contradicted by other passages of Scripture. But there are other texts where it is not conflict with other Scripture that causes the

---

38. So, e.g., F. F. Bruce, *The Book of Acts*, rev. ed. (Grand Rapids: Eerdmans, 1988), 170.

problem. The problem is rather that the passage is unusually difficult to make sense of even on its own. Here the way to deal with problems is to take the sum of the evidence provided by the individual interpretive tools (literary context, historical-cultural background, word studies, etc.) and decide which combination yields the most convincing interpretation. Again, we must allow for more than one interpretation to possibly be correct. When we have finished our inductive interpretive work and then consult scholarly opinion, we dare not dismiss any of the options without giving the evidence for them a fair hearing. Even the major published translations of such passages are tentative enough in some of their conclusions that the English versions often include footnotes alerting the reader to alternate renderings.[39] We will again use the full arsenal of tools introduced so far, including historical-cultural (esp. Old Testament) background, literary context, word studies, and grammar study. In this case, the passage will require the interpreter even to solve an issue of where an apparent quotation begins and ends.

Interpretive uncertainties regarding James 4:5–6 can be summarized as follows: (1) A grammatical issue immediately presents itself because it is unclear whether the neuter noun τὸ πνεῦμα (spirit/Spirit) is nominative or accusative, leaving the interpreter to decide if it is the subject or the direct object of the verb ἐπιποθεῖ (he/it desires, yearns for). Even once an exegete determines whether πνεῦμα is the subject or direct object, he or she must decide if it is the animating force placed in humanity at creation (i.e., the human spirit) or if it refers to the Holy Spirit. (2) A word study becomes necessary for the words ἐπιποθέω and φθόνος because in the Greek Bible ἐπιποθέω is almost always used with positive connotations, while φθόνος (envy, jealousy) is always used negatively. Since πρὸς φθόνον (enviously, jealously) is used to modify ἐπιποθεῖ, the interpreter has a decision to make. The two words must both be used either positively or negatively, and one's decision on this issue will help determine the subject of the verb ἐπιποθεῖ. If the words have positive connotations (i.e., "yearns jealously"), it seems likely that God or the Holy Spirit functions as the subject. If, however, they have negative connotations (i.e., "desires enviously" or "envies intensely"), the human spirit is the more suitable subject, especially given James's tirade against the community's unacceptable behavior in 4:1–4. (3) Finally, the interpreter must inquire about the "Scripture" James refers to in verse 5a and then seems to quote in verse 5b, because nothing in the Old Testament corresponds to the words James "cites." This will be the one step in finding the meaning of this passage where we will want to read most widely in the secondary literature—to find as many proposals as possible for the quotation James uses. Each of these three items creates an interpretive problem in its

39. In this case, the NIV and TNIV give two different options and the preferred one has changed from the NIV to the TNIV. Clearly the decisions are quite difficult!

own right; taken together, as they must be due to their interrelationships, they make one downright perplexing interpretive problem.[40]

While understanding that τὸ πνεῦμα presents a grammatical issue, because we are identifying whether it is functioning as the subject or the direct object, we must also use the literary context, and even our word studies, to help determine what James has in mind. So we will postpone the issue for now and return to it after we have considered the most likely meanings for the words φθόνον and ἐπιποθεῖ. However, we need to remember our concentric circles of context as well (see p. 95), because words cannot be defined apart from their literary contexts.[41] Were we able to locate an Old Testament passage from which James was directly quoting, we would have to take that other author's usage into account also, but that is not the case here.

Since φθόνος occurs only here in James, a word study employing diachrony as well as synchrony is necessary (recall above, p. 123). As just noted, the New Testament uses are decisively negative. Φθόνος expresses human envy that is responsible for Jesus's betrayal in the Gospels (Matt. 27:18; Mark 15:10), appears in lists of vices that should never characterize a Christian's life (Rom. 1:29; Gal. 5:21 [cf. the verbal form in v. 26]; 1 Pet. 2:1), and is the root of quarrels and malice (1 Tim. 6:4; Titus 3:3) and even competitive preaching (Phil. 1:15).[42] Taken alone, the New Testament evidence casts a decisive vote for the phrase ἐπιποθεῖ πρὸς φθόνον to be translated with the negative connotations of an expression like "envies intensely." Φθόνος does not appear at all in the books of the Septuagint that form the Protestant Old Testament canon. However, φθόνος *can* be found in intertestamental apocryphal and pseudepigraphal writings. Because of these writings' close proximity in time to the New Testament and James's probable familiarity with them, the appearances there become a significant factor for understanding the usage in our current context.

The most significant feature to note in intertestamental usage is that φθόνος and ζῆλος are sometimes used interchangeably (cf. 1 Macc. 8:16; T. *Simeon* 5.4; T. *Gad* 7.2).[43] The reader of James has seen the ζῆλος word group before

40. See further Craig L. Blomberg and Mariam J. Kamell, *James* (Grand Rapids: Zondervan, 2008), 190–93, and the literature cited there. Even as it stands, we have simplified the issues by eliminating the comparatively little-held options of treating vv. 5a and 5b as separate sentences, and/or seeing one or both of these individual clauses as rhetorical questions.

41. In our present case, the word studies of ἐπιποθέω and φθόνος are helpful, but the definition ultimately depends on the literary context—a context that is partly defined by the meaning of the words ἐπιποθεῖ and πρὸς φθόνον.

42. Scriptural references were found in John R. Kohlenberger III, Edward W. Goodrick, and James A. Swanson, *The Greek-English Concordance to the New Testament, with the New International Version* (Grand Rapids: Zondervan, 1997). Once the references were located, we grouped them into categories that provide succinct summaries of the word use. This habit is helpful in any word study where the word appears more than a few times.

43. Douglas J. Moo, *The Letter of James* (Grand Rapids and Cambridge: Eerdmans; Leicester: Apollos, 2000), 190.

and each time has been warned that it is a less-than-admirable quality in a believer (as a noun ["jealousy"] in 3:14, 16; as a verb ["covet"] in 4:2). It would perhaps be easiest to say that James must be speaking of the human spirit that envies intensely because he has used the word with such negative overtones, and in close proximity to the occurrence in 4:5. However, Old Testament, extrabiblical, and New Testament uses of ζῆλος are not quite so homogeneous. Some of the uses in all three historical periods do show some of the negative overtones that are prevalent in the word's usage in the book of James. Yet it should be noted that in Old Testament, extrabiblical, and New Testament appearances, ζῆλος is used also of an appropriate attitude for humanity's pursuit of God and his will (e.g., Num. 25:11; Ps. 69:9 [68:10 LXX]; 119:139 [118:139 LXX]; Song 8:6), and in the Old Testament it is frequently attributed to God himself as his righteous response to Israel's breach of his covenant with them (e.g., Deut. 29:20 [29:19 LXX]; 2 Kings 19:31; Ezek. 16:38; 23:25). In the New Testament, Paul commends some of those to whom he writes for their ζῆλος (Rom. 10:2; 2 Cor. 7:7; 9:2)[44] and claims that he himself is jealous for his hearers with a godly jealousy (2 Cor. 11:2). While the contrasting connotations for ζῆλος do not lend themselves to a definitive understanding of its use in James 4, they open up the possibility that, although James has used the word negatively thus far, he could choose to use it positively in a different context. This in turn allows for the option that φθόνος, especially if used of God, is a permissible character trait.

A study of ἐπιποθέω is needed next to help the interpreter zero in on the specific meaning of these difficult verses. All the New Testament occurrences are unambiguously positive, conveying a longing for worthy things, most often (in the epistles) indicating the mutual longing between Paul and his audiences to see each other (Rom. 1:11; 2 Cor. 9:14; Phil. 1:8; 1 Thess. 3:6; 2 Tim. 1:4; cf. also Phil. 2:26). Peter uses it to command his readers to crave spiritual milk that nourishes a believer into the fullness of his or her salvation (1 Pet. 2:2), while 2 Corinthians 5:2 finds Paul longing not to be unclothed (in death) but further clothed (in the resurrection). It seems, with the exclusively positive usage of ἐπιποθέω and the capability of ζῆλος to function positively where context allows, φθόνος too can be viewed as a positive, divine character trait. If God can display a holy jealousy, he can surely disclose a holy envy. It seems that the best way to take our disputed expression in James 4:5 is as "longs jealously."[45] Now we must turn to the ambiguous subject of the verb ἐπιποθεῖ.

Literary context analysis will be the most helpful tool here, which will in turn influence our decision on whether τὸ πνεῦμα is functioning as the

44. It is notable for our purposes that in Rom. 13:13 Paul prohibits dissension and jealousy (ζῆλος), using the same word he used positively in Rom. 10:2. This certainly leaves the door open for James to use the same idea in different ways, as his immediate literary context allows.

45. So already A. T. Robertson, *Grammar of the Greek New Testament in the Light of Historical Research*, 4th ed. (Nashville: Broadman, 1934), 626.

subject or direct object, and whether it is referring to the human spirit or the Holy Spirit. A look at James 4:1–4, the immediately preceding context for the puzzling verse 5, reveals that the community is under James's scrutiny for quarrelsome and anticommunity behavior.[46] But right before we move into the sticky part of the passage in verse 5, James twice introduces the idea of enmity with God, putting God as a central character in these verses. Since verse 5 begins with the contrastive connective ἤ (or), it is clear that James intends to support the idea he has just introduced in verse 4 with the material in verses 5–6. Therefore, after introducing the idea that people who choose friendship with the world severely compromise their relationship with God, James turns to explain precisely why enmity with God is a bad idea, namely because of God's divine jealousy for the hearts of humans, when the human propensity is often to give their heart to the world.

With the word study conducted and literary context considered, several options for translation of the entire phrase emerge: (1) The first option takes the subject of ἐπιποθεῖ to be God. The entire verse is then rendered, "Or do you think that Scripture says in vain, 'God jealously desires the spirit he caused to dwell in us'?" This fits well in a context in which the audience is aligning itself with the world and so making itself an enemy of God. (2) The second interpretation differs only in its understanding of τὸ πνεῦμα as "the [Holy] Spirit," who dwells within us as believers. This seems less likely, for it would be odd for God jealously to desire his own Spirit. Indeed, the only other place where James uses πνεῦμα is in reference to the deadness of the human body in the absence of the human spirit, the element that animates human life (James 2:26). (3) The third option recognizes the ambiguity of the key words but favors viewing ἐπιποθεῖ πρὸς φθόνον as a negative action, so that the [human] spirit "envies intensely." This makes τὸ πνεῦμα the nominative subject of the sentence, leaving the verb without a direct object. The entire verse would thus read, "Or do you think that Scripture says in vain, 'The [human] spirit which he caused to dwell in us envies intensely'?" Because one word study seems definitive in supporting (1) and the other word studies and literary analysis certainly allow for (1), we would tentatively agree with translations such as the TNIV and NRSV in following the first option listed above: God desires the loyalty of human hearts, the affections of the spirit that he created and placed in them.[47]

46. On which, see esp. Luke T. Johnson, "Friendship with the World/Friendship with God: A Study of Discipleship in James," in *Discipleship in the New Testament*, ed. Fernando Segovia (Philadelphia: Fortress, 1985), 166–83.

47. For a full discussion of the strengths and weaknesses of each of the various options, see Richard Bauckham, "The Spirit of God in Us Loathes Envy: James 4:5," in *The Holy Spirit and Christian Origins*, ed. Graham N. Stanton, Bruce W. Longenecker, and Stephen C. Barton (Grand Rapids and Cambridge: Eerdmans, 2004), 270–81. But Bauckham's own creative proposal seems unlikely at several points.

But we are still not finished with the interpretive problem of the verse. To maintain this interpretation, we must be able to account for the apparent reference to the Old Testament. The formula ἡ γραφὴ λέγει (the Scripture says) in its other appearances in the New Testament overwhelmingly favors a direct and identifiable quotation of the Old Testament in the words that follow (though see John 7:38 for a notable exception). As mentioned earlier, the problem lies in the fact that the words that follow James's introduction cannot be found either in the Old Testament or in any existing extracanonical writing. Some scholars have hypothesized that James is citing some unknown version of the Old Testament[48] or some lost apocryphal document.[49] These hypotheses are not falsifiable, but neither are they highly likely, especially since all other Old Testament quotations in James can be found in extant versions of the Old Testament, particularly of the LXX. Even those scholars who support one of these options admit that they do so because they find no better option available, not because their stance proves terribly convincing.[50]

A different sort of proposal posits that the words that follow James's introduction are intended to capture only the gist of what a specific passage of Scripture teaches. Because we understand the passage to mean that God jealously desires the human spirit he caused to live in us, there is the possibility that the words allude to a principle that presents itself consistently throughout the Pentateuch and the Prophets (Exod. 20:5; 34:14; Deut. 4:24; Zech. 8:2): God is jealous for his people and he will not tolerate those who consistently relegate him to the periphery of their thoughts and desires.[51]

A recent proposal understands λέγει as introducing an indirect quotation in 5b–6a, so that πρὸς φθόνον ἐπιποθεῖ τὸ πνεῦμα ὃ κατῴκισεν ἐν ἡμῖν, μείζονα δὲ δίδωσιν χάριν is a paraphrase of the direct Old Testament quotation in James 4:6b-c: ὁ θεὸς ὑπερηφάνοις ἀντιτάσσεται, ταπεινοῖς δὲ δίδωσιν χάριν. The result is that "the direct quote that in the New Testament typically follows immediately after the verb of speaking is delayed, but the standard formula does still prepare for a direct citation. What intervenes is an interpretive gloss, a directed paraphrase of the Proverbs 3:34 scripture."[52] The difficult "quota-

48. James H. Ropes, *A Critical and Exegetical Commentary on the Epistle of St. James* (New York: Charles Scribner's Sons, 1916), 262.

49. Peter H. Davids, *The Epistle of James* (Grand Rapids: Eerdmans, 1982), 162; Martin Dibelius, *James*, trans. Heinrich Greeven, 11th rev. ed. (Philadelphia: Fortress, 1976), 222.

50. Cf. the concession made by Davids, *James*, 162: "Naturally, such a hypothesis can hardly be proved since the text is unknown, yet it is probably the best suggestion to date in that . . . no more concrete suggestion has proved acceptable."

51. As just noted, for another New Testament example of a passage that quotes Old Testament ideas using a direct quote formula, see Jesus's words in John 7:38 (cf. also Matt. 2:23 and Gal. 3:22). No single Old Testament passage matches John's words here, but see the ideas in Isa. 58:11 and Proverbs 18:4. For the full argument, see Craig B. Carpenter, "James 4:5 Reconsidered," *New Testament Studies* 46 (2000): 198.

52. Ibid., 200.

tion" in verse 5b then serves as a transitional interpretive paraphrase of the quotation to come that moves James from his previous argument and paves the way for James to cite Proverbs 3:34 directly, to bolster his overall argument. It also makes good sense of James's call to repentance in verses 7–10.[53]

Of the three options (lost Old Testament or apocryphal work, Old Testament allusion, or indirect quotation used to introduce Prov. 3:34 quotation), we find the hypothesis of a lost work to be least convincing precisely because we have no actual positive evidence in its favor. Given that we have two other less speculative positions, this more speculative option should be the first to be jettisoned. At this point in the decision-making process, we believe the exegete stands on defensible ground with either of the remaining approaches. The third option may be slightly more favorable because it makes sense of the introduction that in every other case is followed by a direct quotation. However, a strong enough case can be made that James alludes merely to a theme of Scripture that neither of us is willing to "go to the wall" for the third option. Still, we hope we have demonstrated that rigorous exegetical work can help the most probable interpretations surface.

John 3:3–5

As we noted earlier, there is another kind of disagreement that creates complex interpretive problems. This one is subtle because it may not emerge just from a cursory study of the text or recent secondary literature. However, delving further into the history of interpretation may help unveil additional options. Where there are differing exegetical approaches, there is also an interpretive problem of some sort.

On the one hand, survey of the most recent scholarship on John 3:3–5 will show a fair consensus rejecting the view that the rebirth for which Jesus calls in 3:3, 5 refers (at least in the context of the historical Jesus) to the Christian rite of baptism.[54] On the other hand, most of the church fathers and other commentators throughout history have strongly believed that if not Jesus

---

53. The grammatical difficulty with this decision is that the statement lacks the ὅτι after λέγει that is typical for introducing indirect discourse. For full explanation on how translation as an indirect quote can still be an option in the absence of ὅτι in v. 5, see ibid., 200–201.

54. As recently as the publication of D. A. Carson's major commentary on John in 1991, we can read that "the simple word 'water' is understood by the majority of contemporary commentators to refer to Christian baptism, though there is little agreement amongst them on the relationship between 'water' and 'Spirit'" (Carson, *The Gospel according to John* [Grand Rapids: Eerdmans; Leicester: Apollos, 1991], 192). Since his work, it is difficult to find an influential commentary that is convinced that baptism, either Christian baptism or John the Baptist's baptism, is in view in Jesus's words. Recent commentators reason with Carson that if baptism is in fact in view, it is only secondary to a more primary message that we will expound below in the text of this chapter. Carson, in turn, is indebted to his former teaching assistant, Linda L. Belleville ("'Born of Water and Spirit': John 3:5," *Trinity Journal* 2 [1981]: 125–41) for his preferred interpretation of the text.

than certainly John the Evangelist did intend to refer to water baptism in these two verses. Put differently, the patristic authors often appeared to attribute to biblical characters interpretations that could only have developed at a later time without differentiating the two time periods. And while there is contemporary consensus on what Jesus *did not* mean in these verses, there is much less agreement as to what he *did* mean. Again the interpreter encounters multiple levels of issues. Have we become too enamored with the notion that contemporary scholarly interpretations are necessarily the best ones? Or were there factors in antiquity that kept previous eras of commentators from seeing the Scripture "correctly" at this point? When tempted to write off ancient authors as less educated or intellectually inferior, let us consider the words of church historian Robert Grant:

> We sometimes think that textual, literary, and historical criticism were created in the eighteenth and nineteenth centuries, or that at any rate they were not previously applied to the gospels. By this convenient fiction we can present ourselves with a picture of early Christianity in which we can see faith constantly triumphing over intelligence—a picture attractive, for different reasons, both to the very orthodox and to the very unorthodox. Such an image, either of the ancient world in general or of ancient Christianity in particular, is thoroughly distorted.[55]

If leading orthodox interpreters in eras past have come to conclusions other than ours today, it is not due to intellectual inferiority or lack of discipline. It often has more to do with the lack of developed literary tools and accessibility to wide-ranging information to the degree that we now enjoy. It may be philosophical or cultural factors that biased them in a particular direction, but we dare not discount the possibility that the same has happened to our generation. We must evaluate each proposal, one at a time, on its own merits.

In the case of John 3:3, 5 on being "born again" (or "from above"), the advent and increasing practice of both historical-cultural and literary criticism were the paramount catalysts that encouraged contemporary interpreters to opt against understanding γεννηθῇ ἄνωθεν as a reference to baptism. When an interpreter reads the text in its original context as an accurate summary of a historical conversation that took place between Jesus and Nicodemus, baptism becomes less of a possibility. First, let us consider the literary context of the statement. True, baptism is mentioned in close proximity to 3:3–5 (3:22 and 4:1), and the Gospel has paired water and the Spirit in a baptismal context at the beginning of the account (1:33–34; yet one has to be familiar with the Synoptics to recognize this context). Those facts present themselves as sufficient literary-contextual evidence to understand John 3:5 as referring to baptism. But those are more remote literary contexts. What about the most immediate literary and historical contexts of 3:3–5? These deserve the exegete's fuller attention.

55. Robert M. Grant, *Earliest Lives of Jesus* (New York: Harper, 1961), 38.

The immediate context of Jesus's conversation with Nicodemus makes it difficult to sustain a baptismal interpretation of the text. While it is true that by the time John wrote his Gospel narrative, most likely in the 90s, the rite of Christian baptism was well recognized, that was not yet the case during Jesus's life. In the Gospels, Jesus's disciples are not commissioned to baptize, in the full Christian sense, until the Great Commission after his death and resurrection (Matt. 28:19–20). Additionally, there is no conclusive evidence that the baptism of John the Baptist was so well known that simple referral to water would have conjured up images of John's baptism of repentance for any of the characters in the narrative. In 4:1–3 we learn of a ministry of baptism under Jesus, but we have not arrived at that point in the narrative yet in 3:3–5. If a discourse on the necessity of baptism is the evangelist's final goal, then "this part of the account, at least, becomes a narrative fiction designed to instruct the church [i.e., at a later date] on the importance of baptism."[56] This ultimately would render John a confused storyteller, inasmuch as a few verses later in the conversation (3:10) Jesus is reprimanding Nicodemus for not understanding something that he would not have been able to understand anyway.

However, "born of water and the Spirit" could very easily have led Nicodemus, who was well versed in the Hebrew Scriptures, to recall Ezekiel 36:25–27. These verses recount the promise that in the days of God's new covenant with Israel he would, metaphorically, "sprinkle clean water on" them, cleanse them from all their impurities, and give them a new heart and a new S/spirit. This fits the immediate context of the demand from Jesus, as the one ushering in the messianic age, needed by even as revered a Jewish leader as Nicodemus. By employing carefully the two critical tools of literary context and historical-cultural background, the tide in interpretation of these verses has turned so that a new consensus is reached.[57] So when an interpreter encounters a drastic change in interpretation, he or she may wish to discern if a new exegetical tool entered the scene and will certainly want to weigh the merits of both the traditional and latest interpretation, applying tools to decide which argument makes the most sense in context.

Matthew 2:15

A final illustration raises the whole vexed question of the seemingly unusual uses of the Old Testament in the New. Large books have been devoted to this

---

56. Ibid.

57. For a good sample of the most prominent approaches in the ongoing discussion about this passage, see Carson, *John*, 191–95. In consulting his survey, try to recognize many of the literary-critical steps we have used thus far to see how exegetes solve the problem. There is a grammatical study and word study that help clarify the issue, and also more study of the literary context that takes into account relevant Old Testament passages. The interpretation that sees Ezek. 36 as the key appears to have garnered a majority of contemporary support.

topic alone, and it lies outside of our scope to do more than introduce the issue here and refer readers to fuller treatments for more detailed study.[58] Sometimes the New Testament writer is not intending to evoke an Old Testament text's original meaning but is simply reusing its language in a new situation. Sometimes the author is giving the text a new application. Often the text may vary in wording from the Hebrew Bible because the author is following the LXX, creating a fresh translation from the Hebrew, or mirroring a targum (one of the later paraphrases of the Hebrew Bible) or some other Jewish tradition.[59] But even when it speaks of a certain text being "fulfilled" in the events of Jesus's life either at his first or second coming, we need to recognize that both the Hebrew and Greek words for fulfill (מָלֵא and πληρόω, respectively) can mean something more akin to our "fill full."[60] More precisely, an understanding of typology can go a long way in helping interpreters make sense of New Testament fulfillment quotations that seem to have little, if anything, to do with events previously predicted.[61]

A classic example appears in the infancy narratives of Matthew's Gospel. Do Matthew 2:15 and Hosea 11:1, the verse Matthew here quotes, teach anything similar? It seems a simple question, but it is really rather loaded. The words of each passage are the same, but their meanings are quite different in their respective contexts. In Hosea, the prophet writes, "Out of Egypt I called my son," referring to Israel's exodus from slavery in Egypt. However, when Matthew picks up and employs the same words, it is not Israel being called out of Egypt, it is Jesus. Matthew is using the verse to refer to the return of the Christ child and his family to Israel after they fled to Egypt at the time of Herod the Great's massacre of the babies in and around Bethlehem. And how

58. See Walter C. Kaiser, *The Uses of the Old Testament in the New* (1985; repr. Eugene, OR: Wipf & Stock, 2001); D. A. Carson and H. G. M. Williamson, eds., *It Is Written: Scripture Citing Scripture* (Cambridge: Cambridge University Press, 1988); Richard N. Longenecker, *Biblical Exegesis in the Apostolic Period*, 2nd ed. (Grand Rapids: Eerdmans; Vancouver: Regent College Publishing, 1999); Craig A. Evans, ed., *The Interpretation of Scripture in Early Judaism and Christianity: Studies in Language and Tradition* (Sheffield: Sheffield Academic Press, 2000); Stanley E. Porter, ed., *Hearing the Old Testament in the New Testament* (Grand Rapids and Cambridge: Eerdmans, 2006); and esp. Gregory K. Beale and D. A. Carson, eds., *Commentary on the New Testament Use of the Old Testament* (Grand Rapids: Baker Academic; Nottingham: Apollos, 2007).

59. For the full range of options, see Darrell L. Bock, "Evangelicals and the Use of the Old Testament in the New: Part 1," *Bibliotheca Sacra* 142 (1985): 209–23; for a proposed method by Bock, see idem, "Evangelicals and the Use of the Old Testament in the New: Part 2," *Bibliotheca Sacra* 142 (1985): 306–19. See also Moisés Silva, "The New Testament Use of the Old Testament: Text Form and Authority," in *Scripture and Truth*, ed. D. A. Carson and John D. Woodbridge (1983; repr. Grand Rapids: Baker, 1992), 147–65, 381–86.

60. J. R. Daniel Kirk, "Conceptualising Fulfillment in Matthew," *Tyndale Bulletin* 59 (2008): 77–98.

61. On which, see esp. Leonhard Goppelt, *Typos: The Typological Interpretation of the Old Testament in the New* (1982; repr. Eugene, OR: Wipf & Stock, 2002).

can this be viewed as a fulfillment of a prophecy when Hosea isn't even using future-tense verbs but speaking of a long-past action? It seems that Matthew has just used the Bible in a way that, if imitated by contemporary students of hermeneutics, would earn them a failing grade from their professors.

It will come as no surprise that scholarly opinion spans an entire spectrum when it comes to attempts to make sense of this phenomenon. On the one hand, Barnabas Lindars's approach is virtually equivalent to claiming that the New Testament authors often quoted the Old Testament Scriptures "by ripping texts out of their contexts, abusing them gloriously, repeatedly, and perversely to justify their Christian presuppositions."[62] On the other hand, some are willing simply to give the New Testament authors the benefit of the doubt, passing the interpretive buck by glossing over their strange uses of the Old Testament in the New. Such commentators are willing to concede that they do not know what the New Testament author was trying to accomplish by using the text in such a manner, while simultaneously reaffirming that God knows, and therefore it must be right.[63] Certainly the student will do well to find some middle ground for interpretation that neither frames the evangelists in such a poor light nor claims a shrouded mystery at the first sign of interpretive difficulty.

It is clear in this instance that the words in the original context do not have any predictive or messianic meaning as the prophet originally stated them. Many interpreters throughout history have tried to explain this phenomenon by asserting that Old Testament writers wrote with one intent but, through fuller revelation in later times, the words were picked up by New Testament authors and employed quite differently. This claim works only when God is credited with having something more in mind than what the original authors intended and the New Testament authors were the receptors of this later divine revelation. Such a view is frequently called *sensus plenior*. At first glance, it appears to be an orthodox way to answer the question of how the New Testament authors adapted Old Testament quotes for their own writing.[64] However, the implications for contemporary application are profound. If New Testament authors can use their Scripture (the Old Testament) in ways that

62. This summary of Lindars's thesis from his book *New Testament Apologetic: The Doctrinal Significance of Old Testament Quotations* (Philadelphia: Westminster, 1961) was offered by D. A. Carson in the second of three lectures for the European Leadership Forum on the use of the Old Testament in the New. See http://www.euroleadershipresources.org/Media/Audio/Don_Carson-Use_of_OT_in_NT_2.mp3 (accessed January 19, 2010).

63. Ibid. Even an interpreter as sensible as Richard N. Longenecker argues that we are not allowed to do what the biblical interpreters did in our hermeneutics because we are not inspired. See his "Can We Reproduce the Exegesis of the New Testament?" *Tyndale Bulletin* 21 (1970): 3–38.

64. For a very cautious, evangelical appropriation of *sensus plenior*, see Douglas J. Moo, "The Problem of *Sensus Plenior*," in *Hermeneutics, Authority, and Canon*, ed. D. A. Carson and John D. Woodbridge (1986; repr. Eugene, OR: Wipf & Stock, 2005), 175–211.

were never intended by the original writers and never understandable by the original audiences, there is very little stopping the contemporary interpreter from looking at any portion of both the Old and New Testaments and applying it with unconstrained creativity. The best solution is to understand the ancient Jewish and Greek use of typology. The word τύπος (*typos*, "type") means a pattern or model. One helpful definition is "the recognition of a correspondence between New and Old Testament events, based on a conviction of the unchanging character of the principles of God's working, and a consequent understanding and description of the New Testament event in terms of the Old Testament model."[65] In the theistic worldview of the ancient Mediterranean world, the assumption was that God revealed himself in consistent, discernible ways. For the Christian, it could not have been coincidence that, just as the children of Israel had to come out of Egypt when God gave Moses the revelation on Mount Sinai, now again Jesus, the inaugurator of the new covenant, had to return to Israel from Egypt before he began his ministry. The same God must be disclosing himself in both contexts. The events of old are being "filled full" or given additional meaning, but it is meaning consistent with and even analogous to the original meaning.[66] The apologetic is less straightforward than with direct predictive prophecy and its fulfillment, but no less powerful.

Conclusion

We have only begun to scratch the surface with our examples of the more complex and synthetic issues we have categorized simply as "interpretive problems." Although these issues cannot be solved with a one-step or one-tool methodology, like those surveyed in previous chapters, one element remains consistent. The student must canvass as many of the suggestions by others as possible, compile the various arguments offered, assess their respective strengths and weaknesses, add in his or her own additional lines of inquiry, and come to a conclusion, however tentative, as to the most probable solution. On particularly difficult issues or with those that have a plethora of proposed solutions, ranking the probabilities of the various options often proves helpful. Less likely possibilities can be eliminated first and then more serious scrutiny given to those that remain. The more complex or multifaceted the exegetical conundrum and/or the more competing, orthodox alternatives that seem to

---

65. R. T. France, *The Gospel according to Matthew: A Commentary* (Leicester: Inter-Varsity Press; Grand Rapids: Eerdmans, 1985), 40.

66. For a detailed exposition on the method chosen here and a fuller treatment of the number of alternative solutions offered by scholars for this passage specifically, see Tracy L. Howard, "The Use of Hosea 11:1 in Matthew 2:15: An Alternative Solution," *Bibliotheca Sacra* 143 (1986): 314–328. Cf. also Dan G. McCartney and Peter Enns, "Matthew and Hosea: A Response to John Sailhamer," *Westminster Theological Journal* 63 (2001): 97–105.

have strong support, the more the interpreter, especially the novice, should want to be cautious of embracing any one solution too dogmatically. There is much to be commended in the preacher or teacher who announces, "Here is where I am in my study of this issue. Good and godly interpreters have not achieved consensus. I may be wrong, but this is why I come to the conclusions I do at this time. Think through the issues and decide for yourselves. And check back with me a decade from now to see if I've changed my mind."

8

Outlining

In dealing with literary contexts of texts, we have already introduced the concept of determining the structure of a biblical book and its constituent sections. In dealing with grammar, we have shown how attention to the connective words that link sentences and clauses can help to disclose a basic outline of a short paragraph. Now it is time to reflect more systematically and in detail on how to produce what is often called an exegetical outline from a passage of the New Testament.

Grammatical Layouts for Students with Greek

There are a variety of forms of diagramming sentence structure that work in both English and Greek. One type of form requires identifying how every word in a sentence functions and then placing it on a line or line segment that represents that function. A common approach is to draw a horizontal line beginning at the left-hand margin of a page. From left to right, write the subject of the first clause of the sentence on it; bisect the horizontal line with a short perpendicular line; write the verb on the next part of the horizontal line; if there is a direct object, create another perpendicular line that comes down to the horizontal line without going past it, and then write the direct object. Or, if a predicate complement appears instead, make the dividing line a slight diagonal and then write the complement. Then use diagonal lines angling away from the horizontal line and turning into parallel horizontal lines above and below the main clause to document various modifiers. Thus, "The hungry girl ate the large hamburger" would look like this diagram:

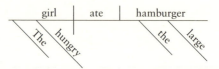

One can quickly imagine how complex the diagram of a sentence of more standard length would become. Numerous textbooks have introduced this kind of diagramming, and Bible software programs are starting to include it.[1] It is our opinion, however, that in the vast majority of instances students do not need this amount of detail. Certainly the exegetical dividends yielded do not seem to correspond to the energy expended first to learn and then to apply the method.

However, a simplified form of a grammatical layout that focuses primarily on entire clauses can be of great benefit in quickly discerning the structure of a passage. An outline that merely places each new independent or dependent clause on a new horizontal line, with a vertical arrow drawn from the beginning of a dependent clause to the word in the independent clause modified, can provide a very helpful visual overview of the passage. An outline can further emerge from the main sections of the text by keeping independent clauses flush with the left-hand margin, while indenting dependent clauses appropriately, and perhaps using some form of bracketing to indicate when two or more independent clauses belong together in a single sentence. Main points in the outline may be labeled with Roman numerals, followed by items labeled with capital letters for the next level of subdivision, followed by entries beginning with Arabic numerals, and so on.[2]

No one inspired version of this method works best in all situations. Outlines were made for students, not students for outlines. But something akin to the following can prove quite useful for a large variety of passages.

---

1. E.g., John D. Grassmick, *Principles and Practice of Greek Exegesis*, rev. ed. (Dallas: Dallas Theological Seminary, 1976); Jay A. Smith, "Sentence Diagramming, Clausal Layouts and Exegetical Outlining: Tracing the Argument," in *Interpreting the New Testament Text: Introduction to the Art and Science of Exegesis*, ed. Darrell L. Bock and Buist M. Fanning (Wheaton: Crossway, 2006), esp. 75–90; Accordance; BibleWorks; and Logos Bible Software. Smith makes a good case for the value of this kind of diagramming. In an ideal world (or in a four-year ThM program), it makes good sense. Most students in shorter degree programs— i.e., no longer than the standard three-year MDiv—probably can't afford the amount of time needed to master the method.

2. With slight modifications, cf. Smith, "Sentence Diagramming," esp. 90–100; Walter C. Kaiser Jr., *Toward an Exegetical Theology: Biblical Exegesis for Preaching and Teaching* (Grand Rapids: Baker, 1981), 99–104, 165–81; Gordon D. Fee, *New Testament Exegesis: A Handbook for Students and Pastors*, 3rd ed. (Louisville: Westminster John Knox, 2002), 41–58; George H. Guthrie and J. Scott Duvall, *Biblical Greek Exegesis* (Grand Rapids: Zondervan, 1998), 27–37; and William J. Larkin, *Greek Is Great Gain: A Method for Exegesis and Exposition* (Eugene, OR: Wipf & Stock, 2008), 48–56.

Sidebar 8.1

Diagramming Greek Sentences

1. On the main line, identify the independent clause (including words or phrases that serve as subject, verb, and direct or indirect objects or predicate complements). Include any one-word modifiers (e.g., individual articles, adjectives, adverbs).
   - Use parentheses or brackets to indicate multiword expressions that function together as a single part of the sentence.
   - Preserve the Greek word order, even when it conflicts with the standard English word order.
2. Above the main line, slightly indented, include conjunctions that connect the clause to what precedes (including postpositive conjunctions) as well as vocative expressions.
3. Below the main line, indent prepositional phrases far enough so that an arrow can be drawn from just before them up to the words in the main line that they modify. Also include on this line any other multiword phrases that elaborate either the subject or the predicate, especially if there is any ambiguity as to what they modify, as well as all subordinate or dependent clauses.
4. Use parallel lines to "stack" parallel parts of speech or parts of a sentence beneath one another, with connecting conjunctions written halfway between and indented slightly farther.
5. Use an equal sign to indicate apposition between two words or expressions written on the same line.
6. Use vertical lines, brackets, or parentheses in the left-hand margin to show that two parallel independent clauses belong together.

A Helpful Method of Diagramming

To begin with, identify the independent clause, complete with subject, verb, and any objects (direct or indirect) or predicate complements that it may contain. On the same horizontal line, put one-word modifiers as well, like individual articles, adjectives, or adverbs. Where entire clauses function as a subject, object, or complement, they can remain on this line too. Putting them in parentheses or brackets can help to show that the multiword expressions contained in them function as a single slot-filler in terms of the parts of a sentence. Preserve the word order of the Greek text for everything on this main line, even if it does not appear in the common *English* word order of subject-verb-object(s)/complement.

Above the main line, slightly indented, can appear any conjunctions that connect the clause to what precedes, including postpositive conjunctions like δέ or γάρ, as well as any vocative expressions that begin with a direct address to the audience. Below the main line, indent prepositional phrases far enough so that an arrow can be drawn from just before them up to the words in the main line that they modify. Prepositional phrases by themselves are either adverbial or adjectival,[3] so normally they will modify either a verb or a noun, but recall that adjectival modifiers can occasionally modify pronouns, and adverbial modifiers occasionally modify adjectives or even other adverbs. Below the main line will also appear any other multiword phrases that elaborate either the subject or the predicate, especially if there is any ambiguity as to what they modify.[4] All subordinate or dependent clauses (multiword expressions with both a subject and a predicate that cannot stand alone) must likewise go below what they modify, with arrows drawn up to the words modified. Like prepositional phrases, dependent clauses will usually be either adjectival or adverbial and thus modify the same kinds of words as just noted.[5] Some clauses may be made up of nothing more than a participle or an infinitival phrase, since these two "moods" are really hybrid forms that have both nominal and verbal features inherent in them.[6] More commonly they will introduce longer clauses that can be kept together on a subordinate line, unless they in turn have dependent phrases or clauses within them.

Where two or more parallel parts of speech or parts of a sentence occur, students may want to "stack" them on parallel lines below one another, with any connecting conjunctions put halfway in between and indented slightly farther. This offers a very quick and convenient visual reminder of the presence of the parallelism. Apposition can be denoted by keeping the words or expression that refer to the same entity together on the same horizontal line but separating them with an equal sign. Vertical lines, brackets, or parentheses can be used at the left-hand margin to show that two parallel independent clauses belong together. Because the goal of these grammatical layouts is to preserve the structure of the text visually, some students may wish to place subordinate elements that occur *prior* to the words they modify on lines *above* what they modify and then draw the arrow preceding the subordinate element *down* to the mainline. Similarly, where modifying words interrupt the terms that go on a given line, students may appreciate inserting ellipses (. . .) to show that something has been left out and moved to a different place in the diagram. Where the Greek text itself contains an ellipsis—a word or words that must

3. Richard A. Young, *Intermediate New Testament Greek: A Linguistic and Exegetical Approach* (Nashville: Broadman & Holman, 1994), 87–88. When introduced by an article, prepositional phrases function to create a larger nominal phrase (i.e., a noun equivalent).

4. As, esp., when the case ending of the modifier does not match that of a noun or pronoun modified. This will normally happen when a noun is qualified by another noun in the genitive or dative case rather than by an adjective.

5. When they are substantival, they simply replace a noun (as subject, object, complement, etc.) and are diagrammed exactly as the corresponding noun would be.

6. Daniel B. Wallace, *Greek Grammar beyond the Basics: An Exegetical Syntax of the New Testament* (Grand Rapids: Zondervan, 1996), 588–89, 613–17.

be supplied in order to complete the thought of a given sentence—a helpful approach is to insert square brackets [ ], with the necessary word or words added inside the brackets.

A Brief Example: Romans 3:25–26

Lists of instructions quickly overwhelm the novice, so it is best to stop at this point and work through a couple of illustrations of the method. Sometimes a single sentence may be complicated enough that it helps to outline it so as to discover its main clause or clauses along with subordinate elements and what they modify. Romans 3:25–26 form such a sentence in the Greek. It occurs in the midst of the theologically crucial paragraph that unpacks the thesis of this, the most theologically rich and detailed of all Paul's letters.[7] Indeed, grammatically the sentence begins with verse 22b and includes the famous verse 23: "for all sinned and are falling short of the glory of God."[8] The sentence continues in verse 24 with a participle of attendant circumstances, grammatically subordinate but conceptually coordinate—"being justified" (or "and are being justified") "freely by his grace through the redemption that [is] in Christ Jesus." Verse 25 then starts with the relative pronoun "whom," which has Jesus as its antecedent. Because all of verses 25–26 will elaborate on this redemption that Christ affords us, if a modern translation is going to break this long, unwieldy sentence at any point, it will be here. The name Jesus (or Christ) can then be substituted for "whom" without any change in meaning. But how are we to understand verses 25–26?

The Greek reads:

[25]ὃν προέθετο ὁ θεὸς ἱλαστήριον διὰ [τῆς] πίστεως ἐν τῷ αὐτοῦ αἵματι εἰς ἔνδειξιν τῆς δικαιοσύνης αὐτοῦ διὰ τὴν πάρεσιν τῶν προγεγονότων ἁμαρτημάτων [26]ἐν τῇ ἀνοχῇ τοῦ θεοῦ, πρὸς τὴν ἔνδειξιν τῆς δικαιοσύνης αὐτοῦ ἐν τῷ νῦν καιρῷ, εἰς τὸ εἶναι αὐτὸν δίκαιον καὶ δικαιοῦντα τὸν ἐκ πίστεως Ἰησοῦ.

The subject, verb, and direct object all appear at the beginning of verse 25, conveniently enough: "God put forward whom [i.e., Jesus]." Ἰλαστήριον (propitiation) then functions as an adverbial accusative of manner.[9] God put Jesus forward *as* a propitiation. As a one-word modifier, it too can

---

7. Cf. C. E. B. Cranfield, *A Critical and Exegetical Commentary on the Epistle to the Romans*, vol. 1 (Edinburgh: T&T Clark, 1975), 199.

8. Unless otherwise indicated, the translations throughout the remainder of this chapter are the authors' own. Here, the verbs translated "sinned" and "are falling short" are aorist and present tense, respectively. The latter is thus more heavily marked (emphasized) according to the theory of verbal aspect. Typical English translations blur this distinction.

9. "Propitiation" is the best English translation of the Greek word, but it is little understood in modern English. Central to its meaning is the concept of a sacrifice that appeases God's wrath. See, e.g., Thomas R. Schreiner, *Romans* (Grand Rapids: Baker, 1998), 190–94.

stay on our main line. But now a long series of subordinate prepositional phrases appears: "through faith," "by his blood," "for a demonstration of his righteousness," "on account of the passing over of sins having been previously committed," "by the forbearance of God," "for the demonstration of his righteousness," and "in the present time." Finally, Paul shifts grammatical forms and concludes verse 26 with an adverbial articular infinitival clause of purpose—"in order that he might be just and justifying the one with faith in Jesus."[10]

The key issue here is what each subordinate phrase (and the final clause) modifies. Given that prepositional phrases can be either adjectival or adverbial, we must always be alert to the possibility of multiple options. Given that a sizable majority of the prepositional phrases in the New Testament appear to be adverbial, we should probably try that option first whenever there is ambiguity.[11] With the first phrase, "through faith," however, the only possible antecedent for an adverbial use is the preceding verb προέθετο ("put forward" or "set forth"). As Douglas Moo succinctly explains, "'Through faith' is not likely to modify 'set forth,' since faith was not the instrument through which God 'set forth' Christ as ἱλαστήριον. Rather, the phrase modifies ἱλαστήριον and indicates the means by which individuals appropriate the benefits of the sacrifice."[12] Particularly with translations that use "in" for the ἐν at the beginning of the next phrase and do not insert a comma before it, it is easy to imagine that Paul proceeds to refer to "faith in his blood." But nowhere else in Scripture is blood ever the object of anyone's faith, so it is best to take this ἐν as instrumental and translate it "by." "By his blood" is then adverbial, modifying "put forward." It is by means of Christ's blood, that is, his shed blood on the cross, that God put him forward as the atoning sacrifice for our sins.[13] Thus far, our diagram becomes:

ὃν προέθετο ὁ θεὸς ἱλαστήριον
⟍   ↑ διὰ [τῆς] πίστεως
   ⎸ ἐν τῷ αὐτοῦ αἵματι

The prepositional phrase "for a demonstration of his righteousness" clearly denotes a purpose, which is an adverbial function, so that εἰς ἔνδειξιν τῆς δικαιοσύνης αὐτοῦ must likewise modify προέθετο. In the next phrase, "on account of the passing over of sins having been previously committed,"

10. There is an important debate about the two uses of "faith" in this passage, as to whether they refer to people's faith in Christ or Christ's faithfulness to his mission, which lies outside the scope of our analysis and does not affect the grammatical layout.
11. Young, *Intermediate New Testament Greek*, 87.
12. Douglas J. Moo, *The Epistle to the Romans* (Grand Rapids and Cambridge: Eerdmans, 1996), 236.
13. Ibid., 237.

"on the account of" is another way to introduce an explanation or rationale for something, and hence we might naturally assume it would introduce another adverbial prepositional phrase. But God did not *put* Jesus *forward* as a propitiation because he had formerly overlooked sin so much as he *demonstrated* his righteousness in so doing.[14] By not having dealt fully with past sins, God could be thought of as unjust, but now he was demonstrating his justice. "For a demonstration," employing a verbal noun, is semantically equivalent to "in order to demonstrate." So "demonstration" can be modified by a prepositional phrase that is grammatically adjectival (because it modifies a noun) but conceptually more or less the same as an adverbial phrase. We must place "on account of the passing over of sins having been previously committed" underneath "demonstration." Our diagram grows to this:

ὃν προέθετο ὁ θεὸς ἱλαστήριον
↑   ↑ διὰ [τῆς] πίστεως
│ ἐν τῷ αὐτοῦ αἵματι
↑ εἰς ἔνδειξιν τῆς δικαιοσύνης αὐτοῦ
    ↑ διὰ τὴν πάρεσιν τῶν προγεγονότων ἁμαρτημάτων

We proceed to verse 26. "By [or in] the forbearance of God" goes naturally with the nearest antecedent clause, giving a rationale for or manner in which God overlooked previous sins. We should place ἐν τῇ ἀνοχῇ τοῦ θεοῦ underneath πάρεσιν, another verbal noun that, when modified, creates an adverbial sense to its adjectival modifier. "For the demonstration of his righteousness" repeats almost verbatim the earlier εἰς phrase, reiterating the same point and going back again to the activity of God's putting forward Christ. If we try to make it modify the activity in the immediately preceding phrase, we end up saying that his passing over sins demonstrated his righteousness, when in fact it was this activity that called that righteousness into question. This is the tipoff that tells us to look farther back in the sentence for what is being modified. "In the present time," though, goes very naturally with the phrase immediately preceding it. This "demonstration" of God's justice is occurring *now*. "In order that he might be just . . ." makes virtually the same point as the two prepositional phrases beginning with εἰς and πρός and should thus be drawn parallel to them. "Just" and "justifying" can be stacked and separated by their conjunction ("and"), while "with faith in Jesus"[15] modifies "the one." We are now ready to complete our grammatical layout of these two verses as follows:

14. Ibid., 237–38.
15. As noted above, justifying this translation goes beyond the scope of our purposes here. For those curious as to how we would do so, see, e.g., R. Barry Matlock, "Detheologizing the Πίστις Χριστοῦ Debate: Cautionary Remarks from a Lexical Semantic Perspective," *Novum Testamentum* 42 (2000): 1–23.

ὃν προέθετο ὁ θεὸς ἱλαστήριον
  ↑   ↑ διὰ [τῆς] πίστεως
  | ἐν τῷ αὐτοῦ αἵματι
  ↑ εἰς ἔνδειξιν τῆς δικαιοσύνης αὐτοῦ
  ↑   ↑διὰ τὴν πάρεσιν τῶν προγεγονότων ἁμαρτημάτων
  | ↑ ἐν τῇ ἀνοχῇ τοῦ θεοῦ
  | πρὸς τὴν ἔνδειξιν τῆς δικαιοσύνης αὐτοῦ
  ↑   ↑ ἐν τῷ νῦν καιρῷ
  | εἰς τὸ εἶναι αὐτὸν ⎡ δίκαιον
              ⎨ καὶ
              ⎣ δικαιοῦντα τὸν
                ↑ ἐκ πίστεως Ἰησοῦ

Visually, we may quickly recognize the main point: God put forward Christ as a propitiation. We see that this action is unpacked in two main ways: how this putting forward was done (by means of the crucifixion) and to what end it was done (to demonstrate God as righteous). The latter point, however, is by far the one Paul highlights because he uses three parallel expressions to say it three times. The first two of these times he further elaborates his remarks with phrases subordinate to the prepositional phrases that carry the repeated thought further. This demonstration (1) was necessary because of God's forbearance that led to him passing over past sins and (2) took place during Paul's day. The only subordinate clauses or phrases we have not accounted for are the first and the last, which create a nice inclusio on the manner in which people receive the benefits of Christ's atonement—through faith in him. What at the outset appeared to be at best a run-on sentence and at worst a jumbled mess has turned out to be coherent, carefully crafted, and a crucial centerpiece of Pauline soteriology.[16]

An Extended Example: James 1:2–8

We promised to return to James 1:5–8 when we introduced it in the context of its connective tissue in our chapter on grammar (chap. 6). Here we can treat all of verses 2 through 8, which the fourth edition of the UBS Greek New Testament keeps together as a single paragraph, to show how a grammatical layout can help us outline an entire passage of preachable length. If, for the sake of illustration, we adopt for the time being the punctuation of this UBS committee, we may begin by separating out individual sentences:

Πᾶσαν χαρὰν ἡγήσασθε, ἀδελφοί μου, ὅταν πειρασμοῖς περιπέσητε ποικίλοις, γινώσκοντες ὅτι τὸ δοκίμιον ὑμῶν τῆς πίστεως κατεργάζεται ὑπομονήν. (vv. 2–3)

---

16. See further, e.g., Thomas R. Schreiner, *Paul: Apostle of God's Glory in Christ* (Downers Grove, IL: InterVarsity; Leicester: Apollos, 2001), 202–3.

ἡ δὲ ὑπομονὴ ἔργον τέλειον ἐχέτω, ἵνα ἦτε τέλειοι καὶ ὁλόκληροι ἐν μηδενὶ λειπόμενοι. (v. 4)

Εἰ δέ τις ὑμῶν λείπεται σοφίας, αἰτείτω παρὰ τοῦ διδόντος θεοῦ πᾶσιν ἁπλῶς καὶ μὴ ὀνειδίζοντος καὶ δοθήσεται αὐτῷ. (v. 5)

αἰτείτω δὲ ἐν πίστει μηδὲν διακρινόμενος· ὁ γὰρ διακρινόμενος ἔοικεν κλύδωνι θαλάσσης ἀνεμιζομένῳ καὶ ῥιπιζομένῳ. (v. 6)

μὴ γὰρ οἰέσθω ὁ ἄνθρωπος ἐκεῖνος ὅτι λήμψεταί τι παρὰ τοῦ κυρίου, ἀνὴρ δίψυχος, ἀκατάστατος ἐν πάσαις ταῖς ὁδοῖς αὐτοῦ. (vv. 7–8)

We now proceed to separate each sentence into its individual clauses. The main, independent clause of the sentence spanning verses 2–3 is the command to "consider it all joy." The two subordinate clauses are adverbial, modifying the verb "consider": "whenever you encounter various trials" is temporal, while "knowing that the testing of your faith produces endurance" is causal.[17] Technically, this second clause itself contains the content clause "that the testing of your faith produces endurance," but a content clause, functioning like a giant direct object, can just stay on the main line with the subject and verb that go with it. The vocative expression of direct address, "my brothers [and sisters]," goes above the main line, slightly indented. So now we have this:

ἀδελφοί μου
πᾶσαν χαρὰν ἡγήσασθε
   ↑ ὅταν πειρασμοῖς περιπέσητε ποικίλοις
   ↑ γινώσκοντες [ὅτι τὸ δοκίμιον ὑμῶν τῆς πίστεως κατεργάζεται
   ὑπομονήν]

Verse 4 likewise contains an independent clause, followed by two dependent clauses. The main idea, again a command, but this time employing the *third-person imperative*, is "let endurance have its perfect work." The subordinate clauses are introduced by a ἵνα of purpose, creating a purpose, or telic, clause answering the question "Why?"[18] Like the dependent clauses in verses 2 and 3, it is again adverbial, modifying the command "let . . . have." To what end should we let endurance have its perfect effect? We should do so in order that we might be whole and complete. The second subordinate clause seems simply to restate the first one, only negatively rather than positively: so that we are

17. Douglas J. Moo, *The Letter of James* (Grand Rapids and Cambridge: Eerdmans; Leicester: Apollos, 2000), 54.
18. Ἵνα clauses can sometimes be content clauses or, rarely, result clauses. But a sizable majority are purpose clauses, so that should usually be the first categorization considered. For the occasional overlapping of these categories, see C. F. D. Moule, *An Idiom Book of New Testament Greek*, rev. ed. (Cambridge: Cambridge University Press, 1959), 142–46.

lacking in nothing.[19] It would be grammatically correct to diagram this sentence exactly like the first one, but if we want to illustrate visually the equation (in grammatical terms, the apposition) between the two clauses, we might choose to put both clauses on the same line separated by an equal sign:

> δὲ
>
> ἡ . . . ὑπομονὴ ἔργον τέλειον ἐχέτω
>
> ↑ ἵνα ἦτε [τέλειοι καὶ ὁλόκληροι] = [ἐν μηδενὶ
>   λειπόμενοι]

The two sets of brackets denote both that we have multiword predicate complements after ἦτε and that it is precisely these two collections of words that are in apposition to each other.

If we choose to go one step further and visually represent the parallelism between the two adjectives, τέλειοι and ὁλόκληροι, we would place them on parallel lines with the conjunction in between and slightly indented:

> τέλειοι
>   καὶ
> ὁλόκληροι

If we want to separate the prepositional phrase "in nothing" from the participle in the last clause, we could diagram it in this way:

> ↓ ἐν μηδενὶ
> λειπόμενοι

Notice that this time the subordinate expression goes above what it modifies, with the arrow drawn down, because it precedes the word it modifies in the order of the sentence. For users of the method who prefer always to see subordinate material *under* what is being modified, they can choose to diagram material that way and sacrifice the sequence of words in the text, visually speaking. However, the initial, simpler diagram above, which does not put either καὶ ὁλόκληροι or ἐν μηδενί on separate lines from the words they modify, still nicely communicates the basic structure of the sentence.

Verse 5 differs from the preceding two sentences in that it begins not with its main clause but with a dependent, conditional clause. All sentences of the form "if . . . then . . ." have the "if" clause as the subordinate clause, adverbially modifying the main clause, which may or may not have an explicit word for "then."[20] So "if anyone of you lacks wisdom" is the subordinate clause in

---

19. Cf. Ralph P. Martin, *James* (Waco: Word, 1986), 17.

20. Stanley E. Porter, *Idioms of the Greek New Testament* (Sheffield: Sheffield Academic Press, 1992), 254.

verse 5, while "let him [or her] ask" introduces the main clause. This third-person imperatival form of "ask" is in turn modified by the prepositional phrase "from God . . ." and "God" is further qualified by the compound (and thus parallel) adjectival participial clauses, "who gives to all generously [or single-mindedly]" and "without mocking [or reproaching]." The last two words of verse 5 form an independent clause all by themselves—"it will be given to him [or her]." But clearly this clause belongs together with the previous as a kind of cause-and-effect or conditional statement itself: "ask . . . and it will be given."[21] So even though these two words should start a new line flush with the left-hand margin with the "and" above and slightly indented, the whole verse belongs together via some kind of bracketing technique. Put all these observations together and James 1:5 should appear as:

δὲ
  ↓ εἰ . . . τις ὑμῶν λείπεται σοφίας
⌈ αἰτείτω
| ↑ παρὰ τοῦ . . . θεοῦ
| ↑ ⌈ διδόντος . . . πᾶσιν ἁπλῶς
⟨   ⟨ καὶ
| ⌊ μὴ ὀνειδίζοντος
| καὶ
⌊ δοθήσεται αὐτῷ

Verse 6 forms the fourth of our five sentences. The same main clause as for the majority of verse 5 is repeated—"let him [or her] ask." The asking is then modified by the short prepositional phrase "in faith." As in verse 4, there are two ways to envision the next dependent clause, "nothing doubting." It could be a second subordinate adverbial modifier stacked underneath "in faith" with the arrow similarly drawn up to "ask." But "nothing doubting" is really the flip side to "in faith," and therefore it is better understood as appositional to "in faith."[22] The second half of verse 6 could be viewed as an independent sentence, although UBS[4] uses a semicolon. Given our comments above on how verses 6b–8 can be seen as three parallel γάρ clauses (the last one elliptical) all modifying "ask" in verse 6a, for the sake of consistency in illustration we will indent verse 6b and treat it as dependent rather than independent: "for the one who doubts is like a wave of a sea." The pair of parallel participles "being blown and being tossed about" both modify "wave," so they will appear stacked underneath "wave" and separated by the "and." All this yields the following:

21. Robert Hanna, *A Grammatical Aid to the Greek New Testament* (Grand Rapids: Baker, 1983), 416, citing A. T. Robertson, *Grammar of the Greek New Testament in the Light of Historical Research*, 4th ed. (Nashville: Broadman, 1934).
22. Cf. James H. Ropes, *A Critical and Exegetical Commentary on the Epistle of St. James* (New York: Charles Scribner's Sons, 1916), 140.

δὲ
αἰτείτω
↑ ἐν πίστει = μηδὲν διακρινόμενος
↑ ὁ γὰρ διακρινόμενος ἔοικεν κλύδωνι θαλάσσης
↑ ⌠ ἀνεμιζομένῳ
  ⎨ καὶ
  ⌡ ῥιπιζομένῳ

Finally, we come to verses 7–8. Punctuated as in UBS[4], they create two independent clauses, asyndetically linked (i.e., without a coordinating conjunction), with the understood "That person is . . ." to be supplied at the beginning of verse 8.[23] But if we are right in suggesting that these are two additional γάρ clauses, then they would be both dependent on verse 6a underneath and intended to the same degree as verse 6b. The ellipsis to be filled in at the beginning of verse 8 would then be *"For* that person is." The clause "that he [or she] will receive anything" in verse 7 is a content clause, akin to a giant direct object of "suppose," while the prepositional phrase "from the Lord" modifies "receive"—answering the question "receive from where (or from whom)?" The adjectives "double-minded" and "unstable" in verse 8 could be stacked as a compound predicate complement or, as we have chosen, could be seen in apposition to each other, especially because James appears to have created the new adjective δίψυχος, literally "double-souled," and then helped to explain it by adding a synonym.[24] The prepositional phrase "in all his [or her] ways" then modifies "unstable." Verses 6–8 now appear thus:

δὲ
αἰτείτω
↑ ἐν πίστει = μηδὲν διακρινόμενος
↑ ὁ γὰρ διακρινόμενος ἔοικεν κλύδωνι θαλάσσης
↑ ⌠ ἀνεμιζομένῳ
  ⎨ καὶ
  ⌡ ῥιπιζομένῳ
↑ μὴ γὰρ οἰέσθω ὁ ἄνθρωπος ἐκεῖνος [ὅτι λήμψεταί τι
                                              ↑ παρὰ τοῦ κυρίου]
↑ [ἐστιν γὰρ] ἀνὴρ δίψυχος = ἀκατάστατος
                              ↑ ἐν πάσαις ταῖς ὁδοῖς αὐτοῦ

23. Here is an excellent example of the inclusive or generic use even of a noun like ἀνήρ (which typically means a "male"), since it is put in parallelism to the clearly inclusive or generic ἄνθρωπος in the preceding verse. Cf. Moo, *James*, 62; J. B. Bauer, "ἀνήρ, ἀνδρός," in *Exegetical Dictionary of the New Testament*, ed. Horst Balz and Gerhard Schneider, 3 vols. (Grand Rapids: Eerdmans, 1990–93), 1:98–99. In fact, Bauer's *first* definition observes, "'Ανήρ can denote any *human being."*

24. Cf. Stanley E. Porter, "Is Δίψυχος (James 1:8; 4:8) a 'Christian' Word?" *Biblica* 41 (1990): 469–98.

Put all of verses 2–8 together and we have this:

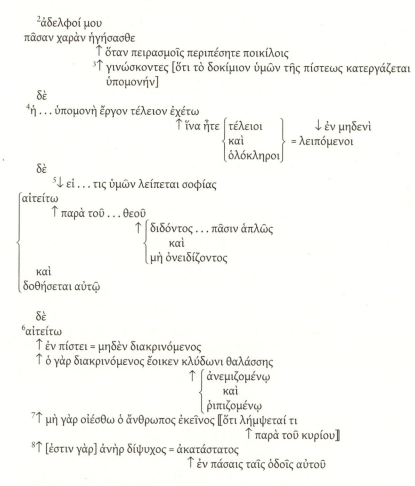

²ἀδελφοί μου
πᾶσαν χαρὰν ἡγήσασθε
  ↑ ὅταν πειρασμοῖς περιπέσητε ποικίλοις
   ³↑ γινώσκοντες [ὅτι τὸ δοκίμιον ὑμῶν τῆς πίστεως κατεργάζεται
       ὑπομονήν]
δὲ
⁴ἡ . . . ὑπομονὴ ἔργον τέλειον ἐχέτω
       ↑ ἵνα ἦτε ⎡τέλειοι ⎤   ↓ ἐν μηδενὶ
              ⎨καὶ   ⎬ = λειπόμενοι
              ⎣ὁλόκληροι⎦
δὲ
⁵↓ εἰ . . . τις ὑμῶν λείπεται σοφίας
⎡αἰτείτω
⎮ ↑ παρὰ τοῦ . . . θεοῦ
⎮   ↑ ⎡διδόντος . . . πᾶσιν ἁπλῶς
⎨   ⎨ καὶ
⎮   ⎣μὴ ὀνειδίζοντος
⎮ καὶ
⎣δοθήσεται αὐτῷ

δὲ
⁶αἰτείτω
  ↑ ἐν πίστει = μηδὲν διακρινόμενος
  ↑ ὁ γὰρ διακρινόμενος ἔοικεν κλύδωνι θαλάσσης
          ↑ ⎡ἀνεμιζομένῳ
            ⎨ καὶ
            ⎣ῥιπιζομένῳ
⁷↑ μὴ γὰρ οἰέσθω ὁ ἄνθρωπος ἐκεῖνος [[ὅτι λήμψεταί τι
                      ↑ παρὰ τοῦ κυρίου]]
⁸↑ [ἐστιν γὰρ] ἀνὴρ δίψυχος = ἀκατάστατος
       ↑ ἐν πάσαις ταῖς ὁδοῖς αὐτοῦ

Moving to an Exegetical Outline

We are now ready to turn our Greek diagram into an English outline. In some passages, beginning the process may be as simple as creating one main point in the English outline for each independent clause in the Greek and subdividing from there. As in Romans 3:25–26, Paul often writes in long-enough sentences that this procedure works for stretches of text that are not too large. James, however, with his more proverb-filled letter,[25] employs many short clauses, so it is important to ask first if any of our independent clauses

25. Indeed, the genre of James imbibes much of wisdom literature and not just epistolary rhetoric. See esp. Mariam J. Kamell, "The Soteriology of James in Light of Earlier Jewish Wisdom Literature" (PhD diss., St. Andrews, 2010).

should be grouped together to form a main point of equal weight as other independent clauses. And, of course, as the UBS text segmentation apparatus beneath the text-critical apparatus at the bottom of each page of the Greek New Testament reminds us, there are at times other logical places to put paragraph or subparagraph divisions besides what the UBS committee chose.

James 1:2–8 reflects one such instance. A majority of commentators sees verses 2–11 as the first opening section (or subsection) of the letter, after the greeting in verse 1. For many within this majority, these verses introduce three key themes in James's letter.[26] (Note again how the larger literary context affects issues of outlining the individual passage, just as we saw above.) Verses 2–11 may thus be subdivided into verses 2–4 on trials, verses 5–8 on wisdom, and verses 9–11 on riches and poverty. If one were using the outlining techniques of this chapter to prepare for preaching a sermon or teaching a Sunday school lesson or Bible study, it might make more sense to tackle all ten of these verses at once. Alternately, if one were proceeding very slowly through the letter, one could do a message for each of the three subsections. But we have begun this illustration deliberately choosing verses 2–8 both to follow the UBS and to create an example with a fair amount of detail but still not overly long. So let us assume we decide that the theme of riches and poverty, given the setting of many in James's audience as being poor day laborers oppressed by rich unbelievers (see 5:1–6), *is* the major issue to which James wants his recipients to apply his principles concerning trials.[27] Now we can collapse the thrust of the letter to (a) a setting of socioeconomic oppression causing trials and (b) the need for wisdom in dealing with them. We will then want to make our first segmentation of verses 2–8 divide the text into verses 2–4 and 5–8.

Next we examine verses 2–4 to see how we want to subdivide them further. Our grammatical layout discloses only two sentences in these three verses (vv. 2–3 and v. 4), so we will naturally try first a subdivision that respects these grammatical units. The independent clauses of these two sentences form two commands: "Consider it all joy" and "Let endurance have its perfect work." The first of these (v. 2a) is modified by the temporal (v. 2b) and causal (v. 3) clauses already noted. So the third level of subdivision in our outline should correspond to them. We begin to imagine something like this:

WISDOM FOR THE TRIALS OF LIFE

I. The Proper Attitude for Coping with Trials (vv. 2–4)
   A. A Settled Mental State of Contentment[28] (vv. 2–3)
      1. In All Difficult Circumstances (v. 2)

26. See further Craig L. Blomberg and Mariam J. Kamell, *James* (Grand Rapids: Zondervan, 2008), 23–27, 43–47.

27. See, e.g., throughout D. Edmond Hiebert, *The Epistle of James: Tests of a Living Faith* (Chicago: Moody, 1979).

28. Note the verbs dealing with thought rather than emotion in the verse. Cf. ibid., 71.

2. Because of the Character They Build (v. 3)
B. Allowing Perseverance Its Complete Work (v. 4)

This may be sufficient for our ministry purposes, depending on what they are. But should we want to subdivide point B, our outline of the Greek would suggest not so much trying to distinguish, say, between "perfect" and "whole" but trying to take each of the expressions in apposition to each other as separate subpoints. The first might be "1. Creating Maturity," and the second could be "2. No Longer Deficient."

The second subparagraph, spanning verses 5–8, requires our attention next. The Greek outline of these verses contains three independent clauses, at least after we made the judgment call to put both explicit γάρ clauses underneath the main clause with which verse 6 begins and to create an implicit, third γάρ clause out of verse 8, similarly subordinate. We have also already seen that the two independent clauses in verse 5 belong together: "let him [or her] ask . . . and it will be given." This leaves two subdivisions of verses 5–8 at the level of capital letters in our outline: verse 5 and verses 6–8. The third level of subdivision, that of Arabic numerals, now lies immediately at hand. A.1 and 2 correspond to the two clauses of verse 5. One might imagine from our layout that B would have to have four subpoints, one for the "in faith" phrase and three for the γάρ clauses. But the γάρ clauses don't explain why to ask per se, but rather why it is important to ask in faith or, conversely, why doubting is so destructive. Given that "in faith" is not a full clause but just a short prepositional phrase that defines the kind of asking the rest of this sentence will be discussing, it makes better sense to keep it with its verb and then have three parallel subpoints.

We are now ready to suggest an exegetical outline for all of verses 2–8 along the following lines:

WISDOM FOR THE TRIALS OF LIFE
I. The Proper Attitude for Coping with Trials (vv. 2–4)
    A. A Settled Mental State of Contentment (vv. 2–3)
        1. In All Difficult Circumstances (v. 2)
        2. Because of the Character They Build (v. 3)
    B. Allowing Perseverance Its Complete Work (v. 4)
        1. Creating Maturity (v. 4a)
        2. No Longer Deficient (v. 4b)
II. Faith in God for Wisdom in Trials (vv. 5–8)
    A. Asking a Gracious God (v. 5)
        1. Especially When Confused (v. 5a)
        2. The Assured Result (v. 5b)

B. The Problems with God-Denying Doubt (vv. 6–8)[29]
   1. Its Instability (v. 6)
   2. Its Ineffectiveness (v. 7)
   3. Its Two-Facedness (v. 8)[30]

Some outline makers will prefer to write each entry in a complete sentence; otherwise, a briefer "tag" may encapsulate the summarized material, even if it doesn't fully explicate a coherent thought. The more that entries, whether complete sentences or shorter headings like the ones above, can avoid reusing many of the words of Scripture itself, the more likely they will reflect conscious thought and understanding on the part of the person producing the outline. The point of creating an exegetical outline is almost always for purposes of preaching or teaching, so anything that will enhance the likelihood of good communication and accurate comprehension is to be prized. At this point in the process, homiletics textbooks typically deal with the next step of sermon development: moving from an exegetical outline to a preaching outline.[31] This lies beyond the scope of our short volume.

Abbreviated Process for Students without Greek

Tragically, many Christian colleges and seminaries have cut back on the amount of the biblical languages they require, and indeed many degree programs require none at all. In almost every instance this does not reflect the faculty's ideals but the realities of the "market." Students seem more likely to enroll in programs with fewer language requirements; these are often shorter degree programs, and therefore they are also less costly. Some of the blame falls on the shoulders of teachers who have not adequately mounted a "propaganda campaign" for the relevance of the languages or taught them in ways that would be most attractive and helpful to students. A lot of the blame falls on churches who hire full-time ministers with significant preaching and teaching components to their job descriptions without the degrees that require the languages and sometimes without degrees at all. As a result, the kinds of exegetical fallacies so trenchantly cataloged and illustrated by D. A. Carson proliferate from pulpits—real,

29. On the kind of doubt that is and is not implied here, see further Blomberg and Kamell, *James*, 52–54.
30. The adjective that literally translates as "double-souled" is usually rendered "double-minded," but since the soul produces actions as well as thoughts, perhaps "two-faced" is an even better dynamic equivalent.
31. On which, see esp. Walter L. Liefeld, *New Testament Exposition: From Text to Sermon* (Grand Rapids: Zondervan, 1984); and Haddon W. Robinson, *Biblical Preaching: The Development and Delivery of Expository Messages* (Grand Rapids: Baker, 1980).

Sidebar 8.2

Tips for Creating Exegetical Outlines without Greek Training

1. Note where the editorial committee chose to put periods in the Greek.
2. Look at either an interlinear New Testament or one of the standard formally equivalent translations and determine what each of the sentences says in English.
3. Look at several English translations and one or more good commentaries, while also thinking through the flow of thought in the text.
4. Note how different translations choose to divide the paragraphs and sentences.
5. Look at other punctuation in the Greek (e.g., commas and raised dots, which represent semicolons) and consider what purpose these marks may serve in the overall structure of the passage (i.e., a major subdivision in the passage, setting off an expression from the rest of the sentence, etc.).
6. Never subdivide a section of text unless you are going to create at least two subdivisions.
7. Be sure that all subpoints cover all parts of the larger unit that they subdivide.
8. When working with narrative material (as opposed to epistles), it is typically less crucial to see precisely which sentences and which parts of sentences are coordinate or subordinate, while it is more crucial to trace the author's flow of thought from paragraph to paragraph.

---

electronic, and virtual—all around the world.[32] The church and the world are the poorer for it.

But even with the best of intentions, it is hard in a busy life to keep one's language skills sharp. Are there any techniques that don't require detailed recall of vocabulary and grammar, even for the person who studied Greek, to say nothing of those who haven't? Yes, there are. It may not have been apparent as we were working through the example from James above, but quite a bit of it could have been discerned even by someone who knew not a word of Greek, even though a working knowledge of the language makes the process a whole lot easier.

James 1:2–8 Again

Consider again our passage, discussed in detail above, and punctuated as in the UBS[4]:

²Πᾶσαν χαρὰν ἡγήσασθε, ἀδελφοί μου, ὅταν πειρασμοῖς περιπέσητε ποικίλοις, ³γινώσκοντες ὅτι τὸ δοκίμιον ὑμῶν τῆς πίστεως κατεργάζεται ὑπομονήν. ⁴ἡ δὲ ὑπομονὴ ἔργον τέλειον ἐχέτω, ἵνα ἦτε τέλειοι καὶ ὁλόκληροι ἐν μηδενὶ λειπόμενοι. ⁵Εἰ δέ τις ὑμῶν λείπεται σοφίας, αἰτείτω παρὰ τοῦ διδόντος θεοῦ πᾶσιν ἁπλῶς καὶ

---

32. D. A. Carson, *Exegetical Fallacies*, 2nd ed. (Grand Rapids: Baker, 1996).

μὴ ὀνειδίζοντος καὶ δοθήσεται αὐτῷ. ⁶αἰτείτω δὲ ἐν πίστει μηδὲν διακρινόμενος· ὁ γὰρ διακρινόμενος ἔοικεν κλύδωνι θαλάσσης ἀνεμιζομένῳ καὶ ῥιπιζομένῳ. ⁷μὴ γὰρ οἰέσθω ὁ ἄνθρωπος ἐκεῖνος ὅτι λήμψεταί τι παρὰ τοῦ κυρίου, ⁸ἀνὴρ δίψυχος, ἀκατάστατος ἐν πάσαις ταῖς ὁδοῖς αὐτοῦ.

Students who know (or remember) nothing of Greek can at least note where the editorial committee chose to put periods. This allows the students to begin to envision an outline of five sentences, namely, verses 2–3, verse 4, verse 5, verse 6, and verses 7–8. They can then look at either an interlinear New Testament or one of the standard formally equivalent translations and determine what each of these five sentences says in English, even if it is not as fluent English as they might like. They can look at several English translations and one or more good commentaries,[33] along with thinking through the flow of thought in the text themselves. They will see the number of scholars who break this single paragraph in the UBS into two paragraphs and may choose to follow suit.[34] The students will see a variety of ways the different translations subdivide verses 2–4 and 5–8, because, as we saw in our chapter on translation (chap. 2), each version has its own objectives with respect to fluency. Less attention, therefore, should be paid to where English translations end sentences and more weight given to the placing of the periods in the Greek text. But keep in mind, even this is the work of a committee; several centuries of the transmission of the manuscripts went by before even the most rudimentary punctuation began to be added.

Let us assume, then, that we have a working outline:

    I. (vv. 2–4)
       A. (vv. 2–3)
       B. (v. 4)
    II. (vv. 5–8)
       A. (v. 5)
       B. (v. 6)
       C. (vv. 7–8)

After consulting the English to see what each of these verses or two-verse groupings says, we ought to wind up with similar entries or titles on the first five lines of the outline as we did above when we were working directly from the Greek. The points of the outline where we may not come up with the same subdivisions will be II.B and C and for any further subdivisions to a third level of outlining that we might desire.

---

33. See the regularly updated commentary section of the New Testament Department Bibliography in the *Denver Journal*, online at www.denverseminary.edu.
34. The student who knows some Greek or recognizes Greek letters will notice that the UBS indicates the same division by using capital, or uncial, letters to begin verses 2 and 5.

But look again at the remaining punctuation within the Greek. In addition to periods, the UBS employs commas, just as in English, and raised dots (as halfway through verse 6), which are Greek semicolons. Semicolons will almost always divide a sentence in the Greek New Testament into its two main subdivisions. Commas are more versatile, but if we use an interlinear we should be able to determine where they appear in the structure of a sentence in all but the most complex or convoluted of Greek sentences. Above, we observe three commas within verses 2–3, all of them in or immediately after verse 2. Since, with only a handful of exceptions, the medieval introduction of verse divisions was done with some discernible logic in mind, we might readily imagine that the comma at the end of verse 2 is more likely a sign of a major subdivision of the sentence that spans verses 2–3 than the two commas earlier in verse 2. If we can use an interlinear to determine that these two earlier commas surround the words that mean "my brothers [and sisters]," we will recognize that, like in English, they merely set this expression off from the rest of the sentence: "Consider it all joy, my brothers [and sisters], when you encounter various trials." These commas will not be a tipoff to a major subdivision of the sentence as is the comma at the end of verse 2. So we can now proceed on the assumption that after I.A our outline will have a 1 (corresponding to v. 2) and a 2 (corresponding to v. 3).

The comma in verse 4, if we follow an interlinear and look at the English, should show us that it is dividing this second sentence of the paragraph into its main clause and a purpose clause. Since independent and dependent clauses are not of equal weight and there is no second dependent clause under the first one as there was in verses 2–3, we might just choose not to subdivide verse 4 at all, or we might recognize, even from the English, the possibility of using the two parts of the purpose clause as flip sides of each other. In verse 5, it should not be hard to discover that the comma separates the "if" clause from the "then" clause (taken together as A.1), while English translations routinely keep the last part of verse ("and it will be given to him [or her]") together with the rest of the verse (which we will outline as A.2).[35]

The place where this exegetical outline is least likely to resemble the one we suggested above based on the Greek is in verses 6–8. Yet, even here, the Greek itself can suggest an alternative.[36] If we accept the UBS committee's

35. Among the major recent translations, the NLT makes verse 5 into two sentences: "If you need wisdom, ask our generous God, and he will give it to you. He will not rebuke you for asking." Even here, "he will give it to you" is kept with the first main clause, "ask our generous God." It is simply the additional descriptor of God as not rebuking that is pulled out in order to avoid a longer, verse-length sentence. And, of course, the NLT is a fully functionally equivalent translation, not at all the formally equivalent kind one should be consulting for this specific exercise.

36. See the punctuation, preserving the period at the end of verse 6 and using a semicolon at the end of v. 7, in the ESV, NIV, TNIV, and NKJV.

punctuation, we will divide verse 6 into the main command ("let him [or her] ask in faith, nothing doubting") and a sole rationale ("for the one who doubts is like a wave of a sea being blown and being tossed about"). Verse 7 will then start an independent clause with its initial "for" (γάρ) more loosely tied to the preceding verse, akin to a coordinating conjunction. Verses 7–8 will then subdivide at the verse break, with the comma after "double-minded" simply separating it from the next adjective, "unstable" (or "restless" or "uncontrollable").[37]

All these observations could yield a plausible continuation of our outline, minus the actual topical headings, and would produce the following:

    I. (vv. 2–4)
      A. (vv. 2–3)
        1. (v. 2)
        2. (v. 3)
      B. (v. 4)[38]
   II. (vv. 5–8)
      A. (v. 5)
        1. (v. 5a)
        2. (v. 5b)
      B. (v. 6)
        1. (v. 6a)
        2. (v. 6b)
      C. (vv. 7–8)
        1. (v. 7)
        2. (v. 8)

The identical entries as before could conceivably be used for all but II.B.1 and C, with II.B.2, C.1, and C.2 corresponding to II.B.1, B.2, and B.3, respectively, on our previous outline. More likely, though, given the different structure, the labels would be a little different throughout the entries for verses 6–8.[39]

Crucial to creating clear, comprehensive exegetical outlines are two important structural features. First, never subdivide a section of text unless you are going to create at least two subdivisions. Writers may choose to

37. Cf. BDAG with Johannes P. Louw and Eugene A. Nida, *A Greek-English Lexicon of the New Testament Based on Semantic Domains*, 2 vols., 2nd ed. (New York: United Bible Societies, 1989), both ad loc.

38. Possibly subdivided into 1 (v. 4a) and 2 (v. 4b).

39. As the Zondervan Exegetical Commentary on the New Testament series emerges, grammatical layouts with the English translation diagrammed according to the Greek structure, along with English exegetical outlines, will appear for each pericope. For James, see already Blomberg and Kamell, *James*. For an excellent example of diagrams for narrative genres, see Grant R. Osborne, *Matthew* (Grand Rapids: Zondervan, 2010).

modify only one part of a sentence with only one subordinate phrase or clause, in which case simply capture the thought of the whole sentence in a single entry. Put another way, if you have a I, you must have a II; if you have an A, you must have a B; if you have a 1, you must have a 2; and so forth. Of course, you can have *more* than two subdivisions, but you cannot have fewer. A moment's thought will make it clear that it is nonsensical to speak of dividing something into one part. All you would have is the original item. Second, be sure that all subpoints cover all parts of the larger unit that they subdivide. It makes no sense to divide a passage spanning verses 24–31 into verses 25–28 and 30–31—what happened to verses 24 and 29? Nor does it make sense to call the larger unit verse 24 and then subdivide it into verses 25–26 and 27–28—those four verses aren't part of verse 24. Neither should subdivisions overlap. If you find yourself dividing verses 12–16 into 12–14 and 14–16, you haven't adequately determined how verse 14 is functioning. Either it belongs only to the first subsection or to the second subsection (e.g., vv. 12–13, vv. 14–16), or it is a hinge verse or separate thought that deserves a line and entry all of its own (yielding vv. 12–13, v. 14, vv. 15–16), or the verse itself should be subdivided (e.g., 12–14a, 14b–16).

An Example from Narrative: Acts 12

By far the most exegetical help afforded by outlines that consider every verse and, at times, half verse, appears in the study of the epistles. In the narrative material of the Gospels and Acts, and to a certain degree, Revelation, individual passages of preachable or teachable length tend to be longer and more episodic in nature. It is not as crucial to see which sentences and which parts of sentences are coordinate or subordinate, as to trace the author's flow of thought from paragraph to paragraph.[40] Of course, Jesus and the apostles regularly "intrude" into the narratives of the Gospels and Acts to give detailed teaching where the close analysis so helpful with letters may bear repeating. But consider a message or lesson from Acts 12, for example, where very little dialogue occurs. The biggest problem from English translations' layout of narrative material is often their use of numerous small paragraphs, including new ones for each new speaker's words, so that one needs to reflect on how they belong together in larger units of thought.[41] Many modern Bible versions do create large divisions of the text and set them off with section headings, but at times these sections are too lengthy to be useful for understanding the detailed flow of thought.

40. Notice how even the labels of the kinds of sentences, clauses, and phrases used in narrative changes in the semantic analysis championed by Guthrie and Duvall, *Biblical Greek Exegesis*, 43–44. One set of categories applies to "events/actions"; another to "argument/discussion." Recall also above, in chap. 6 on grammar, p. 145.

41. The (T)NIV, e.g., divides Acts 12:1–24 into twelve paragraphs.

Thus, the NASB (1997) does not subdivide Acts 12 at all, in terms of section headings, but labels it all "Peter's Arrest and Deliverance." The NET likewise keeps all of chapter 12 together but calls it "James is Killed and Peter Imprisoned." The NIV and TNIV divide Acts 12 into two major sections: verses 1–19a comprise "Peter's Miraculous Escape from Prison," while verses 19b–24 form "Herod's Death." The TNIV recognizes, against the NIV and NET, that verse 25 actually belongs with chapter 13 as its introduction.[42] The section headings disclose the problems that occur when too much of the text is subsumed under one heading. The NASB correctly catches the contrast between Peter's arrest and escape. The NET properly observes the contrast between James's martyrdom and Peter's release. The NIV and TNIV appropriately highlight by their section divisions the contrast between Herod's ruthless behavior while in power and his inability to avoid God's judgment, but the section heading for the first part of the chapter does not alert the reader to this contrast.

What is needed is an outline that does justice to all three of these contrasts. The ESV and HCSB come closest, by dividing the chapter into three parts (vv. 1–5 on James's martyrdom and Peter's imprisonment, 6–19 on Peter's rescue, and 20–25 on Herod's death), which they label with almost identical language. They nevertheless revert back to a more traditional dependence on chapter and verse divisions, thus failing to put Acts 12:25 with chapter 13 where it belongs or putting 12:19b with verses 20–24 as the introduction to the account of Herod's demise. But even dividing the chapter into *three* main subsections doesn't fully disclose its outline. Indeed, that would suggest that a tripartite episodic analysis suffices. What is actually going on, in fact, is a sophisticated set of literary comparisons and contrasts.[43] James is martyred, through no ascribed fault of his own (vv. 1–2), whereas Peter is rescued from prison, despite the unbelief of those praying for him when they first hear the news (vv. 3–19). Peter himself doesn't at first realize or believe what is happening (v. 9) until the angel leaves him and he comes to his senses (v. 11).

The unifying character of the chapter, however, is neither James nor Peter, but Herod Agrippa.[44] First, he appears fully in charge in verses 1–19a. Admittedly, he is unable to prevent the angelic rescue of Peter from prison, but verse 19a forms a clear inclusio with verses 1–2, with Herod ordering executions in both instances—first of James the apostle and then of the guards who failed to prevent Peter's escape. Verses 19b–24, however, tell of God's judgment on

42. Note the summary statement in v. 24, one of six in that separate Acts into its main subsections. Cf. Richard N. Longenecker, "Acts," in *Expositor's Bible Commentary,* ed. Tremper Longman III and David E. Garland, rev. ed. (Grand Rapids: Zondervan, 2005), 10:708–12.

43. Cf. Leland Ryken, *Words of Life: A Literary Introduction to the New Testament* (Grand Rapids: Baker, 1987), 82–87.

44. F. F. Bruce (*The Book of Acts,* rev. ed. [Grand Rapids: Eerdmans, 1988], 232), for example, titles Acts 12:1–24, "Herod Agrippa and the Church."

Herod for accepting acclamation as divine. Indeed, his judgment occurs by the gruesome, slow, and tortuous death of being eaten by worms (v. 23), an event Josephus also recounts and substantially embellishes or at least expands.[45] An outline that does full justice to all these phenomena would have to contain the following main divisions and subdivisions:

I. Herod's Wrath Unleashed on Others (vv. 1–19a)
   A. James's Martyrdom (vv. 1–2)
   B. Peter's Arrest and Escape (vv. 3–19a)
      1. Peter in Prison (vv. 3–5)
      2. Peter Miraculously Released (vv. 6–19a)
         a. Peter Thinks It's a Vision (vv. 6–10)[46]
         b. Peter Understands and Reports to Those Praying (vv. 11–17)
            i. The Ones Praying Don't Yet Understand (vv. 11–15)
            ii. The Ones Praying See and Learn (vv. 16–17)
         c. The Aftermath at the Prison (vv. 18–19a)
II. God's Wrath Unleashed on Herod (vv. 19b–24)

There are only two main sections to the chapter, as dictated by the contrasting positions of the unifying character, Herod. But the second is a short, tightly knit episode, while the first is a much longer, more intricate narrative with four sets of increasingly more embedded contrasts. And each is rich in theological lessons for God's people.[47]

Conclusion

There is no single right way to construct an outline. As we have seen, even when one is producing a grammatical layout that follows the coordination and subordination of clauses and phrases, there will be multiple ways that parallel elements can be grouped together or further subdivided. Occasionally, what is grammatically highlighted is not conceptually prominent, and vice versa. For example, the main clause of James 4:13–14 is "Come now," but this is merely an attention-getting device, much like "Listen up" in colloquial English. One has to keep reading to find the main point of this two-verse sentence. Usually, though, contents and grammar will be closely wedded. When the exegete creates outlines with subdivisions larger than individual sentences, especially in narrative, there will be even greater ambiguity as to where one

45. See Josephus, *Antiquities* 19.343–50.
46. As the text segmentation apparatus in the UBS[4] demonstrates, versions and translations are divided over whether to end the subsection after v. 10 or after v. 11. The outline makes good sense either way.
47. See Darrell L. Bock, *Acts* (Grand Rapids: Baker, 2007), 423–33.

section begins and another ends. Not all biblical writers wrote every part of their compositions with the same amount of structure or the same amount of advance planning. Of all things that commentators differ on, outlines often prove to be the most varied.

But that does not mean that anything goes. There are plenty of ways to do violence to the natural units of thought in a text, of which no competent commentator would approve. And some books or sections of books are clearer in their outlines than others. Even if all our exercises in outlining prove at best to be *approximations* of the authors' original intentions, we learn massive amounts about the inspired writers' thoughts in the process. We run far less risk of emphasizing peripheral items and missing main points. As a student once put it, "Before I came to seminary I did a lot of preaching. I knew you had to look for three main points in a passage. So I read the text and whatever three things struck me the most I preached about. Now I know how to find the points the authors most wanted to stress. And I also know that they may not always be three in number!" When students reach the point where they can take the Greek New Testament—or the English, with a lot of resources and tools to help them understand what the Greek says—and know that they have uncovered what the very grammar of the inspired authors most stresses, they will attain a level of confidence and security in their preaching and teaching that is richly rewarding.

9

Theology

Though few of them realize it at the time, new Christians almost always learn systematic theology before biblical exegesis. Systematic theology "seeks to elaborate the whole and the parts of Scripture, demonstrating their logical (rather than their merely historical) connections and taking full cognizance of the history of doctrine and the contemporary intellectual climate and categories and queries."[1] Children or adults who go through catechetical instruction in a given church will be taught the major doctrines of the Christian faith through the lens of the particular denomination or theological tradition of that church. People coming to faith in Christ in other contexts are often responding to even more-simplified presentations of the gospel in tract or booklet form or from speakers at some kind of evangelistic or outreach event. The most common form of such a presentation is probably one that focuses on God's desire to be in relationship with humanity, our alienation from him, Christ's work on the cross as the solution to humanity's plight, and our need to respond in repentance, faith, and discipleship. Along the way, however embryonically, individuals are exposed to fundamental Christian teachings about God, humanity, sin, salvation, and sanctification. When specific scriptural texts are cited to support such presentations, they are as likely as not to come from the letter to the Romans. Indeed, Romans 1–8 is the clearest sustained presentation of the Christian message in a systematically organized sequence anywhere

1. D. A. Carson, "Unity and Diversity in the New Testament: The Possibility of Systematic Theology," in *Scripture and Truth*, ed. D. A. Carson and John D. Woodbridge (1983; repr. Grand Rapids: Baker, 1992), 69–70.

in Scripture.[2] Such theological preunderstandings can be both a bane and a blessing for exegetes. We will treat both, in that sequence.

The Problems of Systematic Theology Trumping Biblical Exegesis

A natural, if unintended outgrowth of this initial Christian education is that as believers embark on reading entire books and sections of the Bible, they not surprisingly will try to integrate what they are encountering for the first time with what they have already learned about their faith. If they become involved with a church, parachurch organization, Bible study group, or written curriculum that represents only one of various legitimate Christian interpretive traditions, they may not be aware of viable alternatives to what they are being taught. They may not immediately receive help in sifting the more fundamental from the more peripheral elements of Christian doctrine, those elements that historic Christianity has usually deemed nonnegotiable versus those on which Bible-believing Christians often allow for considerable diversity of opinion.[3] All of this influences their reading of any given passage. Part of healthy exegesis is to become aware of these implicit or explicit theological commitments so that they can be evaluated.

Ephesians 2:8–9, for example, is commonly cited in evangelistic settings to make it clear that it is by God's grace through faith in Jesus Christ, not legal works, that a person is saved. If the immediate, literary context of these two verses is not examined, particularly verse 10, Christians may well not realize that Paul goes on instantly to add, "For we are God's handiwork, created in Christ Jesus to do good works, which God prepared in advance for us to do." Paul is scarcely against good works. Indeed, the true believer, empowered by the Spirit, will of necessity perform them as he or she embarks on the process of being transformed into the image of God's Son (2 Cor. 3:18; Rom. 8:29; Eph. 4:24). But it is not the works that save us; rather, they demonstrate the reality of our salvation by grace through faith.[4] Without the balance offered by all three verses of Ephesians 2:8–10, it becomes easy to misinterpret the numerous New Testament passages that teach Christians will be judged according to their works (e.g., Matt. 25:31–46; Rom. 2:6–16; 1 Cor. 3:10–15; 2 Cor.

2. Not surprisingly, James D. G. Dunn organizes his major Pauline theology (*The Theology of Paul the Apostle* [Grand Rapids: Eerdmans, 1998]) along the lines of Rom. 1–8 and then interweaves material from the rest of Paul's letters into his outline of those chapters.

3. In the former category are typically included the authority of Scripture, the Trinitarian nature of God, his major attributes clustered around the concepts of love and justice, the deity of Christ, the sinfulness of humanity despite our creation in God's image, Jesus's atoning work in his crucifixion, his bodily resurrection and exaltation, salvation by God's grace appropriated through faith in Jesus, the role of the Spirit in empowering all believers, Christ's second coming, and the future bodily resurrection of all humanity either to eternal life or eternal destruction.

4. Cf., e.g., Andrew T. Lincoln, *Ephesians* (Dallas: Word, 1990), 113.

Sidebar 9.1

Ways That Systematic Theology Can Trump Biblical Exegesis

- If the immediate, literary context of the verses is not examined
- When textual and contextual features are ignored
- When interpreters fail to observe differences between one biblical writer's or corpus's use of key words or concepts and another's
- If parallel accounts of the same teaching or event are inappropriately harmonized so as to lose sight of the distinctive message of each

---

5:10; James 2:14–26). Some might assume, for example, that there must be a separate judgment in which believers do or do not receive various additional rewards above and beyond "mere" heaven.[5] Others may be misled to think that a changed lifestyle is optional, however desirable it may be. They may speak of Christ becoming Savior at one point in a person's life but only Lord at another time, even though the earliest recorded summary of the Christian confession, endorsed by Paul in Romans 10:9–10, speaks of acknowledging Jesus as Lord.[6]

Consciously or unconsciously, theological systems affect countless exegetical decisions. An interpreter convinced of the Calvinist understanding of "eternal security" or "the perseverance of the saints" will come to the passages in Hebrews warning against committing apostasy (see esp. Heb. 6:4–8; 10:26–31) and reject the apparently straightforward meaning of those texts in which it appears that Christians can repudiate their allegiance to Jesus.[7] Thoroughgoing Arminians will detect no problems in Hebrews but try to avoid the seemingly plain sense of Romans 8:31–39 when it climaxes by maintaining that none of the specified elements in the passage, "nor anything else in all creation, will be able to separate us from the love of God that is in Christ Jesus our Lord" (v. 39), often by insisting that "anything *else*" does not include people themselves, who *can* choose to abandon their prior commitments.[8]

Theological systems will dictate the way individual texts are interpreted, even apart from apparently divergent teachings elsewhere in Scripture. On the one hand, egalitarians will often read Galatians 3:28 ("There is neither Jew

---

5. Contra which, see Craig L. Blomberg, "Degrees of Reward in the Kingdom of Heaven?" *Journal of the Evangelical Theological Society* 35 (1992): 159–72.

6. Contra which, see esp. John F. MacArthur Jr., *The Gospel according to Jesus*, rev. ed. (Grand Rapids: Zondervan, 1994); and idem, *The Gospel according to the Apostles* (Nashville: Nelson, 2000).

7. E.g., Philip E. Hughes, *A Commentary on the Epistle to the Hebrews* (Grand Rapids: Eerdmans, 1977), 206–24, 418–26.

8. E.g., Ben Witherington III with Darlene Hyatt, *Paul's Letter to the Romans: A Socio-Rhetorical Commentary* (Grand Rapids and Cambridge: Eerdmans, 2004), 234.

nor Gentile, neither slave nor free, neither male nor female, for you are all one in Christ Jesus") as if this verse alone settles the debate over whether women can and should exercise all the identical forms of spiritual leadership as men.[9] Complementarians, on the other hand, will often affirm that this refers only to equality (or equal access) with respect to salvation, not to service.[10] Both sides, more often than not, ignore textual and contextual features that should make their claims less sweeping. On the one hand, the passage isn't even primarily about *equality* but about *unity* ("you are all *one*"), which scarcely precludes role differentiation. On the other hand, the immediate context is about that unity being publicly demonstrated in baptism (an egalitarian rite for new believers when compared with Jewish circumcision, which was only for men). If baptism no longer strikes a viewing public as distinctively affirming of women, then Christians in a given culture today need to find other examples, within their overall understanding of biblical teaching on the topic, that will communicate this message. For example, women rather than just men (or "laypeople" rather than just the ordained) could be invited to serve communion or baptize others, since no text in Scripture even remotely suggests any limitations on who can perform these ordinances or sacraments, and this despite a long tradition in some circles of limiting these practices to men and/or ordained clergy.[11]

Systematic theology can prejudice our reading of individual texts also when we fail to observe differences between one biblical writer's or corpus's use of key words or concepts and another's. In this situation, systematic theology trumps biblical *theology*, not just exegesis. Biblical theology may be defined as "that branch of theology whose concern it is to study each corpus of the Scripture in its own right, especially with respect to its place in the history of God's unfolding revelation."[12] Consider the controversial question of whether or not apostles exist in the modern world. Charismatic Christians often correctly observe that Paul includes apostleship as one of the spiritual gifts that God's Spirit gives to whomever he wills during the entire period of church history (cf. Eph. 4:11 with 1 Cor. 12:11 and 1:7). They then look at the profile of an apostle in the Gospels and Acts and assume that there must be gifted individuals today who have a very exalted role of leadership in the church with considerable authority to speak on behalf of God, particularly concerning his will for given individuals' or congregations' lives. Non-charismatics often

9. E.g., Gilbert Bilezikian, *Beyond Sex Roles: What the Bible Says about a Woman's Place in Church and Family*, 3rd ed. (Grand Rapids: Baker, 2006), 94–96.

10. E.g., S. Lewis Johnson, "Role Distinctions in the Church: Galatians 3:28," in *Recovering Biblical Manhood and Womanhood: A Response to Evangelical Feminism*, ed. John Piper and Wayne Grudem (Wheaton: Crossway, 1991), 154–64.

11. Cf. further Ben Witherington III, "Rite and Rights for Women—Galatians 3.28," *New Testament Studies* 27 (1981): 593–604; idem, *Grace in Galatia: A Commentary on Paul's Letter to the Galatians* (Grand Rapids: Eerdmans; Edinburgh: T&T Clark, 1998), 270–81.

12. Carson, "Unity and Diversity in the New Testament," 69.

correctly observe that the criteria for apostleship in Acts 1:21–22—having followed Jesus from the days of John the Baptist onward and being a witness of the resurrection—disqualified anyone from ever being an apostle from sometime early in the second century onward.

As it turns out, each side is often correct in what it observes and wrong in what it infers from its observations. Both sides frequently fail to realize that, with the sole exceptions of Acts 14:4 and 14, the consistent usage of ἀπόστολος (apostle) by the Gospel writers, and especially in Luke-Acts, is to refer to one of the Twelve (including Matthias, Judas's replacement), whereas Paul uses the term, consistent with his understanding of it as a spiritual gift, of a much broader circle of individuals, including himself, Junia, Andronicus, James (the Lord's half-brother), and Epaphroditus.[13] Consistent with the broader use of the term in the Greek language of the day, "apostle" for Paul meant "someone sent on a mission" or, as we might call such a person today, a missionary.[14] Are there apostles today? Yes, in the Pauline sense. No, in the Lukan sense. Each definition must be kept separate and the one must not be used to blur the individual characteristics of the other.

Finally, even parallel accounts of the same teaching or event can be inappropriately harmonized so as to lose sight of the distinctive message of each. In Matthew's more well-known version of the Beatitudes, Jesus begins by blessing the "poor in spirit" (Matt. 5:3). In Luke, however, he declares, "Blessed are you who are poor" (Luke 6:20). Sensing a potential tension between the two forms, most ordinary Western evangelicals who are eager to preserve the unity of Scripture interpret Luke in light of Matthew, rarely the other way around.[15] They believe Luke must have "poor in spirit" in mind when he writes "poor," rather than those who are literally, materially impoverished. After all, most Westerners wouldn't be included if Jesus had in mind (only) the economically poor. A glance at the rest of Luke's Beatitudes, like his corresponding woes, quickly belies this standard approach. Jesus *is* blessing the hungry, the weeping, the persecuted, and he is pronouncing woes on the rich, well fed, laughing, and those of whom everyone speaks well (6:21–26).

Do Matthew's and Luke's versions then simply contradict each other? No, because a word study shows that in the LXX πτωχοί (the plural of the word for "poor" used by both evangelists) frequently translates the Hebrew עֲנָוִים, a term that in its Old Testament contexts often means those who are impov-

---

13. Cf., e.g., D. Müller, "Apostle," in *New International Dictionary of New Testament Theology*, ed. Colin Brown, vol. 1 (Grand Rapids: Zondervan, 1975), 128–35.

14. Cf. Gordon D. Fee, *The First Epistle to the Corinthians* (Grand Rapids: Eerdmans, 1987), 397.

15. So, e.g., Jeff Cook, *Seven: The Deadly Sins and the Beatitudes* (Grand Rapids: Zondervan, 2008), 44, citing Dallas Willard, Robyn Griffith-Jones, and the *Renovaré Spiritual Formation Bible* study notes.

erished but simultaneously turn to God in their distress as their only hope.[16] There is a legitimate harmonization that views these poor as both materially dispossessed and spiritually trusting in God. Even Luke's very "material" slant on the Beatitudes ends with 6:22 in which Jesus blesses those who are hated, excluded, insulted, and rejected "because of the Son of Man," that is, because of their loyalty to Christ. Luke knows there is no automatic spiritual advantage to being poor; if there were, we should never try to help the poor out of their plight![17] But neither can we excise all reference to economic circumstances, even in Matthew. As Dale Bruner so nicely puts it:

> If we say that "blessed are the poor in spirit" means "blessed are the rich, too, if they act humbly," we have spiritualized the text away. On the other hand, if we say "blessed are the poor" means "poor people are happy people," we have secularized the text. . . . Jesus incorporated both Matthew's spirituality and Luke's sociality, getting the best of each.[18]

The Problems of Biblical Exegesis Not Leading to Systematic Theology

This last example of the complex relationship between exegesis and theology forms a good transition to our next category of problems. If one danger in exegesis is to read foreign theology into a text too quickly—whether from an overall system that has some problems, or from another biblical author's different use of concepts or terms, or simply from the exegete not paying careful enough attention to all of the factors already discussed for analyzing a given text—there is an opposite danger as well. Exegetes may stop their work, even after a flawless articulation of a text's meaning, and not reflect on the import of that meaning when it is integrated into the theology of the entire Bible, systematically arranged.

James 3:9 offers an excellent illustration: "With the tongue we praise our Lord and Father, and with it we curse human beings, who have been made in God's likeness." Here James is lamenting the unique duplicity of the human race. Unlike the rest of the created world, in which water is either fresh or salty but not both at the same time, or in which trees bear only one kind of fruit (vv. 11–12), humans can bless God and curse one another in rapid succession (v. 10a). James's main point is to decry such duplicity (v. 10b). But what makes it all the more poignant and inappropriate is that the objects of the cursing—fellow human beings—are the apex of creation, uniquely stamped

16. See, e.g., Donald A. Hagner, *Matthew 1–13* (Dallas: Word, 1993), 91; Rudolf Schnackenburg, *The Gospel of Matthew* (Grand Rapids: Eerdmans, 2002), 47.

17. See esp. Darrell L. Bock, *Luke 1:1–9:50* (Grand Rapids: Baker, 1994), 571–75.

18. Frederick D. Bruner, *Matthew, A Commentary: The Christbook*, rev. ed. (Grand Rapids: Eerdmans, 2004), 159.

with the *imago Dei* ("image of God").[19] The passage's main contribution to biblical teaching has to do with ethics (how we should behave), but it also contributes to theology (what we should believe). We know from Genesis 1:26–27 that God originally created man and woman in his image, in a context that describes their vice regency over creation, but that was before their fall into sin. What about afterward? Colossians 3:10, combined with Ephesians 4:24, makes it clear that believers are being renewed in that image (which also involves growth in righteousness and holiness). What about before someone becomes a Christian? There is not much in Scripture that directly addresses this question, so every hint we get proves welcome. James 3:9 is one of those key hints. Our curses are scarcely limited to fellow Christians; indeed, they are often reserved for unbelievers who attack us. So James must be convinced that even non-Christians continue to have the image of God in them, however marred or effaced it has become due to sin.[20] This gives all humanity a certain inherent dignity, worthy of respect, which the rest of creation does not have. A message on all of James 3:9–12 might make this point only in passing because it is not a major emphasis of the text overall. But a summary of the text's contribution to systematic theology should not neglect it.

If one of the problems of theology trumping exegesis is to obscure legitimate differences among biblical texts and the genuine diversity of perspectives on various topics among the scriptural writers, a key danger of exegesis stopping without full-fledged theological reflection is to *over*emphasize that diversity. Legitimate harmonizations, like the one we saw with Matthew's and Luke's versions of the Beatitudes, either are dismissed too quickly and unnecessarily or are not even considered. Charges of theological contradictions among authors often result when, in fact, they need not.

Take, for instance, Matthew's and Mark's conclusions to their accounts of Jesus walking on the water (Matt. 14:33; Mark 6:51b–52). In Matthew, "those who were in the boat worshiped him, saying, 'Truly you are the Son of God.'" In Mark, "they were completely amazed, for they had not understood about the loaves; their hearts were hardened." Could anyone imagine a more irreconcilable contradiction? Either the disciples understood who Jesus was and therefore worshiped him, or they didn't understand and were spiritually obdurate. But are the options really so diametrically opposite? Even in Matthew's Gospel, it will be two more chapters before Peter is able to confess, "You are the Messiah, the Son of the living God" and have Jesus praise him as not having come to that conclusion on his own but by divine revelation (Matt. 16:16–17). Even then, Peter is unprepared for Jesus's further disclosure that his messianic role will have to involve suffering (vv. 21–23). Apparently, Matthew does not think

19. On which, see esp. G. C. Berkouwer, *Man: The Image of God* (Grand Rapids: Eerdmans, 1962).
20. Likewise John S. Hammett, "Human Nature," in *A Theology for the Church*, ed. Daniel L. Akin (Nashville: B&H, 2007), 353.

that the disciples' worship and acknowledgment of Jesus as God's Son after he walks on the water is sufficient faith to preclude these later phenomena.[21]

If we dare not overestimate how much the disciples in Matthew understood at the end of this pericope, neither should we underestimate how much Mark thought they *did* understand. Curiously, Mark does not say that they failed to understand about Christ's walking on the water, but that they did not understand about *the loaves*—the previous miracle of feeding the five thousand (Mark 6:32–44). Some deeper spiritual insight into the significance of the feeding miracle must be intended, something that probably kept the disciples from expecting Jesus to do anything of the sort again when he is with the later gathering of four thousand hungry people in the wilderness (Mark 8:4).[22] With this, Matthew agrees (Matt. 15:33), further tempering how much credit we give the disciples for fathoming Christ's walking on the sea. Moreover, if we reflect on our own inability to grasp supernatural realities, our frequent unwillingness to credit God for anything that might otherwise have a "natural" explanation, or our divided loyalties in so many walks of life despite our professions of absolute allegiance to Jesus, it is not at all hard to imagine the Twelve at one level worshiping him, and at another level still failing to grasp what was happening due to hard hearts.[23] There need be no irreconcilable contradiction here. But we are still left with the divergent accounts.

When we realize that one of Mark's recurring theological emphases is people's failure to fully understand who Jesus was, including (at times *especially* including) his closest followers, we recognize why Mark incorporated the part he did, phrased the way he crafted it.[24] When we realize that Matthew equally consistently calls attention to his followers' faith, even when it is just very small, we understand more clearly why he included what he did with his own specific wording.[25] We need not jettison the unity of the Scripture at the expense of the diversity or vice versa. A message on either Mark's or Matthew's account should focus on the items they stress without allowing parallel passages to obscure those foci. A biblical theology of these Gospels should highlight the distinctive and dominant theological emphases of each writer, namely, Mark's focus on the disciples' obduracy and Matthew's on their (incipient) faith. But a systematic theology must make room for both. Christian living

21. Cf. Craig S. Keener, *A Socio-Rhetorical Commentary on the Gospel of Matthew* (Grand Rapids and Cambridge: Eerdmans, 2009), 408.

22. Cf. Adela Yarbro Collins, *Mark* (Minneapolis: Fortress, 2007), 336.

23. Robert H. Stein (*Mark* [Grand Rapids: Baker Academic, 2008], 329) points out the places even throughout Mark where the disciples "can also through repentance and faith continue to be Jesus's servants," so that one should not read Mark's reference to hard-heartedness as the only trait exhibited in this context.

24. See esp. Douglas W. Geyer, *Fear, Anomaly, and Uncertainty in the Gospel of Mark* (Lanham, MD, and London: Scarecrow Press, 2000).

25. See esp. Günther Bornkamm, Gerhard Barth, and Heinz J. Held, *Tradition and Interpretation in Matthew* (London: SCM; Philadelphia: Westminster, 1963), 52–57.

this side of eternity will never achieve full understanding, and we will always be compromised by mixed motives and flawed behavior accompanying our worship. But "Son of God" remains a proper title by which to address Jesus, even as our understanding of all that is involved in that concept may grow as we grow in our Christian lives.[26]

The Renaissance of "Theological Interpretation"

In some academic circles today, the "theological interpretation of Scripture" means much more than just asking how a given passage contributes to our understanding of one or more of the major doctrines of the Christian faith. Rather, it can mean any or all of the following: returning to interpretations of passages advanced by Christians in premodern periods of church history, embracing allegorical or symbolic readings of texts more than contemporary exegetes usually advise, reflection and/or meditation on key words or concepts to see how God might speak through them in a blend of spiritual illumination and personal application, interpreting one passage in Scripture with another whether or not there are any historical or literary connections between them, and toning down our claims for just how much of the original meaning of texts *can* be recovered and how much application of those texts can be universalized.[27] Clearly, this is a vast and diverse field and it is not obvious that "theological" is the best umbrella descriptor to attach to it (or that any single adjective applies to all of these approaches).

Of course, we can and should learn from commentators, preachers, and writers from every era and place in church history.[28] The academic guild regularly suffers from the evolutionary assumption that the more recent an idea is, the more likely it is true. At the same time, twenty-first-century Bible students *do* have an unprecedented array of resources, tools, and materials available to help them interpret Scripture accurately, which other generations of believers did not have, and we neglect these resources at our peril when we privilege ancient interpretations at the expense of more recent ones. But, whether modern or ancient, some exegetical criteria must be employed to judge all

26. "Son of God" in first-century Judaism, for example, was often merely a synonym for the Messiah, without overtones of divinity. See esp. John J. Collins, "The Background of the 'Son of God' Text," *Bulletin for Biblical Research* 7 (1997): 51–62.

27. For an excellent overview of all these strands of thought, see Daniel J. Trier, *Introducing Theological Interpretation of Scripture: Recovering a Christian Practice* (Grand Rapids: Baker, 2008).

28. There is a renaissance of interest today in the history of interpretation of individual texts, with good commentary series launched or soon-to-be-launched on such "reception history," or how a given period of time in church history tended to look at a given book. Pride of place thus far goes to Thomas C. Oden, ed., The Ancient Christian Commentary on Scripture series (Downers Grove, IL: InterVarsity).

interpretations—this is what this handbook, along with others of its kind, tries to provide. A detailed examination of the writings of the church fathers, or the theological "doctors" of the Middle Ages, or the major Protestant Reformers, discloses that in every case there is a broad mixture of sensible and well-founded insights into the meanings of texts, legitimate applications to the circumstances of the authors and their addressees, and somewhat fanciful overinterpretations or misapplications of certain passages.[29] Readers who have been taught in introductory hermeneutics classes that premodern writers missed the point most of the time, with respect to sound exegesis, will perhaps be surprised to learn how often these writers make good sense, but the readers will also discover plenty of places where their interpretations probably should not be followed.[30]

As for allegory and symbolism, readers need to discern as best they can where it is present and where it is not, according to the original intention of the author as communicated through the written text to the original audience.[31] People who claim that the "literal" meaning of the text is always the correct or best interpretation *either* mean that they are seeking what the author was actually trying to communicate, so that the literal interpretation of a metaphor is metaphorical (recognizing the metaphor as metaphor) *or else* they are just plain wrong.[32] If Linda asks Joe if she can pick his brain, and Joe interprets the question literally (in the sense of removing some of his cerebral cortex), his answer had better be "No"! But such an interpretation doubtless misunderstands Linda. Meaning has to be determined according to the literary genres, forms, and devices used by a writer, as we discussed under literary context (pp. 102–11). If there is reason to believe that a passage contained allegory, or double meanings of some kind, then that is how it should be interpreted. But "allegorizing"—the reading in of a second or deeper level of meaning where it was not intended—risks eisegesis (reading *into* rather that *out of* the text).[33]

In the case of the New Testament's use of the Old, we must remember that many times the writers are not trying to communicate the original meaning

29. For a good textbook, more nuanced in this respect than many, see Gerald Bray, *Biblical Interpretation Past and Present* (Downers Grove, IL, and Leicester: InterVarsity, 1996).

30. Hopefully avoiding both of these errors is William W. Klein, Craig L. Blomberg, and Robert L. Hubbard Jr., *Introduction to Biblical Interpretation*, rev. ed. (Nashville: Nelson, 2004), 23–62.

31. On this threefold locus of meaning, see ibid., 185–201.

32. G. B. Caird (*The Language and Imagery of the Bible* [London: Duckworth, 1980], 131–33) attributes a large part of this problem to the confusion of "literal" with "real." Both literal and figurative language can refer to real entities, and both can refer to fictional entities. There is no logical correlation between literal and "true," or between metaphorical and "false."

33. See, e.g., Klyne R. Snodgrass, *Stories with Intent: A Comprehensive Guide to the Parables of Jesus* (Grand Rapids and Cambridge: Eerdmans, 2007), 15–17.

of the text; they are giving a contemporary application of some kind.[34] In this kind of context, asking who corresponds to some Old Testament character or element in the New Testament age is very legitimate, as long as we do not confuse original meaning with contemporary significance. Galatians 4:24, for example, reads literally (in the second sense used above), "now these things are being allegorized," probably meaning that Paul's Judaizing opponents have taken the story of Isaac (the freeborn son) and Ishmael (the son born into slavery), sons of Abraham by Sarah and Hagar respectively, and pointed out that the biological descendants of those two sons in the first century are Jews and Gentiles, in that order.[35] Thus Jews are spiritually free (even without Christ) and Gentiles are not (even with Christ), unless they adopt torah. Paul, conversely, completely inverts these claims and argues that it is anyone without Christ who is spiritually enslaved, including those who try to supplement Christ with torah obedience as a requirement for salvation, while Jewish and Gentile Christians alike, trusting solely in God's grace through faith, are spiritually free. Neither the Judaizers nor Paul is *exegeting* the text, but both are trying to apply it. Once we understand their intentions and their logic, we can understand why they come to the conclusions that they do.

However, arguing that the prodigal son's ring given to him when he returned home stood for baptism, that the fattened calf symbolized the Eucharist, or that his new sandals were shoes "fitted with the readiness that comes from the gospel of peace" (Eph. 6:15) seems highly fanciful, not least because nothing in the context of the parable nor in the historical-cultural background of the passage would have led Jesus's original audience to envision these referents. Two out of the three alleged correspondences (the Eucharist and the Pauline missionary armor of Eph. 6:10–20) in fact depend on theological developments or affirmations that had not even occurred yet.[36]

Interpreting Scripture with Scripture, the "analogy of Scripture," or adopting what the ancients called the "rule of faith" (*regula fidei*) is always legitimate when the additional passage being used to interpret a given text would have been known to that text's author.[37] The Old Testament is always potentially relevant to the interpretation of any New Testament text because all of the New Testament authors demonstrate that they were steeped in knowledge of the Hebrew Scriptures. Chronologically earlier New Testament books are po-

---

34. The comprehensive, state-of-the-art work for understanding the use of Old Testament texts in the New Testament is Gregory K. Beale and D. A. Carson, eds., *Commentary on the New Testament Use of the Old Testament* (Grand Rapids: Baker Academic; Nottingham: Apollos, 2007).

35. Richard N. Longenecker, *Galatians* (Dallas: Word, 1990), 198.

36. See further Craig L. Blomberg, *Interpreting the Parables* (Downers Grove, IL, and Leicester: InterVarsity, 1990), 16.

37. A point emphasized esp. by Walter C. Kaiser Jr. (*Toward an Exegetical Theology: Biblical Exegesis for Preaching and Teaching* [Grand Rapids: Baker, 1981], 134–40), which he calls the analogy of antecedent Scripture.

tentially relevant to the interpretation of later New Testament texts, especially if we have reason to believe the later texts' authors were aware of the earlier documents. Matthew and Luke most likely knew Mark, while John probably at least knew the core contents of the narratives found in all three Synoptics.[38] But most of the Pauline Epistles predate the written form of the Gospels, so one cannot automatically assume Paul knew any given Gospel tradition. At the same time, he quotes or alludes to enough of Jesus's sayings or teachings that he clearly has learned from the oral traditions much that would eventually be recorded in the Gospels.[39] The same is true of James.[40] But James may not have known Paul's letters when he wrote.

While it is not legitimate when engaging in exegesis or *biblical* theology to use a biblical text of which a given writer was unaware to interpret that writer's original meaning, *systematic* theology requires an awareness of all relevant Scriptures on a given topic and their organization or systematization into a coherent whole. This use of the rule of faith is fundamental to the theological task.[41] In formulating a comprehensive Christian doctrine of hell, for example, we must take account of how the New Testament, quoting Jesus himself, refers to both outer darkness (Matt. 8:12; 22:13; 25:30) and unquenchable fire (Mark 9:43, 48; Matt. 13:42, 50; 25:41). Taken literally and absolutely, these two descriptors would cancel each other out. This is a good tip-off to their metaphorical nature.[42] Second Thessalonians 1:9 contains a more literal depiction of the life to come of the unrepentant: "They will be punished with everlasting destruction and shut out from the presence of the Lord and from the glory of his might." In other words, they will be eternally separated from God and all things good.[43] But it would be unfair to use 2 Thessalonians 1:9 to interpret any of Jesus's teachings in their original, historical settings (as opposed to their later contexts in the Gospels) because Paul would not author 2 Thessalonians until about twenty years after Jesus's death.[44]

---

38. See esp. Richard Bauckham, "John for Readers of Mark," in *The Gospels for All Christians: Rethinking the Gospel Audiences*, ed. Richard Bauckham (Grand Rapids and Cambridge: Eerdmans, 1998), 147–71.

39. See esp. David Wenham, *Paul: Follower of Jesus or Founder of Christianity?* (Grand Rapids and Cambridge: Eerdmans, 1995).

40. See esp. Peter H. Davids, *The Epistle of James* (Grand Rapids: Eerdmans, 1982), 147–48.

41. Gordon R. Lewis and Bruce A. Demarest, *Integrative Theology*, 3 vols. in 1 (Grand Rapids: Zondervan, 1996), 8.

42. Cf. George E. Ladd, *A Theology of the New Testament*, ed. Donald A. Hagner, rev. ed. (Grand Rapids: Eerdmans, 1993), 196.

43. Cf. Ben Witherington III, *1 and 2 Thessalonians: A Socio-Rhetorical Commentary* (Grand Rapids and Cambridge: Eerdmans, 2006), 196–97.

44. On the assumption of authenticity. If one of Paul's followers wrote the letter in his name, as some scholarship suggests, then its date would be later still.

Postmodern restraint concerning sweeping claims about biblical absolutes or interpreters' ability to recover original meaning likewise has both strengths and weaknesses. Often postmodernism is merely stressing that *applications* of texts to individuals or groups vary widely from one time and place to another. On other occasions, it is stressing that finite, fallen interpreters (i.e., all of us) can at best only approximate original meaning but seldom, if ever, grasp it comprehensively—a view often known as critical realism[45]—with which we heartily concur. But in many instances, postmodernism proves far more pessimistic about our abilities even to capture the gist of another person's communicative acts, especially across the miles and centuries that separate us from the biblical authors. Even if we could capture the author's intent, the argument continues, we can never expect to find a "metanarrative" or any set of timeless propositions that apply to all humans everywhere. These last claims, however, prove self-defeating, because they themselves make absolute claims, in propositional form, about the impossibility of propositional absolutes. The authors of such claims invariably also write as if they intend to be understood—and believed—further undermining their claims. No amount of fascination with interpretive fashion, either very old or very new, can erase the fundamental flaws with these particular tenets of postmodernism.[46]

Legitimate Theology from Valid Exegesis

What then are we commending to our readers that exegetes should do so as to contribute in a valid fashion to either biblical or systematic theology? First, make sure you are familiar with the major categories either of the biblical theology of a given book or author or of systematic theology as a whole. Use standard, published overviews of the topic under study from which to glean this information.[47] In so doing, for example, you will discover that Luke is

45. On which, see esp. Ben F. Meyer, *Reality and Illusion in New Testament Scholarship: A Primer in Critical Realist Hermeneutics* (Collegeville, MN: Liturgical, 1994).

46. See further Douglas R. Groothuis, *Truth Decay: Defending Christianity against the Challenges of Postmodernism* (Downers Grove, IL, and Leicester: InterVarsity, 2000); and Craig G. Bartholomew, "Babel and Derrida: Postmodernism, Language and Biblical Interpretations," *Tyndale Bulletin* 49 (1998): 305–28. Many of the chapters of Paul Copan (*"True for You but Not for Me": Overcoming Objections to Christian Faith*, rev. ed. [Minneapolis: Bethany, 2009]) stress these points as well.

47. Excellent, recent New Testament theologies include I. Howard Marshall, *New Testament Theology: Many Witnesses, One Gospel* (Downers Grove, IL: InterVarsity, 2004); Frank Thielman, *Theology of the New Testament: A Canonical and Synthetic Approach* (Grand Rapids: Zondervan, 2005); and Thomas R. Schreiner, *Theology of the New Testament: Magnifying God in Christ* (Grand Rapids: Baker, 2007). For good, succinct *summaries* of the distinctives of the theologies of each book of the Bible, see Kevin J. Vanhoozer, ed., *Dictionary for Theological Interpretation of the Bible* (Grand Rapids: Baker; London: SPCK, 2005). For excellent, recent systematic theologies, see esp. Millard Erickson, *Christian Theology*, 2nd ed. (Grand Rapids:

generally believed to emphasize such key themes as Jesus's humanity and compassion for the outcasts of society, Jesus as savior and prophet, as the teacher par excellence in parables, and as divine benefactor. Luke stresses more than any other New Testament author, except perhaps James, the need for generous stewardship of material possessions and care for the poor. He particularly highlights the role of the Holy Spirit in the life of Jesus and of his first followers. Luke emphasizes prayer, joy, discipleship as a journey, and the potential for the "Christian age" to be a longer period of time before Christ's return than others may have previously envisioned.[48] So when we come to a text like the parable alternately known as the Unjust Judge or the Persistent Widow (Luke 18:1–8), we will think immediately of the themes of prayer, of God's love for the outcast and dispossessed, and of the seeming delay of the parousia (see v. 8). We will then look to see what this pericope teaches specifically about these topics. Included will likely be statements affirming the importance of persistence in prayer, of justice for those in society who have not received it, and for perseverance in faith even when the Christian life may turn out to be longer or harder than first anticipated.[49]

If we are dealing with a text's contribution to systematic theology, we will start by recognizing the major doctrines of the Christian faith, which are usually broken down into categories such as revelation (both general and special), the nature of God (including treatments of each of the three persons of the Trinity as well as of the Trinity overall), creation and the nature of humanity, sin and its effects, angelology and demonology, salvation (objectively in the work of Christ and subjectively in our appropriation of it), discipleship and growth in the Christian life, the church (its nature, sacraments or ordinances, and leadership structures), and eschatology (last things, both for individuals and at the end of the age). Let's say we are studying Acts 6, a short chapter with just fifteen verses. With this array of doctrines in mind, we will notice that the apostles' actions are designed to create unity instead of conflict in the fledgling church, specifically by inviting a linguistically and culturally unique branch of the community to create its own indigenous leadership to deal with important ministry that is being neglected among their widows.[50] We may well recognize the seeds of a division of labor between those who recognized their role as largely involving the proclamation of God's word and those who would care for very practical matters of service. The verb διακονεῖν (to

---

Baker Academic, 1998); Gordon R. Lewis and Bruce A. Demarest, *Integrative Theology*, 3 vols. in 1 (Grand Rapids: Zondervan, 1996); Stanley J. Grenz, *Theology for the Community of God* (1994; repr. Grand Rapids: Eerdmans; Vancouver: Regent College Publishing, 2000); or Daniel L. Akin, ed., *A Theology for the Church* (Nashville: B&H, 2007).

48. See Craig L. Blomberg, *Jesus and the Gospels: An Introduction and Survey*, 2nd ed. (Nashville: B&H, 2009), 163–70.

49. Cf. Blomberg, *Interpreting the Parables*, 271–74.

50. See further Craig Hill, *Hellenists and Hebrews* (Minneapolis: Fortress, 1992).

Sidebar 9.2

Making Exegetical Contributions to Theology

- Become familiar with the major categories either of the biblical theology of a given book or author or of systematic theology as a whole.
- If a given text's contribution appears difficult to mesh with another text's or author's contribution or with the overall theological system that appears to be emerging from our study of individual passages on a given topic, consider at least two other options before concluding that Scripture simply contradicts itself:
  - Make sure you've not somehow misunderstood the text.
  - Reconsider your overall theological system.
- Be willing to conclude, as a last resort, that contradictory strands of early Christian theology on a given topic are juxtaposed in the New Testament without resolution, while remaining open to the possibility that further study may reveal a plausible solution.

---

serve), used in verse 2 in the expression "to wait on (serve) tables"—not like a modern waiter or server in a restaurant, but in what probably involved door-to-door daily distribution of food to the most destitute in the community—is cognate to the noun διάκονος, from which the later office of "deacon" would derive, distinct from elders or overseers (see esp. 1 Tim. 3:1–15).[51] But from Acts 6:8–15 we realize that the compartmentalization of "job descriptions" was by no means watertight. Stephen, one of the first "deacons" (to apply the term somewhat anachronistically), also became a powerful preacher and theologian, so filled with the Holy Spirit and bold in his proclamation, even in front of the Jewish Sanhedrin (Acts 7), that he became the first recorded martyr for the Christian faith.

From Acts 6:8–15 we note also that Stephen worked miracles (v. 8). If we are aware of the theological debate over whether miracles were limited to the apostles, usually treated in textbooks under the ministry of the Holy Spirit, we might cite this passage as showing that they were not. Under the topic of what it means to be "filled" with the Holy Spirit, we might list something about empowerment for mighty deeds testifying to the nature of Christ's person and the truth of the Gospel.[52] From the charges against Stephen (even though they were apparently so exaggerated that Luke can call them false—v. 13) and his lengthy address in chapter 7, we observe he believed that followers of Jesus, even from Jewish backgrounds, did not need to obey the law in exactly all of

---

51. See further Craig L. Blomberg, *Neither Poverty nor Riches: A Biblical Theology of Possessions* (Leicester and Downers Grove, IL: InterVarsity, 1999), 167–69.

52. See esp. Max Turner, *Power from on High: The Spirit in Israel's Restoration and Witness in Luke-Acts* (Sheffield: Sheffield Academic Press, 1996).

the same ways that they used to, and that this "holy place" (6:13, 14)—the temple—no longer functioned in the same way.[53] As systematic theologians, we can bring this text to bear on later New Testament developments, such as Hebrews' emphasis on Christ's once-for-all sacrifice and the abolition of the need for an earthly temple. We cannot claim that Stephen fully understood everything that would be subsequently revealed to the inspired writers of the New Testament. But in putting together a full theology of the Spirit, of Christ's work for our salvation on the cross, and of the role of the land in the New Testament age, we would do well to incorporate the teachings of Acts 6 into what we have to say.

As long as the contributions of individual texts to larger theological syntheses prove complementary and do not raise any seeming contradictions, we may proceed inductively, in a fairly straightforward fashion. A full list of what each relevant text contributes to a given doctrine can then be organized thematically and we can articulate the Bible's teaching on that topic (or a given part of the Bible's teaching on that topic)—the collection of God's attributes, all the ways the Spirit works in a believer's life, the sequence of events in the end times, and so on. If a given text's contribution appears difficult to mesh with another text's or author's contribution or with the overall theological system that appears to be emerging from our study of individual passages on a given topic, then matters become more complicated. Before concluding that Scripture simply contradicts itself, we should consider at least two other options.[54]

First, we should see if we have misunderstood the text we are exegeting some way. Let us return to our example of Hebrews 6:4–8. Most commentators conclude that Hebrews teaches that true believers can truly abandon their faith and be lost.[55] It is not uncommon for them to add a statement that it is not their mandate as commentators to explain how they would deal with other books that appear to teach the exact opposite. They are simply interpreting *this* book of the Bible. But this really shirks the responsibility that biblical scholars have, in any context, to help readers determine if the book on which they are commenting does or does not contradict other parts of Scripture. In this example, careful exegesis should observe that the writer surrounds verses 4–8 with more optimistic affirmations, hoping that the audience will be able to move beyond elementary instruction and "be taken forward to maturity" (v. 1), and being "convinced of better things in your case—the things that have to do with salvation" (v. 9). But the author's confidence about the truly

---

53. On Acts 7, see esp. John J. Kilgallen, *The Stephen Speech: A Literary and Redactional Study of Acts 7, 2–53* (Rome: Biblical Institute Press, 1976).

54. Similarly, Marshall, *New Testament Theology*, 30–31.

55. For one of the strongest defenses of this interpretation, in light of all the relevant data of Hebrews, see Scot McKnight, "The Warning Passages of Hebrews: A Formal Analysis and Theological Conclusions," *Trinity Journal* 13 (1992): 21–59.

redeemed state of the audience overall does not necessarily mean the author is equally sure about every single participant in those congregations. So, after commending the audience for how they have worked for and loved God and how they have helped God's people (v. 10), the writer adds, "We want *each* of you to show this same diligence" (v. 11).

But what about the descriptors of the people in verses 4–6 for whom it is impossible to be renewed to repentance? Enlightenment (v. 4) suggests cognitive knowledge, not necessarily volitional commitment, while tasting ("the heavenly gift" and "the goodness of the word of God and the powers of the coming age" [vv. 4, 5]) is a metaphor suggesting close contact with an entity without fully embracing it. Sharing (in the Holy Spirit [v. 4]) is the one action that seems hardest to attribute to an unbeliever, but the one other usage in Hebrews of the root word employed for sharing comes in 1:9 (quoting Ps. 45:7) where it refers to "companions"—those in close association with others. If some community members were Jews who were themselves interested in and intrigued by this Jesus of Nazareth, when they joined with the true believers in what are probably a collection of Jewish-Christian house churches in Rome, they would have often looked reasonably indistinguishable from the majority in a milieu in which the lines between Judaism and Jewish Christianity often remained quite fuzzy. Companions of those genuinely filled with the Holy Spirit would surely qualify as companions of the Holy Spirit, without necessarily implying that the Spirit had come to dwell in them too.[56]

Some readers will find this harmonization implausible. Our point is not to mount an extensive defense for it, but merely to show how the perceived tension between Hebrews and other New Testament witnesses on the issue of the perseverance of the saints can lead exegetes to reconsider their interpretation of a given text. The second, more sweeping alternative is to reconsider one's overall theological system. Some, after studying the warning passages in Hebrews intensively, have come to the conclusion that it is easier to adopt an Arminian approach on this issue and to acknowledge that it *is* possible to repudiate salvation, and that texts in other New Testament books that seem to teach otherwise can be more readily dealt with from that point of view than can Hebrews from a Calvinist perspective.[57]

The most drastic option, by the standards of evangelicalism, is to argue that we simply have two contradictory strands of early Christian theology

56. For a detailed defense of this viewpoint, see Roger Nicole, "Some Comments on Hebrews 6:4–6 and the Doctrine of the Perseverance of God with the Saints," in *Current Issues in Biblical and Patristic Interpretation*, ed. Gerald F. Hawthorne (Grand Rapids: Eerdmans, 1975), 355–64. Cf. also Wayne Grudem, "Perseverance of the Saints: A Case Study from Hebrews 6:4–6 and the Other Warning Passages in Hebrews," in *The Grace of God, the Bondage of the Will*, ed. Thomas R. Schreiner and Bruce A. Ware, 2 vols. (Grand Rapids: Baker, 1995), 1:133–82.

57. See esp. I. Howard Marshall, *Kept by the Power of God* (Minneapolis: Bethany, 1969).

on the topic juxtaposed in the New Testament without resolution. This step should be a last resort, especially because the majority of believers for the first seventeen to eighteen centuries of church history, and not a small number even today, especially internationally, have not found such an interpretation necessary. Sometimes exegetes with experience resolving apparent contradictions elsewhere in Scripture, or those who have read plausible resolutions by others, reach a point where it is natural to give a text the benefit of the doubt when there is an apparent contradiction that for the moment defies resolution, rather than concluding that there never will be any plausible solution.[58] This is precisely how interpreters of other ancient works proceed. It is only when a source document regularly proves not to correspond to the hard historical data that one begins to become suspicious and reverses one's hermeneutic— being suspicious of a text's coherence in advance of actually looking at the arguments for its unity or disunity. Particularly when the theological tension appears within one and the same document, it is only proper to allow the benefit of the doubt and not assume that the writer, inspired or not, is flatly self-contradictory in the span of just a few paragraphs or sections of text. We would want our own utterances to be so treated, and we regularly treat non-biblical writers who otherwise show signs of intelligence and coherence such courtesy, until all reasonable alternatives have been exhausted.[59]

Conclusion

Not all passages will contribute crucial information to core theological doctrines. Many will be oriented toward ethics instead. Indeed, the procedures for producing compendia of biblical ethics will find many analogies to what we have described in this chapter for theology. Other passages will inform biblical or systematic theology in only a fairly minor way. Some may suggest that traditional, recent, Western theologies have gaps in them that need to be filled, for example, on topics of spiritual warfare, where an inductive analysis of the New Testament suggests that more needs to be said than one often finds in the existing literature. Or the relative importance given to long-standing topics of theological discussion may be exposed as disproportionately large or small compared with the amount or importance of its treatment in the Bible itself. Depending on how much of a biblical book is taken as a discrete passage for analysis, it is possible occasionally that a text may appear not to contribute anything to our theological understanding. Paul's affirmation in

58. See esp. I. Howard Marshall, *Luke: Historian and Theologian*, 3rd ed. (Downers Grove, IL: InterVarsity, 1998).

59. Except in avant-garde schools of literary interpretation like deconstruction, which stand out precisely because this approach refuses to follow the more ordinary, default method of trying to understand one another's communicative utterances. See further Jeannine K. Brown, *Scripture as Communication: Introducing Biblical Hermeneutics* (Grand Rapids: Baker, 2007).

2 Timothy 3:16 about the relevance of all Scripture was penned long before our existing chapter and verse divisions were introduced. At most, he is saying that every *book* of Scripture, and perhaps every major unit of thought within those books, has theological significance.[60] A single verse of a genealogy, for instance, may contribute little or nothing by itself, only as part of the overall list of ancestors or descendants of a given biblical character.[61] Most Bible teachers and preachers will want to choose passages long and detailed enough that they will contribute to our overall theological "database," and we will want to highlight these contributions in our instruction. Precisely for this reason, exegetes dare not stop without summarizing and reflecting on the nature of the theology of the passages of Scripture they analyze, lest that last piece of work be done only by someone else and the continuity of thought be lost or misunderstood.[62] For the same reason, exegetes also need to reflect on the contemporary application or significance of their texts, as their final step in a complete exegetical process. It is to this final task that we now turn.

60. Interestingly, B. B. Warfield, in his classic exposition *The Inspiration and Authority of the Bible* (Philadelphia: P&R, 1948), 134, declares, "Whether Paul, looking back at the Sacred Scriptures he had just mentioned, makes the assertion he is about to add [in 1 Tim. 3:16–17], of them distributively, of all their parts, or collectively, of their entire mass, is of no moment."

61. Cf., e.g., Craig L. Blomberg, "The Liberation of Illegitimacy: Women and Rulers in Matthew 1–2," *Biblical Theology Bulletin* 21 (1991): 145–50.

62. For similar convictions, see Joel B. Green and Max Turner, eds., *Between Two Horizons: Spanning New Testament Studies and Systematic Theology* (Grand Rapids and Cambridge: Eerdmans, 2000); and the Two Horizons New Testament Commentary series, also from Eerdmans.

10

Application

Most of us have heard it done, and more than a few of us have probably done it: As either teachers or hearers of a passage of Scripture, we feel like we have a pretty good grasp of its meaning and then, in an attempt to make it memorable, the speaker forces the application to the point that it fails to match what the author of the text meant. It may sound something like this:

> So as we consider Paul's powerful words to the Philippians in 4:13, "I can do everything through him who gives me strength," and understand Paul's ability to endure and even be joyful in the trials he encounters as he serves God, remember in your own life that you have God's strength to do the difficult things that you set your mind to. Do you want to be the new CEO in your current place of employment? Work hard and send your resume to human resources; you can do all things through Christ who gives us strength. Are you terrified of heights? Try skydiving; you can do all things through Christ who gives you strength. Have you never experienced the gift of evangelism? Just get out there and start to share your faith, praying for the power of the Spirit, and he will give you that gift. People will come to Christ if you just trust him for the ability.

The error in application here is certainly extreme, but it reflects the kinds of things Christians have actually taught and believed.[1] We can see what happens

---

1. D. A. Carson (*Basics for Believers: An Exposition of Philippians* [Grand Rapids: Baker, 1996], 119) elaborates: "This verse should not be deployed by well-meaning but ill-informed church leaders who are trying to manipulate church members into doing something they really do not think they should do: 'But Mrs. Jones, you can't say no to our invitation to teach ten-year-old boys, just because you've never taught a Sunday School class before or just because you

in the transition from good exegesis to forced application. There is the same inherent danger in the application of any Scripture. In our example, the speaker has a good grasp of the original meaning of the statement. Paul has learned to content himself both in times of want and in times of plenty. Christ gives Paul the strength to endure the ups and downs of ministry as he does God's work.[2] The speaker in our sermon above even concedes that this is the meaning of the statement in Philippians. But in moving from what it meant in Paul's setting to what it means in the audience's life, the whole thing falls apart, and the application violates a number of other principles in Scripture by insisting that we can do *anything we determine to do* through the strength of Christ.[3]

The internationally renowned preacher and homiletics professor Haddon Robinson has made the provocative but probably true statement, "More heresy is preached in application than in Biblical exegesis."[4] What a shame it would be to spend time in lesson preparation, meticulously working through each of the nine topics of biblical exegesis presented in this volume thus far, only to reach the apex of the sermon and have it depart from orthodoxy or even just legitimacy! For this reason we conclude our discussion of New Testament exegesis with the topic of application. This is an indispensable final step in the exegetical process, although it looks and feels remarkably different from the steps we have encountered thus far. It is fairly straightforward to consult historical material, including Bible encyclopedias and New Testament introductions, to get a feel for important features that would have affected the author and audience of biblical passages. Locating the passage's contribution to the author's overall argument is also something that is comparatively

---

feel you have no gifts or calling or interest in this area. After all, Paul teaches us that we can do all things through Christ who gives us strength.' That is horrible." The abuse also occurs in the reverse direction. One of our spouses was a local missions pastor for nine years and regularly had people aggressively soliciting support for missionary work they were bound on performing overseas, notwithstanding their lack of experience or giftedness with similar ministry here at home. All too often they cited Phil. 4:13 to try to bolster their claims.

2. The TNIV recognizes the frequent misinterpretation of the passage and opts for the translation, "I can do all this through him who gives me strength," which departs from the NIV's rendering: "I can do everything through him who gives me strength." While the NIV presents the more formally equivalent translation, the TNIV does a better job of capturing and conveying the original intention (recall our conversation on translations in chap. 2). Cf. Ben Witherington III, *Friendship and Finances in Philippi* (Valley Forge, PA: Trinity Press International, 1994), 129: "Paul is not saying he is superhuman and can *do* anything. In context he is saying he has the inner strength or power to take whatever the world thrusts upon him. This is a very different matter. This verse is not a charter for thinking that one can accomplish anything if one draws on the strength of God."

3. For responsible application of this text, see esp. Dean Flemming, *Philippians* (Kansas City, MO: Beacon Hill, 2009), 247–51, highlighting the need for the average modern Westerner to learn to be content in want.

4. An interview with Haddon Robinson, "The Heresy of Application," *Leadership* 18.4 (1997): 21.

straightforward. In these exegetical steps, we can also check our work against commentaries or other scholarly works to affirm that we are on the right track in the exegetical process of a particular passage. Application, however, makes a sharp departure from these other easier steps. What commentator can help you assess *your* audience and its situation and come up with an application that fits your specific occasion or context? What pastor of another congregation is as much in tune with the needs of those *you* shepherd enough to recommend the most relevant and poignant applications of the text for *them*? Application requires more individual attention and thought on the teacher's behalf than any of the preceding steps. It is the place where responsible and orthodox exegesis can lead either to brilliance or to treachery.

These are some of the reasons why, until recently, biblical scholars have tended to shy away from the subject. Many good interpretive guides devote hundreds of pages to educating the exegete on how to interpret texts of the Bible, only to tack on a couple pages at the end that resemble a pep talk akin to, "Well you're bright enough to have deciphered the meaning of this difficult text. Now apply it in a way that impacts your hearers' lives and motivates change. I'm sure you'll come up with something great!"[5] While this pep talk may be inspiring, it leaves the teacher or preacher with more than a few questions. It is our aim here to propose a method that will help the interpreter of Scripture make the journey from what the text *meant* in the first century to what the text *means* to a given audience today.[6] Or, to use the language of E. D. Hirsch, we want to move from original "meaning" to contemporary "significance."[7]

Recognizing Common Applicational Pitfalls

Among Bible readers there are three main areas where mistakes in application occur.[8] The good news for the exegete is that two of the areas are unlikely to

5. Traditional commentary series often fell victim to this lacuna. Some did not attempt applicational sections at all; others would devote discrete segments to the topic but they would be by far the smallest of all the subdivisions of the commentary. Fortunately, this is changing among many recent series, including The Bible Speaks Today, IVP New Testament Commentary, NIV Application Commentary, Two Horizons New Testament Commentary, and Zondervan Exegetical Commentary on the New Testament.

6. Krister Stendahl made this way of phrasing things famous in his article, "Biblical Theology," in *Interpreter's Dictionary of the Bible*, ed. George A. Buttrick, vol. 1 (Nashville: Abingdon, 1962), 419–22.

7. E. D. Hirsch Jr., *Validity in Interpretation* (New Haven: Yale University Press, 1967); idem, *The Aims of Interpretation* (Chicago: University of Chicago Press, 1978). Kevin Vanhoozer has helpfully refined this even further in terms of speech-act theory, which involves differentiating between a text's locution (what it says) and its perlocution (its intended results). See esp. his *Is There a Meaning in This Text?* (Grand Rapids: Zondervan, 1998).

8. William W. Klein, Craig L. Blomberg, and Robert L. Hubbard Jr., *Introduction to Biblical Interpretation*, rev. ed. (Nashville: Nelson, 2004), 479–82.

Sidebar 10.1

Common Pitfalls in Application

1. Neglect of any context
2. Interpreting the passage in light of the rest of the New Testament book in which it appears, while failing to take into account the full historical and literary contexts
3. Correctly interpreting the passage in light of its literary and historical contexts but bringing its principles to bear on modern circumstances in which they do not apply

---

affect someone who has thoroughly analyzed a passage of Scripture. However, we mention them here because they often plague the personal and devotional Bible reading of some among those we instruct. Pastorally, it is important to know where these interpretations may stem from, so that we can offer gentle guidance in more appropriate ways of Bible reading.

The first problem in application for many readers stems from the total neglect of any context. Akin to using a ouija board or "Bible roulette," a person may throw open the Bible, close his or her eyes and point to a Scripture, and then attempt to let that verse speak into his or her life for specific guidance concerning a pressing decision. A young woman was recently trying to decide whether to move from Denver to Hawaii to attend a discipleship training school there. She had been reading through the book of Revelation for her daily devotions and one morning came to the passage about the great multitude in heaven "wearing white robes and . . . holding palm branches in their hands." As she drove to work later that same morning, the Christian radio station she typically listened to was playing a contemporary praise song that again made reference to palm branches. She took this as the sign she was looking for, to pack her bags and move to the state of islands filled with palm trees.[9]

The second problem is like the first. The reader may interpret the passage in light of the rest of the New Testament book in which it appears, which is a step in the right direction, but then may fail to take into account the full historical and literary contexts. For example, both Colossians and Ephesians feature a household code of conduct written in a form that was common in the first century. In Ephesians 6:5, slaves are commanded to obey their earthly masters with respect and fear, as they would obey Christ. Likewise in Colossians 3:22,

---

9. This is not to say that God cannot work through well-intentioned but terribly flawed means of seeking his will. For the individual who knows no better, God *may* choose to divulge his will through such a method of reading Scripture, but there is hardly any guarantee that he will do so. Those who *do* know better should certainly not seek God's counsel in this fashion. To whom much is given, much shall be required (Luke 12:48). In context, this verse refers to acting wisely based on the amount of knowledge God has granted a person. This would certainly include knowledge of legitimate exegetical methods.

slaves are directed in the same way to obey masters both when they are being watched and when they are out of their masters' sight. Out of context, one could easily conclude that Paul endorses slavery. Not surprisingly, these passages provided considerable ammunition for those who opposed abolitionism at the time of the American Civil War.[10]

What is neglected with regard to historical context is that slavery was a quite different institution in the Roman world in the mid- to late first century than it was in the antebellum South. People would sometimes sell themselves into slavery because it provided better economic standing and offered the protection of their masters. The Roman government provided rights to slaves that American slavery never did, and slaves were often manumitted (or allowed to manumit themselves) by age thirty.[11] In addition, a pro-slavery interpretation fails to take into account the literary context of other epistles, like the letter to Philemon, where it appears that Paul's aim is not only to encourage Philemon to forgive his runaway slave, Onesimus, but also to plead for the master to free his slave altogether now that Onesimus is a full brother in Christ.[12] Why then would Paul not offer outright denunciation of slavery if that is what he intended, and why would he seemingly reinforce slavery by his household codes? It would have proven so countercultural for the New Testament epistles blatantly to repeal such entrenched societal norms, or for Paul to have condemned slavery outright, that the governing authorities might have unleashed unnecessary persecution, even destroying Christianity at its inception. Or it could have altogether undermined the more fundamental spiritual dimension of the good news of the gospel for first-century hearers. Paul knew his audience and his culture well enough to proceed slowly and present the gospel in a way that would best enable the audience to hear the most important part of his message clearly. But as F. F. Bruce has phrased it, "What this letter does is to bring us into an atmosphere in which the institution [of slavery] could only wilt and die."[13] Without understanding these broader historical and literary contexts, readers of Scripture will too often accuse Christians of legitimately deriving support for slavery from the Bible, and then reject Christianity completely as a result.

The third problem area is the error to which interpreters and speakers are most prone, as is represented in our opening example from Philippians 4.

10. Willard M. Swartley, *Slavery, Sabbath, War and Women* (Scottdale, PA, and Kitchener, ON: Herald, 1983), 31–64.

11. For good overviews of slavery in Paul's world, see K. R. Bradley, *Slavery and Society at Rome* (Cambridge and New York: Cambridge University Press, 1994); and Peter Garnsey, *Ideas of Slavery from Aristotle to Augustine* (Cambridge and New York: Cambridge University Press, 1996).

12. E.g., Joseph A. Fitzmyer, *The Letter to Philemon* (New York and London: Doubleday, 2000), 114–15; Markus Barth and Helmut Blanke, *The Letter to Philemon* (Grand Rapids and Cambridge: Eerdmans, 2000), 416–17.

13. F. F. Bruce, *Paul: Apostle of the Heart Set Free* (Grand Rapids: Eerdmans, 1977), 401.

There our hypothetical speaker correctly interpreted the passage in light of its literary and historical contexts but brought its principles to bear on modern circumstances in which they do not apply. In our example, the speaker applied the passage too broadly for his hearers, so that "everything" encompassed the ability to achieve all one desires. Scripture quickly dismisses this interpretation with compelling examples of how all a believer does should be carried out in the context of God's will, not his or her own ambitions (James 4:13–15; Matt. 6:8–14). A quick way to test an application's validity to see if it is sufficiently analogous to the original meaning of the passage is to make sure the application cannot be refuted by anything else in the canon of Scripture. If it is refuted elsewhere, the application fails.

The Nature of Communication

We have hinted at the definition of application throughout the opening pages of this chapter; now it is time to state it more directly. Application has to do with the response of the reader or hearer to the author's meaning of the text.[14] It is the movement from knowing cognitively what to do or believe in light of a passage of Scripture to understanding how to implement that belief or behavior in one's life. As we use the word "application" throughout our treatment here, it primarily deals with the exegete's ability to convey ideas to one's audience about how the meaning of the text should shape individual lives. The word can also connote the action to which the interpreter hopes to move his or her hearers. An effectively presented application, along with the prompting of the Spirit in a believer's life, will result in an active obedience in the context of real life.

Important, Helpful Presuppositions

Before we propose a method for moving from what the text meant to what it means for a contemporary audience, we must state what we have already assumed about the nature of Scripture as communication. How a reader decides to receive a text has as much to do with interpretation as the words that are written on the page. Suppose you receive an unexpected card tucked into your suitcase when you are away from home on the weekend. Your name is on the envelope, and your spouse's signature appears after a thoughtful note inside the card. You will do everything in your interpretive power to figure out exactly what the author of that note meant because he or she is trying to say something directly to you. So you ask, "What does my beloved mean by saying this?" As a reader, you are committed to discerning authorial intent through a text directly for you.[15]

---

14. J. Scott Duvall and J. Daniel Hays, *Journey into God's Word: Your Guide to Understanding and Applying the Bible* (Grand Rapids: Zondervan, 2008), 89.

15. Cf. esp. throughout Jeannine K. Brown, *Scripture as Communication: Introducing Biblical Hermeneutics* (Grand Rapids: Baker, 2007).

Now suppose you found a card without an envelope left in the drawer of the nightstand of your hotel room. You open it, and it is addressed to someone other than you and signed by a name you don't recognize. It is obvious that someone has left this behind, and that it was never intended for you. You may find the words inside sentimental or even discover a poetic expression of love. However, you approach it quite differently than you would a note addressed to you. You may well ask the question, "Does this message have *any* meaning for me?" You will surely skip the parts that don't appeal to you while perhaps admiring the parts that remain. Because the note doesn't directly bear on your life, you have the freedom to pick and choose what you pay any attention to. You have performed one (more conservative) form of "reader-response" interpretation.[16] (A more liberal form might assume it *was* intended for you and twist the meaning of its words so that they seemed to address a situation in your life after all, just as it could take something that *was* intended for you and change the meaning to something the author didn't intend!) Now, on the one hand, we must recognize that none of the biblical books was directly intended to be "our mail." But, on the other hand, to the extent that the New Testament authors knew that their works would be copied quickly and disseminated widely, it *is* fair to look for significance in them for us in the way it would not be with someone else's love letter to a person we don't know.[17]

For an everyday example of the difference in interpretive approaches to the same matter, consider this illustration. You approach an intersection with a red left arrow showing on the traffic light. If you interpret it according to authorial intent, you stop and wait for the green arrow. If you approach it with another kind of reader-response approach in mind, you may slow down, look to see that there are no cars approaching in the oncoming lane, and proceed according to your own schedule. Of course, every driver has more than a few clues that the light should be interpreted according to authorial intent. A $100 traffic citation issued by the city that constructed and controls the traffic light to those who disobey the red arrow's intended meaning is one of the indications that all traffic signs and signals should be interpreted according to authorial intent.[18] Still other forms of communication fall somewhere in between the extremes of "I can take it or leave it" and "This is binding on me."

16. On which, see esp. Vanhoozer, *Is There a Meaning in This Text?* 148–200. Cf. also Stanley E. Porter, "Literary Approaches to the New Testament: From Formalism to Deconstruction and Back," in *Approaches to New Testament Study*, ed. Stanley E. Porter and David Tombs (Sheffield: Sheffield Academic Press, 1995), 77–128.

17. See esp. Richard Bauckham, ed., *The Gospels for All Christians: Rethinking the Gospel Audiences* (Grand Rapids and Cambridge: Eerdmans, 1998). Paul himself refers at times to the exchange of his letters (esp. Col. 4:16), while the so-called General Epistles often made multiple churches intended from the outset, as is explicitly the case with Revelation (see chaps. 2–3).

18. In ordinary acts of human communication, even reader-response critics have to limit the freedoms in interpretation they claim for their literary criticism if they are to be understood by others and if they are to remain responsible, sane members of society.

All readers of Scripture are faced with this spectrum of interpretive options when they approach the biblical text, and each reader will fall somewhere on the spectrum between the practice of pure reader-centered analysis and that of complete reliance on textual or authorial intent. If one reads the Bible as merely a great literary work, full of suggestions for moral living, then one may treat its contents more according to reader-response criticism, choosing very selectively which portions (if any) to apply. If, however, we believe the Bible to be God's special revelation to humanity, written to shape the lives of those who recognize Jesus Christ as Lord, then the task becomes to find out exactly what God meant with every passage of Scripture so that we can apply them to our lives. Our conversation on application (and even the practice of exegesis as presented in this book's ten steps) is firmly rooted in the conviction that God intends to communicate a specific message to us through the pages of Scripture, and so our goal in interpretation is to find what the author meant and means rather than to interpret Scripture based solely on a model in which readers are free to create meaning for themselves.[19]

We have made one other assumption about the nature of communication. With very rare exceptions, communicators intend to accomplish something with their words. Most of us agree that pointless chatter is annoying and a waste of our time. Simple statements are intended to motivate a hearer to something.[20] Consider the example of a family at breakfast. The seven-year-old son asks to be excused from the table, and his father replies, "You didn't even touch your milk." If the child responds, "That's right, I didn't," and then proceeds to empty his glass into the sink and go about the business of the day, his father will hardly be pleased. Implicit in the father's statement may well be the condition, "Before you are allowed to leave the table, you must at least attempt to drink some of that milk." Or imagine, as the children finish up their breakfast, Mom may say, "It's already 8:15!" Everybody at the table knows that means to move as fast as their legs will take them because they're about to miss the bus, and that means trouble. Nobody would say (seriously), "Well, that is interesting information. Thanks, Mom, for reading the clock to us."

Even the small talk exchanged between strangers has a purpose in mind. I might be interviewing a candidate for a job and, when the candidate walks in, I say hello and comment on the beautiful, sunny day it is outside. It is not an aimless comment, even though it is not relevant to whether I will hire the candidate. It is intended to assure the candidate that I share in her humanity, and that, although I'll be asking her questions for the next hour, I can affirm that we are both peers in experiencing our environment similarly, so that our

19. Duvall and Hays, *Journey into God's Word*, 86–87.
20. Daniel M. Doriani, *Putting the Truth to Work: The Theory and Practice of Biblical Application* (Phillipsburg, NJ: P&R Publishing, 2001), 42–44.

playing field is level in that regard. It is an attempt to make the conversation a little less strained and more natural.

Whole conversations are aimed even more carefully at producing identifiable responses. Each party would like to be heard and see the other party respond appropriately in light of the information being given. A person telling his or her spouse about their day at work is not only conveying information but asking the other person to hear the story and respond with sympathy if there was some mild defeat, elation if there was some victory, or to help solve a conflict that was created during the day. Perhaps the only intended purpose is to draw the hearer closer to the communicator by establishing common experience, but be assured that the conversation is purposeful.[21]

If what we have said about speech is true, it is equally true of writing. Although writing is a bit trickier because the author is often not present to clarify ambiguities or combat misinterpretations, the same rules of communication apply, even if the writer's purposes seem veiled upon initial reading. Perhaps writing will not elicit as direct a response as conversation, but it is still intentional. Even entire literary genres have typical purposes: "Poetry ennobles. News reports inform. Lectures educate. Novels entertain. Essays shape opinion and policy."[22]

If all language intends to accomplish something via its utterances, we should expect nothing different from biblical language. Several assertions in the Bible indicate that Scripture is intended to move the believer to action (James 1:22) and that all of it is "God-breathed and is useful for teaching, rebuking, correcting and training in righteousness, so that all God's people may be thoroughly equipped for every good work" (2 Tim. 3:16–17). It is intended to motivate, to generate activity on behalf of God's kingdom.

Dangerous, Misleading Presuppositions

We have approached application with the presupposition that Scripture is communication between God and humanity. On the one hand, we first seek author-intended meaning through the multiple steps of exegesis, and then we subject ourselves to that meaning without excluding anything that at first glance does not seem to benefit us.[23] On the other hand, there are

---

21. Ben Witherington has demonstrated that the substantial majority of New Testament books are "deliberative" in their rhetoric, explicitly aiming to persuade people to certain courses of action. See esp. his *New Testament Rhetoric: An Introductory Guide to the Art of Persuasion in and of the New Testament* (Eugene, OR: Cascade, 2009). The other two species of ancient rhetoric, which account for those portions of the New Testament that are not deliberative in nature, are that of praising or blaming (epideictic) and that of defending or accusing (forensic or apologetic).

22. Doriani, *Putting the Truth to Work*, 44.

23. Vanhoozer (*Is There a Meaning in This Text?*) observes the trinitarian logic inherent in this process: just as an author uses the word to communicate to listeners/readers, so also the Father reveals himself through the Son (the Word) to those illuminated by the Holy Spirit.

several damaging presuppositions that we need to avoid in order to apply the text correctly.

Coming to the text with an agenda is always a danger. While we constantly deal with the hermeneutical spiral of our presuppositions influencing our approach to Scripture and Scripture informing and challenging our presuppositions, an agenda that looks only for certain acceptable features of the text oversteps this natural spiral. If one's sermon on Galatians 3 becomes only a treatise on how, in light of verse 28, women should be allowed to operate in the same leadership capacities as men in the church, one has come to the text with a filter or grid that has not allowed Scripture to speak on its own terms.[24] This principle goes beyond what can be legitimately inferred from this text alone and, even if this were not the case, it does not reflect the *main* thrust or theme of chapter 3 (or even just of vv. 26–29, in which it is more immediately embedded). Similarly, if the average Western pastor preaches the parable of the rich man and Lazarus (Luke 16:19–31) and identifies only with the poor beggar rather than the wealthy man who dines sumptuously every day, one has come wearing blinders, perhaps even unconsciously, that let the rich in one's congregation (in some cases, one's entire audience, when measured by global standards) remain inappropriately comfortable with their wealth. Make sure you read the text on its own terms first, find its original meaning, and then do the work of fitting it into a larger theological framework.

Another presupposition that blinds us to author-intended meaning and therefore causes us to misapply a text involves allowing resources besides the Bible to paint misleading images for us, which we then import to the text. The lyrics of Christian music can misshape our theology, for example. Some songs emphasize the love and grace of God to the exclusion of his justice and hatred for sin. Others focus on God as our best friend without simultaneously sobering us to his perfect holiness and the fear of beholding him in all his power. One popular praise song announces, in the name of God, "Upon this rock, I'll build my kingdom," when Jesus declared he would build his *church*.[25] Do we understand the difference and the significance of the difference, or do we import the changed words of the chorus into our understanding of the

24. Note that this approach is quite different from using Gal. 3:28 as evidence in building a systematic theological stance on the issue of women in leadership in the church. We agree that this text must be included in that discussion, because systematic theology brings all relevant biblical data to bear on a given subject (see above, chap. 9). But Paul's main thrust in this context (vv. 19–29) is that the law was given temporarily to restrict God's people until the messianic age should come. With the arrival of that age we are now free from the law and therefore free from one of the key social barriers that divided humanity into in-groups and out-groups. For an excellent study of how much can and cannot be inferred from verse 28, see Ben Witherington III, "Rite and Rights for Women—Galatians 3.28," *New Testament Studies* 27 (1981): 593–604.

25. Sandi Patty, "Upon This Rock," http://www.gospelmusiclyricsden.com/upon-this-rock-sandi-patty.shtml (accessed June 18, 2009).

text of Matthew 16:18?[26] The classic hymn lyrics, "Jesus shall reign where'er the sun doth its eternal courses run," is explicitly postmillennial. Can premillennialists and amillennialists sing its words with integrity? Does repeated singing of the hymn begin to turn the latter two categories of believers into the former, without their even realizing it, as they approach Scriptures that teach about Jesus's coming triumph?

Art from all ages of history also affects our perception of biblical truths. How many of us in the backs of our minds picture a fair-skinned, blue-eyed Jesus, or Paul knocked off a horse when the Lord spoke to him on the Damascus road? Does viewing paintings of the boy Jesus standing in the temple and discoursing to the Jewish leaders seated around him blind us to the actual words of Luke 2:46 that he was *sitting* among the teachers *listening to them* and *asking them questions*? Maybe even more misleading are portrayals of heaven as little more than fluffy white clouds where angels and believers play harps all day. The Bible presents a very different picture, of the rich glories and grandeurs of a new heavens and a new *earth* (Rev. 21–22), one that is far more diverse and attractive than aimless drifting on clouds for eternity.[27] Hollywood and the media also shape our presuppositions. One silly example that likely affects us all is our perception of Jonah in the belly of the big fish. It's hard not to envision Pinocchio from the Disney movie, perched calmly on a three-legged stool, looking trapped and rather unenthused about being in a whale's belly but otherwise unharmed. However, have you ever stopped long enough to think about what it would really be like to be confined in the large digestive organ of a fish, stomach acid and all? The Pinocchio version is much more palatable, which is one way unbelievers try to domesticate the Bible. But the same is often true of believers, whether in a formal Sunday school curriculum or a popular cartoon like *Veggie Tales*. Their depictions of biblical characters and events are more marketable and less embarrassing, but often less faithful to the text as a result.

A Method for Bringing the Bible to Our Own World

We have laid much groundwork throughout our book to propose a method for taking the author's intended meaning and finding ways to apply it that help one develop the heart and mind of God to think and respond to situa-

26. See esp. George E. Ladd, *A Theology of the New Testament*, ed. Donald A. Hagner, rev. ed. (Grand Rapids: Eerdmans, 1993), 109–17: The church is not the kingdom; the kingdom creates the church; the church witnesses to the kingdom; the church is the instrument of the kingdom; and the church is the custodian of the kingdom.

27. See esp. Tom Wright, *Surprised by Hope: Rethinking Heaven, the Resurrection and the Mission of the Church* (London and New York: HarperCollins, 2008). Cf. also Randy Alcorn, *Heaven* (Wheaton: Tyndale House, 2004).

tions the way God would want one to do.[28] We have alluded in our opening paragraphs to how tricky this step of the exegetical process can be and how little systematic treatment it has received. What, then, exactly is so tricky about the enterprise?

The biggest factor that makes application so hard is that we remain separated from the original recipients of the New Testament documents by two millennia and thousands of miles. The situations that were addressed by the authors were often very different from those we encounter today. Many of us have never been expelled from our homes and homeland like the Jews among the audiences of the letters to the Romans and the Hebrews.[29] Many of us have never had to forgo our right to eat meat because it leads a new Christian to worship idols. And if we meet someone who has, we feel somewhat unable to relate to their experiences. Yet these were huge issues to which letters in the New Testament directly spoke. How are we to apply texts on these topics to drastically different circumstances in our own world?

There are elements of human experience portrayed in the Bible that are universal across time and culture and are much more easily transported to our own world. We sympathize with the human propensity toward sin as it is portrayed in Paul's letters and in many of the biblical narratives, even though we know what Christ has accomplished for us. We feel sorrow for loss, we sometimes have trouble believing in a God we cannot see, and we know what it means to be concerned about food, clothing, and shelter. Many of these items in Scripture resonate so loudly that applications become easier.

Picture a river between two shores. On one side appear the original cultures and times of the biblical authors. On the other is a contemporary audience. In between are the waters that range from calm and shallow to deep and raging. Those passages in which application is easily transferable represent a shallow and slow spot in the river that one might even be able to ford or cross on a path of dry stones.[30] The places where we initially read, scratch our heads, and say, "Now how in the world do we make this relevant to our lives?" are areas where a reliable bridge, one that rises above the danger of flood waters, must be constructed. With this bridge as our metaphor for crossing the deep water between biblical cultures and ours, let us move forward.

28. As in Jack Kuhatschek's definition of application, in *Taking the Guesswork out of Applying the Bible* (Downers Grove, IL: InterVarsity, 1990), 24, which seems less clinical than most, and much more appropriate given our discussion of Scripture's intention to move its hearers to action.

29. As Jews, including Christian Jews, experienced after the edict of Claudius in AD 49.

30. Daniel M. Doriani (*Getting the Message: A Plan for Interpreting and Applying the Bible* [Phillipsburg, NJ: P&R Publishing, 1996], 142–43) likens straightforward application to strolling on a sidewalk from the contemporary world to the ancient world, since very little needs to be reconstructed for the passage to make good sense to the audience. Application can be as easy as walking a paved path from here to there.

The exegetical process thus far has built a solid foundation for our bridge on the other side of the divide. Thorough knowledge of one's own culture and problems that one's audience faces, along with the language they use to explain their human experiences, forms the foundation for the bridge on this side of the divide. It is our hope that the following principles will help interpreters understand exactly what needs to happen for the structure between the two foundations to be erected and crossed. The good news is that virtually all scholars who have researched the topic of application have reached a reasonable consensus on at least the following four principles:

1. Determine the original application(s) intended by the passage.
2. Evaluate the level of specificity of those applications in their original historical situations. If the original applications are transferable across time and space to other audiences, apply them in culturally appropriate ways.
3. If the original applications are not transferable, identify one or more broader cross-cultural principles that the specific elements of the text reflect.
4. Find appropriate applications for today that implement those principles.[31]

We will comment briefly on each of these four steps.

Determining the Original Application

At this point in the exegetical journey, the meaning of a given passage for its original hearers has been determined. All the steps outlined in the previous chapters have been aimed at leading the interpreter to discover what the text meant to its original hearers. Yet even when the original meaning has been reached, a few more questions can be asked of the text to see how the author intended for the audience to *apply* the meaning. Is there a command to obey, an example to follow or to avoid, a promise to claim, a warning to heed, a teaching to act on, or a truth to believe? One or more of these questions will usually be answered by the text.

For example, in Jesus's Sermon on the Mount, he commands his hearers not to worry and gives concrete examples of things that are not worth their worry (Matt. 6:25–34). By asking the questions above, we find several applications.

31. These principles are taken verbatim from Blomberg, Klein, and Hubbard, *Introduction to Biblical Interpretation*, 483. *Four Views on Moving Beyond the Bible to Theology* (ed. Gary T. Meadors [Grand Rapids: Zondervan, 2010]) is actually more about what has traditionally been called application than about theology and does not actually present four necessarily conflicting methods. The "redemptive-historical," "drama-of-redemption," and "redemptive-movement" models all depend and build on the "principlizing" model, which is closest to what we defend here, without excluding the others.

There is the overarching command not to be so preoccupied with taking care of material needs that we miss the kingdom of God. His followers are to act on the example of the birds and the flowers, which do not toil in vain to acquire daily needs. He concludes with the truth that God knows our needs and supplies them, which frees us to seek after the things of God's heart first.[32] We referred previously to Paul's discussion about meat sacrificed to idols in 1 Corinthians 8. Choosing just a few of the questions we recommended above, the application of the text to the original audience emerges. Is there a command? The Corinthians should refrain from their right to eat food that has been sacrificed to idols in situations where it might make newer or less mature Christians stumble in their faith in Christ. Does Paul provide an example? The example to follow is Paul himself, who, as an apostle, knows he has the right to eat the food, and many other rights as well, but would rather refuse to exercise those rights if there is a genuine chance that any action might lead someone to sin (v. 13). Is there a warning? Yes, Paul warns that the exercise of the right to eat meat without concern for what it might cause others to do could actually be a sin against Christ himself (v. 12). The application of the passage to the original audience is not difficult to discern, but a contemporary audience may scratch their heads and wonder what to do in their own lives in light of the original application.[33]

Evaluate the Level of Specificity

Both of the examples above require taking a step beyond discerning the original meaning and application for the audience. Continuing with the example from Matthew 6, it is easy to conclude that the commands in Jesus's teaching were general enough to make the simple hop from one side of the riverbank to the other. The specificity is not so narrow that we have a hard time understanding what we are to do. The interpreter can certainly bring the point a little closer to home by choosing more modern examples of things that people worry about, such as investment portfolios, houses, and cars, but because the general principles for application are already in the text, little more is needed than for the communicator to move the principles into language that the hearers will readily recognize and with examples to which they will relate.[34] There are, however, plenty of passages where the specificity of the application to its original audience makes it downright confusing to the con-

---

32. See further William W. Klein, *Become What You Are: Spiritual Formation according to the Sermon on the Mount* (Milton Keynes, UK, and Tyrone, GA: Authentic, 2006), 175–83.

33. See further Craig Blomberg, *1 Corinthians* (Grand Rapids: Zondervan, 1994), 159–71.

34. For an excellent treatment of this process, see J. Robertson McQuilkin, *Understanding and Applying the Bible: An Introduction to Hermeneutics* (Chicago: Moody, 1983), 255–72. See esp. the flowcharts on pp. 265 and 269.

temporary audience. Consider again 1 Corinthians 8. Because the issue is so specific to the original audience and we as twenty-first-century Westerners have no unambiguously analogical custom, we must proceed to step three of our proposed applicational method in order to make sense of what Scripture is asking contemporary audiences to do as a result of this passage. We will need to find the principle behind the specific command to make the transition from then and there to now and here.

Of course, between the extremes—those passages with applications that clearly transfer from biblical times to ours and those that have no close analogies and require the next step in our application methodology—are passages where the specificity is difficult to discern.[35] Perhaps no issue better demonstrates this than the issue of women's roles in the church. Take the difficult passage 1 Timothy 2:8–15 as an example. Besides Paul's statement, "I do not permit a woman to teach or to assume authority over a man," there are several other commands, including one that asks men to pray while holding up holy hands and one that forbids women to braid their hair with gold or pearls. Now, nearly all commentators agree that someone can pray well without lifting their hands and that, in our culture, there is very little provocative about braided hair, even with jewelry interwoven into it. These were obviously issues that were important in Paul's time and culture in ways they are not for most contemporary audiences. However, often when it is suggested that Paul's command that a woman may not teach or have authority over men is bound by culture and time, the gloves come off and the battle ensues. We don't intend to pursue the exegetical problem any further here, as there are many works that do so

---

35. Responding to the need to create some sort of methodology for interpreting passages where it is difficult to determine whether the biblical author intends changing or unchanging applications, William J. Webb (*Slaves, Women and Homosexuals: Exploring the Hermeneutics of Cultural Analysis* [Downers Grove, IL: InterVarsity, 2001]) proposes a hermeneutic that looks to see if one can find what he calls a "redemptive" trajectory of greater openness to a given practice as one moves through both testaments and the course of God's progressive revelation. If, and only if, such a trajectory is present may the church continue with even greater openness to the practice throughout its history. The resulting hermeneutic finds hints throughout the Bible of increasing freedom for women and slaves (recall our conversation on Philemon above), even though full-fledged freedom for both groups would have proven too subversive in the larger Roman world of the New Testament. The same roadblocks are not found in many contemporary twenty-first-century audiences; in fact, the errant convictions that the Bible actually endorses slavery and misogyny are themselves major obstacles to faith in many current contexts (especially for educated, capable women and African Americans). However, when it comes to homosexual practice, Webb finds no redemptive trajectory or progressive freedom granted throughout the Bible or, for that matter, any passage anywhere permitting the practice. We contend that Webb's hermeneutic as a method is justifiable, but advise considerable care in determining whether a redemptive trajectory is really present. Some, for example, would not see slavery and women's restrictions from certain leadership roles in the Bible as entirely analogous. Others would reject even Webb's methodology, irrespective of its specific applications; see esp. Wayne Grudem, "Should We Move beyond the New Testament to a Better Ethic?" *Journal of the Evangelical Theological Society* 47 (2004): 299–346.

in the type of detail for which we have no space in this book.[36] Additionally, readers now have the tools to do their own exegetical work on the various exegetical conundra that this passage presents. We use it only as an example to say that sometimes passages are difficult enough that the application could go one of several directions, and that passages do not always fit neatly into the categories of universally applicable or culturally specific.

Some hermeneutical approaches prescribe that unless something in the text specifically indicates that a passage teaches timeless truth, readers should assume that the passage is situation-specific. Others insist that unless the text clearly indicates that the content is culture-bound, then the originally intended application remains normative for all believers at all times.[37] The former argument makes it hard, at least in some contexts, to establish the timelessness of even foundational moral principles such as prohibitions against adultery or murder, while the latter would require us to greet each other with a holy kiss (1 Thess. 5:26) or drink wine rather than take an antacid for our upset stomachs (1 Tim. 5:23). We believe that the best approach is somewhere in the middle, so that an exegete should evaluate each passage individually for what might be culturally specific or timeless, even when the author does not directly indicate which of the two is intended.[38]

Let us return now to 1 Corinthians 8 as an example of a passage in which the application in its first-century context seems to have no obvious counterpart for a contemporary Western Christian. The reader must climb the ladder of abstraction[39] to find a way to bridge the gap and can do so by finding the broader cross-cultural principles implicit in the context.[40]

36. See further James R. Beck, ed., *Two Views of Women in Ministry*, rev. ed. (Grand Rapids: Zondervan, 2005). On the complementarian side of the debate, John Piper and Wayne Grudem, eds., *Recovering Biblical Manhood and Womanhood: A Response to Evangelical Feminism* (Wheaton: Crossway, 1991), remains a standard resource. On the egalitarian side, see esp. Ronald W. Pierce and Rebecca M. Groothuis, eds., *Discovering Biblical Equality: Complementarity without Hierarchy* (Downers Grove, IL: InterVarsity, 2004).

37. For an explication of both perspectives, see esp. William J. Larkin Jr., *Culture and Biblical Hermeneutics: Interpreting and Applying the Authoritative Word in a Relativistic Age* (Grand Rapids: Baker, 1988).

38. For ten questions to ask when determining if the application is timeless or culture bound, see Klein, Blomberg, and Hubbard, *Introduction to Biblical Interpretation*, 187–98.

39. Instead of using the image of a bridge, as we do, Webb uses the concept of a ladder to cross the divide, with one leg of the ladder on the original audience's side and the other leg on the side of the contemporary reader. His concept is helpful because it provides a mental image of heights from the text that the interpreter will need to climb to find the closest (lowest rung) common denominator with regard to principle that will link the text to our world. Some texts will require a higher climb (those with original applications that bear little resemblance to contemporary contexts), but our goal is to stay as close to the text as possible and "climb only as high as the text requires us" (*Slaves, Women, and Homosexuals*, 54). See further our discussion below on levels of authority in application.

40. Cf. further Timothy J. Ralston, "Showing the Relevance: Application, Ethics, and Preaching," in *Interpreting the New Testament Text: Introduction to the Art and Science of Exegesis*,

Identify Broader Cross-Cultural Principles

CREATING INITIAL FORMULATIONS OF THE PRINCIPLE

When we zoom out and focus on the larger issue leading to the example of 1 Corinthians 8 and food sacrificed to idols, some of Paul's summary statements help. In verse 9, a broad principle is directly stated: "Be careful, however, that the exercise of your rights does not become a stumbling block to the weak." Paul warns the more mature Christians, who are able to separate the action of eating meat from pagan idol worship, that although they can engage in the practice in good conscience they should curb their right to indulge when there is the threat of leading others who cannot easily make the same distinction to imitate them. The principle then would be that, although the life of a Christian involves great freedom and allows participation in many morally neutral practices, where less mature believers may see these practices and be led into sin, more mature Christians should lay aside their rights out of love for their siblings in Christ.[41]

It is not enough, however, for the exegete to note that a broader principle appears in the text. A good interpreter will delve more deeply to find out why the specific application that was made *did* flow from that principle in its original context. For example, Paul asks women to cover their heads in 1 Corinthians 11. The command seems strange to modern ears and we ask why Paul would issue it. Is it because covering one's head is obviously a righteous and commendable practice for women both in Paul's time and in every culture including ours? Nothing in modern Western societies suggests an obvious reason why the command should be timeless. But that observation alone is inadequate; we must analyze the ancient culture(s) as well. A brief dip into the historical-cultural context of 1 Corinthians will quickly reveal that the command has much more to do with how head coverings signaled a wife's sexual and/or religious fidelity in a world in which infidelity in the context of cultic worship was rampant and often indicated by an uncovered head and/or provocative dress. We deduce from the historical-cultural context and the statement in the text that any appearance that would lead others to question one's sexual purity or allegiance to God should be avoided.[42]

Even after all the exegetical steps explained in this book have been employed, there will be times when the work of an expert commentator will be indispensable. Cases where either the text does not make any direct statement about what the author expects of the audience, or one's own historical-cultural analysis does not provide the cross-cultural principle in the passage, become excellent candidates for consulting a commentary for help. Such help may be

---

ed. Darrell L. Bock and Buist M. Fanning (Wheaton: Crossway, 2006), 293–310.

41. See further Joseph Aldrich, *Life-Style Evangelism* (Portland, OR: Multnomah, 1981), 39–76.

42. See further Blomberg, *1 Corinthians*, 207–26.

found, for instance, in the New International Version Application Commentary (NIVAC) series, which includes in the exegesis of every passage a crucial section called "Bridging Contexts," discussing how to discern broader, cross-cultural principles from the text.[43]

Consider the complex argument of Hebrews 4:1–13. This passage requires every interpretive method we have discussed in order to unpack the idea of entering the rest that Christ has provided for us both now and in eternity. Interpretation of the section is dependent on the author's entire narrative flow (literary criticism) and thorough word studies of "rest" and "obedience," inasmuch as these terms have been prone to eisegesis. The exegete would depend on grammatical studies to understand "rest" as a present and future reality and depend on an outline of the text to differentiate the author's main points of argument from the subordinate points. The passage profoundly shapes the theological topics of Sabbath or rest for Christians and reinterprets the Old Testament Sabbath laws, while verse 12 forms part of every theological discussion of the inspiration of God's word and its authority in a believer's life. These are only a few highlights of the importance of the exegetical steps commended in this book.[44]

Assuming we have done the exegetical work of discerning the meaning of the passage, we find the paradoxical truth that the key to obtaining the rest promised to us by Christ is to "make every effort" (σπουδάζω, "to work hard") at obedience to God as revealed in Christ (v. 11).[45] Here we can return to our questions aimed at discerning original application. There are certainly commands to obey, but they are general principles of obedience versus disobedience, so we move to other questions to see what the author advises the original audience to do. There is the negative example of the Israelites who failed to enter God's rest because of disobedience. Are there promises to claim? Yes, there is the promise that we can enter God's rest, but again this is higher up the ladder of abstraction. Because this text seems to be a theological treatise in which we see very little application to the original audience, it might be tempting to glean only abstract theological principles, or to think that we are ready immediately to move to the final step of deriving *contemporary* application. Even if that were true, the interpreter should still wrestle with the question of originally intended application (step one), perhaps with help of a commentary series like the NIVAC, to make sure that the corresponding contemporary application is as concrete and legitimate as possible.

43. In the NIV Application Commentary series, each section of Scripture in every commentary is treated with three subsections titled "Original Meaning," "Bridging Contexts," and "Contemporary Significance."

44. See further A. T. Lincoln, "Sabbath, Rest, and Eschatology in the New Testament," in *From Sabbath to Lord's Day: A Biblical, Historical and Theological Investigation,* ed. D. A. Carson (Grand Rapids: Zondervan, 1982), 97–120.

45. George H. Guthrie, *Hebrews* (Grand Rapids: Zondervan, 1998), 155.

George Guthrie spends much time in the "Bridging Contexts" section of his volume on Hebrews in the NIVAC working through this process, and he identifies four elements that must factor into an overarching cross-cultural principle: (1) there is a rest that hearers should fear missing; (2) the danger in missing it comes from failing to combine faith with obedience to God's word; (3) the rest consists of ceasing from one's own work and being obedient to God instead; and (4) it is entered now but will be fully consummated at the end of the age.[46] These four points are not quite the same as the four originally intended applications, but they are specific elements of the readers' initial encounter with the text that allow us to create our larger, more abstract principle. Creating a single summary statement, we might suggest that *Christians whose faith does not result in obedience to God's Word but who instead rely on their own work are in grave danger of failing to enter the rest God has for us in this life and the life to come.*

Testing Our Formulations

When interpreters move from details of a text to formulate a statement of the overarching principles, they leave the concrete elements of the passage behind in favor of a statement that is easily transported to a different time and place. Notice that our summary statement of 1 Corinthians 8 left out all references to meat, sacrifice, idols, feasting, and the like, and is packaged in a way that a contemporary audience might hear the statement and generate specific scenarios in their own setting about where that principle might come into play. Once you have an audience that is looking for their own examples of application to real-life situations, it is a short and rewarding jump to the next and final step, which is to give concrete examples of where the text's principles play out in one's own culture. In this final step it is important to make sure that the broader principle captures the entire teaching of the text, and not just part of it. A comprehensive statement of the cross-cultural principle from 1 Corinthians 8:4–13 must thus recognize three elements: (1) the presence of a genuine threat to Christian freedom (vv. 4–6, 8–9, 13); (2) the existence of a potential stumbling block to someone else (vv. 7, 9); (3) the danger of weaker Christian brothers or sisters who might be led into actual sin by imitating the behavior in question (vv. 9–12).[47] A statement that does not acknowledge all of these elements does not capture the full dynamic of the text and easily leads to legalism on the one hand (if element 1 is ignored) or lawlessness on the other hand (if elements 2 and 3 are ignored).

We have already presented four elements that must factor into the cross-cultural principle in Hebrews 4:1–13, identified in George Guthrie's commentary: (1) there is a rest; (2) there is a danger of failing to combine faith

---

46. Ibid., 157–58.
47. Kuhatschek, *Taking the Guesswork out of Applying the Bible*, 68–70.

with obedience; (3) rest consists of ceasing from work and obeying God; and (4) rest is both now and at the end of the age. If we neglect the features of those verses that show us that there is a real danger and therefore a genuine fear in missing out on rest (elements 1 and 2), we might miss the urgency of the author's words and consider entering rest as an option just for some spiritually elite believers. If we fail to note that entering God's rest is a command for both now and eternity (element 4), we could preach that God's rewards are strictly future and that we will toil on earth until Christ's return without hope of any kind of rest. Alternately, we could define rest as solely part of existence in this world and miss the infinitely greater portion of Christ's promise. Worst of all, if we don't define rest in terms of obedience to God's word (element 3), our interpretation may degenerate into a kind of prosperity gospel that pretends that physical rest in this life is always God's will or that we can count on comfortable beds and eight hours of sleep every night as a result of our Christianity. Unless the cross-cultural principles an interpreter formulates incorporate all of the components of the passage, applications may well not be sufficiently analogous to the originally intended ones and can even seriously distort God's intentions for us today.[48]

To double-check, therefore, that cross-cultural principles discerned from texts are accurate and honor the intended meaning of the biblical authors, keep these few tests in mind. First, make sure a given principle has come straight from the text at hand. Fight the temptation to read in concepts from other authors across the canon of Scripture, or to read in anachronistic definitions of terms and concepts. Second, as we have just illustrated, check to see that the principle incorporates all of the main elements of the text and does not conveniently neglect an important component. Third, make sure the principle is not tied to a particular situation but can truly express its original intention in cultures all over the world and throughout history. If you come up with a principle that is true only in urban Chicago but not in sub-Saharan Africa, it is not a fully cross-cultural principle.[49] Likewise, the principle needs to be

48. This is particularly true with passages like this one, where readers are likely to have preconceived notions about the teaching of Scripture overall on a given topic, in this case the Sabbath, and therefore find it hard to notice when an individual passage does not appear to fit their previously accepted synthesis. See further Craig L. Blomberg, "The Sabbath as Fulfilled in Christ," in *Perspectives on the Sabbath*, ed. Chris Donato (Nashville: B&H, forthcoming).

49. Entirely beyond our scope in this volume is the crucial discipline of contextualizing the gospel in new cultures. So often in the history of the church, Christianity as it has existed in one culture has been transported uncritically to another culture without adequate wrestling with the question of which elements of Christian belief and practice should change in a new culture and which should remain the same. For a programmatic treatment of the topic in the New Testament, see Dean Flemming, *Contextualization in the New Testament: Patterns for Theology and Mission* (Downers Grove, IL: InterVarsity, 2005). Increasingly, resource tools for Scripture are emerging that are taking non-Western, nonwhite, and nonandrocentic subcultures more into account. From an evangelical perspective, see esp. Tokunboh Adeyemo, ed., *Africa*

Sidebar 10.2

Checking the Accuracy of Perceived Cross-Cultural Principles

1. Make sure a given principle has come straight from the text at hand.
2. Check to see that the principle incorporates all of the main elements of the text and does not conveniently neglect an important component.
3. Make sure the principle is not tied to a particular situation but can truly express its original intention in cultures all over the world and throughout history.
4. Make sure the principle is in agreement with other comparable principles derivable from the rest of Scripture.
5. Express the principle in one or two sentences with present-tense verbs so that it is memorable and sounds relevant to the audience.

---

relevant to both the biblical and contemporary audiences. Save the cultural specifics for the next step of the applicational process, in which the principle is fleshed out in characters and scenarios that may be totally unique to a specific audience.

Fourth, make sure that the principle is in agreement with other comparable principles derivable from the rest of Scripture. Any principle that contradicts another portion of the biblical text at the same level of abstraction has not been adequately handled by the interpreter and deserves a closer look, possibly with the help of more secondary literature. It is not contradictory to observe that Acts commends helping the Christian poor in one's world by three different means: (a) a common treasury administered by the apostles to which all periodically and voluntarily committed their funds (2:43–47; 4:32–37), (b) subordinate church leaders who regularly distributed food or finances (6:1–7), and (c) a special offering from multiple congregations scattered around the world (Acts 11:27–30; cf. 1 Cor. 16:1–4 and 2 Cor. 8–9). The methods or original applications vary, but the overarching principle of Christians giving generously to help the most materially poor fellow believers in their midst, and around the world, remains constant. What *would* be inappropriate, because it contradicts the principle enunciated in Galatians 6:10 ("Do good to all people, especially to those who belong to the family of believers"), would be to derive the principle from any or all of the three examples in Acts that one must limit Christian giving only to fellow Christians, simply because no unbelievers receive help in those three situations.[50]

Bible Commentary (Nairobi: Word Alive; Grand Rapids: Zondervan, 2006); and Catherine C. Kroeger and Mary J. Evans, eds., *The IVP Women's Bible Commentary* (Downers Grove, IL, and Leicester: InterVarsity, 2002).

50. On all of these passages see further Craig L. Blomberg, *Neither Poverty nor Riches: A Biblical Theology of Possessions* (Leicester and Downers Grove, IL: InterVarsity, 1999), ad loc.

Fifth, express the principle in one or two sentences with present-tense verbs so that it is memorable and seems relevant to the audience. You can thus become familiar enough with the principle to derive several applications and return to it again and again. If you are preaching or teaching the passage, a succinct and attention-grabbing phrasing makes it easier for others to recall it as well. If your principles become too unwieldy, it will be harder for you to work with them and more unlikely that others will grasp their true significance at all.[51]

Find Appropriate Application for Today

We have practiced stepping up and away from the original audiences and the specific actions that the author expected of them, and extracted the principles that help us cross the divide from the biblical world to today. Now we take the final step of moving back down to the concrete level of our contemporary context. This is where the art of knowing one's culture or audience converges with the science of in-depth exegetical work to make the text come alive for people today. The process can consequently create the deeply satisfying sense of having handled God's Word in a way that pleases him. But, as we stressed earlier, it can also be the place where an expositor commits the most grievous errors of making the text say something with which the original author could never have agreed. The hard work is not over until as much care and attention is given to legitimate contemporary application as to all the previous steps in the exegetical method.

In other words, as one learns to exegete Scripture, one must also learn how to exegete culture, so that "a thoroughly trained preacher is first a human being, at home among human beings, and then a scholar, at home among libraries" (today we might add, both real and virtual).[52] Expert pastor and preacher John Stott offers several concrete suggestions that fuel understanding and appropriate interaction with the contemporary world. First, we need to be in the habit of asking questions of people in our spheres of influence. While seasoned exegetes will usually know more about the Bible than those they are teaching, odds are good that the people we pastor will know more about various aspects of life than we do. Therefore, in our conversations we should ask them about their domestic lives, jobs, other areas of professional expertise, and hobbies or recreational interests. Beyond these areas of "doing," we ought to ask questions of "being," finding out what motivates their lives, what roles their Christianity (or other worldviews) play in who they are, and what impedes them in applying faith to life. In addition to listening to others,

---

51. These ideas for formulating principles come from Duvall and Hays, *Journey into God's Word*, 18.

52. John R. W. Stott, *Between Two Worlds: The Art of Preaching in the Twentieth Century* (London: Hodder & Stoughton; Grand Rapids: Eerdmans, 1982), 191.

Sidebar 10.3

Keys to Appropriate Application

1. Make sure that you are responsibly analyzing your culture and the needs of your audience or yourself; develop at least one concrete illustration of how you or your audience can see and respond to the principle you have extracted from the text.
2. Subject possible applications to each element of the cross-cultural principle to be certain that they do not become half-truths and/or destructive tools in the hands of Christians who do not discern their fallacies.

---

the pastor or teacher should be in the habit of learning the daily news, keeping up to a certain extent with popular culture (through television, music, movies, etc.), and reading secular literature (or at least abstracts and book reviews) to understand the major classical and contemporary schools of thought on important, society-shaping movements. Discussion groups often facilitate these kinds of undertakings as well.[53]

Today we must of course add the resources of our digital world, judiciously used and carefully checked, including Internet searches according to key topics, subject-specific video clips, and social-networking sites. Cautious and limited use of all of these resources will enlighten those who are eager to understand popular culture and the interests (and even preoccupations) of many, especially those who are younger than thirty, who have no memories of life before personal computers. These are only a few ideas, but ones that will spark fresh applications of biblical texts as well as key issues that applications of Scripture can and at times must address in the lives of twenty-first-century, technologically savvy individuals.

Study of our contemporary world thus provides a springboard for a few ideas of how the cross-cultural principles from texts might transform our lives and those of our audiences. But again, we must always double-check our work to make sure that we have not misapplied the text. The exegete's biggest defense against misapplication, besides responsible exegesis and careful formulation of cross-cultural principles, is to make sure that the chosen contemporary applications appropriately employ all elements of those cross-cultural principles. Just as we encouraged interpreters to work hard to make sure that the cross-cultural principle accurately represents the entire principle given in the original situation of Scripture, so too here it is critical to make sure that every contemporary application matches each important element in the cross-cultural principle.

---

53. For ideas on how to discipline time so that study of culture can be a priority, see ibid., 201–9. For the entire discussion on ideas for generating points of connection with the everyday life those in one's congregation face, see Stott's full discussion in ibid., 180–210.

Let's return to 1 Corinthians 8. Recall the overall principle from the passage: although the life of a Christian involves great freedom and allows participation in morally neutral practices, whenever less mature believers may see that practice and be led into sin, Christians should consider forfeiting those rights out of love for their siblings in Christ. Then recall the three elements of that principle that must be involved in appropriately analogous contemporary situations: (1) my Christian freedom; (2) a stumbling block; (3) a weaker Christian who could be led to sin.

Unfortunately, 1 Corinthians 8 has frequently been used by almost every individual or group in the church that finds new and counter-cultural expressions of Christian living "offensive."[54] Thus baby boomers (and older people) have appealed to this text in their "worship wars" against younger adults' preferred music styles, even when the lyrics convey a solid, scriptural message. A complaint may sound something like this: "It may be your right to listen to that racket you call music, but I'm offended by it, so you should refrain from what would keep me from stumbling." In this instance, however, the supposed application is missing element 3: those offended in this scenario would never voluntarily listen to the kind of music to which they object and thus be led into any sin, even against their conscience. Even element 2, the stumbling block, in 1 Corinthians 8 is something that causes a person to imitate the morally neutral action and fall into subsequent sin. For the older generation in our hypothetical conversation, something offensive is something that is merely distasteful to them so that they are very unlikely to imitate it. Therefore, we do not have sufficiently similar situations for this to be a correct application of the text. The upshot is often unnecessary legalism that prohibits an otherwise morally neutral action, and reaching the people for Christ for which the new practice was proposed is, tragically, thwarted. Paul would scarcely condone such uses of his writing, given the extent to which he bends over backward to be all things to all people so that by all means he might save some (1 Cor. 9:19–23).

The same would be true of practices like body piercings or the use of tattoos (as long as what is portrayed by the tattoo is not sinful or the location of the piercing too provocative).[55] Members of the church who object

54. Sometimes by people who seem habitually to object to anything nontraditional, leading Garry Friesen and Robin Maxon (*Decision Making and the Will of God* [Portland, OR: Multnomah, 1980], 382–83) to speak of the "professional weaker brother" syndrome, which of course is not at all the kind of person about whom Paul is here concerned.

55. That tattoos are forbidden in Lev. 19:28 raises the entire question, also outside the scope of this book, of the appropriate application of the Old Testament law in the New Testament age. Suffice it to say that the model is similar to what we have described in this chapter, with the added ingredient of understanding how new covenant revelation has or has not altered either the principles of the Old Testament text or their applications. With this example, as the immediate context confirms, tattoos and other cutting of the body "for the dead" formed part of pagan, Canaanite religious ritual and worship. Roy Gane (*Leviticus, Numbers* [Grand Rapids:

to such practice are again normally not the "weaker brothers and sisters" of whom Paul speaks because they wouldn't emulate the practices in question. However, change the situation a bit and picture the tattoos or piercings on a youth pastor. If one or several of the youth under his or her care are likely to be led to imitate the youth worker against their conscience, in disobedience to their parents, or by portraying a pagan symbol, then all elements of the cross-cultural principle *are* present, and the youth pastor should suspend his or her rights to that form of self-expression.

Or consider again Hebrews 4:1–13. Perhaps it seems like a good text to use to remind believers that they need to honor the Sabbath, cease from their work, and attend church every Sunday without exception. But the misapplication alarms should sound loudly at this point. Recall the four elements embedded in this text: (1) the real danger of Christians missing the rest God has for believers, (2) especially when they fail to combine their faith with obedience to God's Word; (3) rest as ceasing from one's own work and obeying God instead; and (4) rest as entered now in part but fully consummated at the end of the age. Our hypothetical application to church attendance potentially misses all four of these elements. This passage is not about Sabbath observance. In fact, it is about something much more difficult and demanding than Sabbath observance. It is about complete and total obedience to the unchanging Word of God, which in the New Testament age arguably no longer requires ceasing from work one day in seven (see Col. 2:16). It does, however, require coming to Christ for the rest he provides twenty-four/seven by full submission to him throughout one's Christian life (Matt. 11:28–30).[56] Our hypothetical (mis)application creates the same problem as insisting on a tithe (giving 10 percent to the Lord's work) without recognizing that the New Testament teaches that God wants far more than just the first 10 percent of one's income. Instead, God expects believers to steward their entire financial, emotional, and spiritual resources because he is ultimately the owner of those resources anyway.[57] Conventional applications of the Sabbath and of tithing unwittingly set the bar for Christians far too low.

Zondervan, 2004], 340) suggests that "verses 27–28 prohibit pagan mourning practices involved in ancestor worship (cf. Deut. 14:1–2; Jer. 48:37)." It is this context, like that of eating idol meat in a pagan worship service in the New Testament, which led to the prohibition. Other issues, of course, come into play in contemporary contexts, like the purpose of the tattoo in the first place, whether it is the best way to treat one's body, etc. But simply quoting Lev. 19:28 should not settle those debates for believers living in the current church age.

56. Cf. further Douglas R. de Lacey, "The Sabbath/Sunday Question and the Law in the Pauline Corpus," in Carson, *From Sabbath to Lord's Day*, 159–95; and D. A. Carson, "Jesus and the Sabbath in the Four Gospels," in ibid., 57–97.

57. See esp. David A Croteau, *You Mean I Don't Have to Tithe? A Deconstruction of Tithing and a Reconstruction of Post-Tithe Giving* (Eugene, OR: Pickwick, 2010). See also Wesley K. Willmer, ed., *A Revolution in Generosity: Transforming Stewards to Be Rich toward God* (Chicago: Moody, 2008).

A better way to apply Hebrews 4:1–13 is to confront the incessant busyness of the American lifestyle and to pose questions such as, How much of what we engage in on a day-to-day basis is aimed at obedience to the word of God? How much of God's Word do we know? Do we know enough to approach situations in life and respond in ways that combine our faith in Christ with obedience to God's Word? How often do we turn to Christ for rest and renewal on a *daily* basis? The urgent often supplants the important, business often trumps family, and recreation and entertainment thwart our best intentions to cultivate our relationship with God. These are the greatest obstacles to the kind of rest on which Hebrews focuses, which is a life centered on Christ and anchored in God's Word—not exemplary church attendance. It is not religious activity, substituting for secular activity, that necessarily helps one enter Christ's rest; instead, it is obedience to the mandate to draw near to God in a relationship with Jesus by immersion in his Word. This rest is begun here on this earth but will be fully realized only when we rest in God's presence at the culmination of history and throughout eternity. Such an application warns readers that rest in the form of relationship with God is not an option for Christians and that we can easily miss relationship with God by focusing on activities in this life that have little to do with true, internalized, and heartfelt obedience to God's Word. Moreover, the rest we cultivate in our lives on earth foreshadows the fully realized rest we will experience in the life to come, if we remain faithful. Now all the elements of the passage are incorporated and we have a legitimate, comprehensive application.

Summarizing our two main points and examples for appropriate application: First, make sure that you are responsibly analyzing your culture and the needs of your audience or yourself. Be intentional about developing at least one concrete illustration, of how you or your audience can see and respond to the principle extracted from the text. Off-the-cuff, thoughtless applications make an otherwise flawless exegesis fall flat. It is well worth your time to work carefully on contemporary significance. It fosters spiritual growth sufficiently for you to stay the course and wrap up excellent exegesis with thoroughly pondered and legitimately derived points of application. Second, as you come up with possible applications, be sure to subject them to each element of the cross-cultural principle to be certain that they do not become half-truths and/or destructive tools in the hands of Christians who do not discern their fallacies.

We should also recall here that there are many different legitimate applications available for a single text. We would never encourage a Christian leader to teach the same text year after year without varying the applications. Longtime congregants will be cheated, and life circumstances change anyway, even when parishioners do not. Daniel Doriani provides a method for finding twenty-eight potential ways that each passage of Scripture might be applied.[58]

---

58. Doriani, *Putting the Truth to Work*, 96.

He asserts that there are seven biblical "sources" for application, ways that the biblical text instructs us, and at least one will occur in most every text of Scripture.[59] The seven sources are rules, ideals, doctrines, narrative (redemptive acts), narrative (exemplary acts), images, and songs/prayers. Many texts will offer several sources of application and most will generate at least two.

The seven sources of application in biblical texts can be developed further by four questions that people ask and the Bible answers. (1) What should I do? That is, what is my *duty*? (2) Who should I be? That is, how do I obtain the *character* that helps me do what is right? (3) To what causes should I devote myself? That is, what *goals* should I pursue? (4) How can I tell truth from error? That is, how can I acquire *discernment*? The words italicized are the four "aspects" of application. The effective teacher will see if the text answers any of these questions; sometimes it will answer several. Thus, if an exegete is running the seven sources of application through the four aspects, each text has the potential to yield up to twenty-eight different insights (though most will not bear quite this much fruit). This, then, is a rich resource for exegetes to use as they reflect on ways in which the material of the Bible intersects the lives of both themselves and others.[60]

Final Thoughts and Conclusion

Whether or not an audience recognizes it, the truth of God applied to their lives in a way that can help them walk in closer relationship with him is the hope of each person who makes the effort to attend instructional Christian gatherings. Haddon Robinson reminds us of the great privilege and serious responsibility of those of us who handle God's Word, especially in public contexts. Scripture at times refers to the spoken word of Christian individuals who bring God's message to others as the very "word of God" itself (see esp. 1 Thess. 2:13; Heb. 4:12). Imagine the great damage that can be done if in our speaking we insist that the Word of God means something that God never intended it to mean.[61] Imagine the great good we can promote when we apply texts well. James 3:1–12 speaks about the power of the tongue in both

59. Doriani concedes that we cannot "claim that the biblical texts generate applications in precisely seven ways, no more, no less" (ibid., 92). Other scholars present shorter or longer lists. Also, these sources should not be confused with genres of Scripture, such as prophecy, poetry, parable, and narrative. Genres identify the forms of whole books, while multiple sources can appear in a book of any one genre.

60. To see the seven sources of application examined in light of the four questions, arranged as a table, see ibid., 96. To find definitions and further helpful study on each of the aspects of application (duty, character, goals, and discernment), along with rules for using each as you apply a text, or to see the method applied to a passage of Scripture, see the entire helpful two-chapter section in ibid., 81–157.

61. Robinson, "Heresy," 26.

of these lights. Remember James's specific warning for Christian leaders in verse 1: "Not many of you should presume to be teachers, my brothers and sisters, because you know that we who teach will be judged more strictly."[62]

Distinguish Levels of Authority

Here it is worth recognizing that our applications will have varying levels of authority. We cannot always assert the same level of confidence in our application of a portion of the Bible, especially as we confront contemporary situations to which the Bible does not directly speak.[63] When we can employ the biblical author's originally intended response in our situation with little or no change, our confidence in application is greatest. When we derive a broader principle with an application that incorporates particular elements of the passage that are timeless, we have the second greatest amount of confidence. Finally, if we have to back away significantly from the text to apply principles in ways that are not actually represented in the text, then we must be the most cautious in how much authority we ascribe to our applications. The more abstract the cross-cultural principle, the greater the room for error in returning to a level of concrete specificity. Remember, when we interpret, we climb up and down the "ladder of abstraction, in which the most abstract ideas are at the highest rungs of a ladder, whereas it is our task to climb only as high as the text requires us."[64]

Haddon Robinson illustrates the problem well:

> We want to have a "Thus saith the Lord" about specific things in people's lives, but we can't always have that. So we need to distinguish between various types of implications from the text. Implications may be necessary, probable, possible, improbable or impossible.
>
> For example, a *necessary* implication of "You shall not commit adultery" is you cannot have a sexual relationship with a person who is not your spouse. A

62. Luke T. Johnson (*The Letter of James* [New York and London: Doubleday, 1995], 263) explains and applies the verse incisively: "Teachers are particularly vulnerable to failures in speech" because the teaching context "provides temptations to virtually every form of evil speech: arrogance and domination over students; anger and pettiness at contradiction or inattention; slander and meanness towards absent opponents; flattery of students for the sake of vainglory."

63. Consider an issue such as doctor-assisted suicide. One can thumb through the pages of Scripture and not find the issue treated at all, simply because it was not an issue for any of the originally intended audiences. Now, this does not mean that the Bible is irrelevant to this issue. Scripture does address topics such as human suffering, the sanctity of life, and the sovereignty of God, and it contains theological principles that should inform our views. Even if specific passages in Scripture cannot be gathered in favor of one side or the other, general principles can be. Here, based on our levels of authority, discussion must be tempered with humility, and we dare not claim the same level of certainty as we should when we apply John 3:16 to our audience's life and ask them to trust in Christ alone for their salvation.

64. Webb, *Slaves, Women and Homosexuals*, 54.

probable implication is you ought to be very careful of strong bonding friendships with a person who is not your spouse. A *possible* implication is that you ought not travel regularly to conventions or other places with a person who is not your spouse. An *improbable* conclusion is you should not at any time have lunch with someone who is not your spouse. An *impossible* implication is you ought not to have dinner with another couple because you are at the same table with a person who is not your spouse.

Too often preachers give a possible implication all the authority of a necessary implication, which is at the level of obedience. Only with necessary implications can you preach, "Thus saith the Lord."[65]

Always Leave Room for the Holy Spirit

When one has worked through the exegetical process, formulated the meaning of the text that the author most likely intended, found principles that are in clear agreement with the statements of Scripture, and then isolated concrete ways in which the truth will interact with the lives of oneself and others, it would seem that one has responsibly handled the interpretive task as comprehensively as possible. However, the absence of a crucial element would mean that the process has still fallen short of God's ideals. To what degree has the Holy Spirit been involved in the lives of those to whom the text is applied and throughout the process of exegesis? The applications that will be the most poignant will come from texts and lessons in which exegetes have let the Spirit use God's Word to work in their own lives. This process should be transparently communicated to audiences so that they can see how the text has caught hold of one's heart and wrought change. If we as teachers and pastors are committed to letting the Spirit bring change based on the passages we are studying, we will not have to rely on the snazziest movie clips, the most relevant songs, or the best stories to use as illustrations. While these tools can help reinforce the text's main points, the greatest transformation in others' lives will come from our willingness to show them how a given passage applies in our own lives, how we have allowed the Spirit to help us model effective application, and how important we recognize the application is, as the Spirit has touched both our heads and our hearts.

While we turn to the Holy Spirit throughout the process of interpretation, we still have our work cut out for us. There are things that the Spirit does not do. The Spirit does not give new revelation on par with Scripture, guarantee that our interpretations are infallible, or give insights that no one else has ever had and with which no one will ever agree. The Spirit does not bypass the normal human processes of communication, enabling us to claim that "For God so loved the world that he sent his only Son" really means, "Give me all your money, preferably in fresh $100 bills!" The Spirit does not miraculously enable us to read biblical Greek and Hebrew and analyze it grammatically

---

65. Robinson, "Heresy," 26 (italics in original).

without having studied those languages. Above all, the Spirit does not force us to obey God in applying Scripture to our lives. The Spirit may remind, motivate, lend power, and create circumstances that encourage us to do so, but the onus remains on us actually to accept this empowerment and follow through. A pastor or teacher cannot prompt that behavior in any of his or her hearers merely by eloquence, charisma, or passion. As the Spirit has superintended the process of writing the words of Scripture and illuminated believers to understand Scripture and lead godly lives, so too the Spirit must guide the exegete's study and determination of the text's meaning and application. The Spirit empowers us subsequently to obey and implement those applications, without ever overruling our human freedom to rebel. Christians must choose to obey. So pray for yourselves and all those under your spheres of influence not only to have hearts that understand and mouths that communicate the truths of Scripture, but also to have hands and feet that respond appropriately. In doing so we will "not merely listen to the word and so deceive" ourselves, but by our responsible teaching and matching obedience, we will enable ourselves and our hearers to "do what it says" (James 1:22).[66]

---

66. On the roles of faith, obedience, and the Spirit in the interpretive process, see further Klein, Blomberg, and Hubbard, *Introduction to Biblical Interpretation*, 136–42.

Summary

A thorough exegesis of a given passage will proceed through all of the following steps. Apart from formal writing assignments, most studies will be more selective, based on the form and contents of the specific passage and the purpose of the study. But a complete checklist, akin to the following, can enable exegetes to think quickly through all possible steps and make sure they have not skipped anything important.

Textual Criticism

Determine if there are any significant textual variants worth study. The UBS Greek New Testament will be the most helpful tool here.

Identify the most important external manuscript evidence for each reading, determining which has the strongest support based on the combination of age, reliability, and quantity of manuscripts.

Assess the internal evidence for each reading, considering both transcriptional and intrinsic evidence. In other words, ask both which readings are more likely to have reflected scribal alterations and which one the original author most likely wrote. The simplest rule of thumb for this pair of steps is to determine which reading is most likely to have generated the other ones.

Translation and Translations

Whether you are creating your own translation or choosing from among existing translations, identify the purpose of the exercise.

If the goal is to achieve as literal a translation as possible, within the confines of grammatically acceptable English, aim for formal equivalence or utilize a translation like the NASB, NRSV, ESV, or (while being aware of the text-critical deficiencies of it) the NKJV.

If the goal is to achieve as fluent and understandable a translation among the broadest cross section of English-language speakers or readers, aim for dynamic equivalence or utilize a translation like the NLT, GNT, or (especially for British English) the REB.

If the goal is to achieve the best balance between literal translation and fluent English, aim for a mediating position between fully formal and fully dynamic equivalence or utilize a translation like the TNIV, NIV, HCSB, NAB, or NJB (recognizing the Catholic origins of the latter two, if that matters for your purposes). For public reading and study, among reasonably sized and diverse audiences, this is usually the optimal goal.

Historical-Cultural Context

Identify the author, date, audience, location of author, location of audience, and other circumstances of both author and audience that initially produced the book of the Bible in which your passage appears, to the extent that we are able to recover that information.

If the interpretation of the passage varies significantly depending on disputed matters of historical background, investigate the disputed issues further. Otherwise, determine the significance of the undisputed information for your text and move on.

Identify the key concepts in your passage that will be significantly illuminated by further understanding of the ancient Jewish and/or Greco-Roman history or culture and do extra research on those topics, assessing the significance for your passage.

Be sure to include historical, political, religious, social, and sociological issues for potential analysis and use the appropriate reference works accordingly.

Literary Context

Read the passages immediately preceding and following the one you are studying. Evaluate how they impinge on the interpretation of your text.

Formulate a probable outline of the entire biblical book. Locate your passage and its immediate context in the book's overall narrative flow and discover any additional implications for interpreting your text.

Note any figures of speech or other literary devices that affect interpretation. See if narrative criticism helps clarify any of the elements of the passage by considering plot, characterization, narrative time, climax, and the like.

Word Studies

Identify unusual, controversial, or theologically important words that merit further study.

Determine each word's range of meanings in classical Greek, in the LXX, in Hellenistic or Koine Greek, and in the New Testament. If the word occurs frequently in the author or book at hand, pay special attention to these uses.

From the full range of possible meanings, taking special note of the most common ones (especially in the book or author at hand), come to a conclusion about which best fits in the context of your passage.

Grammar

Identify unusual, controversial, or theologically important grammatical constructions that merit further study.

For any ambiguous forms, list the full range of suggestions made by commentators, grammarians, and other scholars as to the identification of each. Include any options that seem probable to you, even if you don't find them supported elsewhere.

Evaluate the arguments for and against the various alternatives and determine the most probable classifications in the immediate contexts.

Interpretive Problems

Formulate the remaining, more synthetic, exegetical problems that cannot be solved merely by one of the above steps.

Determine which combination of the above steps permits a solution of each of these problems and perform the necessary exegetical study.

Where multiple plausible solutions remain, use a process of elimination to narrow down to your preferred solution. Look for the most agreed-on, straightforward exegetical decisions that can be made and use these to exclude other, less likely options.

Where a clear-cut solution does not emerge, rank in order of probability the options that remain. Hold your views tentatively, especially when they in turn impact other important exegetical debates from your text.

Outlining

Based as much on the structure of the Greek text as possible, identify the number and location of complete sentences in your passage.

If there are too many for each to represent a separate main point of an outline, group those that belong together chronologically, thematically, or episodically. Then subdivide from there until you get at least to the level of the individual sentence.

If there are too few for each to represent a separate main point of an outline, subdivide according to the natural divisions of one or more of the sentences. Separate at the points where sentences combine independent clauses, and again at the next level for dependent clauses or prepositional phrases.

Perform the latter kinds of subdivision even when one point per sentence for your outline works well.

Create in your own words appropriate outline headings for each section and subsection, and include the relevant verses contained in each part.

Theology

With the major categories of systematic theology in mind, itemize the ones about which your passage has something to say.

Formulate what your text contributes to an understanding of each of the doctrines on which it impinges.

If apparent contradictions with other biblical passages emerge in the process, reevaluate your understanding of the text and, if necessary, of the other passages. Survey a cross section of how others have resolved the apparent contradiction, and modify your systematic theological synthesis in light of your best resolution of the problems.

Application

Determine as best as possible the originally intended application(s) of your text.

If a changed contemporary context makes the same application(s) impossible or uncertain, identify the cross-cultural theological principle(s) on which each application is based.

Climb the "ladder of abstraction" just as far as is necessary to uncover such principles but no further.

Look for different, contemporary applications of the cross-cultural principle(s) that accomplish the same goals as the originally intended applications.

Appendix

Checklist for Doing Biblical Exegesis

Textual Criticism (Chapter 1)

☐ List any significant textual variants worth study.

☐ Review the external evidence for each reading.

___ Select the reading with the strongest support (based on the combination of age, reliability, and quantity of manuscripts).

☐ Review the internal evidence for each reading.

___ Identify the transcriptional evidence (which readings are more likely to have reflected scribal alterations).

___ Identify the intrinsic evidence (which readings the original author most likely wrote).

___ Select the reading most likely to have generated the other ones.

Translation and Translations (Chapter 2)

☐ Translate the text.

___ For a *literal* translation, aim for formal equivalence or use the NASB, NRSV, ESV, or NKJV (be aware of the text-critical deficiencies of the NKJV).

___ For a *fluent and understandable* translation aim, for dynamic equivalence, or use the NLT, GNT, or (especially for British English) REB.

___ For the *best balance* between literal translation and fluent English, aim for a mediating position between fully formal and fully dynamic equivalence or use the TNIV, NIV, HCSB, NAB, or NJB.

Historical-Cultural Context (Chapter 3)

☐ List the date, author, audience, location of author, circumstances of author, location of audience, and circumstances of audience for the passage.

☐ List and research key concepts in the passage that will be significantly illuminated by further understanding of ancient Jewish and/or Greco-Roman history and culture.

Literary Context (Chapter 4)

☐ Read the passages immediately preceding and following the one you are studying.

☐ Evaluate how they impinge on the interpretation of your text.

☐ Formulate a probable outline of the entire biblical book.

___ Locate your passage and its immediate context in the book's overall narrative flow and discover any additional implications for interpreting your text.

☐ Note any figures of speech or other literary devices that affect interpretation.

___ Consider plot, characterization, narrative time, climax, etc., to see if narrative criticism helps clarify any of the elements of the passage.

Word Studies (Chapter 5)

☐ Identify unusual, controversial, or theologically important words.

☐ Determine each word's range of meanings.

___ Consider classical Greek, the Septuagint, Hellenistic or Koine Greek, and the New Testament.

___ If the word occurs frequently in the author or book at hand, pay special attention to these uses.

☐ Select the meaning that best fits in the context of your passage for each word.

Grammar (Chapter 6)

☐ Identify unusual, controversial, or theologically important grammatical constructions.

☐ List the range of solutions to each made by commentators, grammarians, etc.

☐ Evaluate the arguments for and against the alternatives and identify the most probable classifications in the immediate contexts.

Interpretive Problems (Chapter 7)

☐ Formulate the remaining, more synthetic, exegetical problems.

☐ Determine which combination of the above steps permits a solution to each of these problems and perform the necessary exegetical study.

☐ Use a process of elimination to narrow down to a preferred solution where multiple plausible solutions remain.

__ Look for the most agreed-on, straightforward exegetical decisions that can be made and use these to exclude less likely options.

☐ Rank in order of probability the options that remain when an obvious solution does not emerge.

Outlining (Chapter 8)

☐ Identify the number and location of complete sentences in your passage.

☐ Make each sentence the main point of an outline.

__ If there are *too many* sentences for each to represent a main point of an outline, group them chronologically, thematically, or episodically. Subdivide from there until you get at least to the level of the individual sentence.

__ If there are *too few* sentences for each to represent a main point of an outline, subdivide according to the natural divisions of one or more of the sentences. Separate at the points where sentences combine independent clauses, and again at the next level for dependent clauses or prepositional phrases.

☐ Create subpoints for the outline.

__ Subdivide according to the natural divisions of the sentence.

__ Separate at the points where sentences combine independent clauses, and again at the next level for dependent clauses or prepositional phrases.

☐ Write the main points and subpoints in your own words and include the relevant verses contained in each part.

Theology (Chapter 9)

☐ List the categories of systematic theology about which your passage has something to say.

☐ Formulate what your text contributes to an understanding of each of the doctrines on which it impinges.

☐ If apparent contradictions with other biblical passages emerge, reevaluate your understanding of the text and, if necessary, of the other passages.

___ Survey a cross section of how others have resolved the apparent contradiction.

___ Modify your systematic theological synthesis in light of your best resolution of the problems.

Application (Chapter 10)

☐ Determine as best as possible the originally intended application(s) of your text.

☐ If a changed contemporary context makes the same application(s) impossible or uncertain, identify the cross-cultural theological principle(s) on which each application is based.

___ Climb the "ladder of abstraction" just as far as is necessary to uncover such principles but no further.

☐ Look for different, contemporary applications of the cross-cultural principle(s) that accomplish the same goals as the originally intended applications.

Select Bibliography

Various items are helpful in more than one category, but we have listed each only once, in an area in which they are particularly helpful.

Textual Criticism

Aland, Kurt, and Barbara Aland. *The Text of the New Testament*. Rev. ed. Grand Rapids: Eerdmans, 1989.

Black, David A. *New Testament Textual Criticism: A Concise Guide*. Grand Rapids: Baker, 1994.

Greenlee, J. Harold. *Introduction to New Testament Textual Criticism*. Rev. ed. Peabody, MA: Hendrickson, 1995.

Jones, Timothy P. *Misquoting Truth: A Guide to the Fallacies of Bart Ehrman's Misquoting Jesus*. Downers Grove, IL: InterVarsity, 2007.

Metzger, Bruce M. *A Textual Commentary on the Greek New Testament*. 2nd ed. Stuttgart: Deutsche Bibelgesellschaft/German Bible Society, 1994.

Metzger, Bruce M., and Bart D. Ehrman. *The Text of the New Testament: Its Transmission, Corruption, and Restoration*. 4th ed. New York and Oxford: Oxford University Press, 2004.

Omanson, Roger L. *A Textual Guide to the Greek New Testament*. Stuttgart: German Bible Society, 2006.

Parker, D. C. *An Introduction to the New Testament Manuscripts and Their Texts*. Cambridge: Cambridge University Press, 2008.

Wegner, Paul D. *A Student's Guide to Textual Criticism of the Bible: Its History, Methods and Results*. Downers Grove, IL: InterVarsity, 2006.

Translation and Translations

Beekman, John, and John Callow. *Translating the Word of God*. Grand Rapids: Zondervan, 1974.

Carson, D. A. *The Inclusive-Language Debate: A Plea for Realism*. Grand Rapids: Baker, 1998.

Cotterell, Peter, and Max Turner. *Linguistics and Biblical Interpretation*. Leicester and Downers Grove, IL: InterVarsity, 1989.

Fee, Gordon D., and Mark L. Strauss. *How to Choose a Translation for All Its Worth*. Grand Rapids: Zondervan, 2007.

Lewis, Jack P. *The English Bible from KJV to NIV: A History and Evaluation*. 2nd ed. Grand Rapids: Baker, 1991.

Metzger, Bruce M. *The Bible in Translation: Ancient and English Versions*. Grand Rapids: Baker Academic, 2001.

Nida, Eugene A., and Johannes P. Louw. *Lexical Semantics of the Greek New Testament*. Atlanta: Scholars Press, 1992.

Strauss, Mark L. *Distorting Scripture? The Challenge of Bible Translation and Gender Accuracy*. Downers Grove, IL, and Leicester: InterVarsity, 1998.

Wegner, Paul D. *The Journey from Texts to Translations: The Origin and Development of the Bible*. Grand Rapids: Baker, 1999.

White, James R. *The King James Only Controversy: Can You Trust the Modern Translations?* 2nd ed. Minneapolis: Bethany, 2009.

Historical-Cultural Context

Bell, Albert A., Jr. *A Guide to the New Testament World*. Scottdale, PA, and Waterloo, ON: Herald, 1994.

Blasi, Anthony J., Jean Duhaime, and Paul-André Turcotte, eds. *Handbook of Early Christianity: Social-Science Approaches*. Walnut Creek, CA: Altamira Press, 2002.

Burge, Gary M., Lynn H. Cohick, and Gene L. Green. *The New Testament in Antiquity: A Survey of the New Testament within Its Cultural Context*. Grand Rapids: Zondervan, 2009.

Carson, D. A., and Douglas J. Moo. *An Introduction to the New Testament*. 2nd ed. Grand Rapids: Zondervan, 2005.

De Silva, David A. *Honor, Patronage, Kinship and Purity: Unlocking New Testament Culture*. Downers Grove, IL, and Leicester: InterVarsity, 2000.

———. *An Introduction to the New Testament: Context, Methods and Ministry Formation*. Downers Grove, IL: InterVarsity, 2004.

Evans, Craig A., and Stanley E. Porter, eds. *Dictionary of New Testament Background*. Downers Grove, IL, and Leicester: InterVarsity, 2000.

Ferguson, Everett. *Backgrounds of Early Christianity*. 3rd ed. Grand Rapids: Eerdmans, 2003.

Keener, Craig S. *The IVP Biblical Background Commentary: New Testament*. Downers Grove, IL, and Leicester: InterVarsity, 1993.

Neyrey, Jerome H., and Eric C. Stewart, eds. *The Social World of the New Testament: Insights and Models*. Peabody, MA: Hendrickson, 2008.

Witherington, Ben, III. *New Testament History: A Narrative Account*. Grand Rapids: Baker Academic, 2001.

Literary Context

Bailey, James L., and Lyle D. Vander Broek. *Literary Forms in the New Testament: A Handbook*. Louisville: Westminster John Knox, 1992.

Bullinger, E. W. *Figures of Speech Used in the Bible: Explained and Illustrated*. 1898. Reprint, Grand Rapids: Baker, 2003.

Caird, G. B. *The Language and Imagery of the Bible*. London: Duckworth, 1980.

Duvall, J. Scott, and J. Daniel Hays. *Grasping God's Word: A Hands-On Approach to Reading, Interpreting, and Applying the Bible*. 2nd ed. Grand Rapids: Zondervan, 2005.

Osborne, Grant R., and Stephen B. Woodward. *Handbook for Bible Study*. Grand Rapids: Baker, 1979.

Powell, Mark A. *What Is Narrative Criticism?* Minneapolis: Fortress, 1990.

Resseguie, James L. *Narrative Criticism of the New Testament: An Introduction*. Grand Rapids: Baker Academic, 2005.

Witherington, Ben, III. *New Testament Rhetoric: An Introductory Guide to the Art of Persuasion in and of the New Testament*. Eugene, OR: Cascade, 2009.

Word Studies

Balz, Heinrich, and Gerhard Schneider, eds. *Exegetical Dictionary of the New Testament*. 3 vols. Grand Rapids: Eerdmans, 1990–93.

Bauer, Walter, Frederick W. Danker, William F. Arndt, and F. Wilbur Gingrich, eds. *A Greek-English Lexicon of the New Testament and Other Early Christian Literature*. 3rd ed. Chicago: University of Chicago Press, 2000.

Brown, Colin, ed. *The New International Dictionary of New Testament Theology*. 4 vols. Grand Rapids: Zondervan, 1975–85.

Kittel, Gerhard, and Gerhard Friedrich, eds. *Theological Dictionary of the New Testament*. 10 vols. Grand Rapids: Eerdmans, 1964–76.

Liddell, H. G., and Robert Scott. *A Greek-English Lexicon*. 9th ed. Oxford: Clarendon, 1996.

Louw, Johannes P., and Eugene A. Nida. *A Greek-English Lexicon of the New Testament Based on Semantic Domains*. 2 vols. 2nd ed. New York: United Bible Societies, 1989.

Marshall, I. Howard, ed. *Moulton and Geden Concordance to the Greek New Testament*. 6th ed. New York: Continuum, 2002.

Mounce, William D., ed. *Mounce's Complete Expository Dictionary of Old and New Testament Words*. Grand Rapids: Zondervan, 2006.

Verbrugge, Verlyn D. *The NIV Theological Dictionary of New Testament Words*. Grand Rapids: Zondervan, 2000.

Grammar

Black, David A. *It's Still Greek to Me: An Easy-to-Understand Guide to Intermediate Greek*. Grand Rapids: Baker, 1998.

Blass, Friedrich, Albert Debrunner, and Robert W. Funk. *A Greek Grammar of the New Testament and Other Early Christian Literature*. Chicago: University of Chicago Press, 1961.

Carson, D. A. *Exegetical Fallacies*. 2nd ed. Grand Rapids: Baker, 1996.

Porter, Stanley E. *Idioms of the Greek New Testament*. Sheffield: Sheffield Academic Press, 1992.

Rogers, Cleon L., Jr., and Cleon L. Rogers III. *The New Linguistic and Exegetical Key to the Greek New Testament*. Grand Rapids: Zondervan, 1998.

Silva, Moisés. *Biblical Words and Their Meaning: An Introduction to Lexical Semantics*. Rev. ed. Grand Rapids: Zondervan, 1994.

Wallace, Daniel B. *The Basics of New Testament Syntax*. Grand Rapids: Zondervan, 2000.

———. *Greek Grammar beyond the Basics*. Grand Rapids: Zondervan, 1996.

Young, Richard A. *Intermediate New Testament Greek*. Nashville: Broadman & Holman, 1994.

Zerwick, Maximilian. *Biblical Greek: Illustrated by Examples*. Rome: Biblical Institute Press, 1963.

Interpretive Problems

Beale, Gregory K., and D. A. Carson, eds. *Commentary on the New Testament Use of the Old Testament*. Grand Rapids: Baker Academic; Nottingham: Apollos, 2007.

Black, David A., and David S. Dockery, eds. *Interpreting the New Testament*. Nashville: Broadman & Holman, 2001.

Bock, Darrell L., and Buist M. Fanning, eds. *Interpreting the New Testament Text: Introduction to the Art and Science of Exegesis*. Wheaton: Crossway, 2006.

Carson, D. A., and John D. Woodbridge, eds. *Hermeneutics, Authority, and Canon*. 1986. Reprint, Eugene, OR: Wipf & Stock, 2005.

Green, Joel B., ed. *Hearing the New Testament: Strategies for Interpretation*. Rev. ed. Grand Rapids: Eerdmans; Carlisle: Paternoster, 2010.

Klein, William W., Craig L. Blomberg, and Robert L. Hubbard Jr. *Introduction to Biblical Interpretation*. Rev. ed. Nashville: Nelson, 2004.

Osborne, Grant R. *The Hermeneutical Spiral: A Comprehensive Introduction to Biblical Interpretation*. Rev. ed. Downers Grove, IL, and Leicester: InterVarsity, 2006.

Porter, Stanley E., ed. *A Handbook to the Exegesis of the New Testament*. Leiden and Boston: Brill, 2002.

Outlining

Fee, Gordon D. *New Testament Exegesis: A Handbook for Students and Pastors*. 3rd ed. Louisville: Westminster John Knox, 2002.

Grassmick, John D. *Principles and Practice of Greek Exegesis*. Rev. ed. Dallas: Dallas Theological Seminary, 1976.

Guthrie, George H., and J. Scott Duvall. *Biblical Greek Exegesis*. Grand Rapids: Zondervan, 1998

Kaiser, Walter C., Jr. *Toward an Exegetical Theology*. Grand Rapids: Baker, 1983.

Larkin, William J. *Greek Is Great Gain: A Method for Exegesis and Exposition*. Eugene, OR: Wipf & Stock, 2008.

Liefeld, Walter L. *New Testament Exposition: From Text to Sermon*. Grand Rapids: Zondervan, 1984.

Robinson, Haddon W. *Biblical Preaching: The Development and Delivery of Expository Messages*. Grand Rapids: Baker, 1980.

Ryken, Leland. *Words of Life: A Literary Introduction to the New Testament*. Grand Rapids: Baker, 1987.

Theology

Akin, Daniel L., ed. *A Theology for the Church*. Nashville: B&H, 2007.

Erickson, Millard J. *Christian Theology*. 2nd ed. Grand Rapids: Baker Academic, 1998.

Green, Joel B., and Max Turner, eds. *Between Two Horizons: Spanning New Testament Studies and Systematic Theology*. Grand Rapids and Cambridge: Eerdmans, 2000.

Helyer, Larry. *The Witness of Jesus, Paul and John: An Exploration in Biblical Theology*. Downers Grove, IL: InterVarsity, 2008.

Ladd, George E. *A Theology of the New Testament*. Ed. Donald A. Hagner. Rev. ed. Grand Rapids: Eerdmans, 1993.

Marshall, I. Howard. *New Testament Theology: Many Witnesses, One Gospel*. Downers Grove, IL, and Leicester: InterVarsity, 2004.

Schreiner, Thomas R. *New Testament Theology: Magnifying God in Christ*. Grand Rapids: Baker; Nottingham: Apollos, 2008.

Thielman, Frank. *New Testament Theology: A Canonical and Synthetic Approach*. Grand Rapids: Zondervan, 2005.

Treier, Daniel J. *Introducing Theological Interpretation of Scripture: Recovering a Christian Practice*. Grand Rapids: Baker Academic, 2008.

Witherington, Ben, III. *The Indelible Image: The Theological and Ethical Thought World of the New Testament*. 2 vols. Downers Grove, IL: InterVarsity, 2009–10.

Application

Brown, Jeannine K. *Scripture as Communication: Introducing Biblical Hermeneutics*. Grand Rapids: Baker Academic, 2007.

Doriani, Daniel M. *Getting the Message: A Plan for Interpreting and Applying the Bible*. Phillipsburg, NJ: P&R Publishing, 1996.

———. *Putting the Truth to Work: The Theory and Practice of Biblical Application*. Phillipsburg, NJ: P&R Publishing, 2001.

Duvall, J. Scott, and J. Daniel Hays. *Journey into God's Word: Your Guide to Understanding and Applying the Bible*. Grand Rapids: Zondervan, 2008.

Flemming, Dean. *Contextualization in the New Testament: Patterns for Theology and Mission*. Downers Grove, IL, and Leicester: InterVarsity, 2005.

Kantzer, Kenneth S., ed. *Applying the Scriptures*. Grand Rapids: Zondervan, 1987.

Kuhatschek, Jack. *Taking the Guesswork out of Applying the Bible*. Downers Grove, IL: InterVarsity, 1990.

Meadors, Gary T., ed. *Four Views on Moving Beyond the Bible to Theology.* Grand Rapids: Zondervan, 2010.

Larkin, William J., Jr. *Culture and Biblical Hermeneutics: Interpreting and Applying the Authoritative Word in a Relativistic Age.* Grand Rapids: Baker, 1988.

Vanhoozer, Kevin J. *Is There a Meaning in This Text? The Bible, the Reader, and the Morality of Literary Knowledge.* Grand Rapids: Zondervan, 1998.

Webb, William J. *Slaves, Women and Homosexuals: Exploring the Hermeneutics of Cultural Analysis.* Downers Grove, IL, and Leicester: InterVarsity, 2001.

Scripture Index

Subject Index